KU-607-757

MOZART'S OPERAS

Rudolph Angermüller

QM LIBRARY (MILE END)

MOZART'S OPERAS

Preface and translation by Stewart Spencer

RIZZOLI
NEW YORK

QM LIBRARY
(MILE END)

GOETHE
INSTITUT
LONDON

WITHDRAWN FROM
GOETHE INSTITUTE LIBRARY

78
(052)
Moz

89 - 39

Translated from the German:
Mozart—Die Opern von der Uraufführung bis heute

Copyright 1988 © Office du Livre S.A., Fribourg, Switzerland

English translation: Copyright © 1988 Office du Livre S.A.

First published in the United States of America in 1988 by
Rizzoli International Publications, Inc.
597 Fifth Avenue, New York, NY 10017

All rights reserved.
No part of this book may be reproduced in any manner whatsoever
without permission of Rizzoli International Publications, Inc.

Library of Congress Cataloging-in-Publication Data

Angermüller, Rudolph.
   Mozart's operas.

   Bibliography: p.
   Includes index.
   1. Mozart, Wolfgang Amadeus, 1756-1791. Operas.
ML410.M9A8 1988   782.1'092'4   88-42743
ISBN 0-8478-0993-5

Printed in Japan

Contents

Preface 7

Acknowledgments 9

Die Schuldigkeit des Ersten Gebots 11

Apollo et Hyacinthus 15

Bastien and Bastienne 19

La Finta Semplice 25

Mitridate, Rè di Ponto 31

Betulia liberata 37

Ascanio in Alba 41

Il Sogno di Scipione 46

Lucio Silla 49

La Finta Giardiniera 59

Il Rè Pastore 71

Zaide (The Seraglio) 75

Idomeneo 79

The Abduction from the Seraglio 97

L'Oca del Cairo 118

Lo Sposo Deluso ossia
La Rivalità di Tre Donne
per un Solo Amante 123

Der Schauspieldirektor 129

The Marriage of Figaro 133

Il Dissoluto Punito
o sia Il Don Giovanni 163

Così fan tutte o sia
La Scuola degli Amanti 197

The Magic Flute 222

La Clemenza di Tito 261

Select Bibliography 276

Index 283

Photo Credits 295

Preface

Although some critics among Mozart's contemporaries found his music too audacious and too complex for the ordinary listener to follow, his obituary notices unanimously acknowledged his greatness. It is the development toward this greatness as a dramatic composer that the present study traces. The year of his death, 1791, acts as a nodal point in a narrative that moves backward in time across Mozart's life and forward to the present day. In examining the genesis of each of his works for the stage, we gain an insight into his evolution as a music dramatist, from the earliest attempts at sacred Singspiel, school drama, *opera buffa*, *opera seria*, and *festa teatrale*, to the later works with libretti by Lorenzo Da Ponte, and, finally, to *The Magic Flute* and *La Clemenza di Tito*. Excerpts from Mozart's letters show us something of his working methods and help to dispel the myth that the work of art sprang fully fashioned from the composer's brain. We also see Mozart concerned to find suitable libretti, his dramatic flair and pragmatic sense of the theater, and, above all, his infectious enthusiasm and self-assurance.

Although it would be an exaggeration to say that the history of the German-speaking theater is the production history of Mozart's operas, there is no denying that Mozart is the first classic composer of opera in the sense that his works, once performed, have never been absent from the repertory. Already during his lifetime operas such as *Don Giovanni* and *The Magic Flute* established themselves as the cornerstones of every German opera house program. Other countries were relatively slow to follow: in England *The Marriage of Figaro* was not heard until 1812 and in New York not until 1824. (Not until 1858 was it given there in Italian.) Mozart's Italian operas were performed in Italy during the early nineteenth century, only because Milan, Venice, and Florence were under Austrian rule. In general, Italian audiences preferred their Rossini; Verdi considered Mozart a *quartettista*, a composer of chamber music rather than music drama.

In Germany too, Mozart was eclipsed for a time by the shadows of Beethoven and Wagner: Beethoven had claimed to be unable to write an opera on such "frivolous and immoral" subjects as *Figaro* and *Don Giovanni*, and, however admiringly Wagner may have spoken of the "transfigured, suffering, sorrowing human beings" that people Mozart's operas, those operas belonged to a bygone age, part of a Hegelian process of which the Wagnerian art-work of the future was to be the inevitable synthesis and successor.

The English writer on music, Edward J. Dent, dated the revival of European interest in Mozart to the Mozart festivals that began in Munich in 1896 under the stage direction of Ernst von Possart and the conductorship of Hermann Levi; but perhaps an even greater impetus was given by Salzburg which first admitted Mozart's stage works into its Festival repertory in 1922. Since then the world has flocked to the composer's birthplace to see authoritative performances of *The Abduction from the Seraglio, The Marriage of Figaro, Don Giovanni, Così fan tutte* and *The Magic Flute*. With their portrayal of human weaknesses and passions

Preface

transfigured by the redeeming beauty of forgiveness, these works transcend the Enlightenment origins of their humanitarian message and will always speak to us with the timeless voice of hope and fear.

A further chapter in Salzburg's history opened in 1956 with the first of an annual series of Mozart Weeks in which lesser known works that were drawn from the Neue Mozart-Ausgabe (New Mozart Edition) were performed. Gradually all of Mozart's earlier works have been performed and recorded, culminating in *Die Schuldigkeit des Ersten Gebots* in 1987 and *Betulia liberata* in 1988. Other theaters have followed Salzburg's lead, encouraged not only by a more general acceptance of the conventions of *opera seria* but by a revival of interest in the lesser works of eighteenth- and early nineteenth-century operatic composers. While the independent merits of these works may continue to be a matter for debate, their importance for our understanding of Mozart's later *œuvre* cannot be overestimated. For here we find him already master of his art, expressing the classical conflict of joy and pain, contentment and terror, compressing violent emotion into the constraints of classical form and yet bending the melody to suit the text. At the same time, the early involvement with the contrasting genres of *opera seria* on the one hand and *opera buffa* on the other provides a clue to the variety of the later works.

Mozart was especially fortunate in his choice of Lorenzo Da Ponte as the librettist of *The Marriage of Figaro, Don Giovanni,* and *Così fan tutte*: for Da Ponte, as we know from his memoirs, tailored his libretti to suit the composers for whom they were written. He provided Mozart with three plots that contain many traditional elements of *opera buffa,* yet permitting a new seriousness of approach on the composer's part. The result is a triptych of operas in which comedy and tragedy have never been more finely balanced, a tension that wrenches the listener from laughter to tears, and back again, within moments. In *The Magic Flute,* the gap between tragedy and farce has grown even wider, so much so that the work—as the history of its performances attests—has all too often been dismissed as a mixture of suburban pantomime and solemn platitude made bearable only by the beauty of Mozart's music. Yet the naïveté and the solemnity are reconciled in the dance-like *allegro* with which the work concludes, an ending that can be seen as the summation of Mozart's musical and dramatic gifts. It is also an expression of that search for self-knowledge predicated by *Così fan tutte,* and, what one writer has called, "the quest of the human soul for both inner harmony and enlightenment." As such Mozart's final German opera, and by implication the rest of his dramatic *œuvre,* may perhaps be of even greater relevance to us in 1991 than they were to the composer's contemporaries in 1791.

London, 1988   Stewart Spencer

Acknowledgments

Without the Department of Theater Studies at the International Mozart Foundation in Salzburg, the present volume would have been much the poorer. Valuable and, in some cases, previously unpublished documents from this collection have been used here. Numerous nineteenth- and twentieth-century documents were made accessible by the Institut für Theater-, Film- und Fernsehwissenschaft at the University of Cologne. My sincere thanks are due to Herr Helmut Grosse for his cooperation and unending willingness to help. It is also a pleasure to record the constant kindness of Herr Hans Jaklitsch of the Salzburg Festival archives.

The following theaters have kindly placed archival material at my disposal: Berlin (West and East), Bregenz, Brussels, Budapest, Buenos Aires, Cologne, Dresden, Düsseldorf, Edinburgh, Freiburg im Breisgau, Geneva, Glyndebourne, Hagen, Hamburg, Kassel, London, Lyons, Milan, Munich, New York, Paris, Salzburg (Festival, Landestheater and Marionette Theater), Ulm, Vienna, Wiesbaden, Wuppertal, and Zurich.

In gathering documentary material I have been assisted by the following archives, libraries, and museums: Frankfurt am Main (Stadtgeschichtliches Archiv), Milan (Pinacoteca Brera), Mannheim (Reiss-Museum), Munich (Theatermuseum), Paris (Bibliothèque Nationale, Bibliothèque et Archives de l'Opéra, and Arsenal), Stuttgart (Staatsgalerie), and Vienna (Österreichische Nationalbibliothek and Historisches Museum der Stadt Wien).

A number of photographers and private individuals have also provided me with material and with permission to publish it. Warmest thanks are due to the translators of my text: Mme. Geneviève Geffray (Salzburg) for the French edition and Mr. Stewart Spencer (London) for the English edition. I owe many of my ideas to my publishers, Office du Livre, and especially to the late Jean Hirschen. Their editorial care has been wholly in the composer's spirit: *finis coronat opus*.

Rudolph Angermüller

Ignatz Anton v. Weiser

Handelsmann und Bürgermeister zu Salzburg von 1772–1775

Ignaz Anton von Weiser, the librettist of *Die Schuldigkeit des Ersten Gebots*. Lithograph by Sebastian Stief based on a lost oil portrait

Die Schuldigkeit des Ersten Gebots

Sacred Singspiel

Throughout the seventeenth and eighteenth centuries the prince-archbishops of Salzburg showed a particular predilection for the theater. Grand operatic spectacles, organized by the personnel of their own Court Chapel, were presented on festive occasions at court. Of especial significance for Salzburg's musical life was a genre of school drama whose aims were chiefly pedagogic and moral. The students were given an opportunity to show their skill at acting and public speaking, and the librettists, who were principally Benedictine instructors, took the subject matter for their texts from the Bible, from the lives of the saints, and from church history. Mythological and historical themes were also a popular choice for these *ludi scenici*. The staging was always a resplendent affair, and the lavish sets would pay homage to the country's ruler, lending a sense of occasion to the end of term celebrations, and honoring the feast days of the University's patron saints. Initially music played only a modest part in school dramas. Relatively brief choruses were soon followed by dance interludes; and, finally, arias and entire music-dramatic complexes found their way into the genre. The music served two functions: on the one hand it illustrated the events on stage, and on the other it appealed to the listener's imagination.

Structurally a sacred Singspiel differs little from a school opera. Its subject matter is sacred, and its main accent is placed on allegorical figures. Its florid language, aiming at rhetorical effect and wholly indebted to the Baroque Age, reveals the poetic abilities of local writers. Performances are known to have taken place in Salzburg in St. Peter's, in the Cathedral, on the Nonnberg, and in the Residenz. Composers such as Johann Ernst Eberlin, Anton Cajetan Adlgasser, and Michael Haydn, in addition to Leopold Mozart, all made valuable contributions to the genre of school opera. For the eleven-year-old Wolfgang Mozart they were the models whose experience in handling this genre he himself was able to draw on.

It was customary in Salzburg for a sacred Singspiel to be divided up among a number of composers. There were, accordingly, three local composers entrusted with the task of setting *Die Schuldigkeit des Ersten und fürnehmsten Gebots* (The Obligation of the First and Most Eminent Commandment: cf. St. Mark 12:30, "And thou shalt love the Lord thy God with all thy heart, and with all thy soul, and with all thy mind, and with all thy strength: this is the first commandment"). The three composers were Mozart, Michael Haydn, and Anton Adlgasser. At the time of writing the whereabouts of the music to the second and third parts remain unknown.

The text, published by Johann Joseph Mayr's heirs in Salzburg in 1767, was by Ignaz Anton von Weiser, an eminent member of the local middle classes and a textile merchant, who had performed sterling service as town councilman and who held office as Salzburg's mayor from 1772 to 1774.

The aim and purport of the poem is made clear in the preface to the printed text, a piece written in the ornate language that is typical of the time: "That there is no more perilous spiritual state than lukewarmness in the

K. 35

First part of a sacred Singspiel with words by Ignaz Anton Weiser. Completed in Salzburg at the beginning of March 1767. First performed in the Prince-Archbishops' Residenz in Salzburg on Thursday, March 12, 1767 at 7 p.m. Autograph score: Windsor Castle, Royal Library.

11

Die Schuldigkeit

Des ersten und fürnehmsten Gebottes Marc. 12. v. 30.

Du sollst den HErrn, deinen GOtt lieben von ganzen deinem Herzen, von deiner ganzen Seel, von deinem ganzen Gemüth, und aus allen deinen Kräften.

In dreyen Theilen

zur Erwegung vorgestellt

von J. A. W.

Erster Theil in Musik gebracht von Herrn Wolfgang Mozard, alt 10. Jahr.

Zweyter Theil von Herrn Johann Michael Heiden, Hochfürstl. Concertmeistern.

Dritter Theil von Herrn Anton Cajetan Adlgasser, Hochfürstl. Kammer = Componist = und Organisten.

SALZBURG,

Gedruckt bey Johann Joseph Mayrs, Hof = und Akademischen Buchdruckers, und Buchhandl. sel. Erbinn, 1767.

Title page of the libretto of Die Schuldigkeit des Ersten Gebots

The action takes place in the pleasant setting of an orchard and small wood. The lukewarm Christian is discovered asleep in a thicket of flowers. It is Justice's task to chastise the slothful and reward the pious. Christian Spirit bewails the lukewarm faith of the sons of men, and declares that only a few have chosen the path of righteousness. For Compassion it is the first and greatest and most important commandment to love the Lord God from the depths of one's soul. Ostentation, sensuality, selfishness, and vainglory are common idols that mankind prizes more highly than his creator. According to Christian Spirit, mankind will not become clearsighted until confronted by the actual torments and terrors of hell. Justice desires to improve mankind and to use the lukewarm Christian as a means of proving her case. Christian awakens. Spirit of the World warns him against believing in dreams, otherwise he would already have taken his own life out of fear and apprehension. An unknown voice has robbed Christian of his peace of mind. Spirit of the World bids him enjoy life, insisting that Christian Spirit's words are marked by foolish simplicity. Christian Spirit appears, disguised as a physician. Christian asks him to cure his grief, his fear, and his terror. Spirit of the World offers him instead a more agreeable medicine: a fair glimpse of a beautiful woman, food and drink, gambling and hunting will chase away all his grief. Christian Spirit promises to care for Christian's health and for his soul's ease, if only he follows his advice. Christian Spirit gives him a sealed folio. All who perform their Christian duty will never perish. Once again Spirit of the World seeks to seduce Christian, but the latter rejects all affluence and declares himself a zealous Christian. Christian Spirit determines to grant the lukewarm Christian justice and compassion.

pursuance of our soul's salvation is most assuredly confirmed for us by that same divine truth that is expressed in the words of the secret Revelation of St. John 3: 15, 16: "I know thy works, that thou art neither cold nor hot: I would thou wert cold or hot. So then, because thou art lukewarm, and neither cold nor hot, I will spue thee out of my mouth."

Characters and résumé of the plot

The characters personifying these conflicting values are Justice (soprano), Compassion (soprano), Weltgeist (Spirit of the World, soprano), Christgeist (Christian Spirit, tenor), Christian (tenor).

Origins and premiere of the opera

One wonders if there was not an intermediary who obtained this commission for Mozart. Ostensibly, the prince-archbishop of Salzburg, Sigismund Christoph von Schrattenbach did not believe in the successes enjoyed by the young Mozart on his tour of western Europe between June 9, 1763 and November 29, 1766. Accordingly, or so writers on Mozart have alleged, the prince-archbishop had the boy locked up for a week in order to test his abilities as a composer. It is difficult,

Die Schuldigkeit des Ersten Gebots

Salzburg, Mozart Week given by the International Mozarteum Foundation in collaboration with the Salzburg Landestheater, January 23, 1987 (Great Hall of Salzburg University) Justice: Diane Jennings. Christian: Karl Lobensommer. Christgeist: Josef Köstlinger. Weltgeist: Angelika Luz. Compassion: Kathleen Cassello. Producer: Werner Hollweg. Designer: Florian Parbs. Conductor: Hanns-Martin Schneidt Parbs set the action on a large disc, emphasizing the tellurian aspect of the work. Large masking draperies surrounded the stage and symbolized the etherial element.

however, to relate this anecdote to *Die Schuldigkeit des Ersten Gebots*, although the facts might better fit the "Funeral Music" K. 42, which is both shorter in length, having 39 manuscript sides, and requires only two singing roles and modest orchestral forces. *Die Schuldigkeit des Ersten Gebots*, a much more multilayered work musically, can scarcely have been written in the space of a week, since it is unlikely that the eleven-year-old Mozart could have completed 106 folios (recto and verso) in so short a period of time. There can be no question of work produced under examination conditions, since almost without exception the text of the recitatives was written by Leopold Mozart, who also took it upon himself to touch up some of the arias and to add dynamic markings in the full score. Wolfgang most probably wrote K. 35 in Salzburg in February and March 1767.

As for the first performance, the diary of the Salzburg Benedictine monk Father Beda Hübner of St. Peter's contains the following entry dated March 12, 1767: "XIIma Martij Thursday, after evening prayers at court today an oratorio was performed in the so-called Rittersaal by five persons, namely, three female singers and two men, Herr Meisner and Herr Spizeder. The German text was written by Herr Weiser, a merchant and councilman, and the music was composed by Wolfgang Mozart, a boy of 10 [!]." The performers were members of the Salzburg Court Chapel. The initially lukewarm but thereafter zealous Christian was taken by Joseph Meissner, a bass singer. Christian Spirit was played by Franz Anton Spitzeder, Court tenor from 1760 until his death, and voice and keyboard teacher at the Salzburg Kapellhaus. Spirit of the World was sung by Maria Anna Fesemayr, whom Mozart gave away when she married Adlgasser in 1769 and who was said to be an accomplished actress capable of performing difficult roles with bravura. Divine Compassion was performed by Maria Magdalena Lipp, a Court singer from 1765 until 1803. She married Michael Haydn on August 17, 1768. Maria Anna Braunhofer sang the role of Divine Justice. She too held a Court appointment from 1765 until 1803, and, like Maria Lipp, was one of the prince-archbishop's favorites, and thus performed regularly.

Schrattenbach was undoubtedly pleased with his young fellow citizen's composition. According to the records of the Salzburg treasury for March 18, 1767, "18th. To little Mozart for composing the music of an oratorio a 12-ducat gold medallion ... 60f."

In writing *Die Schuldigkeit des Ersten Gebots* Mozart not only enriched the Salzburg sacred Singspiel repertory, he also showed that he could assimilate local traditions and adapt them to suit his own stylistic ends.

The first modern production of K. 35 took place in the Great Hall of Salzburg University on January 23, 1987 as part of the 1987 Mozart Week. It was organized by the Mozarteum International Foundation in collaboration with the Salzburg Landestheater.

Wuppertal Stadttheater,
January 25, 1942
Producer: Heinrich Köhler-
Helffrich. Designer: Heinrich
Wendel. Conductor: Karl
Egon Glückselig
A classical production style
which made a virtue of
wartime necessity

Apollo et Hyacinthus

School drama set to music

Following his success abroad Mozart was invited to demonstrate his abilities in his hometown of Salzburg too. *Apollo et Hyacinthus* was commissioned by the town's University, an institution with which the composer's father Leopold was already on the best of terms. Many of his pupils attended the University high school, where the theater played an important part in the school's activities. Not only were the students trained in rhetoric, but the theater also represented a form of entertainment and festive ceremonial in the school curriculum. The young Mozart had first come into contact with the University theater on September 1 and 3, 1761 when as a five-year-old boy he had appeared as an extra in performances of the Latin school drama *Sigismundes Hungariae Rex* with words by Jakob Anton Wimmer and music by Johann Ernst Eberlin. As a rule school performances were given at the end of the academic year, although the term time itself was by no means unusual. In 1767 the University arranged for its fourth-year students or "syntaxians" to present a performance "ex voto." (Details of the promise or vow are not known.) The author of the piece was Rufinus Widl, a Dominican monk from the monastery of Seeon. He had been born at Frauenwörth on the Chiemsee on September 26, 1731, and had taught philosophy for a number of years in Freising before being appointed high-school teacher in Salzburg in 1763. In the fall of that year he assumed responsibility for the first-year students or "rudimentalists," following them through their course until 1767, when they entered the fourth year.

Widl wrote the Latin tragedy *Clementia Croesi* for a performance planned for the summer term, interpolating a musical *intermedio* into the text of his spoken drama and thus introducing a subplot into the work. The task of setting the *intermedio* to music was entrusted to Widl's fellow citizen, the eleven-year-old Wolfgang Mozart, who—it will be remembered—never enrolled at a school or university in the whole of his life.

Preparations for the performances are known to have been taken in hand by at least April 29, 1767. On May 1 mass was held in the University Church (Collegiate Church), the platform in the Great Hall being unusable because of the elaborate sets. Stage rehearsals were held on May 10, 11, and 12. The school records for May 13 report, "Wednesday. Morning school ended early to allow for a blood-letting session [a customary practice at this time not only for sick pupils but also for healthy ones]. After the midday meal the syntaxians' play was performed in keeping with our promise; written by their excellent teacher and admirably presented by his pupils, it afforded the liveliest pleasure. I congratulate their excellent teacher on his great acclaim. Moreover, the music by Herr Wolfgang Mozart, an eleven-year-old boy, met with general approbation; in the evening he gave us excellent proof of his musical skill on the keyboard."

Cast list and résumé of the plot

The libretto, published by the Salzburg University printer and bookseller Joseph Mair, lists the following *personae in musica*: Oeba-

K. 38

A Latin *intermedio* for performance with the school drama *Clementia Croesi* by Father Rufinus Widl OSB. First performed in the Great Hall of Salzburg University on May 13, 1767. Autograph score: West Berlin, Staatsbibliothek Preussischer Kulturbesitz.

Apollo et Hyacinthus

Salzburg Marionette
Theater, July 16, 1935
Designer: Count Franz
Schaffkotsch
Set model showing the
epiphany of Apollo

lus, King of Lacedaemonia: The excellent and erudite Herr Matthias Stadler, student of moral theology and law [tenor, 22 years old]; Melia, Oebalus's daughter: Felix Fuchs, chapel chorister and grammar-class pupil [boy soprano, 15 years old]; Hyacinthus, Oebalus's son: Christian Enzinger, chapel chorister and first-year student [boy soprano, 12 years old]; Apollo, entertained by Oebalus as his guest: Johann Ernst, chapel chorister [boy contralto, 12 years old]; Zephyrus, Hyacinthus's confidant: Joseph Vonderthon, fourth-year pupil [boy contralto, 17 years old]; first Priest of Apollo: Joseph Bründl, poetry-class pupil [bass (?), 18 years old]; second Priest of Apollo: Jakob Moser, fourth-year pupil

[bass (?), 16 years old]. The performance was a great success, but, apart from this single amateur airing, the work was not heard again during Mozart's lifetime.

Act I. A sacrificial altar dedicated to Apollo occupies the center of the stage. Hyacinthus draws Zephyrus's attention to the sacrifices that are shortly to be made to the god. Zephyrus criticizes the Lacedaemonians for their exaggerated veneration of Apollo, and makes no secret of his jealousy of the latter.

Oebalus and Melia enter. A sacrifice is offered up to the god, but not accepted: a thunderbolt destroys the altar. Hyacinthus attempts to console the dismayed Oebalus, claiming that the gods are not always so serious. Apollo appears, disguised as a shepherd: he announces that he has been banished by Jupiter and has therefore come to seek Oebalus's friendship, which the king readily grants him. Melia and Apollo feel a mutual attraction. The god assures Hyacinthus of his undying friendship.

Act II. Oebalus informs his daughter that Apollo has sued for her hand in marriage. Melia is overjoyed at the prospect. Zephyrus arrives with the terrible news that Apollo has killed Hyacinthus with a discus during a sports contest held on the banks of the Euratos. He advises Oebalus to banish the

Linz Landestheater (Maria
Günzel-Dworski Opera
School), April 16, 1937
Apollo: Flora Janisch.
Hyacinthus: Trude Haudek.
Melia: Jetti Topitz-Feiler.
Oebalus: Erwin Euller.
Producer: Maria Günzel-
Dworski. Conductor: Paul
Günzel
The *intermedio* was per-
formed in a revised version
by Roland Tenschert.

Salzburg Marionette Theater, January 25, 1975 Producer: Klaus Gmeiner. Designer: Günther Schneider-Siemssen. Costumes: Friedl Aicher. Puppet heads: Josef Magnus. Prose dialogue translated into German by Walther Kraus
The Salzburg Marionettes first produced *Apollo et Hyacinthus* in early July 1935 in a German translation by Roland Tenschert. The work was restaged, in a new production, in 1946; and in 1975 Klaus Gmeiner used the "illusionistic possibilities of the puppet stage not only to exploit the depth of stage available and give visual expression to the different levels of reality that exist between gods and humans, but to employ effects such as Hyacinthus's transformation into a flower or the collapse of the temple to achieve a theatrical vitality which, by and large, obviated the risk of making the work appear static," Gottfried Kraus wrote in *Das Kleine Welttheater. Die Salzburger Marionetten* (Salzburg-Munich 1988).

god from the land. Believing his rival is no longer a threat, Zephyrus proceeds to sue for Melia's hand, and confirms her in the belief that Apollo is her brother's murderer. Apollo, however, has seen that it was Zephyrus himself who killed Hyacinthus, and turns the murderer into a wind that Eolus then confines in a cave at Apollo's behest. Melia, who continues to think that Apollo has murdered her brother, is incensed at the god's latest cruelty. Apollo remains in hiding, waiting for Melia's anger to abate.

ACT III.   The dying Hyacinthus reveals that it was not Apollo but Zephyrus who murdered him. Oebalus and Melia lament his death and express their regret at the unjustified affront to Apollo. The god appears. Such is his love for Hyacinthus he transforms the dead youth's body into a flower. He forgives Oebalus and Melia, and accepts the latter's renewed offer of marriage, promising to remain in Lacedaemonia as her husband.

Performances of the opera

It is noteworthy that Mozart later reused an abbreviated form of the Oebalus-Melia duet, "Natus cadit, atque Deus" (No. 8), in his F major Symphony K. 43. *Apollo et Hyacinthus* was published as part of the old Mozart Edition in March 1879, and was reedited in 1959 for the Neue Mozart-Ausgabe.

A musical arrangement of the work by Karl Schleifer was published in Munich and London in 1936. (The rewritten German text by Irmgard von Dincklage was printed by Bärenreiter in Kassel in 1941-42.) Erika Mann rewrote Schleifer's stage adaptation for the Mitteldeutscher Verlag of Halle/Saale. Other German translations include those of Roland Tenschert in 1937, Father Stephan Schaller (produced for the Mozart bicentenary in Ettal), and Walther Kraus, who translated the Latin text for a booklet accompanying Deutsche Grammophon's 1981 recording.

There appear to have been no performances of *Apollo et Hyacinthus* between Mozart's lifetime and the twentieth century, when productions have included ones at the Salzburg Marionette Theater on July 16, 1935, designed by Franz Schaffkotsch, and at the Linz Landestheater on April 16, 1937 in a production by the Maria Günzel-Dworski Opera School based on Tenschert's performing version. The work was also staged by the Wuppertal Stadttheater on January 25, 1942, again using Tenschert's version. The producer was Heinrich Köhler-Helffrich, the designer Heinz Wendel, and the conductor Karl Eugen Glückselig. The Augsburg Puppenkiste (Oemichens Marionettentheater) took up the piece in the fall of 1974. A concert performance under Leopold Hager was given in the Grosses Festspielhaus in Salzburg on January 23, 1981.

Hagen, Städtische Bühne,
1980-81
Bastienne: Patricia Raine.
Colas: Peter Leug. Bastien:
Carmen Mommaer.
Final scene. Thanks to Colas's cunning ruse, Bastien
and Bastienne are recon-
ciled: "Children! Children!
Rain and storm / A fair
new day portend. / My
magic skills have brought
You gladness without end."

Bastien and Bastienne

Origins of the libretto

In its choice of subject Mozart's *Bastien and Bastienne* is closely bound up with the *intermède Le Devin du village* by Jean-Jacques Rousseau first performed in Fontainebleau on October 18, 1752. Rousseau's piece was one of the great operatic successes of the Paris Académie Royale de Musique (better known as the Paris Opéra) during the second half of the eighteenth and first third of the nineteenth century. Between March 1, 1753 and June 3, 1829 *Le Devin du village* received 544 performances there. Although Mozart was in Paris in 1763-64 and again in 1766, he could not have seen Rousseau's *intermède* then, since the work was currently out of the repertory.

On Wednesday, September 26, 1753, after *Le Devin du village* had been performed thirty-three times at the Académie Royale de Musique, the Comédiens Italiens Ordinaires du Roi (more commonly known as the Comédie Italienne) presented a parody of Rousseau's piece under the title *Les Amours de Bastien et Bastienne*. The authors of the parody were Charles-Simon and Marie-Justine-Benoîte Favart, together with Harny de Guerville. Their intention was not to pour scorn on the original, since their parody is totally lacking in humorous references or allusions to contemporary events. The version by Favart and Harny is rather an adaptation in which members of the country's rural population appear in a realistic setting, speaking and singing in their dialects.

Les Amours de Bastien et Bastienne was a familiar piece to Viennese audiences. It was performed in Laxenburg on June 16, 1755 and in Vienna on July 5, 1755. Count Giacomo Durazzo, who had come to Vienna in 1749 as Genoese ambassador to the city following a stay in Paris, was appointed *directeur des spectacles* in 1754 and is known to have ordered the parody to be performed at the Vienna Burgtheater. His period as director coincided with the appointment there of the actor, translator, and topographer Friedrich Wilhelm Weiskern, and it was presumably on Durazzo's instructions that Weiskern translated *Les Amours de Bastien et Bastienne* in 1764.

A comparison between the French and German texts reveals that the monologues and dialogues have been translated almost word for word, whereas the arias and ensemble passages (where the text is predetermined by the music) are somewhat freer. Although Weiskern's translation is fairly accurate, he has failed to reflect the nuances of his French source. For all that he had mastered classical French, he appears not to have known what to make of the language of the peasants and lower orders which is imitated in the play, and he has failed to appreciate the often wicked parodies that the work contains. As Weiskern indicates in his note to the translation, three of the numbers (11, 12, and 13) are by the actor Johann Heinrich Friedrich Müller, whom Durazzo engaged in 1763.

The Weiskern-Müller translation was soon taken up into the repertory of various professional children's theaters including the Berner Troupe, which had made a name for itself throughout the whole of Europe during the 1760s and 1770s. The company first

K. 50 (46b)

Singspiel in one act. Words by Friedrich Wilhelm Weiskern, Johann Heinrich Friedrich Müller, and Johann Andreas Schachtner, based on the French source *Les Amours de Bastien et Bastienne* by Marie-Justine-Benoîte Favart, Charles-Simon Favart, and Harny de Guerville. Begun in Salzburg (?) in 1767 (?) and completed in Vienna in 1768. First documented performance: Architektenhaus in Berlin, October 2, 1890. Autograph score: Cracow, Biblioteka Jagiellońska.

visited Salzburg in 1766. There is evidence that Berner had Johann Baptist Savio's *Bastienne* in his repertoire. Savio, who had been director of music in Prague in the early 1760s, was responsible for the new airs in *Bastienne*. And so it is understandable that the French airs do not appear in the 1763 Prague libretto of *Les Amours de Bastien et Bastienne*, since they were replaced in the Bohemian capital by newly composed numbers. Savio presumably got to know the Weiskern-Müller translation in Vienna and then set their words to his own music.

Did Mozart hear *Bastienne* in Salzburg? Two questions need to be clarified: Firstly, did Berner perform *Bastien and Bastienne* in Salzburg? (The chroniclers of the time do not say.) And, secondly if Berner *did* perform the piece in Salzburg, did Mozart see it? Again, the sources leave us in the dark. Nonetheless, it may be assumed that Mozart, and more especially his father, who was hoping for a successful piece from his son's pen, got to know the whole complex of *Bastienne* texts in Salzburg. The young Mozart may well have been inspired by the subject matter, although Savio's music must have left him very dissatisfied. Possibly Mozart drew the attention of Salzburg's court trumpeter Johann Andreas Schachtner to the Weiskern-Müller translation, or perhaps it was the other way round. At all events, Schachtner was a close family friend of the Mozarts (Leopold was a witness at his wedding) and by 1766 he already had a number of poetic successes to his credit. No documentary evidence has survived to explain the background of Schachtner's version of *Bastienne*.

Mozart may have begun work on his German operetta in Salzburg as early as 1767. It is certainly a possibility, not least because Leopold Mozart does not mention the work in his correspondence between September 22, 1767 and November 12, 1768. If *Bastien and Bastienne* had already been started in Salzburg, there would have been no reason to write from Vienna to inform Mozart's landlord Johann Lorenz Hagenauer of something already well-known in professional circles.

Schachtner's technique in adapting the version by Weiskern and Müller extended to the following points: Schachtner versified Weiskern's prose dialogue and left unaltered the only rhyming passage (Recitativo accompagnato No. 14). The texts of Weiskern's arias were basically retained word for word with only occasional improvements for reasons of metrical smoothness. Schachtner made further improvements by removing everything that got in the way of the meaning, and adapted the text to suit the dramatic situation. Colas's magic formula (No. 10) was rewritten. The secco recitatives that Mozart composed around 1770 (the recitatives intended for Colas are notated in the alto clef in the autograph score, whereas the remainder of Colas's part is written in the bass clef) were all versified by Schachtner. By the same token, all the dialogue passages *not* set by Mozart were also turned into verse. A comparison of the arias and ensemble passages by Weiskern, Müller, and Schachtner with the text as set by Mozart leads to the following observation: Nos. 1, 6, 8, 9, and 14-16 are based on Weiskern's translation, Nos. 11 and 13 on Müller's, and Nos. 4 and 12 on Schachtner's. Nos. 2, 5, 7, and 10 are a mixture of Weiskern and Schachtner. Schachtner's versification of the prose passages in the version by Weiskern and Müller strikes us nowadays as clumsy and somewhat amateurish.

Our comparison of the two versions allows us to posit the following stages of composition: Mozart began work on the version by Weiskern and Müller, yet while composing the individual vocal numbers, he had recourse to Schachtner's adaptation (cf. Nos. 4 and 12, which are based on Schachtner). Having completed all the vocal numbers, Mozart corrected Weiskern's version of 5, 7, and 10 and brought it into line with Schachtner's translation. For whatever reasons, however, Mozart was not consistent in adopting Schachtner's changes: nos. 1, 6, 8, 9, and 14-16 were left in Weiskern's version, no. 13 in Müller's version. In all probability the surviving recitatives were composed after around 1770 and were based on Schachtner's versified text. Whether Mozart also set the remainder of Schachtner's versified dialogue we are unable to say, since no evidence exists to support or refute the claim. If he really wrote only the familiar recitatives, then Schachtner's dialogue passages were only partially set to music. Mozart evidently did not compose the individual numbers in the order in which they appear in the score. Nos. 4 and 12 seem to have been written later than nos. 13 to 16.

Characters and résumé of the plot

Bastienne, a shepherdess (soprano); Bastien, her lover (tenor); Colas, believed to be a

Salzburg Marionette Theater, 1913
This set model is on permanent exhibition in the house where Mozart was born in Salzburg. The academic sculptor Professor Anton Aicher presented Mozart's *Bastien and Bastienne* at a carnival event organized by "Gral," an artists' co-operative in Salzburg. The performance, which took place in the town's Hotel Bristol on February 27, 1913, launched the Salzburg Marionette Theater on its successful international career. Gretl Aicher, the granddaughter of the founder, wrote on the occasion of the theater's 75th anniversary in February 1988, "For me marionettes are living creatures for which you can feel fervent affection, with which you can identify whole-heartedly and unreservedly, and with which you can become one in music and movement." The Salzburg Marionette Theater has always been committed to performing Mozart's works.

magician (bass). Several shepherds and shepherdesses.

The action takes place in a village with a field in the distance. Bastienne is downcast because she believes herself abandoned by her lover Bastien. Colas enters over a hill, playing his bagpipes. Bastienne seeks his advice, confiding that Bastien has been bedazzled by "another woman's gifts," the woman in question being a noblewoman from the nearby castle. Colas tells the young shepherdess that women must behave thoughtlessly toward their lovers and appear to be fickle, the better to arouse the other's jealousy. Colas describes the couple as a true marvel: such innocence could scarcely be found anywhere else but in the country. Tired of his noblewoman's empty flatteries, Bastien determines to return to his Bastienne. Colas pretends that she has taken another lover and bidden farewell to Bastien. The latter remains convinced that Colas is spinning him a tale. Colas consults his book of spells and revives the hapless lover's flagging hopes. Bastien settles down to await his lover, but when she arrives, it is to reject his advances. Both of them boast of their "new" lovers, Bastienne of a young and well-to-do gentleman, Bastien of his beautiful lady of the castle. When Bastienne continues to ignore his entreaties, Bastien announces his decision to die. But the two of them are reconciled when they recall the beautiful times they have spent together. They sing in radiant praise of Colas's skill as a great and wise magician.

Performances of the "operetta"

The theory advanced in many biographies of Mozart that *Bastien and Bastienne* was written for the garden theater of the Viennese magnetist and physician Dr. Anton Mesmer is untenable. Mesmer's theater, an open-air stage hewn out of beech hedges, had not been completed by 1768. Or might it perhaps have been the case that, because of the lateness of the season, the performance in October 1768 took place in what Georg Nikolaus Nissen called Mesmer's "summer-house," that is, in the rooms of Mesmer's country house? Nissen speaks of a "society theater," in other words an amateur company, not a garden theater or open-air stage. Or was *Bastien and Bastienne* not given in Vienna at all at that time? Contemporary sources leave us in the dark on all of these questions. The first documented performance of this German "operetta," as Leopold Mozart called the piece, took place on October 2, 1890 (!) as part of a double bill with Mendelssohn's *Die Heimkehr aus der Fremde*. The performance was organized by the Society of Opera Friends in Berlin and given in the city's Architektenhaus. It was produced by Ferdinand von Stantz, former director of the Royal Opera in Berlin. In 1891 Max Kalbeck wrote

Bastien and Bastienne

Salzburg Festival, August 3, 1928, guest performance by the Leningrad Opera Studio in the Salzburg Landestheater
Bastienne: Lydia Schuk. Colas: Vladimir Talankin. Bastien: Vassily Tichy. Producer and designer: Emanuel Kaplan. Costumes: Ekaterina Petrova. Conductor: Serge Elzin. Prologue, epilogue, and textual revisions by Emanuel Kaplan and Arkady Orel
The Leningrad Opera Studio was the first foreign company to visit the Salzburg Festival in 1928. In addition to Mozart's *Bastien and Bastienne*, they performed Bernhard Paumgartner's *Die Höhle von Salamanca*, Alexander Dargomyzhsky's *The Stone Guest*, and Nikolai Rimsky-Korsakov's *Kashchey The Immortal*. In this production Mozart's Singspiel was subjected to a constructivist interpretation.

a new text and dialogue for K. 50, and in 1900 Henry Gauthier-Villars and Georges Hartmann produced a French version of the work. Rainer Simons adapted the piece for the Vienna Volksoper in 1906. Carlo Rossi translated Weiskern's text for a production in Venice in 1914, and Faixà translated Schachtner's version for Madrid about 1915. Weiskern's text was rendered into English by Olga Paul and into Flemish by Korneel Goosens, the latter for a puppet production first seen at the Royal Art Society in Antwerp on May 9, 1942. In 1957 Bernhard Sönnerstedt produced a translation for Stockholm Radio; in 1962 Max Leavitt translated Weiskern's version into English; and in 1969 Basil Swift adapted the work for a production in Pennsylvania.

Since *Bastien and Bastienne* is not long enough to provide a whole evening's entertainment, the piece has often been coupled together with other short works. Marionette theaters and student companies in particular have welcomed the Singspiel into their repertories. The Leningrad Opera Studio under the direction of Boris Asaf'yev gave guest performances of the work at the Salzburg Festival on August 3, 4, and 10, 1928. In 1969 and 1970 the work was given in the Salzburg Residenz, together with Giovanni Battista Pergolesi's *La serva padrona*, as part of the Salzburg Festival.

The score was first published in March 1879 within the framework of the old Mozart Edition. The editor was Franz Wüllner. It was reedited by the present author for the Neue Mozart-Ausgabe in 1974. The conductor Leopold Hager later wrote music for the recitatives which Mozart himself had left unset. His version was first heard at a concert performance given in the Great Hall of the Mozarteum in Salzburg on February 1, 1976 as part of the 1976 Mozart Week.

Salzburg Festival, July 31, 1969 (Residenz)
Colas: Peter van der Bilt.
Bastien: Thomas Lehrberger.
Bastienne: Ileana Cotrubas.
Producer and designer: Ladislav Štros. Costumes: Marcel Pokorný. Conductor: Leopold Hager
"It is the merit of this performance in the Residenz courtyard to have given adequate expression, both theatrically and musically, to the purity and naive perfection of *Bastien and Bastienne*. The small revolving stage, with its stylized pavilion, ... is admirably suited to a work that maintains such an ideal synthesis between lively realism and stylization. The three characters, the magician Colas in velvet green, the shepherdess Bastienne seen in silhouette as a Rococo porcelain figure, and the somewhat more strongly delineated Bastien were all clearly contrasted with each other, without their harmless game being in any way overburdened with the intellectual profundity of a production concept," Gottfried Kraus reported in the *Salzburger Nachrichten* of August 2, 1969.

LA
FINTA SEMPLICE.
DRAMMA GIOCOSO
PER MUSICA,
DA RAPPRESENTARSI IN CORTE,
PER ORDINE
DI S. A. REVERENDISSIMA
MONSIGNOR
SIGISMONDO
ARCIVESCOVO
E PRENCIPE
DI SALISBURGO:
PRENCIPE DEL S. R. I.
LEGATO NATO DELLA S. S. A.
PRIMATE DELLA GERMANIA,
E DELL'ANTICHISSIMA FAMIGLIA
DEI CONTI DI
SCHRATTENBACH
&c. &c.

Yd

SALISBURGO:
Nella Stamparia di Corte 1769.

1316

Title page of the Salzburg
libretto of *La Finta
Semplice*

La Finta Semplice

Composing for a Viennese audience

Mozart's second stay in Vienna from September 11, 1767 to January 5, 1769 was something of a family outing, marked as it was by the presence of his father Leopold, his mother Anna Maria, and his sister Nannerl. It was principally intended to provide him with an opportunity to write an opera for the Imperial and Royal capital of the Austro-Hungarian Dual Monarchy. It was no doubt due to the general thift of *tout* Vienna and of the Emperor Joseph II that at the 1768 carnival the city's glittering balls and social gatherings were organized not by the Imperial Court but in public halls and at the expense of private individuals. As a result, famous virtuosos were less in demand than usual, and the organizers of society balls and other spectacles were concerned first and foremost about their profit levels, not least because of the high taxes that they had to pay to the Imperial household.

In a letter dated January 30-February 3, 1768 and addressed to his landlord in Salzburg, Johann Lorenz Hagenauer, Leopold revealed that Wolfgang was to write an opera for Vienna—"and what sort of an uproar do you suppose has secretly arisen among the composers here? – what? – today it is a [Christoph Willibald] Gluck and tomorrow a boy of 12 who is seen sitting at a keyboard and conducting his opera?—yes, in spite of all their grudging envy! I have even won over Gluck to our side, so that, although he is not altogether whole-hearted, he dare not show what he really thinks, since our patrons are his too, and in order to secure ourselves with regard to the *acteurs*, who generally cause the composer the greatest annoyance, I have taken up the matter with them myself, and one of them has given me all the suggestions himself. But to tell the truth, the initial idea of getting Wolfgangerl to write an opera came from the Emperor himself, since he twice asked Wolfgangerl if he would like to compose an opera and conduct it himself. Of course he said yes, but the Emperor could say nothing more in the matter since the opera is the sole concern of [Giuseppe] Affligio [Afflisio]. The consequences of this undertaking (if God helps us to bring it about) are so great but at the same time so easy to predict that they do not need spelling out...." The opera, according to Leopold, was not a "short *opera buffa*, but one lasting at least two and a half to three hours..., since there are excellent people here for an *opera buffa*."

Giuseppe Afflisio was a key figure in Vienna's theatrical life in 1768. He had leased the Burgtheater and Kärntnertortheater on May 16, 1767, the lease to run until Shrove Tuesday 1769. As "lessor of the local theatrical spectacles" he was contractually obliged "to provide the two theaters entrusted to his care with good German, French, and Italian spectacles in accordance with the terms of his proposal." In other words, his contract allowed him to engage whichever performers he wished, although he was required to retain the services of existing members of the company at least until their contracts had expired.

On March 30, 1768 Leopold Mozart was able to venture the opinion that things would turn

K. 51 (46a)

Opera buffa in three acts. Words by Carlo Goldoni and Marco Coltellini. Written in Vienna between April and July 1768. First performed in Salzburg in 1769 (?). Autograph score: Act I Cracow, Biblioteka Jagiellońska. Acts II and III West Berlin Staatsbibliothek Preussischer Kulturbesitz.

out well for the new opera and that it would receive its first performance after Joseph II's return from Hungary. By May 20, he was anticipating a performance in June. On June 29, however, we find him writing to Hagenauer that "envy has broken forth on every side," and on July 30, he wrote to say that all of Vienna's composers, with Gluck at their head, had left no stone unturned in their efforts "to hinder the progress of this opera. The singers were incited and the orchestra stirred up against us, everything was done to prevent the performances of this opera from going ahead.... In the meantime it was being put about by certain persons that the music was not worth a rap, while others were saying that the music did not fit the words or the meter, since the boy did not understand the Italian language sufficiently well."

The hope that *La Finta Semplice* would finally be performed in Vienna in August proved unfounded, and so, when Leopold was granted an audience with Joseph II on September 21, he handed the Emperor a *species facti* or letter of complaint, accusing the impresario of preventing a performance of the work from taking place. Above all he complained of intrigues against Wolfgang, and expressed his regret that, in spite of a positive response on the part of the court and various influential individuals, the opera was not to be staged after all. Hagenauer, too, was told of the petition: "His Excellency Count [Johann Wenzel] Spork [*directeur des spectacles* from 1764] has already been entrusted with the task of inquiring into the affair, and Afflisio has been ordered to justify himself; in addition to the 100 ducats for the opera, I am also demanding reimbursement of all the expenses etc. that I have incurred here so far.... The Emperor was most gracious and promised that our case would be justly dealt with."

Cast list and résumé of the plot

The most famous singers available in Vienna in 1768 were due to have sung in *La Finta Semplice*. The cast would have included Clementina Poggi (later Baglioni) as Rosina (soprano), a Hungarian baroness and Fracasso's sister, who pretends to be the simple-minded heroine of the title; Francesco Carat(t)oli as Don Cassandro (bass), a wealthy landowner from Cremona, who is a conceited and miserly man of honour and the brother of Don Polidoro; Gioacchino Cari-baldi (or Garibaldi) as Don Polidoro (tenor), Don Cassandro's younger brother and, like him, a conceited man of honor; Teresa Eberhardi as Giacinta (soprano), the sister of Don Cassandro and Don Polidoro; Antonia Bernasconi as Ninetta (soprano), Giacinta's chambermaid; Filippo Laschi as Fracasso (tenor), Rosina's brother and a captain in the Hungarian troops stationed in the region of Cremona; and Domenico Poggi as Simone (bass), Fracasso's sergeant-at-arms.

The action takes place on Don Cassandro's estate near Cremona.

ACT I. Fracasso and Simone have been billeted for the last two months at the home of two wealthy bachelor brothers, Don Cassandro and Don Polidoro. Fracasso has fallen in love with their sister Giacinta, while Simone has set his sights on Giacinta's maid, Ninetta. The two brothers are unaware of what is going on under their very noses. Don Cassandro is a boor, conceited about his money, his good looks, and his intelligence. Having once been betrayed by his sister-in-law, he now plays the part of the misogynist, tyrannizing the household. Don Polidoro lives in continual fear of his brother's rages, however much he would prefer to run after the girls. Ninetta suggests that the brothers will be cured by falling in love with Fracasso's sister, Rosina, who is currently on her way to visit Fracasso. Simone is instructed to put Rosina in touch with Ninetta, who in turn will advise her on what to do when she arrives. Simone leaves, complaining that no woman is worth such trouble. Giacinta picks up his theme: having been left on the shelf for many years, she would be happy to marry *any* man—just so long as he knows his place.

Don Cassandro comes bustling in. He has heard that Fracasso's sister is expected, but he refuses steadfastly to allow a strange woman into the house. He has made up his mind to live and die a bachelor. Fracasso replies by singing of the inescapable charms of women.

The scene changes to Cassandro's study, where Ninetta welcomes Rosina and exhorts her to ensure that the two "idiots" (as she calls Don Polidoro and Don Cassandro) fall in love with her. Don Polidoro enters. Normally timid, he wastes no time in pressing his suit on Rosina who promises to be faithful to him. The two women leave as Don Cassandro is heard approaching.

Salzburg Landestheater, January 21, 1956 (Mozart Week)
Rosina: Dorothea Siebert. Simone: Walter Raninger. Polidoro: August Jaresch. Cassandro: Alois Perner-storfer. Ninetta: Karin Küster. Adapted and translated into German as *Das schlaue Mädchen* by Bernhard Paumgartner. Producer: Géza Rech. Designer: Stefan Hlawa. Conductor: Bernhard Paumgartner
Finale of Act II. "The basic principle was to allow Mozart-Goldoni to speak in all their natural simplicity, and, apart from necessary cuts and minor adjustments, not to alter or 'revise' anything. It is only right that the recitative, as the primary means of conveying the plot and the wittily pointed dialogue, should have an important role to play in this small-scale musical comedy. The German translation stuck as closely as possible to the original, reflecting the popular and pleasantly pithy diction of the great Venetian dramatist," according to R. Purgmaaten's program note.

Don Polidoro informs his brother that he has fallen in love with the Hungarian baroness. Cassandro warns him off, but Polidoro is not to be discouraged: the mere sight of a woman, he says, is enough to inflame him. He leaves. Cassandro muses briefly on this unexpected turn, before being joined by Rosina. He immediately sets about wooing her but grows covetously distrustful when she asks him to give her the ring he is wearing. Eventually, she manages to trick him out of it. Rather than let the precious object out of his sight, Cassandro, much against his better judgment, invites Rosina to sup with him that evening.

ACT II.   While their masters are at dinner, Ninetta and Simone discuss the merits of an ideal spouse: Ninetta wants a complaisant husband, while Simone favors a more violent approach: "When someone won't love you or makes you jealous, it's time to use the stick."

Giacinta enters, begging Simone to go and restore order at the dinner table, where the two brothers are engaged in a drunken squabble. But Simone has scarcely left when Polidoro arrives. The quarrel, it appears, is over Cassandro's ring. Giacinta advises Polidoro to give Rosina an even more beautiful ring; in that way he will be sure of her affections. But Polidoro has a better present: a baby boy. For Rosina, he claims, has already agreed to marry him. Ninetta suggests that he had

better get a move on, since Rosina is on the point of leaving for good: Cassandro has forbidden the baroness to talk to Polidoro.

The scene changes to a drawing room. Alone, Rosina prays that she may not feel love's torments. Polidoro arrives, anxious to obtain her promise of marriage. But Rosina will not be rushed: she must first test her prospective bridegroom. They are interrupted by Cassandro, who insists that he is "not tipsy, just a trifle merry," though Rosina counters that he stinks of wine and tells him to sit at the opposite end of the room. Don Cassandro duly sits down and promptly falls asleep. Rosina seizes her chance to replace the ring on his finger.

Fracasso enters and Cassandro renews his demands for the return of the ring. Since Cassandro is clearly wearing the ring himself, Fracasso takes this as a slight to his family's honor and challenges Cassandro to a duel. Rosina manages to pacify her brother.

A new intrigue is now set in motion: since Fracasso needs Cassandro's consent to marry Giacinta, he decides to abduct her (with her approval). This, he hopes, will force Cassandro's hand. And, sure enough, when Cassandro enters and is told that Giacinta and Ninetta have disappeared, taking all the family fortune with them, he agrees that whoever brings his sister home shall receive her hand in marriage.

ACT III.   Simone and Ninetta look forward to married life. Don Cassandro presses

27

La Finta Semplice

Salzburg Festival, August 5, 1960 (Residenz)
Giacinta: Bianca-Maria Casoni. Fracasso: Manfred Schmidt. Producer: Georg Reinhardt. Designer: Heinrich Wendel. Costumes: Xenia Chris. Conductor: Bernhard Conz
"The designer Heinrich Wendel had to forgo his favorite device of a spiral staircase, but at least made use of flights of steps to structure the small stage area. For the rest, he packaged the piece as a pastoral play, making it tasteful if not entirely plausible. Georg Reinhardt's production was neither good nor bad, being virtually non-existent.... The new Festival chairman, Hofrat Bernhard Paumgartner, was responsible for the edition used and also, unfortunately, for the German translation. In the interests of the respect which his life's work otherwise merits, he would have done better to have spared himself, and especially us, the effort that went into preparing it," Manfred Vogel wrote in the *Frankfurter Nachtausgabe* of August 10, 1960.

Rosina to reveal which of the brothers she prefers. She demurs, continuing to tease them both. Only when Ninetta and Giacinta have returned with Fracasso and Simone, demanding realization of their promised marriages and gaining the brothers' forgiveness for the deception practiced on them, does she reveal her love for Don Cassandro. The three couples are reconciled, and only Don Polidoro is left on his own.

Performances of the opera

Two arguments may be adduced in support of the claim that a performance of *La Finta Semplice* took place in Salzburg in 1769: firstly, the libretto was published in the city in 1769; and, secondly, Mozart's manuscript score contains alterations dating from that year. Even today writers on *La Finta Semplice* are still to be found maintaining that the opera was first performed on May 1, 1769 in the small Court Theater of the Salzburg Residenz. No contemporary source has yet come to light to confirm this date, and it must be remembered that, according to the diary of Father Benedictine Beda Seeauer, Prince-Archbishop Schrattenbach was in Hallein, not far from Salzburg, on May 1. However,

we may still conclude from the above-mentioned libretto, for which the court itself was responsible, that a performance of Mozart's *La Finta Semplice* did indeed take place in Salzburg in 1769. There is no direct evidence of any performance material from Salzburg, but the fact that this existed is clear from passages in letters by Leopold Mozart (December 17, 1769) and Nannerl Berchtold von Sonnenburg (March 23, 1800).

The singers named in the Salzburg libretto were among the most illustrious members of the prince-archbishop's ensemble. Rosina was sung by Maria Magdalena Lipp, Don Cassandro by Joseph Hornung, Don Polidoro by Franz Anton Spitzeder, Giacinta by Maria Anna Braunhofer, Ninetta by Maria Anna Fesemayr, Fracasso by Joseph Meissner, and Simone by Felix Winter.

Sources of the libretto and history of performances

It is not known for certain who selected the libretto of *La Finta Semplice* for Mozart, although it may be supposed that Afflisio had a say in the matter, advised perhaps by the Imperial Court poet Marco Coltellini. The text is based on Carlo Goldoni's *dramma giacoso*,

La Finta Semplice, first performed during the 1764 carnival in the Teatro Giustiniani di S. Moisè in Venice with music by Salvatore Perillo. Goldoni's piece, evidently written in Paris, was in turn modeled on *La Fausse Agnès ou Le Poète campagnard* of 1734 by Philippe Néricault Destouches. Destouches' comedy was well-known in Italy, having been translated into Italian by Duchessa Maria Vittoria Serbelloni under the title *Il Poeta di Villa*. Afflisio invited Coltellini to adapt Goldoni's text for Vienna, and if we compare the two versions, we may observe not only the similarities but also certain basic differences. Above all, the third act is more theatrically effective and operatically apposite in Coltellini's version, and the finale is more successful in terms of the drama.

When Mozart composed *La Finta Semplice* in 1768, he had yet to set foot on Italian soil, which makes it all the more astonishing that the twelve-year-old Austrian had so excellent a grasp of the Italian language, and that he was able to do justice to that supreme law of *opera buffa*—textual intelligibility. This first *opera buffa* by Mozart already contains clearly structured arias and finales, and brings out the nuances of emotion that are implied by the text. Precisely because the words meant so much to him, the young composer was able to write a complex accompaniment, but one in which the instrumental writing always matches the vocal line. Of course, the work also contains much that is obvious and imitative, since Mozart has adapted his style to suit the *buffa* taste of his

time. But even if he often writes "conventional" music, he knows what the genre demands, and knows, moreover, how to exploit the whole gamut of styles from the popular to the earthily comical, while at the same time paying homage to the fashionable distinction between the naïve and the sentimental in art. The orchestral writing is highly varied, and far surpasses the everyday achievements of other contemporary opera composers.

Apart from a single performance in Salzburg, *La Finta Semplice* was not heard again during Mozart's lifetime. In 1921 the opera was revised by Anton Rudolph under the title *Die verstellte Einfalt* for a German-language production in Karlsruhe (the text was published there in 1933). And a Danish version based on Rudolph's revision was published by Wilhelm Hansen of Copenhagen in 1923. A revised version, in Italian and German, by Bernhard Paumgartner was performed in Italian in the Salzburg Landestheater on January 21, 1956, and in 1960 the piece was taken up by the Salzburg Festival and performed in the Residenz in Paumgartner's version. Povl Ingerslev-Jensen translated the opera into Danish in 1969 for a production in Copenhagen, where it was performed under the title *Underfundig uskyld*. A literal German translation was published by the author of the present volume in 1982; and on January 21, 1983 a concert performance of *La Finta Semplice* was given in the Grosses Festspielhaus in Salzburg as part of the 1983 Mozart Week. The performing edition used was that of the Neue Mozart-Ausgabe.

Zurich Opera at the Schwetzingen Festival, May 4, 1983 Sifare: Ann Murray. Aspasia: Yvonne Kenny. Producer and designer: Jean-Pierre Ponnelle. Costumes: Pet Halmen. Conductor: Nikolaus Harnoncourt. Scene in Act I. "As with *Idomeneo* and *Lucio Silla*, the designer Jean-Pierre Ponnelle has found a unique solution to the problem of staging this work: since the libretto ... is based on an Italian translation of a *tragédie* by Racine, he has located the action within a kind of decorative 'historicism' at the very time that Racine was writing. His scenery points to the theater of the Baroque, and he structures it with Baroque flats which can be moved and changed in seconds. The predominant color is a warm sepia, effectively and cleverly varied in its contrastive use of light and shade. Pet Halmen's costumes are of a Baroque magnificence; plumes sway on royal heads, and lordly figures strut to and fro majestically, if not a little pompously, on their built-up shoes," wrote Gerold Fierz in *Musica*, 1983.

Mitridate, Rè di Ponto

History of the *Mitridate* libretti

On March 12, 1770—during Mozart's first visit to Italy from December 13, 1769 to March 28, 1771—the fourteen-year-old composer received a "scrittura" or operatic commission from Count Carlo di Firmian, Governor-General of the Austrian province of Lombardy and nephew of the former Salzburg prince-archbishop, inviting him to write an opera to open the 1780-81 season at Milan's Regio Ducal Teatro. The fee was fixed at 100 gold florins plus free board during his stay in the Lombard capital.

Mozart did not learn what subject he would be setting to music until July 27. This was the day on which he was handed the libretto to *Mitridate, Rè di Ponto*, an existing text that was the work of one of the members of Turin's Accademia dei Trasformatori, Vittorio Amedeo Cigna-Santi. The theme was already an acknowledged success in the literary and musical world. The Italian operatic stage in particular favored themes from Roman history. Mithradates VI Eupator, a tyrannical ruler from pre-Christian Asia Minor who inflicted three wars on the Roman Empire, provided a popular subject with which to glorify the Imperium Romanum.

All the *Mitridate* libretti of the eighteenth and nineteenth centuries are based on the five-act *tragédie Mithridate* by Jean Racine, first performed in the Hôtel de Bourgogne in Paris on January 13, 1673. Racine had aimed at achieving human truths and finely observed characterization. His oriental despot is essentially a figure out of Corneille, a typical ruler who dominates the tragedy. Intrigue and dénouement are similarly indebted to Corneille. The dying tyrant triumphs over his own baser nature, and unites the lovers whom he had earlier cursed. But the passions that the individual characters feel and which motivate the action are typically Racinean in that what the dramatist exposes are human weaknesses. At the beginning of the play a tragic outcome seems inevitable. The real crisis is precipitated by the false report that Mithridate gives out concerning his death. The French essayist Jean de La Bruyère once said that Corneille depicts men as they ought to be, Racine as they are. In other words, Racine conveys a subtler understanding of mankind.

The Bolognese composer Giuseppe Aldroandini wrote a *Mitridate in Sebastia* in 1702 for the Teatro Regio in Turin; *Mitridate Eupatore* was the title which Alessandro Scarlatti gave to the work that he wrote for Venice in 1707; in 1723 Benedetto Pasqualio wrote a *Mitridate, Rè di Ponto Vincitor di Se Stesso* for the Teatro Grimani in Venice; and in 1728 Antonio Caldara composed a *Mitridate* for Vienna. Two settings of the libretto date from 1730, the first by Giovanni Antonio Giai for Turin, the second by Nicola Porpora for Rome. In the early 1760s Giuseppe Parini, the librettist of *Ascanio in Alba*, orator at Milan University and resident poet at the Milanese court, translated Racine's *tragédie* into Italian. Cigna-Santi refashioned the material and turned it into an effective opera text. His version had already been set by Quirino Gasparini in 1767 for the Teatro Regio in Turin before Mozart was entrusted with it in 1770. In his treatment of the cruel

K. 87 (74a)

Opera seria in three acts. Words by Vittorio Amedeo Cigna-Santi. Begun in Bologna on September 29, 1770. First performed in the Regio Ducal Teatro in Milan on December 26, 1770. Autograph score missing; only sketches and first drafts have survived and are preserved in the Bibliothèque Nationale in Paris (Département de la Musique).

Salzburg Festival, August 7, 1971 (Felsenreitschule). Producer: Wolfgang Weber. Designer: Peter Heyduck. Conductor: Leopold Hager Sets for Act I. Wolfgang Weber relied principally on a static dramaturgy.

and cunning Pontic tyrant, Cigna-Santi adapted the subject matter along Metastasian lines, viewing the classical world of the first century B.C. through Baroque eyes. Contemporaries were impressed above all by the libretto's rhetorical heroism, by the introduction of a love intrigue, and by its contrastive dramatic effects.

Angelo Tarchi produced his *Mitridate, Rè di Ponto* in Rome's Teatro delle Dame in 1785, and almost a century later the old *opera seria* theme was still inspiring composers: Emilio Serrano y Ruiz set Mithradates's cruel end to music for a production in Burgos in 1881.

Cast list and résumé of the plot

Mitridate (tenor), King of Pontus and other countries, in love with Aspasia: Guglielmo d'Ettore; Aspasia (soprano), betrothed to Mitridate and already proclaimed his queen: Antonia Bernasconi; Sifare (male soprano), son of Mitridate and Stratonica, in love with Aspasia: Pietro Benedetti; Farnace (male alto), Mitridate's eldest son, also in love in Aspasia: Giuseppe Cicognani; Ismene (soprano), daughter of the King of Parthia and Farnace's beloved: Anna Francesca Varese; Marzio (tenor), Roman Tribune and friend of Farnace: Gaspare Bassano; Arbate (male soprano), governor of Ninfea: Pietro Muschietti.

ACT I. Farnace, Mitridate's first-born son and governor of Pontus, and Sifare, his son by his marriage to Stratonica, Princess of Colchis, have arrived in the royal city of Ninfea. The report has reached them that their father has fallen in battle against the Romans. The brothers are political enemies—Farnace is a friend of the Romans, whereas Sifare is on the side of the Greeks—but both of them love the Greek princess Aspasia. She, however, has been promised in marriage to their father. Farnace sues for her love, thus obliging her to seek the protection of Sifare, whom she had previously loved in secret. A furious argument develops between the brothers but it is brought to an end by the return of their father, who brings Farnace a bride in the person of the Parthian princess, Ismene.

Mitridate was himself the author of the report that he had died. He now realizes that both his sons have been suing for Aspasia's hand. Arbate confirms that Farnace loves Aspasia. Beside himself with anger and jealousy, Mitridate resolves to destroy his sons.

ACT II. Ismene complains to Mitridate about Farnace's attitude to her: the king decides to kill his son, but Ismene refuses to countenance such a punishment. Mitridate is determined to marry Aspasia there and then, and Sifare is sent to inform her of his father's wishes. Sifare and Aspasia confess their love for each other. She demands, however, that he avoid her sight henceforth, since she insists that she exists only to fulfill her obligations towards his father. Mitridate confers with his sons on how to make good the defeat he has suffered at the hands of the Romans. Sifare declares his willingness to take up arms against the Empire. Marzio brings an offer of peace from Rome, which Farnace is inclined to accept. Mitridate suspects his son of collaborating with the enemy, and has Farnace thrown into prison. Ismene tries in vain to mediate. Farnace makes no secret of his conspiratorial links with Rome, but he accuses Sifare of attempting to win Aspasia's heart for himself. In order to test the truth of Farnace's accusations, Mitridate cunningly assures him that he is ceding Aspasia to Sifare, whereupon Aspasia joyfully confesses her love to Sifare. The latter is arrested, and both sons are condemned to death. Aspasia begs Sifare to kill her, but he is resolved to die alone, and entreats her to forget him and to ascend the throne with his father. They prefer to die rather than to be parted.

ACT III. Ismene attempts to persuade Mitridate to abandon his cruel resolve. In vain. Mitridate is prepared to show clemency only if Aspasia returns to him, but the latter rejects his demand. Arbate reports the approach of an army of Romans. Mitridate resolves that, before he marches into battle, both his sons and Aspasia shall die. Aspasia is prepared to drink the cup of poison to its bitter dregs. Sifare, freed by Ismene, succeeds in preventing Aspasia from killing herself. He determines to support his father in battle against the Romans and thus justify his escape from prison. Farnace, held captive in a tower in the city, has been freed by Marzio. The tribune suggests that Farnace ascend the throne in place of his defeated father and reign as Rome's ally. Seized by remorse,

however, Farnace resolves to renounce both Aspasia and the throne. To prevent himself from falling into the hands of the Romans, Mitridate has run on his own sword. As he lies dying in the courtyard of the royal palace, he names Sifare his successor; Aspasia shall be his wife. He has learned from Ismene that Farnace has set fire to the enemy ships and forced the Roman fleet to retire: in consequence, he extends his forgiveness to Farnace, too. The opera ends with a chorus of revenge directed against the despotic rule of the Romans.

Composing the opera

Mozart was allowed only five months to write his first opera for Italy, and so there was no time to be lost if the lengthy score was to be delivered to the performers on time; and it was the singers whose needs had to be met above all else. Contemporary practice required and expected that the latter exercise an influence over their arias: their roles would be written to suit their "flexible" throats. Mozart certainly had problems with his singers while he was working on *Mitridate*. The final distribution of the roles was not known until October. No other opera by Mozart has so many different versions, sketches, fragments, and variants of the individual numbers. The singer entrusted

Salzburg Festival, August 7, 1971 (Felsenreitschule) Sifare: Arleen Augér. Aspasia: Edda Moser. Farnace: Helen Watts. Producer: Wolfgang Weber. Designer: Peter Heyduck. Conductor: Leopold Hager
Act I, Scene 7. "Salzburg went to a lot of trouble over *Mitridate*," John Higgins wrote in *Opera* magazine (Festival edition, 1971). "The cast on paper, led by Peter Schreier, Pilar Lorengar, and Edda Moser, was strong. Wolfgang Weber and his designer, Peter Heyduck, had clearly been given a reasonable budget: the arcades and cloisters of the Felsenreitschule were carefully obscured with sheets of crinkly glass reflecting and simultaneously absorbing metallic light from lamps with green, blue, and purple filters; there were quantities of supers, all well dressed, who had nothing to do but stand and listen. But it added up to an unsatisfactory evening.... Despite the obvious affection Leopold Hager and the Salzburg Mozarteum revealed for the score its performance was not much to the taste of the Festival audience."

with the role of Aspasia did not trust the *maestro* but planned, instead, to create a brilliant impression by interpolating arias from Gasparini's *Mitridate*. Not until she set eyes on Mozart's score and saw the pieces he had written specially for her did she admit to being "beside herself for joy." After an orchestral rehearsal on December 17, the copyist expressed his own private satisfaction since, as Mozart reported, a successful opera often meant "more money for the copyist through selling and distributing the arias than the kapellmeister got for composing them."

Meanwhile, intrigues were being plotted behind the young composer's back: ten days before the first performance it was being suggested that such a young boy—and a German to wit—could not possibly write an Italian opera, since, although regarded as a great virtuoso—he allegedly lacked the "*chiaro ed oscuro* that is necessary in the theater." Mozart taught his would-be critics a lesson: following the orchestral rehearsal in Milan's Sala di Ridotto all disparaging gossip was silenced, and the first performance was a sensational success. Leopold Mozart wrote to his wife in Salzburg on December 29, "God be praised, the first performance of the opera took place on the 26th to general acclaim: and two things which have never before happened in Milan occurred, namely, that (contrary to the usual custom of a first night) an aria by the prima donna was repeated, although normally at a first performance the audience never calls out 'f[u]ora,' and secondly, after almost all the arias, with the exception of a mere handful delle ultime Parti, there was the most tremendous applause and cries of Viva il Maestro, viva il Maestrino after the aria concerned."

Of the second performance on December 27 Leopold wrote, "On the 27th two arias of the prima donna were repeated: and since it was Thursday, with Friday to follow, they had to try to keep things short, otherwise the duet [No. 18] would also have been repeated, such was the noise that was beginning to be made. But most of the audience still wanted to have some supper at home, and the opera with its three ballets [by Francesco Caselli] lasts a good six hours: the ballets are now going to be shortened, since they last a good two hours. How we wished that you and Nannerl could have had the pleasure of seeing the opera!—Never within living memory has there been such a desire to see a first opera in Milan as there was on this occasion; there was such terrible disagreement beforehand, with two people saying that the opera would be good, and ten others insisting that they knew in advance it would be a botched job, others again that it was a hotchpotch, and yet others that the music was German and barbarous. Patronage is of no use here in helping an opera to win acclaim, since everyone who goes to see it insists on getting his money's worth, and speaking, shouting, and criticizing as much as he likes. Patronage was useful in our own case, and indeed was necessary if the work was not to be prevented from being heard, and if the maestro was not to find obstacles placed in his way while he was working on the opera, or later during the rehearsals, and if, finally, certain malicious individuals among the orchestra members and cast were not to play tricks on him."

On January 2, 1771 Giuseppe Parini informed the readers of the *Gazzetta di Milano* that the audience had been well satisfied, the sets tasteful, and the music excellent. A number of Aspasia's arias, he went on, expressed real passion and moved the listeners' hearts.

Structure of the opera

Mitridate, Rè di Ponto is a number opera. It contains 25 separate numbers, not including the Overture. The entire opera, moreover, boasts only a single duet (No. 18) and one chorus (No. 25), which is in fact not so much a chorus as a quintet performed by the soloists at the end of the work.

Hermann Abert claimed that Mozart was, emotionally, not equal to the task of composing *Mitridate*; and Alfred Einstein once wrote that Leopold Mozart ought to have advised his son, "Keep your hands off it! It's beyond your abilities. Wait till you're more mature, since it's the best *opera seria* libretto you'll ever get your hands on." But Einstein's reproach inevitably begs the question how Mozart's Italian career would have developed if he had turned down this *scrittura*. What did Mozart achieve here? He remained within the conventions of the genre, met the challenge that had been set him, and delivered the work he had been asked to write.

Opera seria presupposes an abstract formalism and rigorous schematicism in matters of musical form. Immutable human qualities such as goodness, wisdom, magnanimity, bravery, and black-hued malice have to be depicted here. The action is divided into precisely regulated entrances and exits, and the situation on stage culminates in the individual aria that dominates the work as a whole. *Opera seria* involves a stylistic unity that precludes the possibility of experimentation. Music, words, costumes, sets, gesture, stage, and auditorium are subject to the stylistic principles of all Baroque art. As yet, Mozart neither wished nor was able to depict characters of flesh and blood as he would do later in *The Marriage of Figaro*. Indeed, it would have been a mistake for him to have done so in Milan in 1770, when the audience, expecting a quite specific genre, would have felt snubbed by anything different. Mozart showed brilliant skill in adapting his style to suit that of the neo-Neapolitan school, and, as was usual on such occasions, for whole stretches on end pushed all question of his own personality into the background.

An entirely personal note, however, is struck in Aspasia's G minor aria "Nel sen mi palpita" (No. 4) which expresses the heroine's grief and melancholy and which thereby becomes the heart of the entire work. Other pieces that are permeated by unmistakably Mozartian characteristics include Mitridate's entrance *cavata* "Se di lauri il crine" (No. 8), Sifare's aria "Lungi da te, mio ben" (No. 13), and the duet for Aspasia and Sifare scored *(inter alia)* for four horns, "Se viver non degg'io" (No. 18). Such features become increasingly pronounced and constitute the Mozart whom we know and recognize. In composing the individual numbers Mozart drew upon all the musical forms that were then available to him—da capo aria, shortened da capo, and two-part cavatina. The arias are structured in terms of both recitative and arioso, giving scope for "affections" and moments of repose. The young composer's never-ending stream of invention and new ideas prevent him from achieving a sense of inner unity in some of the individual numbers. The coloratura passages are not yet used to express psychological processes and often fail to match the words, serving rather to show off the singer's bel canto line and his or her virtuosity. Unlike the Italian composers of the time, Mozart lavished great care on the secco recitatives. Whereas the aria gravitates around a single principal emotion, the *recitativo secco* follows the dynamic development of the plot; it is well declaimed in *Mitridate* and always reflects the emotional state of the actor concerned. Leopold Mozart

will undoubtedly have advised his son in writing the opera.

The fourteen-year-old Mozart entered new compositional territory with *Mitridate, Rè di Ponto*, but he accomplished the task brilliantly. Without denying convention or destroying the generic type, he made himself familiar with the genre of *opera seria*, and delivered the goods as requested.

Without the need to experiment, Mozart scored an immediate success in the international opera world and in a large opera house of European caliber.

The Neue Mozart-Ausgabe published the score in 1966 in an edition by Luigi Ferdinando Tagliavini, and it was this edition which served as the basis for the 1971 Salzburg Festival production of the work, premiered in the Felsenreitschule on August 7, 1971. Ernst Poettgen staged the opera for the Deutsche Oper am Rhein in Düsseldorf during the company's 1971-72 season. A concert performance was given in the Grosses Festspielhaus in Salzburg on January 21, 1977 as part of the 1977 Mozart Week; a gramophone recording of the production followed later that same year. Important stagings of the work include those seen at the 1983 Schwetzingen Festival, and at the Teatro Olimpico in Vicenza and the Gran Teatro La Fenice in Venice, both in 1984. The 1985 Zurich Opera production was conducted by Nikolaus Harnoncourt; Jean-Pierre Ponnelle directed and designed the sets, and Pet Halmen designed the costumes.

Deutsche Oper am Rhein, Düsseldorf, 1971-72 (October 23, 1971) Aspasia: Meredith Zara. Sifare: Rachel Yakar. Producer: Ernst Poettgen. Designer: Ruodi Barth. Costumes: Jan Skalicky. Conductor: Günther Wich Scene in Act I. "Ernst Poettgen's production did not even attempt to present a realistic or even illusionistic staging, but, supported by Ruodi Barth as set designer and Jan Skalicky as costume designer, provided decorative tableaux illustrative of particular 'affects,' in which the singers and audience could concentrate uninterruptedly on the musical content that was being conveyed. Since brief, spoken summaries of the plot were interpolated between each complex of scenes, the audience knew, even without being able to understand Italian, what was going on all the time. In other words, Poettgen chose a kind of exhibition method, somewhere between opera and *concerto scenico*, and the success of the production certainly justified his decision," Horst Koegler wrote in *Musica*, 1971.

Salzburg Mozart Week given by the International Mozarteum Foundation in collaboration with the Salzburg Landestheater, January 25, 1988 (Great Hall of the University) Giuditta (Jutta Geister) and the chorus of the Salzburg Landestheater (chorus master: Ernst Raffelsberger). Producer: Ernst Poettgen. Designer: Gerhard Jax. Costumes: Susanne Birke. Conductor: Walter Hagen-Groll "My idea is to elucidate the dramaturgy of the piece, as determined by the sequence of musical numbers, and to set it within a precise framework. The authentic account contained in the Bible is of use here. There is a translation made in Augsburg in 1776 that was also being used in St. Peter's in Salzburg at this period, and it is from this that I have taken the Book of Judith and incorporated it into our own production. At the same time, the relatively few real secco recitatives have been dropped. In this way the listener experiences the story directly through the spoken word.... Within the dramaturgy of the work, it seemed to me especially important, now that we had embarked in the direction of a religious message, to use the newly gained element of language in such a way that this language leads us, logically, into the densest moments of the action—such as the exact chronology of Judith's deed—while at the same time remaining fully contained by the musical aspect of the work," Ernst Poettgen explained in his program note.

Betulia liberata

The biblical background of the libretto

Whereas *opera seria* took its subject matter from classical history and mythology, the *azione sacra* or oratorio drew repeatedly on the Holy Scriptures. The source of *Betulia liberata* is the apocryphal Book of Judith, an account of the life of Judith in sixteen chapters formerly included in the Old Testament. In it the following incident is recounted: Nebuchadnezzar has declared war on the Medes, but he is not supported by the western states of Syria, Arabia, and Palestine. Having subdued the Medes, he resolves to punish the western states for their lack of assistance. The latter submit, with the exception of the Jews who are represented by the town of Betulia. Holofernes sets out with his troops to wage war on the Jews. Achior the Ammonite introduces him to the history and religion of the Jewish nation, and encourages him to attack the country in order to determine whether Jehovah will protect them or not. Angered by Achior's remarks, Holofernes hands the Ammonite over to the Jews. He lays siege to Betulia and cuts off the town's water supply. After five days the Jews consider whether or not to surrender. Judith decides to go to Holofernes's camp with her maid. He receives her well and gives a banquet at which he drinks too much. Judith kills him, and brings his head back to Betulia. The Assyrians are defeated, Judith launches into a hymn of praise and is honored by her fellow citizens. She dies at the age of 105.

The Book of Judith cannot lay claim to historical truth, and is more of a historical novel characterized by religious and nationalist fervor and poetic verve. Nebuchadnezzar, who destroyed Jerusalem and its temple, ruled Babylon from 606 to 562 B.C. The Assyrian empire crumbled in 610 B.C. A certain Holofernes is known from a later period as commander of the combined armies of Artaxerxes Ochus (Artaxerxes III) in a campaign waged by the Persians against the Egyptians. The author may have wished to draw a pseudonymous veil over historical events, or it may even have been his purpose to promulgate a fictional tale of didactic value. Students of religious history date the Book of Judith to the third century B.C. The narrative follows certain dramatic rules: Judith herself does not appear until chapter eight, so that the action develops at a leisurely pace until then. The opening chapters set the scene. The background is described first, after which the reader's attention is increasingly focused and finally concentrated upon the tragedy's point of departure.

Among the critics of Judith's action were first and foremost the moralist writers of the day. In order to achieve a laudable aim she used illegitimate means, namely, falsehood, seduction, and murder. But the Book of Judith is a piece of theology. In the hand of God the well-to-do widow becomes an agent of justice, a single episode within the wider framework of God's mighty plan. She is treated as an exemplary figure, as someone who devoutly observes the laws. Holofernes's pride leads to his humiliation and to a pitiful end. Judith is seen as a perfect human embodiment of the Judaic ideal. And Christianity, too, expressed its admiration for this

K. 118 (74c)

Azione sacre in two parts by Pietro Metastasio. Written in Salzburg in the summer of 1771. Autograph score with additions by Leopold Mozart. Act I Deutsche Staatsbibliothek in East Berlin, Act II Staatsbibliothek Preussischer Kulturbesitz in West Berlin.

Betulia liberata

Jewish heroine, albeit at a very late date. Her chastity in widowhood was compared to Christian purity.

Performances of the "oratorio"

We have only sketchy information concerning the genesis of *Betulia liberata*. Leopold Mozart and his son are known to have left Venice for their first visit to Italy and to have arrived in Padua on March 13, 1771. They spent the night at the Palazzo Pesaro. While in Padua Wolfgang played on a cembalo belonging to the oboist, composer, and voice teacher Giovanni Ferrandini and on the S. Giustina organ, an instrument much admired by Goethe during his stay in the northern Italian town in 1786. The young composer also paid a visit on Francesco Antonio Vallotti, a music theorist and kapellmeister with whom Padre Giambattista Martini was in regular correspondence. The same day, March 13, Mozart received a commission or "scrittura" to write an oratorio for Padua. On the 14th Leopold wrote from Vicenza to inform his wife that Mozart had been given "work" and that he "had to write an oratorio for Padua, which can be done as and when he likes." A good four months later, on July 19, 1771, we find Leopold writing from Salzburg to Count Giovanni Luca Pallavicini-Centurioni in Bologna, revealing that the oratorio had been commissioned by the Padua music lover Don Giuseppe Ximenes de Principi d'Aragona. Ximenes used to hold musical gatherings in his palazzo (as a rule it was oratorios and cantatas that were performed), and he was in lively correspondence with the leading music theorist of the day, Padre Martini. One of Ximenes's surviving works is the text to the cantata *Il deliro umano* published in Padua in 1768. In other words, the oratorio was commissioned by an important figure in Padua's musical life. Ximenes would no doubt have preferred it if Mozart had completed the work by Holy Week 1771. But the composer is unlikely to have made any progress on it during his return journey from Padua to Salzburg, which lasted from March 14 to 28, 1771. We can probably conclude from this that *Betulia liberata* was written in Salzburg after the Mozarts' return there in the summer of 1771.

The above-mentioned letter from Leopold Mozart to Count Luca Pallavicini also reveals that the text of the oratorio was by Pietro Metastasio and that during their second visit to Italy between August 13 and December 15, 1771, the Mozarts had thought of sending the autograph score from Verona to Padua for it to be copied there. On their return journey from Milan (where *Ascanio in Alba* was performed on October 17) they hoped to hear a rehearsal of the oratorio in Padua. We do not know whether Mozart sent the manuscript to Padua or whether he attended a rehearsal there. Contemporary sources maintain an equally impenetrable silence on the question of a performance of the work. What is certain is that a *Betulia liberata* by Giuseppe Calegari was performed in Padua in 1771, and it may well be that Calegari's composition replaced Mozart's, either because the latter's setting was in some way unacceptable or because it arrived too late. In the absence of any documentary evidence we cannot be sure.

Structural differences between oratorio and opera

It was standard practice in Italy until around 1770 to replace operas by oratorios during the period of Lent, a custom which has resulted in countless oratorios surviving from that time. The oratorio differs fundamentally in its structure from the *opera seria*. It is conceived and designed in two parts, whereas the *opera seria* typically has three acts, and the action is limited in the former genre since the love intrique—a regular feature of *opere serie*—is lacking. The chorus plays a more central role, and ensembles and *recitativi accompagnati* are found more frequently than in *opere serie*. The recitative is generally composed to reflect the librettist's expressive aims. Both halves end with a chorus, often homophonic in style. Oratorio is designed rather to clarify the inner conflicts of the protagonists, to round out the characters, and to offer a believable biblical and religious experience. It appeals to the listener's imagination in a way that opera cannot, not least because it depicts things which, because of the rules of *bienséance*, could not be presented on stage. By about 1770 the oratorio no longer fulfilled a liturgical function and had become a kind of *opera seria* without costumes and scenery. Indeed, oratorio had grown so like *opera seria* that a distinction can be sought only in its subject matter and dramaturgical conception. The text of Mozart's *Betulia liberata* is by Pietro Metastasio, whose works derive their inspiration more especially from the spirit of eighteenth-century music. He liked to depict antithetical characters, and to distinguish vice from virtue as darkness from light. His emotions or "affects" are subjected to courtly convention, and his arias correspond to a certain typology (simile aria, revenge aria, lament, and so on). The Emperor Karl VI had commissioned the text of *Betulia liberata* from Metastasio in 1734, and the work was heard the same year in the Vienna Court Chapel in a setting by Georg Reutter the Younger. Numerous later composers set the text to music, even after Mozart had done so. In his critical edition of Metastasio, Bruno Brunelli lists over thirty settings of the Judith story based on Metastasio's text alone.

Characters and résumé of the plot

Ozìa, prince of Betulia (tenor); Judith, Manasse's widow (contralto); Amital, Israelite noblewoman (soprano); Achior, prince of the Ammonites (bass); Cabri, leader of the people (soprano); Carmi, leader of the people (soprano); chorus of townspeople.

PART ONE. Nebuchadnezzar's army commander, the Assyrian captain Holofernes, has laid siege to Betulia. Ozìa exhorts his troops not to lose heart. One of the leaders of the people, Cabri, and an Israelite noblewoman, Amital, tell of the fear that has taken hold of Betulia: all the townspeople believe death is at hand, friends and kinsmen embrace, bidding each other a last farewell. Ozìa reminds the others that Jehovah has always stood by the people of Israel and helped them with miracles. Holofernes, he continues, had been threatening Betulia for a long time but did not dare attack the town. They should regard that as a sign of God's favor. Cabri points out that the town's water supply is running short since Holofernes has gained control of the source. Amital reproaches Ozìa for his indecisiveness, bidding him negotiate with the Assyrians and thus reduce the population's sufferings. She demands that he hand over Betulia to the Assyrians without delay. Ozìa asks for five days' grace, in the hope that Jehovah will perhaps confirm the glory of His name during that time. Judith, Manasse's God-fearing widow, emerges from a four-year period of self-imposed hiding, where she has spent her nights in prayer and her days in fasting, despising the wealth and beauty which heaven had granted her. She exhorts

Ozìa not to hand over Betulia, promising instead to provide him with help. The people of Israel should trust in Jehovah, she tells him. Ozìa asks Judith to pray to Jehovah for mercy, forgiveness, and counsel. She places her trust in Ozìa and devises a plan whereby he is to wait for her at sunset at the town gate. Carmi, one of the leaders of the people, drags in a prisoner left behind by the enemy. It is Achior, prince of the Ammonites. Achior reveals that he has told Holofernes the history of the chosen people and explained that Jehovah is forever on their side: only if Israel were unfaithful to its God would Holofernes be certain of victory; but as long as it stands before Him pure in heart, he—Achior—saw no prospect of success. Consumed by anger, Holofernes had hounded him out of the Assyrian camp and sent him to Betulia to be killed with the Betulians. Ozìa offers Achior refuge in his house. Judith appears. She has cast aside her widow's weeds and is now resplendently attired. She orders Ozìa to open the town gates: she intends leaving the town, unarmed, at sunset, together with her companion.

PART TWO. Ozìa seeks to convince Achior that there is only one true God. Amital expresses her dismay that the situation has not altered. Their complaints have become less vocal, their pain more intense. Judith appears. Jehovah has kept his promise. She tells how she succeeded in winning Holofernes's confidence and at the same time aroused his feelings for her. Following a meal at which he had drunk too much, she struck off his head with his sword. She describes her action in detail. Achior is converted to Judaism: he swears he will love and acknowledge no other God save the God of Abraham. Amital confesses to having offended against God's divine mercy. Carmi announces that, following Holofernes's death, the Assyrians have worn themselves out in flight. Judith is honored as Israel's savior, although she points out that their hymn of thanks should rather be directed at Jehovah alone.

Structure of the oratorio

Mozart's *Betulia liberata* is written in the style of *opera seria*, a style almost indistinguishable from that of contemporary Neapolitan oratorio, and especially that of Johann Adolf Hasse. The heroic subject matter of the piece demanded musical forms similar to those of *opera seria*. In consequence what we find in Mozart's score is a tripartite overture, da capo and bravura arias, and *recitativi secchi* and *accompagnati*. Particular attention has been devoted to the instrumental writing, and Mozart also involves the chorus in the action, as Gluck did, giving its members an independent life and setting them off from the background. The musical form and structure give an inner profundity to the sacred subject matter.

The overture in D minor reflects the atmosphere of the *azione sacra*, mirroring the disconsolate mood of the Jewish people. It is striking that there is no thematic contrast in the opening movement; instead the thematic relationship between the outer movements works almost like a link. Gluck's overture to *Alceste* may perhaps have served as a model for the fifteen-year-old Mozart. The arias are richly scored, with the wind in particular being integrated into the structure. Judith's vocal line is in some ways a preliminary study for Giunia's part in *Lucio Silla*, composed in 1772. Mozart shows a preference for concertante arias with abbreviated repeat sections, reflecting his wish to avoid wearying and boring his singers and listeners with long da capo repeats. The character arias that are interwoven into the plot are psychologically sophisticated, and Judith's monologue (No. 8) is especially skillful in its orchestration, in addition to containing a number of ear-catching modulations. The extravagant coloratura of individual arias points the way to Mozart's Italian masterpieces.

The recitatives reveal particular care on the composer's part. At the beginning of Part Two, the dispute between Ozìa and Achior on the subject of polytheism and monotheism illustrates the speakers' gestures by means of short instrumental phrases. Judith describes her action in killing Holofernes in a long yet tensely expectant *recitativo accompagnato*.

The chorus scenes (Nos. 4, 6, 9 and 16) are characterized by their homophonic writing, strident sounds, declamatory phrases and passionate orchestral figures. They are also directly connected with the action. Nos. 4 and 6 employ simple but highly effective homo-phonic writing to express the people's despair. No. 9 underlines the Jews' astonishment at Judith's heroic action and the resultant sense of inspiration. No. 16 is a hymn in praise of the Betulians' new-found freedom. Subjective feeling becomes inseparable here from ecclesiastical objectivity. The final chorus is based on the ninth church mode or *tonus peregrinus* associated with Psalm 113, *In exitu Israel de Aegypto*. The same cantus firmus recurs in Mozart's *Requiem* K. 626 at the words "Te decet hymnus." Another composer to interweave church modes into his choruses is Johann Adolf Hasse, who used the chorale "O Lamb of God" in the Pilgrims' Chorus of his *Santa Elena*.

Gerhard Croll has shown that the four-part melody of the final chorus (No. 16) is not by Mozart, but has been taken over from a piece by Michael Haydn that had been written a year previously. Haydn's tragedy *Pietas christiana* with words by Florian Reichssiegel had been performed in the Great Hall of Salzburg University on August 31, 1770. The work contains two choruses, the first of which was appropriated by Mozart for use in his *Betulia liberata*. With the exception of a few changes necessitated by the new text, Mozart's choral writing is identical to that of Haydn's chorus. Why Mozart should have copied or borrowed in this way we do not know.

In his *Betulia liberata* Mozart pulled out all the stops, so to speak, and painted a lively picture using a highly colorful palette in order to show that he could effortlessly adapt his style to suit oratorio and complete his commissioned "work" without any difficulty.

The full score of *Betulia liberata* was published by Breitkopf & Härtel of Leipzig in December 1882 in the old Mozart Edition, and the work was taken up into the Neue Mozart-Ausgabe in 1960. A concert performance of the *azione sacra* was given in Salzburg's Grosses Festspielhaus on January 29, 1978 as part of the 1978 Mozart Week. The first ever staging of the oratorio was seen in the Great Hall of Salzburg University on January 25 and 27, 1988 as part of the 1988 Mozart Week.

Ascanio in Alba

Father Leopold's reports to Mother

On March 18, 1771 Leopold wrote from Verona to inform his wife (who had remained behind in Salzburg) that he had received a letter from Milan which had arrived the previous day and which had announced that a further missive was on its way to him from Vienna; this second letter, however, would not reach him until after his return to Salzburg from Italy. According to Leopold, it "will not only fill you with amazement, but will bring our son imperishable honor." The letter in question contained a commission from the Empress Maria Theresa for a *serenata teatrale* to be written for the politically important wedding between the seventeen-year-old Archduke Ferdinand of Austria, the third son of the Emperor Franz I and brother of the later Emperor Leopold II, and Princess Maria Beatrice Ricciarda of Modena, of the House of Este. On July 19, 1771 Leopold wrote to Margrave Giovanni Luca Pallavicini, who had been in the service of Austria since 1731 and a field marshal since 1754, informing the latter that he and his son Wolfgang were expected in Milan at the beginning of September in order to comply with the conditions of the commission. The oldest of Maria Theresa's "maîtres de musique," Johann Adolf Hasse, was to compose the festival opera, while her youngest composer was to write the serenata.

The libretto of *Ascanio in Alba* had still not been approved by the Austrian Court on August 24, 1771. This was the day on which Leopold wrote to his wife to report that they were "awaiting the poem with dreadful anxie-ty, for until it arrives it is impossible to make a start on the costumes and scenery, or to arrange the stage, etc. The Archduke will arrive in Milan on the 15th of October and, the moment he alights from his carriage, he will go straight to the Cathedral and get married." The libretto finally arrived in Milan on Thursday, August 30. But Wolfgang "has not yet written anything apart from the overture, which is a relatively long allegro followed by an andante that has to be danced, but by only a few people; then, instead of the final allegro, there is a kind of contredanse and chorus, to be sung and danced at the same time. Well, he will have a fair amount of work to do during the coming month." And in September Leopold writes that "our minds are on other things at present, since the poem arrived late and was still in the poet's hands until two days ago on account of various changes that he wanted to make. I hope it will turn out well: but Wolfg. now has his hands full, since he also has to write the ballet which links together the two acts or parts."

As early as September 13 Leopold was able to report back to Salzburg that "With God's help Wolfgang will have completely finished the serenata in twelve days' time, though really it is more of an *azione teatrale* in two parts. The recitatives, with and without instrumental accompaniment, are all finished, as are the choruses, of which there are eight, and of which five are also danced. We saw the dances being rehearsed today, and marveled at the hard work of the two ballet masters, Pick [Carlo Le Picq, also spelt Lepic and Lepik] and [Jean] Fabier [a colleague of Le Picq's]. The first scene is Venus coming

K. 111

Festa teatrale in due atti. Words by Giuseppe Parini. Begun in Milan at the end of August 1771, and completed there on September 23, 1771. First performed at the Regio Ducal Teatro, Milan, on October 17, 1771. Autograph score: West Berlin, Staatsbibliothek Preussischer Kulturbesitz.

out of the clouds, accompanied by genii and graces. The andante of the sinfonia is danced by eleven women, that is, eight genii and the graces, or eight graces and three goddesses. The final allegro of the sinfonia is a chorus for thirty-two singers, that is, eight sopranos, eight contraltos, eight tenors and eight basses, and is also danced by sixteen persons, eight women, eight men. There is another chorus of shepherds and shepherdesses, sung by a different group. And then there are choruses for the shepherds alone, in other words, tenors and basses; and other choruses of shepherdesses, in other words, sopranos and contraltos. In the final scene they all appear together, genii, graces, shepherds, shepherdesses, singers, and dancers of both sexes, and all of them dance the final chorus. This does not include the solo dancers, that is, M. Pick, Mme. Binetti, M. Fabier and Mlle. Blache. The short solos, which come during the choruses, either between two sopranos, or between alto and soprano etc., are also interspersed with solos for dancers, male and female. The characters in the cantata are: La Venere, Signora Falchini, seconda donna. Ascanio, Signor Manz[u]oli, primo uomo. Silvia, Signora Girelli, prima donna. Aceste, sacerdote, Signor Tibaldi, tenor. Fauno, Pastore, Signor Solzi, secondo uomo."

"The serenata will be rehearsed at the end of the coming week," we learn from a letter dated September 21; "and the first rehearsal of the recitatives is on Monday, with chorus rehearsals on the remaining days. Wolfg. will have completed the whole work by Monday or Tuesday at the latest." The choruses were rehearsed on September 27, and the first full rehearsal with music was held on the 28th. Further rehearsals took place on October 4, 8, 11, and 14. The work, Leopold informed his wife, was "really a short opera." The singers, whom he described as "most excellent and sensible people," had all visited the composer: "everyone is extremely kind and shows the greatest respect for Wolfgang." The Archduke Ferdinand, Governor and Captain General of Lombardy by profession, arrived in Milan on October 15, and the wedding took place the same day in the city's cathedral. The formal ceremonies began on the 16th with Hasse's final stage work *Il Ruggiero ovvero L'eroica gratitudine* (words by Pietro Metastasio), while Mozart's *Ascanio in Alba* was premiered on the 17th in Milan's Regio Ducal Teatro. The townspeople did not come off badly either: three hundred other couples were married and fed

by the Empress during this period. A magnificent procession of carriages drove through the town on its way to the performance of Mozart's serenata, and carnival processions, horse races, and chariot races also found general approval. The townspeople were entertained with a *cuccagna*, where the wine flowed from four fountains.

Wolfgang's *festa teatrale* was destined to enjoy a considerable success. Further performances were planned for October 19, 24, 27, and 28. The Milanese nobility kept stopping the Mozarts in the street in order to congratulate them, and the Archduke ordered two extra copies of the 465-page score. Hasse's *opera seria* simply did not pose a threat to Mozart: as Leopold wrote to Salzburg on October 19, "In short, I really cannot say how sorry I am that Wolfg.'s serenata has killed Hasse's opera." For his own part, Hasse is said to have described Mozart's success to the Abbate Giovanni Maria Ortes, a musical friend and writer, in terms that show a complete want of jealousy: "This boy will mean that we are all forgotten." Even if his words are apocryphal, they indicate the general enthusiasm that was felt for the young composer. The newly-wed couple attended the performance on the 24th and honored Mozart with cries of "bravissimo maestro," while Count Luca Pallavicini sent a letter of congratulation from Bologna. In addition to a respectable fee, the composer received a watch studded with diamonds.

The libretto was the work of Abbate Giuseppe Parini, orator at the University of Milan, resident poet at the Milan Court Theater and a writer of satires; it was intended, as it were, to congratulate the married couple, to wish them well, and to pay them homage on stage. The *festa teatrale* is a legitimate descendant of the pastoral play, the main influences being the *Aminta* of Torquato Tasso and *Il Pastor fido* by Giovan Battista Guarini. In its dramaturgy *Ascanio in Alba* may be described as Baroque. Mozart's serenata was the focus of interest in Milan during this period of pomp and ceremony, and it placed in the shade all the parades and processions; the garlanded streets and squares were forgotten. Festive procession and festival drama were closely associated. The enlightened Abbate Parini, influenced in part by the Imperial Court poet Pietro Metastasio and in part by the ideas of Francesco Algarotti and Ranieri de Calzabigi, once wrote that the theater should be domi-

Salzburg Festival, August 1, 1967 (Residenz)
Aceste: Werner Krenn. Venus: Simone Mangelsdorff. Silvia: Edith Gabry. Ascanio: Gertrude Jahn. Producer: Hellmut Matiasek. Designer: Ekkehard Grübler. Conductor: Leopold Hager

Final scene. "Death sentence" was the title which Gerhard Mayer gave to his review in the *Wochenpresse* of August 9, 1967. "Mozart caused an entirely natural sensation with his early works. In many of them—and by no means in all of those that were written for the mass requirements of contemporary courts—there is even a distant rumbling of his future genius. But it is impossible to turn back the clock, except for study purposes in seminars. Once the public has discovered the mature genius, it will no longer be interested in the 'previously future genius,' unless the boy has left behind works that are still of interest in themselves. This is all that matters in the theater. And who, apart from the arranger Bernhard Paumgartner, could really claim that he would tolerate this *Ascanio* on any stage if this tentative experiment on the part of a 15-year-old were not listed in Köchel? To present it nowadays ... to a varied audience is tantamount to pronouncing a death sentence on almost everyone concerned."

nated by "the piety and sanctity of custom, the dignity of solemn celebrations, the maturity of ministers, the good manners of women and noblemen, the magnificence of clothes, the radiance of candles, and the charm and elegance of decoration." The scenery, by the Galliari brothers, Bernardino, Fabrizio, and Giovanni Antonio, was also Baroque in style. It is said to have been so attractive visually that *Ascanio in Alba* stood out among all the other plays that were being performed. As an allegory, it paid homage to Maria Theresa in the figure of Venus, while her son Ferdinand is not difficult to recognize in the figure of Ascanio. In his description of the wedding ceremonies, published in Milan in 1824, Parini noted that the music for *Ascanio in Alba* had been written by the young Mozart and that the composer's abilities had already ensured his reputation in various European lands.

Cast list and résumé of the plot

La Venere (Venus) (soprano), Gertrude Falchini; Ascanio (male soprano), her son, Giovanni Manzuoli; Silvia (soprano), a nymph descended from Hercules, Maria Antonia Girelli-Aguilar; Aceste (tenor), priest, Giuseppe Tibaldi; Fauno (male soprano), leader of the shepherds, Adamo Solzi. Chorus of genii, chorus. Chorus of shepherds, chorus of menfolk. Chorus of shepherdesses, chorus of womenfolk.

The action takes place in the open countryside. In the center of the stage is a rustic altar with an image of a strange beast representing Alba. Between the surrounding oak trees the spectator can glimpse pleasantly rolling countryside bounded by distant hills.

PART I. Venus (symbolizing Maria Theresa) descends from the heavens with her son Ascanio (representing for Ferdinand). She intends to found a new city—Alba Longa—in the very region where she once spent a time of happiness with Aeneas. Graces, genii, amoretti, and nymphs pay homage to the goddess with their singing and dancing. She appoints Ascanio ruler of Alba; she has already chosen a bride for him from the line of

Hercules, a nymph by the name of Silvia. Brought up by the priest Aceste, Silvia has repeatedly seen the god Amor appearing to her in dreams in the figure of Ascanio. She has come to love the young man. Ascanio must now test Silvia's love for him. The goddess disappears with her retinue into the clouds. Ascanio is left alone; he yearns for his beloved. Led by Fauno, shepherds and shepherdesses offer up their thanks to the merciful goddess. Fauno tells Ascanio that a sacrifice will be made to Venus that very day. He hopes that the promise of a new ruler will also be fulfilled. Aceste announces the birth of a new city: it will be founded by Venus and Ascanio, and will be called Alba. In place of lowly shepherds' houses, sacred fanes will arise, temples for the Muses, and bastions against enemies and wild animals. Asked by Fauno who he is, Ascanio admits himself to be a stranger, but says that he has come to visit the fabled beauties of Latium. When Aceste and Silvia arrive, Fauno advises Ascanio to conceal himself among the shepherds, since strangers are not allowed to approach the virgin nymph. The shepherds and shepherdesses celebrate the beauty and purity of Diana. The priest tells Silvia that, with the goddess's consent, she will marry Ascanio that very day. Silvia is thunderstruck. She admits her respect for Ascanio, but says she can never love him. Her heart belongs to a youth who has appeared to her in a dream. Aceste comforts her: the goddess has shown her the image of her future husband; she must trust in Venus. Aceste bids Silvia and the shepherds prepare to receive the goddess. A sacrifice will welcome her and her son. The shepherds repeat their hymn of supplication. Ascanio is entranced by Silvia's beauty and charm, but Venus demands that, before revealing himself to the nymph, he must test her moral virtues. She leads him to a hill and shows him the genii transforming the grove into a magnificent temple, the very first building in the newly-founded city of Alba Longa.

PART II. Silvia praises the newly-founded city as the work of the gods. She yearns to see her lover. Ascanio arrives. They recognize each other, but dare not speak. Fauno enters. He invites Ascanio to the sacrifice and to be a witness at Silvia's wedding. Thunderstruck, Silvia assumes that the stranger is not Ascanio after all, and falls to the ground in a faint. Ascanio regrets that he is unable to reveal who he is. Silvia recovers conscious-

ness, and insists that she will renounce the stranger and obey her duty. Ascanio throws himself at Silvia's feet, but she spurns him and flees. He is dismayed at the nymph's behavior. When Silvia describes her predicament to Aceste, he praises her for her nobility of character. The clouds part, and Venus appears in her chariot. She takes Ascanio in her arms and commends the young couple to increase the town and to bring joy to their subjects through justice and love. Aceste thanks the goddess in the name of the townspeople, and Venus flies back to Olympus to the sound of general rejoicing.

Critical reception of the opera

Writers on Mozart have paid scant attention to the music of *Ascanio in Alba*, the general opinion being that Mozart had little new to offer in this bucolic work and that the serenata does not mark any advance in the composer's progress as a music dramatist. However, Mozart himself regarded *Ascanio in Alba* as immensely attractive and special. After all, the composer had not yet had the opportunity in any of his previous stage works to write a grandiose pastoral play with choral and ballet sections, and with arias of a predominantly pastoral character. *Ascanio in Alba* was a new and imposing task for the young composer. If we compare Mozart's score with that of Hasse's *Ruggiero*, we will note a particularly sophisticated handling of the orchestration in the case of the fifteen-year-old Mozart. With Hasse the wind instruments are used for dynamic intensity, whereas in Mozart they take on an independent existence, and are deployed autonomously. Mozart's orchestral writing is light and bright in texture and, as such, in marked contrast to the Baroque style that typifies Hasse and *his* generation. Above all, Mozart works with contrasts, fully exploiting the dualism between subject and countersubject and allowing symphonic elements to find their way into music written for the stage. Inwardness is a word that comes to mind in describing one of the elements that distinguishes *Ascanio in Alba*. Even at this date Mozart identifies with his dramatic characters, giving them—consciously or unconsciously—human features. He uses large-scale form in his arias, often playing with it, while his solo numbers impress through their elegant thematic writing. As Hans Engel has said, the aria form in *Ascanio in Alba* has "taken on the form of an instrumental concerto." The strong preference for the chorus may well be a concession to Viennese tradition, certainly the combination of singing and dancing was far from everyday practice for Milanese audiences. *Ascanio in Alba* should not be regarded as an occasional composition in Mozart's dramatic *œuvre*, since the *festa teatrale* reveals Mozart's development as a man of the theater.

Editions and performances

The first printed score of *Ascanio in Alba* appeared in May 1879 within the framework of the old Mozart Edition published by Breitkopf & Härtel of Leipzig. The new edition, edited by Luigi Ferdinando Tagliavini, was published by the Neue Mozart-Ausgabe in 1956. Bernhard Paumgartner revised and staged the work in Italian for the Salzburg Landestheater; it was premiered on January 25, 1958 as part of the 1958 Mozart Week and performed in the opera studio of the Mozarteum by the Camerata Academica, conducted by Robert Kuppelwieser and designed by Gustav Vargo.

The opera was first performed at the Salzburg Festival on August 1, 1967 in the courtyard of the Salzburg Residenz. A concert performance, conducted by Leopold Hager, was given in the Grosses Festspielhaus in Salzburg on January 23, 1976 as part of the 1976 Mozart Week, and the performance was later recorded. A further production of the *festa teatrale* was given in the Teatro Olimpico in Vicenza on July 3, 1983.

Il Sogno di Scipione

K. 126

Azione teatrale by Pietro Metastasio. Composed in Salzburg, probably between April and August 1771. Autograph score: Staatsbibliothek Preussischer Kulturbesitz in West Berlin.

Occasions for an operatic composition

The names of two of Salzburg's prince-archbishops, Count Sigismund Christoph von Schrattenbach and Count Hieronymus Colloredo, are closely bound up with the *azione teatrale Il Sogno di Scipione* (Scipio's Dream). When Mozart returned to Salzburg from his second Italian expedition on December 15, 1771, Schrattenbach was already dying. Philological investigations have revealed that the composer had originally intended *Il Sogno di Scipione* to mark the fiftieth anniversary of Schrattenbach's ordination, which was due to fall on January 10, 1772. The prince-archbishop's sudden death on December 16, 1771 prevented the *azione teatrale* from being performed at court. Mozart revised the work for the enthronement of Schrattenbach's successor, Hieronymus Colloredo, on April 29, 1772, and altered the dedication from "Sigismondo" to "Girolamo" (Hieronymus). The libretto is by Pietro Metastasio, and had been written in 1735 for the birthday celebrations of Emperor Karl VI.

Characters and résumé of the plot

Scipio, a Roman general (tenor); Costanza (soprano); Fortuna (soprano); Publio, Scipio's adoptive grandfather (tenor); Emilio, Scipio's father (tenor); Licenza (soprano); chorus of fallen heroes.

The action takes place in Africa in the empire of Massinissa. The Roman general Publius Cornelius Scipio Aemilianus, best known as the captor of Carthage, has fallen asleep in the palace of King Massinissa of Numidia. Costanza and Fortuna appear before him in his dream, praising their respective gifts and inviting Scipio to chose one or other of them to guide him through his life. Confused by these ghostly apparitions, Scipio begs time to consider his decision, and demands to know where he is. Costanza and Fortuna declare their readiness to reply to his questions. He discovers that he is in the Elysian Fields, and that the unusual but melodic sound that he can hear is the harmony of the spheres that is imperceptible on earth since it transcends the power of the human senses. Scipio expresses a wish to know who inhabits these immortal abodes. Fallen Roman heroes appear, including his dead ancestors, Emilio and Publio, his father and grandfather. He is invited to follow them and bid them welcome. Scipio starts up in terror, only to be admonished for doing so. Publio explains that only his limbs are dead, but that his spirit and soul live on. All who, in life, sacrificed themselves to their fatherland had the fairest "dwellings" in heaven. Publio exhorts his grandson to lead a virtuous life, for only thus can he be accepted into the ranks of heavenly heroes. Fortuna, impatient of Scipio's many questions, insists that he reach a decision, but Costanza allows him to question her further, for only when in full possession of all the facts can he come to the right decision. Scipio discovers his father Emilio, who permits his son a glimpse of the tiny earth as seen from the starry vault of heaven. Scipio at once understands the futility of all human endeavor and the insignificance of human ostentation. He desires to remain with his father, but Costanza and Fortuna are unable to meet his request. His ancestors remind him of the need to fulfill his duty to Rome and his fatherland. Scipio bows his head to fate's decree, but is still obliged to choose between one or the other goddess. He asks his father's advice, but the latter declines to deprive his son of the "honor of making a choice." Fortuna presses him for a reply, declaring that all his emprises will founder if fortune does not attend him in future. He asks her whether there is no power greater than the whim of fortune. Costanza beckons him: she alone can stand in Fortuna's way. Scipio accordingly decides in Costanza's favor, unafraid of Fortuna's vengeance. The goddess of fortune vents her wrath in thunder and lightning, and thus reveals her true face to Scipio. He wakes up and realizes it was all a dream, but feels in his heart that Costanza was real. Licenza (a theatrical epilogue addressed to the audience) enters as Homage personified and announces the allegory's moral in the form of a direct address. The virtues of Prince-Archbishop Colloredo are compared to those of Scipio. But whereas Scipio was praised with mere words, the country's ruler deserves and demands his people's affection. It is an otiose exercise to *listen* to tales of exemplary virtue from out of the past, when that selfsame virtue is plain to *see* in the person of Colloredo. The chorus wishes the new prince-archbishop a serenely peaceful rule: may his mitre and heart be spared the fickleness of the goddess Fortuna.

Editions and performances

The first full printed score of *Il Sogno di Scipione* was published by Breitkopf & Härtel in Leipzig in August 1880 within the framework of the old Mozart Edition; the work was reedited in 1977 as part of the Neue Mozart-Ausgabe. A concert performance of the work, conducted by Leopold Hager, was given in the Grosses Festspielhaus in Salzburg on January 20, 1979, 208 years after its first performance. The piece has yet to be staged.

Salzburg Festival, July 28, 1964 (Residenz)
Lucio Silla: William Dooley.
Giunia: Melitta Muszely.
Producer: Christoph Groszer.
Designer: Ekkehard Grübler.
Conductor: Bernhard Conz
Scene in Act I. In the original opera the part of Lucio Silla is scored for a tenor, but it was sung here by a bass-baritone.

Lucio Silla

Success spurs new commission

Following the successful first performances of Mozart's *Mitridate, Rè di Ponto*, the *associati* of Milan's Regio Ducal Teatro decided on March 4, 1771 to commission a second opera from the young Salzburg composer, this time for the 1772-73 carnival season. The contract was signed by the theater's director Federico Castiglione and required Mozart to have completed the recitatives of his new opera by October 1772, in return for which he would be paid a substantial fee and given free board in the city. He was to arrive in Milan in November and write the arias and ensembles for the individual singers *in situ*, and he was also contractually obliged to attend all the rehearsals.

We cannot say for certain who suggested the text to Mozart. It was probably an Italian offer, and certainly Wolfgang himself is scarcely likely to have influenced the choice.

The text of *Lucio Silla*, the last of his operas written for Italy, is by Giovanni de Gamerra, a native of Leghorn, where he had taken holy orders as Abbate, before studying law in Pisa and then deciding on a life of soldiery in 1765, when he became "Tenente nelle Armi di Sua Maestà Imperiale." In addition to a number of opera libretti, Gamerra wrote a genre of sentimental tragedy that was all the rage in Europe in the second half of the eighteenth century. In 1775 we find Gamerra in Vienna, where he was Court poet, and in 1786 he announced his plans to found a tragicomic National Theater in Naples.

Mozart had already begun work on the recitatives in Salzburg in October 1772, but he was later obliged to change these passages, and in some cases to rewrite them completely, after Gamerra had sent his libretto to the Imperial and Royal Court poet Pietro Metastasio in Vienna. Presumably Gamerra sought Metastasio's approval because he still felt unsure of himself in the art of libretto-writing. His first text appears to have been *L'Armida*, performed in Milan in 1771 and 1772. Metastasio improved and altered Gamerra's text, and added an entire new scene in the second act.

Episodes from Roman history are typical of *opera seria*. In this case there was ample opportunity to develop grand heroic characters, but also to introduce emotions such as envy and resentment, intrigue and jealousy.

Lucius Cornelius Sulla—the classical pronunciation of the name was later changed to Sülla and then to Sylla, and spelt Sylla in French and Silla in Italian—is an enigmatic and somewhat shady character from pre-Christian Roman history. Together with Gaius Marius, a general of genius and *homo novus*, he waged war on the Cimbri and Teutones, defeating the latter in 102 B.C. at Aquae Sextiae (Aix) and the former the following year at Vercellae (Vercelli), thereby averting the first Germanic offensive against the Roman Empire. In 92 B.C. Sulla went as propraetor to Cilicia with the task of persuading Mithradates VI of Pontus to restore Cappadocia to Ariobarzanes, one of Rome's dependants in Asia. (Mithradates, it will be remembered, was the subject of Mozart's first Italian opera.) In 83 B.C., after numerous

K. 135

Dramma per musica in three acts. Words by Giovanni de Gamerra. Written in Salzburg and Milan in the fall of 1772. First performed at the Regio Ducal Teatro in Milan on December 26, 1772. Autograph score: Cracow, Biblioteka Jagiellońska.

victories over enemies both outside and inside the Empire, Sulla had himself elected dictator for life and invested with unlimited power. He was utterly vindictive in dealing with his enemies, and a sense of humanity was totally alien to him. Never have justice and humanity toward Roman communities been so disdained as they were under Sulla's dictatorship. He arrogated all judicial power to himself, and the life and possessions of every Roman citizen were placed in his hands. In 79 B.C. he renounced his dictatorship. According to Plutarch's account, "Sulla placed so much trust in his actions—far more so than in his good fortune—that he gave up his dictatorship of his own accord and restored to the common people the right to elect its consuls. Indeed, he did not even apply for the office of consul, but wandered round the marketplace like any ordinary citizen. He offered to requite all who called him to account, and he sacrificed a tenth of his wealth to Hercules. He entertained the populace to lavish banquets at which there was much eating and drinking at his own expense."

Composing the opera

Accompanied by his father, Mozart set off for Milan on October 24, arriving in the Lombardy capital about midday on November 4. Of all the singers who were to appear in Mozart's new opera, only two were present in Milan in early November, Felicità Suardi, who was to sing Lucio Cinna, and Giuseppe Onofrio, the Aufidio. Mozart spent the first half of November altering and rewriting the recitatives and also wrote the choruses "Furor di queste urne" (No. 6), "Se gloria in crin ti cinse" (No. 17), and "Il gran Silla che Roma in seno" (No. 23), together with the Overture, but he had to delay work on the arias and ensembles since the principal singers, whom he had to take account of both vocally and dramatically, were still absent. On November 21, 1772 Leopold Mozart wrote to his wife in Salzburg to report that the *primo uomo*, Venanzio Rauzzini, who was to sing the part of Cecilio, had finally arrived in Milan. Rauzzini, a castrato soprano, had been in the service of the Elector of Bavaria Maximilian III Joseph since 1765, having made his debut in Rome the previous year. London heard him in 1774. Mozart wrote the motet "Exsultate, jubilate," K. 165, for him in Milan shortly before January 16, 1773; it was first performed in the Church of the Theatines on the 17th. In the above-mentioned letter, Leopold remarks that, "There is now even more for Wolfgang to do, and things are livening up considerably." On November 28, he wrote that most of the people who were interested in the opera were still in the country and would not return to the city until the season began. Not even the Archduke Ferdinand had arrived in Milan yet. That same day (November 28), the *prima donna* Anna de Amicis Buonsolazzi, who was to create the part of Giunia, had set off for Milan from Venice: "only now can work begin in earnest," Leopold commented; "not much has been done to date." Apart from the above-mentioned recitatives, choruses, and overture, Mozart had so far written only the opening aria for Cecilio "Il tenero momento" (No. 2), a number which Leopold described as incomparable: the *primo uomo* was said to sing like an angel. Anna de Amicis arrived in Milan on December 4: "her journey from Venice to Milan by mail coach with six horses took a week, so flooded and dirty were the roads," Leopold reported to his wife on the 5th. This was the third time that the Mozarts had met the singer, who was a pupil of Vittoria Tesi. Their first meeting had been in Mainz in 1763, and their second in Naples in 1770. In a letter from Rome dated April 21, 1770, Mozart had already felt able to describe her to his sister as a good friend and acquaintance, and on May 29, 1770 he wrote to Nannerl from Naples, reporting that de Amicis had sung "à meraviglio" at a rehearsal of an opera by Niccolò Jommelli. In other words Mozart had at his disposal a distinguished and renowned singer who was on a friendly footing with him. Difficulties over the casting of the title role arose in early December. The tenor Signor Cordoni, who was to have sung the part of Lucio Silla, suddenly fell ill and handed back his part. "And so we have sent the theater secretary to Turin by special post-chaise, and a courier has been despatched to Bologna," Leopold told his wife on December 5, "in order to find some other decent tenor, who must not only be a good singer, but more especially be a good actor and cut an attractive figure, in order to perform Lucia Silla creditably. Since the prima donna did not arrive until yesterday and the tenor is still unknown, it is easy to appreciate in the circumstances that the major and most important part of the opera has yet to be written. Now we shall really get going in earnest." How pressed Mozart was for time emerges from the postscript which he added to his father's letter of December 5: "I still have 14 numbers to write, and then I'll have finished. Of course, the trio ["Quell'orgoglioso sdegno," No. 18] and duet ["D'Eliso in sen m'attendi," No. 7] can be reckoned as four pieces. I cannot write much, for I've nothing to tell you, and secondly I don't know what I could write since all my thoughts are on my opera and I risk sending you an entire aria rather than words." Three weeks before the opera's premiere only nine numbers out of twenty-three had been written: the rest had still to be composed and memorized by the singers, in addition to being copied out.

On December 12—the Mozarts were "in good health, God be praised"—Mozart informed his wife that Wolfgang was now "hard at work." "These blessed theater people leave everything to the last minute. The tenor [Bassano Morgnoni], who is coming from Turin, belongs to the King's Cappella, and is expected on the 14th or 15th; only then can his four arias be written for him. [Presumably lack of time obliged Mozart to reduce this number to two, "Il desio di vendetta," No. 5, and "D'ogni pietà mi spoglio," No. 13.] Signora de Amicis sends greetings to you both. She is quite extraordinarily pleased with the 3 arias that she has received so far. Wolfg. has introduced into her principal aria ["Ah se il crudel periglio," No. 11] passages which are new and quite special and astonishingly difficult; she sings them amazingly well, and we are on the friendliest and most intimate terms with her. I am writing with a poor pen and ink, since Wolf., who is writing at another table, has the good ink." The first rehearsal of the recitatives took place that same day, Saturday, December 12. The second was scheduled to take place as soon as Morgnoni arrived in Milan. The tenor finally arrived in the city on Thursday, December 17. Meanwhile, there had been three recitative rehearsals, which had taken place regardless of Morgnoni's belated arrival. On December 18 Leopold told his wife that Wolfgang had already written two arias for Morgnoni (see above), but that two were still outstanding. The second of these arias (No. 13) was completed at 11 o'clock on the evening of the 18th. At this point, a week before the premiere, Mozart was evidently still thinking of giving the tenor another two arias. The first stage rehearsal with orchestra took place on Saturday December 19 at 9.30. When it was over, the Mozarts dined with Albert Michael von Mayr, the Archduke's Paymaster General.

The second orchestral rehearsal was held on Sunday the 20th; and on Monday, and on the two following days, the Mozarts spent the evening at the house of Count Firmian "with all the nobility." As Leopold told his wife in a letter of December 26, "there was continuous vocal and instrumental music being played here every evening from 5 o'clock until 11 at night. We were among those invited, and Wolfg. played every evening. On the third day in particular [December 23] Wolfg. had to perform immediately Their Royal Highnesses came in, and at their special request. And both Their Royal Highnesses spoke for a long time with us." The city was decked out for Christmas, as Leopold went on to report: "On all three evenings the foremost houses were lit with great torches, in the church towers close to Count Firmian's house the bells played certain pieces like the carillons in the Netherlands, and in the street there was music with trumpets and drums, these were the festivities which were held in Milan to mark the elevation of His Eminence the Bishop of Passau [Leopold III, Count Ernst Firmian] to the dignity of Cardinal."

A further rehearsal took place on Tuesday December 22, and the first dress rehearsal followed on the Wednesday. According to Leopold, it "passed off so well that we can hope for an outstanding success. The music alone lasts four hours, without the ballets." Anna de Amicis as Giunia seems to have been especially memorable. In his letter of December 26, Leopold praises her in the following words: "De Amicis is our best friend, she sings and acts like an angel, and is extremely pleased because Wolfg. has served her uncommonly well. Both you and the whole of Salzb[urg] would be amazed if you could hear her." On Christmas Eve the Mozarts were guests of Count Firmian's steward Don Fernando Germani at a "celebratory supper." The premiere of *Lucio Silla* took place on the second day after Christmas. The Mozarts had lunch with Frau Marianne d'Asti von Astenburg, the daughter of Leopold Troger, who was an official at the Governor General's court in Milan.

The sets for *Lucio Silla* were created by the Galliari brothers, and the costumes by Francesco Motta and Giovanni Mazza. Three ballets were included in the opera, *La Gelosia del Serraglio* (music partly written by Josef Starzer), *La Scuola di Negromanzia*, and *La Giaconna*. The first and third of these ballets were choreographed by Carlo Le Picq, the second by Giuseppe Salamoni.

Lucio Silla

Cast list and résumé of the plot

Lucio Silla (tenor), dictator, Bassano Morgnoni; Giunia (soprano), daughter of Gaius Marius and betrothed to Cecilio, Anna de Amicis Buonsolazzi; Cecilio (male soprano), proscribed senator, Venanzio Rauzzini; Lucio Cinna (soprano), Roman patrician, friend of Cecilio and secret enemy of Lucio Silla, Felicità Suardi; Celia (soprano), sister of Lucio Silla, Daniella Mienci; Aufidio (tenor), tribune and friend of Lucio Silla, Giuseppe Onofrio.

ACT I. Lonely spot on the banks of the Tiber. Trees and ruins. In the distance the Quirinal, one of Rome's seven hills, can be seen, surmounted by a small temple. Lucio Silla, victor in the Roman wars against Mithradates, has banished the Senator Cecilio, who is betrothed to Giunia, the daughter of his enemy Marius. Cecilio has returned to Rome in secret in order to discover the fate of his betrothed. Cinna tells him that Silla has maliciously put about the news of his death in order to win Giunia as his bride. Cinna advises Cecilio to await his lover near the mausoleum of fallen heroes, where she habitually comes in the course of the day. The scene changes to Giunia's apartments in Sulla's palace. Here, under the watchful eye of statues of Roman heroines, Silla confers with his sister Celia on ways to win Giunia's love. Giunia enters. She rejects Silla's suit, preferring to remain loyal to her dead lover Cecilio. She would rather be dead than accept Silla's hand. Silla resolves to kill Giunia for spurning his love. The third scene is set in an imposing but somewhat gloomy vestibule at the entrance to the catacombs: memorials to Roman heroes rise up out of the darkness. Cecilio is waiting impatiently for Giunia. When she enters, he conceals himself behind Marius's funerary urn. Standing beside her father's urn, she laments the deaths of Marius and Cecilio. To her astonishment Cecilio emerges from his hiding place. At first she thinks he is a ghost, but then recognizes him as her betrothed.

ACT II. An archway adorned with military trophies. Aufidio advises Silla to tell the populace and senate that Giunia is his betrothed. She would then not dare to oppose him. Silla is prepared to follow Aufidio's advice, but his conscience holds him back. Celia tells her brother that her attempts to intercede with Giunia have been in vain. Silla then promises to unite her in marriage with Cinna, her lover. Cecilio rushes in, eager to kill Silla, having been egged on to vengeance by the ghost of Gaius Marius who had appeared to him in a dream. But Cinna discourages him from perpetrating so ill-considered a deed, pointing out that, by doing so, he would jeopardize Giunia's life. Cinna's thoughts turn to revenge, and he betrays Silla's plans to Giunia, advising her to marry Silla and kill the dictator on her nuptial couch. Giunia, however, finds the thought of so insidious a murder repellent, and so Cinna resolves to kill Silla himself. The scene changes to the Hanging Gardens. Giunia tells Silla that she would rather die than become his wife. In spite of Silla's threats Giunia begs Cecilio to remain calm and to stay in hiding. He must trust her. She will beg the senate to show her lover mercy and clemency. A further change of scene brings us to the Capitol. Silla informs the populace and senate of his plans to marry Giunia. She, however, forcefully rejects his offer. To general dismay Cecilio enters and confronts the assembly with his drawn sword. He is disarmed and thrown into chains. Cinna, in turn, enters with his sword drawn, but, realizing that Cecilio's plan has failed, he pretends that he has come to protect Silla. Silla announces that Cecilio shall die the next day.

ACT III. The forecourt of the dungeons. Cinna informs the shackled Cecilio that he has failed in his attempt to kill Silla. There is little hope of deliverance. But Cecilio believes that Celia may pacify Silla's heart. Giunia is ready to die with her lover. Aufidio enters to fetch Cecilio. Giunia, ready to follow her lover in death, is tormented by baleful thoughts of death. The scene changes to a hall in the palace. Silla makes it clear that he is determined to avenge himself on his enemy, and that his heart knows no mercy. He insists that, as a proscribed senator, Cecilio had secretly dared to break the laws. He had tried to murder him in the presence of his soldiers. Giunia accuses Silla of murdering her betrothed, and invites the populace to exact vengeance. Silla replies, "Listen to me, Giunia. Revile me if you still can. This godless Silla, this haughty tyrant whom all despised, wants Cecilio to live and to be your husband. I know now that innocence and heartfelt virtue bring more welcome peace than all deceptive splendor." Silla even forgives Cinna, who, filled with remorse, admits his attempt on the dictator's life; he and Celia are united. Silla

Regio Ducal Teatro, Milan, 1772
Set designs by Fabrizio Galliari: "Rovine" (Act I, Scene 1) and "Sepolcri" (Act I, Scene 3)
Fabrizio Galliari's magnificent sets mark the transition from Rococo to classical designs. The center and downstage areas receive particular emphasis.

renounces his power and restores freedom to Rome. All shower him with praise and glory, and acclaim him as victor.

Leopold gives an account of the premiere in a letter to his wife of January 2, 1773:

"A Happy New Year!

I forgot to wish you a Happy New Year when I last wrote, since I was not only in a hurry but in a state of confusion and absent-mindedness, as we were just on the point of leaving for the theater. The opera passed off successfully, although on the first evening a number of very annoying incidents took place. The first such incident was that the opera, which generally starts one hour after the bells have rung for vespers, started three hours late on this occasion, in other words, about 8 o'clock by German time, and it did not end until 2 in the morning. The Archduke [Ferdinand] did not rise from his midday meal until shortly before the bells began ringing, and he then had another five letters or New Year greetings to write in his own hand to Their Majesties the Emperor [Joseph II, Ferdinand's brother] and the Empress [Maria Theresa], and, nota bene, he writes very slowly, etc. etc.

"Well, you can imagine, the whole theater was so full by half past five that no one else could get in. The singers are always very nervous the first evening at having to perform before such a distinguished audience. But the terrified singers, together with the orchestra and the whole of the audience, many of them standing, had to wait impatiently in the heat for three hours for the opera to begin.

"Secondly, you must know that the tenor [Bassano Morgnoni], whom we had to take in desperation, is a church singer from Lodi [where Mozart wrote his first string quartet, K. 80], who has never acted on such a distinguished stage before; he has appeared on stage as primo tenore only a couple of times in Lodi and was only engaged a week before the performance. In her first aria [No. 4], the prima donna Anna de Amicis should expect him to show her a gesture of anger, but he performed this angry gesture in such an exaggerated way that it looked as though he was about to box her ears and knock off her nose with his fist, which made the audience laugh. Carried along by her own enthusiasm, Signora de Amicis did not realize at first why the audience was laughing, and she was taken aback and initially did not know who was being laughed at, so that she did not sing well

for the rest of the evening, because she was also jealous that the primo uomo [Venanzio Rauzzini] was applauded by the Archduchess the moment he came on stage. This was a typical trick of the kind that castratos play, since he had arranged for the Archduchess to be told that, such was his fear, he would be unable to sing, his intention being to ensure that the court would then encourage and applaud him. In order to console her, Signora de Amicis was summoned to Court at around noon the next day, and she had an audience with Their Royal Highnesses which lasted for a whole hour, only then did the opera begin to go well, and although the theater is normally very empty for a first opera, the first six performances (today [January 2] is the seventh) were so full that it was scarcely possible to slip in, and the prima donna generally has the upper hand, with her arias having to be repeated. Madame d'Asti, at whose house I am writing, sends her greetings and wishes you a Happy New Year. Please convey our greetings to all our dear friends, both male and female. Inside and outside the house, we kiss you many millions of times. I am your old Mzt. Wolfg. sends his special greetings, we are well, thank God."

Critical reception of the opera

The Milanese audience appears to have liked Mozart's opera. On January 9, 1773 Leopold was able to tell his wife, "the opera, praise God, is going incomparably well, so that the theater is astonishingly full every day, although people do not normally come to a first opera in large numbers unless it receives special acclaim. Arias are repeated every day, and since the first night the opera has gained daily in popularity and has won increasing acclaim, indeed, Count [Carlo Ercole] Castelbarco has presented my son with a gold watch with a beautiful golden chain, and a sedan chair and a gold lantern. And so you can have yourself transported in the chair and Bölzl-mayr can light the way for you." By January 16, 1773 Lucio Silla had been given seventeen times. Since Mozart's opera was such a success, the second opera of the season, Il Sismano nel Mogol by Giovanni Paisiello could not be performed until January 30. On January 23 Leopold wrote to tell his wife that Lucio Silla had now been given twenty-six times: "the theater is astonishingly full every day. The rest of the time is being kept free for the second opera [Il Sismano nel Mogol], on

Zurich Opera, February 28, 1981
Cecilio: Ann Murray. Giunia: Edita Gruberova. Lucio Silla: Eric Tappy. Cinna: Jill Gomez. Celia: Rachel Yakar. Producer and designer: Jean-Pierre Ponnelle. Costumes: Pet Halmen. Conductor: Nikolaus Harnoncourt

The finale during a rehearsal. "[Ponnelle] decided against a unit set, and retained only the imposing entrance from his *Idomeneo* production, using, instead, a series of flats that could be flown in and out to create an illusionistic staging which gave the impression of depth and a classical ambiance. The flats were painted with designs based on engravings by Piranesi and Bibiena, and provided a traditional view of classical antiquity typical of the eighteenth century, for whom ancient Rome was a place of imagined perfection and ruins. By the same token, Ponnelle depicted the classical characters as courtly figures from Mozart's time, but motivated by living and, to a certain extent, 'timeless' human passions. In his handling of the characters, Ponnelle succeeded in producing a synthesis between statuesque attitudes and emotional expressive gestures," according to Wolfgang Schreiber in *Musica*, 1981.

Fridays and one or two holy days there are no performances. I have sent Wolfgang's opera to the Grand Duke [Leopold of Tuscany] in Florence. Even if there is nothing to hope for from that quarter, I still hope he may recommend us. But if it is all in vain, I do not suppose we shall go under, God will help us, and I already have other plans."

Mozart himself commented on Paisiello's opera—something of a rival to his own *Lucio Silla*—in a letter to his sister of January 23, 1773: "The first rehearsal of the second opera took place yesterday evening, but I heard only the first act, since it was late and I left at the beginning of the second act. There are to be twenty-four horses and a large crowd on stage in this opera, so that it will be a miracle if some accident does not happen. I like the music, but I do not know whether the public will like it."

The fact that Mozart thought highly of *Lucio Silla* is clear from performances of individual numbers from the work. On January 23, 1778 he set out with Fridolin Weber and his daughter Aloisia, Mozart's later sister-in-law, for Kirchheim-Bolanden, where they stayed for several days at the court of Princess Caroline von Nassau-Weilburg. During their visit, Aloisia, who had fallen in love with Mozart, sang two of Giunia's arias, "Dalla sponda tenebrosa," No. 4, and "Ah se il crudel periglio," No. 11. At an *accademia* held

at Johann Christian Cannabich's Aloisia sang arias Nos. 11 and 16, "Parto m'affretto." On March 23, 1783 Therese Teyber sang No. 16 at Mozart's great *accademia* in the Vienna Burgtheater.

There is no record of any further complete performance of *Lucio Silla* during the eighteenth or nineteenth centuries. The first printed score appeared in August 1880 in the framework of the old Mozart Edition. The Neue Mozart-Ausgabe, edited by Kathleen Kuzmick Hansell, appeared in 1986.

Later settings of Gamerra's text include those by Johann Christian Bach for the Mannheim Court Theater (premiered on November 4, 1773) and Pasquale Anfossi for the Teatro di S. Samuele in Venice (Ascension 1774). The first performance of Mozart's *Lucio Silla* in the present century was given by the Prague Theater on December 14, 1929. It was performed in the Residenz at Salzburg as part of the 1964 Salzburg Festival. A concert performance of the opera was given in the Grosses Festspielhaus on January 24, 1975, when the conductor was Leopold Hager. The performance was later recorded. Jean-Pierre Ponnelle staged the opera in Zurich in 1981; Patrice Chéreau for La Scala, Milan (June 5, 1984), for the Théâtre des Amandiers in Nanterre (September 30, 1984), and for the Opéra National de Belgique.

Lucio Silla

Opéra National de Belgique, Brussels, January 22, 1985 (Théâtre Royal de la Monnaie)
Lucio Silla: Anthony Rolfe Johnson. Giunia: Lella Cuberli. Producer: Patrice Chéreau. Designer: Richard Peduzzi. Costumes: Jacques Schmidt. Conductor: Sylvain Cambreling
Patrice Chéreau emphasized the geometrical nature of the plot by dressing the characters in black Rococo uniforms and having their actions reflected by groups of accompanying extras who evoked the impression of echoes or shadows. A gray sliding wall that kept on changing shape provided the background for this *opera seria*, which Chéreau transformed into a tragedy.

Structure of the opera

Mozart appears not to have given his complete approval to Gamerra's libretto, since he came closer to the essential drama of the theme than the poet had done, and expressed more, in terms of his music, than the text demanded. Mozart's subjective view of music and drama in *Lucio Silla* has been described by Théodore Wyzewa and Georges de Saint-Foix, among others, as a "grande crise romantique." But attempts have also been made to attribute the work to a *Sturm und Drang* phase in the composer's operatic output. What is decisive, however, as Leopold Conrad has pointed out in *Mozarts Dramaturgie der Oper*, is that Mozart was working within the framework of Baroque dramaturgy. The contrasts of mood which typify the score are to be understood in the Baroque sense of a contrastive dynamism, a contrastive dynamism which is of course colored in a wholly Mozartian way. What is striking about *Lucio Silla* are the subjective moods that reflect the darker sides of the individual's emotional life, but also the full-scale vocal numbers that are given to secondary characters and which both diverge from *opera seria* practice and give greater emphasis to the protagonists.

The role of Lucio Silla is clearly less important than that of the other characters. The value of an aria and the overall role often depended in *opera seria* upon the vocal resources of the singer in question. Mozart did not know until the last moment for whom he was tailoring the part, and so it is not surprising that those sections of the role which were written before the singer's arrival turned out to be relatively conventional, in that they show the protagonist as a run-of-the-mill villain. The arias reveal repeated inequalities: on the one hand Mozart, following convention, wrote the aria that the singer desired, while on the other there are certain solo numbers that have been written without regard for the singer or listener and which reveal the character's inner life.

One of the high points of the score—in dramatic terms it is the crisis that takes place in Act I, Scene 7—is the confrontation between Cecilio and Giunio in a *luogo sepolcrale molto oscuro*. This meeting, which belongs in the arsenal of popular *ombra* scenes, has been furnished with all the musical means at Mozart's disposal: the key of E flat major, the use of syncopation and tremolo effects, wind instruments in their lowest register recalling the sound of ghosts, unusual harmonies, bold and tense transitions, and new instrumental phrases all contribute to the overall atmosphere. More than the individual characters, it is the chorus that carries the action forward, a technique which Mozart may well have learned from Gluck.

The closing trio in Act II, "Quell'orgoglioso sdegno," No. 18, depicts the clearly differentiated psychological state of the three characters: Silla is the angry and domineering dictator, and Cecilio passionately defiant, while Giunia confesses her love. Giunia's solo scene in Act III has tragic greatness to it: she calls on her father's shade and announces her willingness to die. According to Alfred Einstein, her final aria, "Fra i pensier," No. 22, is "short and simple in form, without any virtuoso ornamentation, but so deeply felt that it would do honour to the role of Donna Anna." Mozart explored Giunia's role in depth: she diverges from the traditional type of *opera seria* lover.

Mozart followed the demands of his time and retained the rule that required recitative to be followed by aria, "in order to arouse every passion in the spectator." Theorists demanded that the aria should show the relevant affection at its optimum strength; it was a delaying factor, not intended to further the course of the action. According to the poet Christoph Martin Wieland, the action could not be sung but only acted. In other words, the more complicated an opera's action, the less room there was for singing.

Lucio Silla is the first of Mozart's operas in which the composer devoted his particular attention to the *recitativo accompagnato*. Conventional *recitativi secchi* are replaced by *recitativi accompagnati* which shed light on the emotional state of the character in question. At the same time, *Lucio Silla* is (as far as we know) the last of Mozart's operas in which the overture was written before the rest of the work. In comparison to his first Italian opera *Mitridate*, the opera orchestra in *Lucio Silla* is much more ambitious. Events on stage are accompanied and interpreted instrumentally, as it were. The orchestral writing is now more rounded: the first and second violins go their separate ways, the violas break away from the bass and are often divided, and the wind instruments are given expressive motifs and characteristic tonal effects. Many numbers give the impression of being symphonic compositions with obbligato vocal accompaniment.

With *Lucio Silla* Mozart bade farewell not only to Italy but also to his youth. In completing his commission, he broke the chain of convention. It is difficult to understand how Mozart's music could have entranced the Milanese public while eliciting no further commission for an opera from him. How much he himself wanted such a commission is clear from a letter that he wrote from Mannheim on February 4, 1778 in which he begged his father, "Please do your utmost to arrange for us [Wolfgang and Aloisia Weber] to come to Italy. You know my greatest desire is to write operas."

Title page of a vocal score
of *La Finta Giardiniera*
with German words, pub-
lished in Mannheim by Carl
Ferdinand Heckel, 1829

La Finta Giardiniera

Breaking new ground

A three-act *dramma giocoso* by Pasquale Anfossi *La Finta Giardiniera*, was first performed at Rome's Teatro delle Dame on December 26 (?), 1773. The libretto was probably by Abbate Giuseppe Petrosellini, Secretary to Prince Giustiniani and later Gentleman of the Privy Bedchamber at the Vatican. He was elected a member of the Accademia Quirina in 1761, of the Accademia degli Infecondi in 1764 and of the Accademia Aborigeni in 1779. His most famous libretto was the one he wrote for Giovanni Paisiello's *Il Barbiere di Siviglia* (1782).

From a literary point of view, the text of *La Finta Giardiniera* belongs to the genre of *drame bourgeois*: in doing so it conforms to the theoretical demand formulated in the preface to the printed libretto of Francesco Bianchi's opera *Il Disertore Francese* (Venice 1784): "A new genre has been formed of late out of *opera seria* and *opera buffa*, a genre which has been tried out with great success in France. It is called 'drama' or 'melodrama.' It takes as its theme tender and terrible emotions with a general plot, not heroic figures, but persons who are sometimes drawn from the common people."

Mozart's setting of *La Finta Giardiniera* is based upon Petrosellini's libretto, which has it source in a text by Raniero de Calzabigi. A comparison between the text set by Mozart and Petrosellini's libretto, discovered in Rome in 1976 by the present author, makes it palpably clear that the Salzburg composer must have had the Roman libretto in his hands while writing the opera. With few exceptions—cuts in the recitatives in the second and third acts and the suppression of two arias in the third act—Mozart set the Roman libretto as it stood.

Who obtained the Munich commission for Mozart in the summer or fall of 1774? Joseph Heinz Eibl assumes that it was the Bishop of Chiemsee, Count Ferdinand Christoph Waldburg-Zeil, who for many years was in charge of the affairs of the Salzburg archbishopric. He became canon in Salzburg on September 13, 1745 and dean in 1753, before being appointed Bishop of Chiemsee in 1772. He was a lifelong patron of Mozart's. Robert Münster, on the other hand, argues that Mozart received the *scrittura* from Count Joseph Anton von Seeau, the Elector Maxmilian's Controller of Opera. The two views are not mutually exclusive. It is entirely possible that Count Waldburg-Zeil suggested that the young Salzburg composer should write the new opera; the definitive commission would have come from the appropriate authority, in other words, from the theater intendant Seeau himself.

Wolfgang and his father Leopold set off for Munich on December 6, 1774, with parts of the opera—principally the recitatives—already included in their luggage. The first news that Leopold reported back to his wife in Salzburg was to the effect that there was nothing at present that he could tell her about the opera: "Not until today did we get to know the people here, all of whom were very polite, especially His Excellency Count [Joseph Anton] Seeau." On December 14 Leopold was able to venture the opinion that the opera would be rehearsed before Christ-

K. 196

Dramma giocoso in three acts. Words by Giuseppe Petrosellini (?). German translation by Johann Franz Joseph Stierle the Elder (?). Begun in Salzburg in September 1774. First performed at the Salvatortheater in Munich on January 13, 1775 (in Italian), and in Augsburg on May 1 (?), 1780 (adapted as a Singspiel in German). Autograph score: Act I missing; Acts II and III in Cracow, Biblioteka Jagiellońska.

mas and that the first performance would take place on December 29. On the 28th, however, we learn that, "On the very day that you were both with His Ex. Ct. Sauerau [Seeau], the first rehearsal of Wolfg.'s opera was held at 10 in the morning and was so well received that it has been postponed until the 5th of January 1775 so that the singers can learn their parts properly and, once they have the music in their heads, act with greater confidence, so that the opera is not ruined in consequence. To have had it ready by December 29 would have been overhasty. In short! the music is proving astonishingly popular, and so it will be performed on the 5th of January. Everything now depends upon the stage production, which we hope will be a success, since the actors are not ill-disposed toward us." And on December 30 Leopold again wrote to his wife, "Nannerl will arrive just in time for the opera, since she'll get here on Wednesday afternoon [January 4] and it is being performed on Thursday [January 5]. If Herr von Mölk [probably Franz von Mölk] comes too, he will see it as well; but if he comes later, he will not see it until Easter, because after that date no more operettas will be performed in the theater, but only in the Salla di Ridotta, where only intermezzi will be given.... I must tell you that Maestro Tozi [Antonio Tozzi] who this year is writing the *opera seria*, wrote an *opera buffa* at exactly this time last year, and made such an effort to write it well that it killed off the *opera seria* [*Achille in Sciro*] which Maestro Sales [Pietro Pompeo Sales] had written, so that Sales' opera no longer found any real favor. Now, as chance will have it, Wolfgang's opera is being done before Tozi's opera. And when people heard the first rehearsal, they all said that Tozi was being paid back in his own coin, since Wolfg.'s opera would kill off Tozi's opera. I do not like this sort of thing, and am trying to silence such remarks as much as possible by protesting endlessly: but the whole orchestra and everyone who heard the rehearsal say that they have never heard a more beautiful composition in which all the arias are beautiful. Wherever we go, they already know. Basta! God will ensure that everything turns out all right in the end."

However, the first performance of *La Finta Giardiniera* did not take place as planned on January 5. What the reasons were for the postponement we can only surmise: perhaps more rehearsals were necessary than had first been provided for, perhaps it was wished to see Tozzi's official carnival opera *Orfeo ed Euridice* before Mozart's *dramma giocoso*, or perhaps the decision was influenced by the proposed visit to Munich by the Salzburg Prince-Archbishop Count Hieronymus Collodero. A new date was fixed for the premiere, as we learn from Leopold's letter to his wife of January 5, "You will have heard from Herr Schulz [a tenor in the Salzburg Court Chapel] that Wolfg.'s opera is not to be performed until the 13th." On the 11th Wolfgang himself took up his pen and wrote to his mother, "All three of us are very well, praise God. I cannot write very much since I must leave in a moment for the rehearsal. The dress rehearsal is tomorrow, and on Friday the 13th it will be performed in the Salvatortheater. Mamma need not worry, everything will go well."

Mozart was heavily and decisively involved in the rehearsals for *La Finta Giardiniera*, although he did not conduct the performances. The Munich orchestra contained about twenty-three musicians and is said to have been in some disarray. Exact details concerning the cast of Mozart's opera are not known. The only name we know for certain is that of Rosa Manservisi, who created the part of Sandrina. She was a member of Seeau's Opera Buffa company from 1772 until 1776. Contemporaries praised her voice and musicality: Charles Burney, who heard her in Munich in the summer of 1772, wrote that, "Her figure is pleasant, her voice, although not strong, is melodious, there is nothing common about her manner, she remains in tune, and never offends the ear."

Characters and résumé of the plot

Don Anchise, Podestà of Lagonero, in love with Sandrina (tenor); Marchesa Violante Onesti, in love with Count Belfiore, believed dead but disguised as a gardener under the name of Sandrina (soprano); Count Belfiore, earlier in love with Violante, now with Arminda (tenor); Arminda, lady from Milan, earlier in love with the knight Ramiro, now promised as bride to Count Belfiore (soprano); Cavalier Ramiro, in love with Arminda but rejected by her (male soprano); Serpetta, chambermaid to the Podestà and in love with him (soprano); Roberto, Violante's servant, disguised as a gardener, in love with Serpetta but ignored by her (bass).

The action takes place on the Podestà's estates at Lagonero. Before the curtain rises: in a fit of jealousy Count Belfiore has injured his beloved, the Marchesa Violante. Believing himself to have killed her, the Count has fled. Violante has set off with her servant Roberto in search of him. They are both taken on as gardeners by the Podestà (a kind of provincial governor) of Lagonero, she under the name of Sandrina, he as Nardo. The Podestà soon falls in love with the beautiful garden girl and neglects his housekeeper Serpetta, whose favors Nardo courts in vain. The knight Ramiro, who is staying with the Podestà as his guest, was once in love with his host's niece Arminda. But she had sent him packing and become engaged to Count Belfiore.

ACT I. The inhabitants of Lagonero are awaiting the arrival of Arminda, whose betrothal is to be celebrated with a great banquet. Each of the characters expresses his or her feelings: Ramiro admits to the Podestà that he is tormented by unrequited love, Sandrina broods on her fate, and Nardo sees himself spurned by Serpetta. The Podestà orders Nardo and Serpetta to withdraw; left alone with Sandrina, he declares his love for her. The latter is evasive, and is supported in her response by the jealous Serpetta. The Podestà does not know whether to feel joy, fear, or hope. Sandrina tells Nardo that she intends to leave Lagonero in order to escape from the Podestà's unwanted attentions. Ramiro laments the infidelity of women, Sandrina that of men. Nardo, for his part, is head over heels in love with Serpetta and is dismayed by her dismissive attitude and hard-heartedness. Arminda, who has just arrived, proves capricious, and inquires whether her bridegroom is also well-mannered. Belfiore welcomes her as his bride and praises her beauty. She calmly informs him that, if her husband is unfaithful, she will personally take him to task. The Count and the Podestà praise Arminda's tenderness, beauty, charm and sagacity. Belfiore asserts that women run after him in droves in order to set eyes on his handsome features, and boasts of his nobility, wealth, and ancestry. He claims to be related to the greatest monarchs in the world. Serpetta refuses to remain in the house a moment longer, since she is being overworked by Arminda. Nardo has overheard Serpetta's complaints and confesses his love for her. But she turns him down. Sandrina bewails her fate. Believing her to be the garden girl, Arminda tells her that she is going to marry Belfiore. Sandrina is so shocked by this revelation that she faints. Arminda calls on Belfiore to help, leaving the unconscious Sandrina with him while she

goes in search of her smelling-salts. On returning she encounters her earlier lover Ramiro. The four lovers recognize each other, much to their mutual embarrassment. The Podestà hurries in and demands an explanation, but in vain; both couples leave. Hoping to make the Podestà jealous, Serpetta tells him that she has seen Belfiore and Sandrina in a tender embrace. He withdraws in order to observe them from afar. Belfiore attempts to persuade Sandrina to reveal her true identity as Violante. She begins by denying who she is, but then forgets herself and reproaches him for his infidelity. He falls to her feet in remorse just as Arminda and Ramiro return. The rest of the characters rush in and heap Belfiore and Ramiro with reproaches. Belfiore is overcome with embarrassment, not knowing whether to choose Sandrina or Arminda. The act ends in confusion.

ACT II. Ramiro reproaches Arminda for preferring the Count for reasons of social prestige. Belfiore comes looking for Sandrina. On seeing Arminda, he pretends it was she whom he was seeking. But she sees through his deceitful disguise and leaves him in her anger, although, as she confesses, she still loves him. Serpetta advises the Count to beg Arminda's forgiveness and kiss her hand. The Count leaves, and Nardo enters. He courts her in Italian, French, and English, and she submits to his entreaties. Sandrina still loves Belfiore, in spite of herself. He comes upon her unawares in the garden, and she showers him with reproaches. He begs her to recall their old love, but she tells him that she knew Violante and has merely told him of the latter's feelings. Confused, he tenderly apologises to Sandrina and tries to kiss her hand. Instead, he seizes the hand of the Podestà who has crept in to eavesdrop on their conversation. The latter begins by reproaching Sandrina, but then declares his love for her, a declaration which she attempts to evade. Ramiro appears with a warrant for the arrest of Belfiore for the murder of Violante Onesti. He demands that the Podestà launch an inquiry. The latter announces that the wedding with Arminda is off, an announcement which gives Ramiro renewed hope. The Podestà questions the Count, who makes contradictory statements and thus increases the suspicion that he is the murderer. Sandrina enters to defend the Count. She declares that she is Violante Onesti: she had been merely wounded, not killed. No one believes that she is Violante. Left alone with

La Finta Giardiniera

Théâtre Montansier, Versailles, May 17, 1963
Nardo: Louis Noguera. Sandrina: Jacqueline Brumaire. Arminda: Jane Berbié. Serpetta: Margaret Mas. Belfiore: Rémy Corazza. Ramiro: André Mallabrera. The Podestà: Jean Giraudeau. Producer: Georges Hirsch. Designer: Bernard Daydé. Conductor: André Girard
An abstract forest for the finale of Act II, stretching out over the performers like a tent

the Count, who once again confesses his love for her, she insists that she is *not* Violante and had only pretended to be in order to save him. Belfiore is confused and dismayed. Serpetta reports that Sandrina has fled, but she tells Nardo that Arminda has had her abducted to a place of hiding in the nearby woods in order to prevent her from interrupting her wedding with Belfiore. The scene changes to a rocky and deserted spot. Sandrina is in a state of despair. She hopes to save her own miserable life by seeking refuge in a cave. Guided there by Nardo, Belfiore arrives, followed by the Podestà, both in search of Sandrina. Hard on their heels come Arminda and Serpetta, anxious to establish whether Sandrina is in the forest. In the darkness the Podestà stumbles into Arminda, Belfiore into Serpetta. Both men believe they are speaking to Sandrina. Only Nardo recognizes her. Ramiro appears with torches, determined to tear Belfiore from Arminda's arms. A scene of general recognition and deep embarrassment ensues. There are reproaches on all sides. Sandrina and the Count lose their reason, believing themselves to have been turned into mythical beings.

ACT III.   Serpetta makes fun of Nardo. The Count and Sandrina importune him, but he manages to escape. The Podestà dismisses first Serpetta, then Arminda, who insists upon marrying the Count, and finally Ramiro, who comes to demand Arminda's hand in marriage. The scene changes to a garden where Belfiore and Sandrina are lying asleep. They awaken, cured of their madness, and recognize each other. Sandrina lends an ear to Belfiore's wooing. Arminda is prepared to offer her hand to Ramiro. Serpetta chooses Nardo. Only the Podestà is left behind, determined not to marry until he has found another Sandrina.

Critical reception of the opera

Mozart himself gives us a graphic account of the premiere of *La Finta Giardiniera* in a letter to his mother dated January 14, 1775: "Thank God! My opera was performed yesterday, the 13th; and it turned out so well that it is impossible for me to describe the noise to Mamma. In the first place, the theater was packed to the rafters, so that a good many people were turned away. After every aria there was the most frightening noise with clapping and shouts of 'Viva Maestro.'" Leopold describes the unprecedented success which the opera enjoyed in a letter of January 18. The exuberant father singles out the fact that the nobility had praised the opera and offered Wolfgang "the most enthusiastic congratulations."

A second performance of *La Finta Giardiniera* took place on February 2, not in the Salvatortheater on this occasion but in the Sala di Ridotta. Leopold reported on the performance in a letter to his wife: "Wolfg.'s opera has been performed again, but it had to

Théâtre des Champs-Elysées, Paris, May 5, 1965
Belfiore: Eric Tappy. Sandrina: Teresa Stich-Randall. Nardo: Guy Godin. The Podestà: Jean Giraudeau. Serpetta: Nicole Broissin. Arminda: Jane Berbié. Ramiro: André Mallabrera. Producer: Georges Hirsch. Designer: Bernard Daydé. Conductor: André Girard. Performing version by Pierre Sabatier
Finale of Act I. The designer used the two parasols to create additional perspectives and acting areas, which in turn allowed the producer to clarify the complex action.

be cut because the soprano was ill. I could write a good deal about this woman: she was dreadful." It is not known what cuts were involved, since the performing material in question has not survived. The third and final performance of *La Finta Giardiniera* took place on March 2 in Munich, when the audience included the Elector Maximilian III Joseph.

Mozart revised the Italian text of *La Finta Giardiniera* in the fall and winter of 1779-80. It was translated into German, probably by the buffo bass Johann Franz Joseph Stierle, a member of Johann Böhm's traveling company and well known as an interpreter of earnest old men, tyrants, and father figures. Mozart made various cuts, more especially to parts of the second and third acts.

Böhm's company was in Augsburg between March 28 and May 19, 1780, and it was probably here that they performed the German version of *La Finta Giardiniera* under the title *Die verstellte Gärtnerin* (The Disguised Garden Girl). A second performance took place in Augsburg on May 17 or 18. It is not certain who conducted the Augsburg performances, although it may well have been Anton Mayr, who was then music director of Böhm's company. Nor do we know who the singers were at the Augsburg performances, since no playbills have survived. Böhm performed *Sandrina oder Die verstellte Gärtnerin* in Frankfurt am Main on April 2, 1782, and the opera was given there again on September 12, this time under the title of *Die*

edle Gärtnerin (The Noble Garden Girl). Other performances known to have taken place during Mozart's lifetime include German-language productions in Frankfurt am Main and Mainz, both in 1789.

A German-language performance of the opera was given in Prague on March 10, 1796; and on February 25, 1797 it was staged as *Die Schöne Gärtnerin* (The Beautiful Garden Girl) in the Silesian town of Oels. In 1800 J.P. Thonus of Leipzig published a two-volume selection in German of arias and choruses from the comic opera *Die Gärtnerin aus Liebe* (The Garden Girl out of Love); following Thonus's premature death the two volumes were acquired in 1801 by Hoffmeister & Kühnel of Leipzig. A vocal score of *Die Gärtnerin aus Liebe* was published in 1829 by Carl Ferdinand Heckel of Mannheim; and in May 1881 *La Finta Giardiniera* was published by Breitkopf & Härtel of Leipzig in the old Mozart Edition. Some ten years later Richard Kleinmichel prepared a revised German version of *La Finta Giardiniera* which was published by Bartholomäus Senff of Leipzig. Also in 1891 Max Kalbeck and Johann Nepomuk Fuchs provided the opera with a new text and dialogue for a production in Vienna. The libretto for this version was published the following year by Adolph W. Künast of Vienna. Breitkopf & Härtel published a libretto for *Die Gärtnerin aus Liebe* in 1893. There was one further nineteenth-century piano arrangement of the work which was published by J. Brieff in

La Finta Giardiniera

Salzburg Festival, August 1, 1965 (Residenz)
Don Anchise: Cesare Curzi. Sandrina: Colette Boky. Count Belfiore: Donald Grobe. Nardo: Thomas Tipton. Serpetta: Graziella Sciutti. Arminda: Jean Cook. Don Ramiro: Evelyn La Bruce. Producer: Ernst Poettgen. Designer: Leni Bauer-Ecsy. Conductor: Bernhard Conz

Finale of Act II. "The great merit of Bernhard Paum-gartner's adaptation lies in polishing up the German text, reinstating the recitatives and bringing them into line with the rest of the score, and making minor dramaturgical improvements such as suppressing the embarrassing theme of madness. On the other hand, it is difficult to understand how a Mozartian of Paumgartner's stature could have made such arbitrary changes to the score as to destroy its formal structure and delineation of character: arias have been transposed and given to different characters, important and significant numbers have been cut, the sequence of events has been destroyed, and the interplay of dramatic contrasts has been eroded....
The production went even further in eroding the work's outlines. Instead of the clear and passionate realism that would have been appropriate here but which is clearly unattainable on a stylized stage, the producer Ernst Poettgen and his designer Leni Bauer-Ecsy presented us with a sugary sweet pseudo-Rococo animated by dancing extras. It marked a relapse into the aesthetic approach of 1880 which really ought not to be tolerated any longer in Salzburg," Werner Oehlmann wrote in the Berlin *Tagesspiegel* of August 8, 1965.

St. Petersburg. Universal Edition of Vienna and Leipzig published Oscar Bie's one-act (!) revision of *Die Gärtnerin aus Liebe* in 1911. Rudolf and Ludwig Berger (Bamberger) prepared a German adaptation of *La Finta Giardiniera* for a production in Mainz in 1915, the same year in which Bie's version was performed in Darmstadt. In 1917 Anton Rudolph provided the piece with a new text and dialogue, and the libretto was published by Ferdinand Zierfuss of Munich. This version was seen in Karlsruhe in 1918. Rudolf Bechtold & Comp. of Wiesbaden published Berger's and Bie's version in 1927. Also around 1927 a typewritten English translation of the opera by F. Harrison Dowd was published in New York under the title *The Love Game*; it was based on Rudolph's adaptation. In 1928 Siegfried Anheisser prepared a two-act version of *Die Gärtnerin aus Liebe* for German radio (published by Rufu-Verlag G.m.b.H of Cologne). Anheisser's German translation and adaptation was performed in Munich during the 1934-35 season, with sets by Leo Pasetti. The libretto was published by the Deutscher Musikverlag in der NS-Kulturgemeinde in Berlin. Karl Schleifer's score of *La Finta Giardiniera* (with an enlarged orchestra based on the Oels manuscript) was published in Hamburg and Berlin in 1956. The text and staging instructions were prepared by Ernst Legal and Hans Henny Jahnn using the Italian text of Raniero de Calzabigi.

Richard Petzold wrote an introduction to the libretto. The piece was performed in May 1963 in the Château de Versailles, and in May 1965 in the Théâtre des Champs-Elysées in Paris. In 1965 Bernhard Paumgartner revised the work musically and dramatically in a version that was performed at the 1965 Salzburg Festival in the Residenz. In 1972 Hans Schmidt-Isserstedt recorded *Die Gärtnerin aus Liebe* with the orchestra of North German Radio (Hamburg). In 1978 both the Italian and German versions of the opera were edited by the present author and Dietrich Berke and published within the framework of the Neue Mozart-Ausgabe. Only since this date has it been possible to perform both versions in an authentic text. In 1979 the author translated the Italian text of *La Finta Giardiniera* into German in a literal translation. The Bavarian State Opera performed the original German version of the opera at the Schwetzingen Festival on May 24, 1979, before transferring the production to the Munich Opera Festival and presenting it in the Cuvilliés Theater on July 9, 1979. On December 23 of the same year the Salzburg Landestheater was the second theater to stage the original German version of the work. The Italian version was first heard in a concert performance at the 1980 Salzburg Mozart Week, when it was conducted by Leopold Hager; the performance was later recorded. There were staged

Bavarian State Opera, Munich, July 9, 1979 (Cuvilliés Theater) Belfiore: Claes H. Ahnsjö. The Podestà: Karl-Ernst Mercker. Serpetta: Julia Conwell. Producer: Ferruccio Soleri. Designer: Ezio Frigerio. Costumes: Mauro Pagano. Conductor: Bernhard Klee Scene in Act I. The ornate magnificence of the scenery and costumes was typical of the production's general extravagance. The singers moved with choreographically calculated precision and struck posturing attitudes.

Bavarian State Opera, Munich, July 9, 1979 (Cuvilliés Theater) Serpetta: Julia Conwell. The Podestà: Karl-Ernst Mercker. Sandrina: Patricia Wise. Ramiro: Daphne Evangelatos. Producer: Ferruccio Soleri. Designer: Ezio Frigerio. Costumes: Mauro Pagano. Conductor: Bernhard Klee Finale of Act I

La Finta Giardiniera

Städtische Bühne, Hagen,
1982-83 (March 5, 1983)
Belfiore: Reinhard Liesenheimer. Serpetta: Patricia
Raine. The Podestà: Hannes
Brock
Act I, Scene 8. The Podestà
asks the Count how he finds
his niece. Serpetta serves
the two men.

productions at the Städtische Bühnen Hagen on March 5, 1983 (the producer was Samy Molcho and the designer Timm Zorn) and at the 1984 Aix-en-Provence Festival, when the producers were Gildas Bourdet and Alain Milianti, the designer Françoise Chevalier, and the conductor Semyon Bychkov. The most important production to date to have used the Neue Mozart-Ausgabe is the one first seen at the Théâtre Royal du Parc in Brussels on April 15, 1986.

Structure of the opera

For long stretches of *La Finta Giardiniera* we find Mozart speaking a musical language all of his own. Melody, harmony and rhythms already contain pointers towards the great Viennese operas that were to follow. "It is Mozart in the run-up to Mozart," Horst Koegler wrote in *Musica* on the occasion of the Schwetzingen production of the opera. This work of an eighteen year old, he went on, revealed "constant lightning flashes in the music—not only the various pre-echoes of Belmonte's ardent idealism, of Constanze's grief, of Donna Elvira's hysteria, of Pamina's and Papageno's 'Schnelle Füsse, rascher Mut,' but also a prophetic pointer to the

sextet from *Don Giovanni*—this opening up of the ground beneath our feet, the uncertainty of feeling which the music signals—and hence the fact that there are still fourteen and a half years to go before the French Revolution. The rumbling noise is not that of the Third Estate, but of pent-up emotions."

The text that Mozart set marks a new departure in the development of *opera buffa*. It includes *parti serie* and *parti buffe*, both of which demand their own individual characterization. What Mozart has set is basically a *drame bourgeois* in the mould of Denis Diderot, a genre which was intended to offer the spectator a world of feelings both solemn and not so solemn. By drawing upon these two emotional spheres, the composer enriched the genre of *opera buffa* both instrumentally and formally, so that it was no longer subject to a single unified scheme. In consequence the way was open for Mozart to write an opera of immense diversity.

There is diversity of aria form, each individual form being a projection of the character concerned and of the relevant dramatic situation. Thus we find strophic form, binary dal segno aria (AA), contrasting aria (AB), rondo-form, and ternary da capo aria (ABA). Binary arias are the preserve first and foremost of

66

the *parti buffe. Recitativi accompagnati* are used only at decisive moments and are reserved for the protagonists. The Podestà, Serpetta, and Nardo are straight from the world of the *commedia dell'arte*. The Podestà is modeled on the old Pantalone, the duped fool who falls in love with a girl whom he cannot have. In addition, a figure of official-dom is made fun of here. The foolish village mayor was a favorite figure of improvised comedy and *opera buffa*. It is curious, none-theless, that Mozart wrote the part for a tenor, since the Podestà's ancestral line goes back to the buffo bass. The instrumental aria "Dentro il mio petto" (No. 3) is a bravura piece in which text and music are in complete harmony. The qualities of individual instruments such as flute, oboe, viola, kettledrum, trumpet, double bass, and bassoon reflect the Podestà's emotional state. Affected dignity is conveyed by the aria "Una damina, una nipote" (No. 17), which is almost a prelimi-nary study for Bartolo's aria "La vendetta" in *The Marriage of Figaro* (No. 4). And the Podestà, or "Amtshauptmann," as he is called in the German text, reveals the predicament in which he finds himself in his aria "Mio padrone, io dir volevo" (No. 25), where the listener is struck by the independent treat-ment of the orchestra and by the way in which Mozart never allows the Podestà to complete a sentence, such is the man's unease.

Serpetta is coquettish, spiteful and jealous, but basically no more than a stereotype lacking the individuality of Mozart's later soubrette characters. There is a superficial, mischievous, and sometimes even conven-tional tone to such arias as "Appena mi vedon" (No. 10), in spite of its pointers to Despina's "Una donna a quindici anni" (*Così fan tutte* No. 19), and "Chi vuol godere il mondo" (No. 20) which, although it contains pre-echoes of *The Marriage of Figaro*, cer-tainly does not turn Serpetta into a Susanna. Nardo, the "honorable booby," as Alfred Einstein called him, shows picturesque quali-ties in his gigue-like aria "A forza di martelli" (No. 5), where he makes it clear that he is incapable of tempering women's egoism. The singer is required to show histrionic and even linguistic talent in the aria "Con un vezzo all'Italiana" (No. 14): he begins by playing the part of a besotted Italian, then shows his respects for Serpetta in a richly ornamented French minuet, and finally attempts to win her heart with his stiffly formal English.

The character of Sandrina is revealed in a variety of nuances. In her aria "Noi donne poverine" (No. 4), for example, she appears buffo-like and mischievous, superficial and lacking genuine emotion. She is Zerlina here, rather than Sandrina. By contrast, the fashionable simile aria "Gema la tortorella" (No. 11) is individually colored and even heartfelt. It bears features of tearful senti-mentality and already anticipates the more mature opera composer of *The Marriage of Figaro* and *Don Giovanni*. The rondo-like aria "Una voce sento al core" (No. 16) is entirely structured around the textual opposi-tion between goodness and inner conflict: the two emotions are sharply outlined here, the one in a style recalling Mozart's Blondchen, the other in the style of *opera seria*. Also part of the *opera seria* arsensal is the highly emotional lament "Crudeli, fermate" (No. 21). Sandrina reveals herself here as a tho-roughgoing heroine, a point underlined by the resigned minor key in which the piece is written. The binary cavatina "Ah dal pianto, dal singhiozzo" (No. 22), with its declamatory writing for the voice and restless orchestral accompaniment, similarly ends on a note of hopelessness. Both pieces form an integral part of the second act and go well beyond the scope of an *opera buffa*. A serious element, not to be construed as parody, gains the upper hand, and reveals the true feelings of the female protagonist.

Sandrina's counterpart, Count Belfiore, is a typical cavalier, who already reveals the lyrical features of a Belmonte in his first aria "Che beltà, che leggiadria" (No. 6), with its theme of love. There is only a short distance from here to Tamino's Portrait Aria. That his

Festival d'Aix-en-Provence, July 16, 1984
Sandrina: Roberta Alexan-der. Belfiore: John Aler. Producers: Gildas Bourdet and Alain Milianti. Designer: Gildas Bourdet. Costumes: Françoise Chevalier. Con-ductor: Semyon Bychkov
"The cast was dazzling," Tony Mayer wrote in *Opera* magazine (Festival edition, 1984). "The young American soprano Roberta Alexander played the double part of Sandrina (the pseudo-gar-dener) and Violante.... The male trio was no less bril-liant. It included the Amer-ican John Aler, a wonderfully light and bright singer; the well-known Britisher An-thony Rolfe Johnson as a charmingly humorous Pod-està; and the young Swiss, Gilles Cachemaille, a vintage valet by no means unequal to his master. All these youthful and gifted singers, cleverly directed by Gildas Bourdet and Alain Milianti, disported themselves on the terraces and stairs of a splendid marble palace, whose richly sculptured ceiling was supported by four tall, purple marble columns."

La Finta Giardiniera

Opéra de Lyon, April 6, 1985
Belfiore: Neil Rosenshein.
Arminda: Julia Faulkner.
Producer: Gildas Bourdet.
Designer: Françoise Che-
valier. Conductor: Semyon
Bychkov
Belfiore woos Arminda,
bowing low "as though to
his princess and queen."

feelings for Sandrina are more genuine than those for Arminda is made clear by the aria "Care pupille, pupille belle" (No. 15). By contrast, the Count's recitative and aria "Ah non partir... Già divento freddo" (No. 19) is intended as a parody, the protagonist behaving here in a comically mad fashion. Effective are the two duets for Sandrina and the Count, "Da bravi seguitate" (No. 24) and "Dove mai son... Tu mi lasci" (No. 27). One of the most poetic passages in the work is the awakening of the two lovers to the strains of sweet music. A *dolce sinfonia* leads from the world of dreams to the world of reality.

The second couple, Arminda and Ramiro, reveal different characteristics. Arminda is capricious, spiteful, and even violent at times. Her austere passion is evident, for example, in her *seria*-like G minor aria "Vorrei punirti indegno" (No. 13), which points forward to the figure of Elettra in *Idomeneo*, still five years in the future. A more coquettish and cunning side to her character emerges from her opening aria "Si promette facilmente" (No. 7). Ramiro, the loyal and doting lover, is a throwback to *opera seria*, the typical castrato whose da capo arias abound in coloratura writing. His simile aria "Se l'augellin sen fugge" (No. 2) is well sustained in the *seria* tradition, while his difficult and deeply-felt *larghetto* aria "Dolce d'amor compagna speranza" is aimed exclusively at his genuine love for Arminda. Outbursts of anger characterize his *agitato* aria in C minor, "Va pure ad altri in braccio" (No. 26). The finales to the first and second acts go beyond the scope of contemporary *opera buffa* with their 530 and 478 measures respectively. In both finales, moreover, the participants are individually characterized. The finale to Act I, although not contrapuntally structured, reveals symphonic greatness and shows the way to the two extended finales in *The Marriage of Figaro*. Mozart is receptive to moods here, filling stereotypical situations with pulsating life and individualizing them. He turns his characters into human beings who make no secret of their emotions and moods.

La Finta Giardiniera did not find a place for itself in the eighteenth-century *buffa* repertory. In Munich it was shelved after only three performances. And in Paris, which Mozart visited from March to September 1778, there was no attempt to stage the work at all, although contemporary *opere buffe* were regularly seen here. In contrast to Anfossi's work, which was performed throughout Europe, *La Finta Giardiniera* remained a passing attraction. It has been left to present-day productions to reveal Mozart's inventiveness and imaginative power and to recognize the psychological and dramatic depth of his handling of the subject.

Opéra National de Belgique, Brussels, April 15, 1986 (Théâtre Royal du Parc) The Podestà: Ugo Benelli. Sandrina: Britt-Marie Aruhn/Joanna Kozlowska. Belfiore: Marek Torzewski/Barry McCauley. Arminda: Barbara Madra/Malvina Major. Ramiro: Lani Poulson. Serpetta: Elzbieta Szmytka. Nardo: J. Patrick Raftery. Producers: Karl-Ernst and Ursel Herrmann. Designer: Karl-Ernst Herrmann. Conductor: Sylvain Cambreling

Finale of Act II. This production was also seen at the 1986 Vienna Festival and during the 1987 Mozart Week in Salzburg. "Herrmann's unit set made allowance for the simple stage facilities without in any way giving the impression of limited means or provisional arrangements. A scattering of young birch trees, which bent over at an angle during the nighttime storm, formed a natural setting reminiscent of Peter Stein's production of *Summerfolk* or Fellini's *Amarcord*. The insoluble

tension between nature and social 'unnaturalness' provided the narrative's basic ironical and dramatic theme. The music was often reduced to lengthy silences, when the only noises to be heard were mysterious natural sounds, chirping crickets, croaking frogs, and cawing ravens. Light and shade were starkly contrasted.... Herrmann's painstakingly detailed work allowed comedy and tragedy to oscillate freely," Hans-Klaus Jungheinrich wrote in *Musica*, 1986.

Il Rè Pastore

Contemporary compositions abound

Pietro Metastasio, poet to the Imperial Court in Vienna, completed his libretto to *Il Rè Pastore* on April 18, 1751. As he wrote to inform Francesco Algarotti in Berlin, the work was intended to be staged as an opera in the fall of 1751 before an audience of "dame e cavalieri." The first performance took place on October 27, 1751 before the Viennese Court at Schönbrunn. The music was by Giuseppe Bonno, who was later to become kapellmeister to the Viennese Court. Shortly after the premiere, the court poet wrote to the famous castrato Carlo Broschi, known as Farinelli, informing him that, "*Il Rè Pastore* is cheerful, tender, charming, and brief, and, as a whole, it has all the qualities that constitute an opera. The music is so graceful, so apt and so cheerful.... it was exceedingly well received." What is arguably the poet's finest lyric work had already been set to music by a series of famous contemporary composers before Mozart turned his hand to it in 1775. The list of the earlier composers includes Johann Friedrich Agricola (Berlin 1752), Giuseppe Sarti (Venice 1753), Johann Adolf Hasse (Dresden 1755), Francesco Antonio Uttini (Stockholm 1755), Christoph Willibald Gluck (Vienna 1756), Antonio Mazzoni (Bologna 1757), Baldassare Galuppi (Milan 1758), Giovanni Battista Lampugnani (Milan 1758), Giuseppe Zonca (Munich 1760), Niccolò Jommelli (Stuttgart 1764) and Pietro Guglielmi (Turin 1765).

Composing the opera

Mozart received a new commission for an opera immediately after his return to Salz-burg from Munich at the beginning of March 1775. Two dramatic works were to be prepared for a visit that the Archduke Maximilian Franz, the youngest son of the Empress Maria Theresa and future Elector of Cologne, was to pay to the town on the Salzach. The Archduke left Vienna on his way to Italy on April 20 and the following day arrived in Salzburg, where he stayed at the Prince-Archbishop's Residenz. A *serenata a 5 voci*, "Gli Orti Esperidi," with words by Metastasio and music by the Neapolitan court kapellmeister in Salzburg, Domenico Fischietti, was performed on April 22, and on the 23rd Mozart's serenata *Il Rè Pastore* was heard for the first time. Entries relating to both works are to be found in the private diary of Johann Baptist Joachim Ferdinand von Schiedenhofen auf Stumm und Triebenbach, Court Councillor in Salzburg and later Regional Chancellor, and in the travel diary of Archduke Maximilian. Schiedenhofen wrote on April 22, "In the evening I went to Court with Herr Stadtsindicus [Joseph Benedikt Loes] for the serenada by Signor Fischietti in which the castrato Consoli and the flutist Becke from Munich were engaged." The flutist Johann Baptist Becke and the castrato Tommaso Consoli had come to Salzburg from Munich as a result of negotiations undertaken by Leopold Mozart. On April 23, 1775 we read in Schiedenhofen's account, "In the evening to Court for the serenada prepared by the young Mozart." And an entry in the Archduke Maximilian's travel diary for the same day reads, "Sunday the 23rd ... As on the previous day the evening ended with a *musique-concert* and supper in the palace, but in regard to the concert there was this distinction, by way of a change, that, whereas the well-known kapellmeister Fischietti had written the music for the previous evening,

K 208

Serenata in two acts. Words by Pietro Metastasio. Composed in Salzburg in the spring of 1775. First performed in the Prince-Archbishop's Residenz on April 23, 1775. Autograph score: Cracow, Biblioteka Jagiellońska.

71

on this occasion the music for the cantata had been written by the no less famous Mozart." It is striking that both works were written for five voices and that both were settings of texts by Metastasio. Are we to imagine that a musical competition was held here between the Court kapellmeister and the second concertmaster, as Mozart was at this time in Salzburg? We know only that the castrato Consoli took the part of Aminta. Since neither a playbill nor a libretto for the Salzburg performance has survived, we are thrown back on hypothesis in determining who the other singers were. It is probable, however, that, apart from Consoli, the four remaining singers were recruited from the Salzburg Court Chapel. The following names are likely candidates for the female roles of Elisa and Tamiri: Maria Anna Fesemayr, later Adlgasser, Maria Anna Braunhofer, and Maria Magdalena Lipp, later married to Michael Haydn; for the tenor roles of Alessandro and Agenore: Franz Anton Spitzeder and Felix Hofstätter. For the violin solo in Aminta's rondo aria "L'amerò sarò costante" (No. 10), only two names can be considered, the first concertmaster of the Court Chapel, Michael Haydn, and the second concertmaster, Wolfgang Amadeus Mozart. The flute soli in Alessandro's aria "Se vincendo vi rendo felici" (No. 9) were written in all probability with the Munich flute virtuoso Johann Baptist Becke specially in mind.

The most striking feature of the work is the detailed instrumental writing. The overture, written in a single movement, passes straight into the first scene, as was customary in any school drama. The dramaturgy of *Il Rè Pastore* rests essentially upon the contrast between recitative and aria. Mozart has often been taken to task for having neglected the characterization of the individual singers in his serenata, and for having written an excessively conventional type of *recitativo secco*. It must be emphasized, however, that Mozart wrote entirely within the style of the genre and conformed to the prescribed tradition. On closer examination, a work which has often been treated somewhat dismissively can be shown to contain features that recur in Mozart's more mature operas. One thinks especially of the melodic writing that is so typical of the composer. That Mozart himself thought highly of *Il Rè Pastore* emerges from the fact that in October 1777 he sent the work to his "good and true friend" Joseph Mysliweczek, and that he performed the Overture at an *accademia* at the Mann-

heim home of Johann Christian Cannabich on February 13, 1778.

Characters and résumé of the plot

Alessandro, King of Macedonia (tenor); Aminta, shepherd, in love with Elisa, and, unknown to himself, legitimate heir to the kingdom of Sidon (male soprano); Elisa, noble Phoenician girl, descended from Cadmus, in love with Aminta (soprano); Tamiri, daughter of the tyrannical King Strato, and in love with Agenore (soprano); Agenore, Sidonian nobleman, friend of Alessandro and in love with Tamiri (tenor).

Alexander (Alessandro) the Great, King of Macedonia, has conquered the town of Sidon. Following the suicide of the tyrant Strato, he has resolved to crown the son of the last legitimate king, Abdalonymus. This son, however, is living as a shepherd under the name of Aminta, unknown to the world and in ignorance of his true identity. He loves Elisa, a young noblewoman from Phoenicia and a descendant of Cadmus. At the very moment that Aminta receives her father's permission to marry Elisa, Agenore, a Sidonian nobleman and friend of Alexander the Great, offers Aminta the royal crown of Sidon at the bidding of his lord and master. Alexander intends Aminta to marry Tamiri, the daughter of the late tyrant Strato, who is secretly in love with Agenore. Various intrigues develop out of this constellation of characters. Vacillating between virtue and love, Aminta finally renounces the throne out of his love for Elisa. Tamiri confesses her love for Agenore. Moved by so much nobility, Alexander unites the two couples; he installs Aminta as the legitimate ruler of Sidon and promises another kingdom to Agenore.

Metastasio's three-act libretto was compressed into two acts for Salzburg. The first act takes place in a rural area in the vicinity of Sidon, the Phoenician capital, the second opens in Alexander the Great's encampment, outside his tent, after which the scene changes to a luxuriantly overgrown rocky grotto, and finally to the courtyard of the Temple of Hercules in Sidon. What is striking is that the text, as set by Mozart, has been cut at the very points where it could have served to instruct its princely auditor, Archduke Maximilian Franz, in the lessons of royal behavior. One thinks, for example, of the sentiment placed in Alexander's mouth: "A king can perform the finest feats of war and justice through another's hand, but to penetrate the secrets of a human heart and to distinguish supressed truth from lies is a great duty that is enjoined upon the king alone," or of Elisa's "My liege, let it be with your consent that a loyal shepherd finds greater favor with me than a faithful king."

The first printed score of *Il Rè Pastore* was published in March 1879 in the framework of the old Mozart Edition. It was taken up into the Neue Mozart-Ausgabe in 1985 in an edition by Pierluigi Petrobelli and Wolfgang Rehm. M.F. Browne translated the serenata into English in 1917 under the title *The Royal Shepherd*, and in 1930 Siegfried Anheisser translated it into German. Gramophone recordings of the work appeared in 1967 and 1974, conducted respectively by Denis Vaughan and Leopold Hager.

Salzburg Festival, August 8, 1968 (Residenz)
Zaide: Ingeborg Hallstein. Gomaz: Horst Laubenthal. Allazim: Barry McDaniel. Sultan Soliman: James Harper. Osmin: Robert Granzer. Slave: Monique Lobasà. Zarem: Sepp Scheepers. Producer: Gandolf Buschbeck. Designer: Erni Kniepert. Conductor: Bernard Conz

Final scene. "The seraglio in which the fair Zaide is held captive is symbolized by a large birdcage in the 1968 Salzburg Festival production. It stands in the middle of the wooden stage in the Residenzhof; little doves from Hellbrunn preen themselves and flutter around, billing and cooing undisturbed by the bright lights, while the Sultan's slaves sleep stretched out on the wooden boards.... Erni Kniepert had the aforementioned cage removed and replaced for the second act by a large silk tent, nobly Ottoman in style, which the slaves, evidently experienced campers, put up during the intermission. It provided an elegant background for the fairy-tale costumes of Zaide and the Sultan (who wore a plume instead of a horse's tail on his turban). Frau Kniepert was rather more sparing in the colors and ideas which she brought to the other singers' costumes," wrote Dr. Hehn in the *Salzburger Volksblatt* of August 10, 1968.

Zaide (The Seraglio)

Origins of the opera

The fragmentary Singspiel *Zaide* (*The Seraglio*) dates from 1779-80, a dating which emerges from both the handwriting of the autograph score and from other stylistic evidence. In other words, the piece was begun during the period between Mozart's return to Salzburg from his successful visit to Paris in mid January 1779, and November 5, 1780, the date on which Mozart left Salzburg to start rehearsing *Idomeneo* in Munich. The work has come down to us without title or dialogue: the former was supplied by the Offenbach publisher Johann Anton André, who published a full score and vocal score of the piece in 1838. André also wrote an Overture and Finale for *Zaide*, and the German musicologist Friedrich Carl Gollmick supplied the missing parts of the libretto.

It is not known for whom Mozart wrote *Zaide*: there is no evidence that he received a commission to compose the piece. However, two theater companies made guest appearances in Salzburg in 1779-80, and in both cases Mozart was in close contact with their managers. The company of Johann Heinrich Böhm played in the town from April 4 until May or June 1779 and from September 1779 to March 1780: and the company of Emanuel Schikaneder probably appeared there in July and August 1780 and again from September 17, 1780 to February 27, 1781, during which time it gave ninety-three performances.

Writers on Mozart disagree as to who encouraged Mozart to write *Zaide*. A number favor the influence of Böhm and Schikaneder. Walter Senn has attempted to show that *Zaide* was "Mozart's first, abortive attempt to make his voice heard at the new German Theater in Vienna, the 'National Singspiel' of Emperor Joseph II." Certainly, a cursory glance at Mozart's correspondence reveals passages which suggest plans for a performance of *Zaide* in Vienna. On December 11, 1780 Leopold Mozart wrote to his son in Munich, "As for Schachtner's drama there's nothing to be done at present, since the theaters are closed [Maria Theresa had died on November 29, 1780, and all Vienna's theaters were closed during the period of Court mourning], and there is nothing to be done with the Emperor, who usually interests himself in everything connected with the theater. It is better like this, since the music is in any case not yet completely finished, and who knows what sort of opportunity this may yet give you of coming to Vienna." Mozart is clearly thinking in this passage of a German National Theater, or rather of the German National Singspiel which had been established in 1776 by Joseph II, but which ceased to operate at the end of the 1782-83 season.

The composer seems to have realized that *Zaide* would not catch on in Vienna and that the libretto would fall short of Viennese demands. He wrote from the city on April 18, 1781, "Nothing has come of Schachtner's operetta—for the same reason that I have often mentioned. The young Stephani [Johann Gottlieb Stephanie the Younger] is going to give me a new piece, and, as he says, a good one [it was to be *The Abduction from the Seraglio*]: he'll send it to me if I am no longer here, I have to admit that Stephani was

K. 344 (336b)

German Singspiel in eight scenes. Words by Johann Andreas Schachtner. Written in Salzburg in 1779-80. First performed in the Stadttheater, Frankfurt am Main, on January 27, 1866. Autograph score: West Berlin, Staatsbibliothek Preussischer Kulturbesitz.

Zaide (The Seraglio)

right. I only said that, with the exception of the long dialogues, which can easily be altered, the piece [*Zaide*] is very good, but not for Vienna, where people prefer comic pieces." Together with the plan to write a new and improved German Singspiel Mozart may well have abandoned the hope of seeing *Zaide* performed.

Not until the nineteenth century was the piece first staged. It was premiered in Frankfurt am Main on January 27, 1866 in an adaptation by Friedrich Carl Gollmick; the Overture and closing section were by Johann Anton André. Robert Hirschfeld revised the work for Vienna, where it was performed on October 4, 1902 in a production designed by Heinrich Lefler. In 1915 Anton Rudolph arranged *Zaide* for Mannheim, and on May 5, 1917 Karlsruhe took the work into its repertory. Schwetzingen followed in 1938. There have been several productions since the end of the Second World War, including the Salzburg Festival in 1968 and the Vienna Festival in 1983. William B. Ober translated the Singspiel into English in 1952 (there is also an undated English translation by Julian Budden), and Fritz Tutenberg and Kurt Diemann adapted the piece in Salzburg in 1955. The old Mozart Edition published the work in January 1881, the Neue Mozart-Ausgabe in 1957.

As with many of his plays, Schachtner used a particular source in preparing his libretto for *Zaide*, and although the libretto has not survived, his source was discovered by Alfred Einstein in the Vienna National Library in 1935-36. The title page of the work in question reads, "Ein musikalisches / Singspiel, / genannt: / Das Serail. / Oder: / Die unvermuthete Zusammenkunft in der / Sclaverey zwischen Vater, Tochter / und Sohn. / Botzen, / gedruckt bey Karl Joseph Weiss, Stadt- und / Mercantil-Buchdrucker, / 1779." (A Musical Singspiel entitled: The Seraglio, Or The Unexpected Meeting of Father, Daughter, and Son in Slavery. Bolzano, published by Karl Joseph Weiss, Municipal and Mercantile Bookseller, 1779.) The composer of this Singspiel was Haydn's librettist Franz Karl Frieberth. Frieberth for his part based his text upon *Das Serail* by the theater manager Franz Josef Sebastiani.

Characters and résumé of the plot

Zaide (soprano); Gomatz (tenor); Allazim (bass); Sultan Soliman (tenor); Osmin (bass); four slaves (tenor); guards (tenor and bass); Zaram, captain of the guard (speaking role).

The European Gomatz has fallen into the hands of the Sultan Soliman and set to work in the Sultan's seraglio. He laments his fate in a melodrama. While in the seraglio Gomatz has won the love of Zaide who is loved in turn by the Sultan Soliman; she, however, spurns the latter's passionate advances. Zaide confesses her love for Gomatz; both realize that they come from Europe and that they have suffered a similar fate. They enter into league with the seraglio guard, Allazim, who represents the enlightened Moslem. He obtains Turkish clothes for the two Europeans and all three set off in flight. The refugees are brought back to the seraglio. Soliman refuses to be swayed either by Zaide's entreaties and steadfastness or by Allazim's warnings, or even by the lovers' unshakable loyalty. His thoughts turn to vengeance. In what way a *lieto fine* or happy ending is brought about is not clear from the existing sources.

Mozart extends the scope of his operatic style both musically and dramatically in *Zaide*. He writes in an arioso style for virtuoso voices, and in a melodramatic style for singing actors. The work's ten arias are elaborately structured, richly instrumented, and often provided with grandiose introductions. The composer always adheres to the principle of contrast here and brings out the individual character of the figures concerned. Whereas the whole of the first act revolves around the relationship between Gomatz and Zaide, radiating tender and heartfelt emotions, the changing situation in the second act is determined by the Sultan's jealous rage, by Zaide's decision to die, and by Allazim's penchant for moralizing.

The female protagonist Zaide has been alloted three arias. Nos. 3, 12, and 13. The serenely intimate G major aria "Ruhe sanft, mein holdes Leben" (No. 3) with oboe and bassoon soli and divided violas recalls French models written in the style of Grétry. The A major simile aria "Trostlos schluchzet Philomele" (No. 12) is an andantino rondo accompanied by strings alone. Poetic and idyllic in mood it reveals descriptive features. The histrionically heroic G minor da capo aria "Tiger! wetze nur die Klauen" (No. 13) is wholly indebted to the intellectual movement of *Sturm und Drang* and calculated to be as expressive as possible. The listener's attention is caught and held by the freely interpolated cry of "Tiger!" The animal's fury is

Vienna Festival 1983 (Theater an der Wien) Sultan Soliman (Werner Hollweg) and his retinue. Producer: Werner Hollweg. Designer: Hannes Rader. Conductor: Leopold Hager Werner Hollweg's principal concern was to give this fragmentary work a contemporary relevance. Günther Schatzdorfer wrote a narrative around it, emphasizing the theme of hostility to foreign workers. A Schikaneder-like theater principal is convinced of the opera's quality by his lover and a wardrobe master. This intermezzo, which mostly took place in the auditorium, provided the work with a tidy conclusion.

depicted by means of rearing figures and hurrying *tremoli*. In the deeply-felt central section, a *larghetto* reminiscent of Gluck, Zaide turns to her lover Gomatz. This G minor aria points the way ahead not only to Constanze's "Traurigkeit" but also to Pamina's "Ach, ich fühl's."

In his eccentric B flat major aria "Rase, Schicksal, wüte immer" (No. 4), a number determined by its sharply dotted rhythms, Gomatz introduces himself as a noble European, his words recalling the text of Tamino's Portrait Aria ("dieses Bild macht alles gut": "this portrait requites me for everything"). Gomatz's second aria, "Herr und Freund, wie dank' ich dir" (No. 6) reveals the joy that he feels at being rescued, his "loving heart" recalling that of Belmonte.

New for Mozart is his use of melodrama in Nos. 2 and 9. It is a genre that the composer got to know more especially in Mannheim in 1778. Melodrama, a combination of declamation and orchestral commentary, has its origins in France, particularly in Jean-Jacques Rousseau's *Pygmalion* of 1770. It required good, if not virtuoso, singing actors who knew how to declaim and mime. Mozart draws a contrast in these melodramas between the spoken word and music, aiming in the process at verbal intelligibility.

Bavarian State Opera, Munich, July 25, 1975 (Cuvilliés Theater) Idamante: Claes H. Ahnsjö. Ilia: Lilian Sukis. Elettra: Julia Varady. Idomeneo: Hermann Winkler. Bavarian State Opera Chorus. Producer: Peter Brenner. Designer: Ekkehard Grübler. Conductor: Wolfgang Sawallisch

Scene in Act III. "Peter Brenner showed an honest attempt to present as much as possible of the plot by means of a revolving stage, projections, and scrims, and, wherever the drama falters or fails, to probe the emotional lives of the virtually static characters. Torn between gripping theater and historical reminiscences, he contrasted turbulent choral scenes with processions of successful teams of oarsmen, leather-clad heroes with Furies and Masks, forceful action with frozen sublimity.... The set and costume designer Ekkehard Grübler attempted a similar compromise in his choice of dull shades of velvety red, creating a decoratively symbolic space above which the wild sea-god Neptune hovered on a four-horsed chariot. Initially we saw Crete on stage, exposed to the sea's injustices, but as the action developed on its hesitant course, the stage picture brightened and grew less violent, producing a grandiose and pleasantly abstract antiquity typical of the Baroque theater. The radiant glow from the orchestra pit was offset by the crimson pomp on stage," Karl Schumann wrote in *Musica*, 1975.

Idomeneo

Carnival in Munich

At some point during the course of 1780 Mozart received a commission to compose an opera for the 1780-81 carnival season in Munich. Who suggested Mozart's name is not known. It is generally assumed that Johann Christian Cannabich, music director at the Mannheim Court and a friend of Mozart's, and Anton Raaff, Court singer and first interpreter of the role of Idomeneo, prevailed upon Countess Josepha von Paumgarten to intercede on Mozart's behalf with the Elector Karl Theodor. The latter will have instructed Count Joseph Anton Seeau, Intendant or Controller of Operatic and Dramatic Performances at the Electoral Court, to convey the *scrittura* to Mozart.

Nor do we know who chose Gianbattista Varesco as librettist, although it was presumably Mozart himself. Varesco was baptized in Trento on November 25, 1735, and from 1753 to 1756 he attended the Jesuit College in the town and took minor orders. In 1766 he applied for an appointment with the Salzburg prince-archbishop Count Sigismund Christoph von Schrattenbach.

Schrattenbach was happy to take him on, not least because Varesco, in addition to being a priest, was also a musician. His salary was 100 gulden per annum—Mozart earned 150—in return for which Varesco was expected to "make himself available in the Court Chapel." As a priest his chief responsibility was to attend to the altar of St. Nicholas in the Cathedral. Privileges that Varesco had enjoyed under Schrattenbach were drastically curtailed by Schrattenbach's successor,

prince-archbishop Count Hieronymus von Colloredo. Mozart's librettist died a pauper on August 25, 1805 in Salzburg's St. John's Hospice (now the regional hospital).

In 1784, in his *Journey Through the Bavarian District*, Johann Pezzl worte that Varesco's plays were dominated by "the sort of wit that we associate with the breviary and hagiography, and with the school and monastery." Certainly, there is no denying that Varesco's schooling was grounded in the Jesuits' *ratio atque institutio*. Familiar with the works of the Church Fathers and equipped with a knowledge of medieval literature, he had studied grammar, rhetoric, and the humanities, learned Greek and Latin, and read Virgil and Homer in the original. At the Jesuit College in Trento he was instructed to write poems based upon classical models.

During the course of 1780 the Munich Court conveyed to Varesco a detailed plan for producing a libretto, in return for which he was to be paid the sum of 90 gulden. The text of *Idomeneo* was then translated into German by the Salzburg Court trumpeter, Johann Andreas Schachtner, who was a friend of Mozart's and who received 45 gulden for his pains. What Mozart himself received for the work we do not know, but we can assume that it was in the region of 200 gulden, a sum which Wolfgang considered too little. For a "payment such as this one cannot leave one's score behind," his father Leopold commented mockingly. Certainly Mozart did not relinquish his autograph score to the Munich Court, but kept it safe in Vienna.

Mozart left Salzburg on November 5, 1780 and made his way via Wasserburg-am-Inn to

K.366

Dramma per musica in three acts. Words by Gianbattista Varesco. Music begun in Salzburg in the fall of 1780. First performed at the Court Theater (Cuvilliés Theater), Munich, on January 29, 1781. Autograph score: Acts I and II: Crakow, Biblioteka Jagiellońska; Act III: West Berlin, Staatsbibliothek Preussischer Kulturbesitz.

Idomeneo

Munich to prepare for the premiere of *Idomeneo* there. When he arrived in the Bavarian capital at around 1 o'clock on the afternoon of the 6th, the score was far from being sufficiently complete for rehearsals to begin at once. Having taken rooms on the second floor of 6 Burgstrasse (with a certain Herr Fiat), Mozart went to pay a call on the Intendant Count Joseph von Seeau that same evening, but did not find him at home. Not until the following day could he and the flutist Johann Baptist Becke obtain an audience with the Count.

Composing the opera

A glance at the correspondence relating to *Idomeneo*, most of which is now preserved in the Library of the International Mozart Foundation in Salzburg, reveals that the composer was involved in a constant round of revisions, alterations, rewriting, and rehearsals. The opera was not ready musically until January 18, 1781, and the premiere took place on the 29th.

As early as November 8 Mozart had requested his librettist to make changes to Ilia's second-act aria "Se il padre perdei." Nor was the composer entirely satisfied with his performers; only his Ilia, Dorothea Wendling, met with his approval. By November 8 he had still to meet the Idamante, the castrato Vincenzo Dal Prato, but knew only that the singer's breath often gave out in the middle of an aria; even worse, "he has never been on any stage." Raaff, he observed, "is like a statue."

On November 11 Leopold Mozart returned "the book and the plan, so that His Ex. Count Seeau may see that everything has been done as instructed. A complete copy of the text will follow in a week's time, showing how Abb. Varesco wants it to be printed: it will also include the necessary notes."

On November 12 Seeau introduced Mozart to the Elector Karl Theodor, and on the following day the composer dined at Seeau's in the company of Cannabich, the Italian set-designer Lorenzo Quaglio, and the balletmaster Jean-Pierre Legrand. It was a "working lunch," arranged to discuss the future progress of the opera and to fix a date for the first performance.

In mid-November there were problems with Raaff and Dal Prato. In view of the singer's age, Mozart felt obliged to cut one of Raaff's arias. "But I shall have to teach the entire opera to my molto amato castrato del Prato. He is incapable of improvising an effective cadenza; and such an uneven voice...." Only the Elettra, Elisabeth Wendling had gone through her arias "Tutte nel cor vi sento" and "Idol mio, se ritroso" "half a dozen times—she is well satisfied."

Of the balletmaster Legrand, whom Mozart visited on November 22, the composer thought very little, describing him as "a terrible talker and *seccatore* [bore]," whose incessant chatter had made Mozart miss his mail coach.

On November 26 Mozart dined with the tenor Domenico de Panzacchi, the Arbace, and discussed with him the problem of the "subterranean voice": "Tell me, don't you think that the speech of the subterranean voice is too long? Consider it carefully. Imagine the theater, the voice must be terrifying—it must be penetrating—people must believe that it really exists—how can it produce this effect if the speech is too long and if the listeners become more and more convinced that it means nothing? If the speech of the Ghost in Hamlet were not so long, it would be even more effective. This speech here is very easy to cut, and will gain more in the process than it loses."

The instrumentation of the opera was uppermost in Mozart's mind when he wrote to his father on November 29: "For the march in Act II, which is heard in the distance, I need mutes for the trumpets and horns of a kind that is unobtainable here. Could you send me one of each by the next mail coach, so that I can have them copied here?"

On December 1 there was a rehearsal of Act I, which went well, according to the composer, in spite of the fact that, in addition to the wind instruments, they had only six violins. "I cannot tell you," he admitted to his father, "how delighted and astonished everybody was. But I never thought it would be otherwise; for I can assure you that I went to this rehearsal feeling as calm as if I had been invited out to dinner. Count Sensheim [Joseph Maria von Seinsheim] said to me, 'I assure you that I had expected a great deal from you—but I really did not expect that.'"

A second rehearsal was planned for a week later, when twelve violins were expected. A rehearsal of Acts I and II was held on December 16 from 5 until 8 in the evening, as we learn from Mozart's letter of that date to his father: "Acts I and II are being rehearsed this afternoon—again in the Count's apart-

Vienna Court Opera, October 25, 1879 Franz Gaul's costume designs for Idomeneo and Ilia. The designs are classical Greek in style. Franz Gaul was costume painter at the Vienna Court Theaters from 1868 to 1879. From 1879 to 1900 he was head of design at the Vienna Court Opera and the theater's senior technical inspector. His work shows evidence of a late Romantic and realist aesthetic.

ments; then we shall have only a chamber rehearsal of Act III—and then go straight to the theater—the rehearsal keeps on being postponed because of the copyist—which has put Count Sensheim into a devil of a rage.

"As for having the score copied, I did not need to be overfastidious, but simply told the Count straight out that it was always the custom in Mannheim (where the kapellmeister was certainly well paid) for him to have the original score returned to him—and the reason why the copying has been done all the more quickly here (for the first act has already been copied) is because Danzig [Innozenz Danzi] (the cellist) is getting on in years and would certainly not be able to read my small notes at night. As for the so-called popularity of the piece, you do not need to worry, for there is music for every kind of person in my opera; excepting only people with long ears."

His verdict on the rehearsal was entirely positive: "the latest rehearsal, like the first, went off very well—and the orchestra, together with all the audience, discovered to their delight that the second act was incomparably stronger than the first in its expressiveness and novelty—the 2 acts are to be rehearsed again next Saturday. But this time in a large room at Court, as we have long

desired, since there is far too little space at Count Seeau's—the Elector will listen to the rehearsal (incognito) from an adjoining room—but we shall have to rehearse for all we are worth, as Cannabich said to me—at the last rehearsal he was dripping with sweat."

The rehearsal in question took place on the day before Christmas Eve 1780: "the last rehearsal was splendid—it was in a large room at Court, the Elector was there too—this time we rehearsed with the whole orchestra (I mean with as many players as there is room for in the opera house). After the first act the Elector called out bravo in a very loud voice. And when I went over to kiss his hand, he said the opera will be charming and will certainly do me credit. As he did not know whether he could stay long enough, we had to perform the concertante aria ["Se il padre perdei"] and the thunderstorm at the beginning of the second act. At the end of it he again expressed his approval in the kindest manner and said with a laugh, no one would think such great things could be hidden in so small a head. And early the next day he praised my opera very highly at the levee. The next rehearsal will probably be in the theater. By the way, Beckè [Becke] told me a few days ago that he had again written to you after the last rehearsal but one and had mentioned, among other things, that in Raaff's aria in the second act the music and words were at odds—'so I have been told,' he sais, 'I know too little Italian—is that true?'—'If only you had asked me first and written afterward—I have to say that whoever told you so knows too little Italian.' The aria is well adapted to the words—one can hear the *mare*—and the *mare funesto*—and passagework is used for the word *minacciar*, since it is wholly expressive of the idea of *minacciar*, of something threatening. And in any case it is the most splendid aria in the opera, and has already won general approval.... Let me tell you, Raaff is the best and most honest fellow in the world, but so obsessed with slovenly routine that I could often weep tears of blood;—as a result it is very difficult to write for him,—but also very easy, if you like, and if I choose to write everyday arias. Take, for example, the first aria 'Vedròmi intorno' etc.: when you hear it, you will say that it is good, and that it is beautiful—but if I had written it for Zonca [Giovanni Battista Zonca], it would be even better suited to the words. He likes everything to be cut and dried—pays no heed to expression. I have now had problems with him over the quartet ['Andrò ramingo e solo']. The more I think of this quartet, as performed in the theater, the more effective I think it will be. And everyone who has heard it played on the clavier has liked it. Only Raaff thinks it will be ineffective. When we were by ourselves, he said to me, 'Non c'è da spianar la voce [It's impossible to smoothe out the voice]—it's too confining'—as if in a quartet the words should not be spoken much more than sung—he does not understand such things. I merely said, 'My very dear friend, if I knew of a single note in this quartet that could be altered, I would do so at once. But there is nothing in this opera that I like as much as this quartet; once you have heard it together with the rest, you are bound to change your mind. I have made every effort to serve you well in your 2 arias—and shall do so in the third as well—and hope to succeed—but as far as trios and quartets are concerned, the composer must have a free hand.' At which he said he was satisfied. He was recently very annoyed about some of the words in his final aria: *rinvigorir*—and *ringiovenir*—particularly *vienmi a rinvigorir*—five i's—it is true that at the end of an aria this is very disagreeable."

After Christmas Mozart confirmed that he had received Schachtner's German translation of the libretto, and the following day (the 28th) he held a rehearsal for the recitatives and quartet at the home of the flutist Johann Baptist Wendling.

He wrote to his father on December 30 to wish him a premature "Happy New Year," apologizing for writing so little but explaining that he was "up to his eyes in work." "I have not quite finished the third act, and then—since there is no extra ballet but only a divertissement appropriate to the opera—I have been given the honor of writing that as well. But I am pleased to be able to do so, since all the music will now be by a single composer. The third act will turn out to be at least as good as the first two—in fact, I believe, infinitely better—and I think it may be said with some justification, *finis coronat opus*.

"The Elector was so pleased by the recent rehearsal that, as I wrote to tell you the other day, he praised my opera very highly at his levee the next morning—and again at Court in the evening. And I know from a reliable source that, on the same evening after the rehearsal, he spoke of my music with everyone who came to see him, saying, 'I was quite surprised—never before has a piece of music made such an impression on me;—it is magnifique.'"

The third act was rehearsed in mid-January, and the first rehearsal of the recitatives was held in the theater on the 18th!!! The final dress rehearsal took place on January 27, Mozart's twenty-fifth birthday, and was attended by the composer's father and sister Nannerl.

Almost no contemporary reports have survived describing the premiere of *Idomeneo*. The *Münchener Staats-, Gelehrte, und Vermischte Nachrichten* noted that, "Authorship, music and translation all smack of Salzburg. The decorations, more especially the view of the maritime harbor and Neptune's temple, were masterpieces of ingenuity on the part of our famous local theater architect, Court Councillor Lorenzo Quaglio, and were the object of universal admiration."

An amateur performance of *Idomeneo* was given in the private mansion of Prince Karl Auersperg in Vienna on March 13, 1786, a performance for which Mozart made extensive revisions to his score and wrote two new numbers, a duet for soprano and tenor, "Spiegarti non poss'io" K.489, and a *scena* and rondo for tenor and violin solo, "Non più, tutto ascoltai...Non temer, amato bene" K. 490.

Characters and résumé of the plot

Idomeneo, King of Crete (tenor); Idamante, his son (male soprano); Ilia, Trojan princess, daughter of Priam (soprano); Elettra, daughter of King Agamemnon of Argos (soprano); Arbace, Idomeneo's confidant (tenor); High Priest of Neptune (tenor); La Voce (Voice of Neptune [Oracle]) (bass); chorus.

ACT I.   Following the fall of Troy, Idomeneo, King of Crete, returns home. Among the inhabitants of his royal palace in Cydon (Cydonia) is Ilia, daughter of the dead Trojan king, Priam, and a prisoner of Crete. Ilia is in love with Idomeneo's son, Idamante, but insists upon preserving the honor of Troy. On learning of his father's return, Idamante has freed the Trojan prisoners and declared his love for Ilia. She has reluctantly rejected him. The Trojans and Cretans are moved by gratitude to celebrate peace. Also present at the royal court of Cydon is Elettra (Electra), the daughter of Agamemnon; she has fled to Crete in order to escape from Aegisthus, who has seized power in Argos during her father's absence in the Trojan Wars. Elettra is promised in marriage to Idamante; his clemency towards the Trojan prisoners incurs her displeasure. Idomeneo's confidant, Arbace, puts about the false report that the King has been shipwrecked and that Neptune has destroyed the returning fleet at the very entrance to the sheltering harbor. Elettra is in despair at this news, believing herself the victim of a general conspiracy. Afraid that, as the new king, Idamante will choose Ilia as his wife, she threatens to destroy them both.—Idomeneo's fleet is close to foundering, and his crew is in extreme danger. A mimed scene follows in which Neptune appears at sea and gestures the winds to withdraw to their caves. The sea grows gradually calmer. On seeing the sea-god, Idomeneo implores his help. Neptune fixes him with his dark and threatening eyes, then sinks beneath the waves and disappears. "Eccoci salvi alfin," Idomeneo drags himself ashore, safe at last from the storm. He has appeased the angry god with a vow: the first human being whom he sees on land will be sacrificed to Neptune. And the first person to greet him is his son Idamante, who recognizes his father with joy and contentment. Idomeneo, however, turns away in agitation, forbidding his son to follow him. Saddened by his father's incomprehensible severity, Idamante remains behind. An intermezzo follows. The sea is now calm, and the Cretan army, which has returned to Cydon with Idomeneo, comes ashore. The warriors sing in honor of Neptune. Cretan women hurry in to welcome the safe return of their menfolk, and all give expression to their mutual joy in a dance.

ACT II.   Idomeneo confers with his confidant Arbace on ways to circumvent his vow and save Idamante. He resolves to send his son to Argos together with Elettra, where she will ascend the Mycenean throne. Arbace is instructed to inform them of Idomeneo's decree, and he promises to obey the command. Ilia welcomes Idomeneo and assures the king of her loyalty, acknowledging him as

IDOMENEO   1.AKT 2.BILD

Vienna State Opera, April 16, 1931
Producer: Lothar Wallerstein. Conductor: Richard Strauss
Alfred Roller's set design and technical drawing for Act I, Scene 2. The acting area is delimited by Roller's famous "towers," first seen at the Vienna Court Opera in the 1906 production of *Don Giovanni*. They allow rapid scene changes, but also underline the work's basic unity. In the background is an elaborately laid-out French garden.

Idomeneo

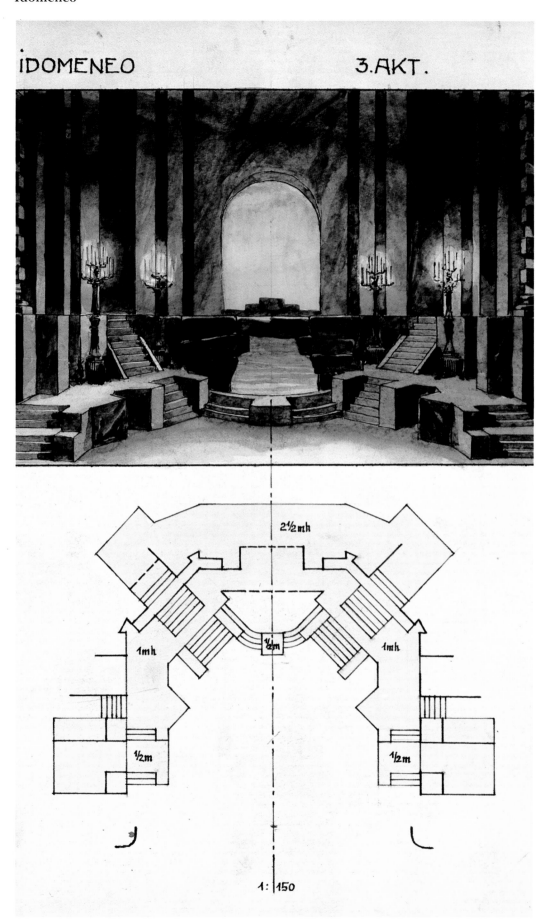

Vienna State Opera,
April 16, 1931
Producer: Lothar Waller-
stein. Conductor: Richard
Strauss
Alfred Roller's set design
and technical drawing for
Act III. The set is dominated
visually by a large gateway
looking out over the sea.
Roller's "towers" once again
delimit the stage, but the
flight of steps is the determining influence for this
act. Roller uses colors with
a symbolic and suggestive
value.

84

Nationaltheater, Mannheim, June 14, 1931
Producer: Richard Hein. Conductor: Joseph Rosenstock. Revised version by Lothar Wallerstein and Richard Strauss
Eduard Löffler's set design for Act I, Scene 7. Löffler interpreted the work as a Baroque opera. He introduced many realistic elements into his sets, but his view of the piece is on the whole traditional and certainly owes nothing to the "Neue Sachlichkeit" of his time.

ENTWURF ZU MOZARTS ,JDOMENEO' VIERTES BILD

Nationaltheater, Munich, 1936 (revival of 1931 production)
Producer: Kurt Barré. Conductor: Karl Tutein
Leo Pasetti's set-design for Act I, Scene 4 ("Coast"). Scene at the harbor after the sea has grown calm again. Idomeneo approaches the beach, lost in thought. His ship can be seen in the background.

Idomeneo

Stadttheater, Breslau, 1930-31
The painter, sculptor, set-designer, and graphic artist Hans Wildermann designed the sets for a production of *Idomeneo* in Breslau in 1930-31. From 1926 to 1936 he was professor at the city's State Academy for Art and Craft, in addition to designing sets for the Stadttheater and running the theater's design department. His sets are heavily architectural in style and use set-pieces that are often arranged along Cubist lines.

her father. Crete, she says, is now her second home. Idomeneo suspects that Ilia loves Idamante, and feels all the more dismayed by this knowledge. Elettra thanks Idomeneo. With her rival no longer close at hand, she hopes to win Idamante for herself by dint of her caresses and blandishments. Preparations are made for the couple to leave. Elettra is triumphant. Just as she and Idamante are on the point of embarking, a storm suddenly blows up. It increases in violence, and the sea rises. Thunder and lightning add to the fury of the elements, and the ships are struck by thunderbolts. A terrible monster emerges from the waves. Idomeneo admits his deceit and sin. He offers himself as a sacrifice in order to save the innocent couple. The storm continues unabated. The Cretans flee in terror.

ACT III. Ilia confides her love to the gently caressing zephyrs. Idamante enters and complains that his father is avoiding him and that she, Ilia, spurns him. He intends to seek death in battling with the monster that Neptune has sent. Ilia thereupon confesses her love. The lovers are surprised by Idomeneo and Elettra. Once again Idomeneo orders his son to leave Crete. Arbace announces that the townspeople are approaching with the High Priest, demanding to be rid of the sea-monster. Arbace bewails Cydon's unhappy lot and begs the gods to show forgiveness. Accompanied by the townspeople, the High Priest enters and confronts Idomeneo, insisting that the latter's vow be honored in order to save the country from further ruin, and demanding to know the victim's name. Idomeneo names his own son, and the townspeople express their general grief. Priests prepare the sacrifice. Idomeneo and the priests are ready to perform the deed. Arbace arrives to report that Idamante has slain the sea-monster. Idamante has learned of his father's vow and is ready to die. As Idomeneo is on the point of killing his son, Ilia rushes up to the altar, demanding to die at Idamante's side. A voice proclaims, "Idomeneo shall cease to reign; Idamante shall be king, and Ilia his bride." Consumed by anger, Elettra storms away. Idomeneo proclaims peace and allegiance to the gods' decree. The Cretans celebrate the coronation of their new king. The opera ends with a ballet, K. 367.

Structure of the opera

Idomeneo occupies a key position in Mozart's *œuvre* and is a turning-point in his operatic career. In it he bursts asunder the bonds of conventional *opera seria* and invests the genre with individual features, combining Baroque and subjective stylistic elements, making *opera seria* and its stereotyped characters less rigid, and creating a scenically representative work of artistic freedom and boldness which embraces both dramatic and lyric extremes of expression. The musical vocabulary that is deployed here reveals Italian, French, and German elements, and demonstrates the cosmopolitanism of the twenty-five-year-old composer who has assimilated and synthesized all the various European stylistic characteristics.

The work is conceived for singers trained in the Italian tradition, its basic structure being formed by recitative and aria: the former frequently loses its *secco* character and passes over into the more permissive area of *recitativo accompagnato*, while the arias are predominantly binary in form, seeking to intensify the musical expression and using Italianate melody and coloratura writing to depict psychological processes that reflect the emotional state of the individual character concerned. The tradition of French *tragédie lyrique* that Mozart was able to study in Paris in 1778 is revealed not only by his handling of the chorus, by the scenes involving priests, by the oracular pronouncement and by the orchestral recitatives, but also by his introduction of marches and processions and by the elaborately structured ballet music both within the work and at the end of the drama. It is to the Electoral Ballet Company that we owe the individual choreographic features of the work and the great closing orchestral suite, K.367, which is an integral part of the opera. In writing *Idomeneo*, Mozart was not concerned to portray the rationalism of Gluckian characters but rather to create subjective individuals, each with his or her own emotional life and depth of sensitive expression. The chorus—both dynamic and theatrical—functions as extras, as a catalyst in the action, and as a distant chorus, but is always closely bound up with the plot, and has lost its static, decorative aspect.

Idomeneo impresses with its rich and brilliant orchestral fabric. No restrictions were imposed on the composer in Munich in writing for the orchestra, for, unlike Salzburg, he was dealing with a topflight international orchestra recently transferred to Munich from Mannheim, with whom he could practice orchestral techniques learned in Paris and Mannheim, creating a sensual tonal impression, accompanying and emphasizing the vocal writing, and devising picturesque details. Thus we find—for the first time in any Mozart opera—a provision for clarinets, while he also writes for four separate horns, and introduces trombones for the oracular pronouncement and a piccolo for the storm.

Varesco's verbose libretto borrows from French libretti of the time as well as from Pietro Metastasio. The reduction in the number of characters to five is entirely in the spirit of Metastasio. Varesco has worked his humanist and Jesuit background into the piece, and also introduced elements of classical antiquity and medieval Christianity, elements which Mozart himself was at pains to digest intellectually.

Idomeneo is one of the works that was misunderstood by musicologists and theater directors throughout the nineteenth century and even as recently as the end of the Second World War. It was subjected to numerous revisions, and not until the 1970s did it enter public consciousness in its original form. Neither an engraved full score nor a printed vocal score of the work appeared during Mozart's lifetime. The first vocal score was published by Schmidt und Rau of Leipzig in 1796-97 and was the work of Johann Wenzel. The piece is identified on the title page as an "Opera Seria." Shortly afterwards, in 1797, August Eberhard Müller prepared a vocal score with an Italian and German libretto; described as a "serious opera," it was published by Breitkopf & Härtel of Leipzig. In 1798 David Apell, a member of the Upper

Chamber and Intendant of the Kassel Court Theater, prepared a German translation of the opera for a vocal score which was marketed by Nicolaus Simrock in Bonn. This version was performed in Kassel, in German, on January 1, 1802. The Leipzig *Allgemeine musikalische Zeitung* reported on the performance on February 17, 1802: "Our theater has risked an undertaking which no other German stage has yet attempted by presenting Mozart's Idomeneus on stage, and if we are to be at all fair, we must admit that it was with great success." The report went on to say that Mozart's "sublime and profound music" was reserved, however, for the "better sections of the audience." It was no doubt noticed in Kassel that *Idomeneo* stretched the resources of a provincial theater. Not all the roles were filled in a way "appropriate to so grand an opera." The acting of Madame Hassloch, brought in from Hamburg to sing

Vienna State Opera, April 16, 1931 Idomeneo: Josef Kahlenberg. Elettra: Maria Nemeth. Idamante: Eva Hadrabová. Producer: Lothar Wallerstein. Designer: Alfred Roller. Conductor: Richard Strauss. Words and music revised by Lothar Wallerstein and Richard Strauss Scene in Act II. The picture in the background shows a scene from the Trojan Wars.

Residenztheater, Munich, June 15, 1931 Idomeneo: Fritz Krauss. Idamantes: Sabine Offermann. Producer: Kurt Barré. Designer: Leo Pasetti. Conductor: Hans Knappertsbusch

Idomeneo

Salzburg Festival, July 27, 1951 (Felsenreitschule) Idomeneo (Rudolf Schock) with the chorus of Cretan men and women. Producer: Josef Gielen. Designer: Caspar Neher. Conductor: Georg Solti

Intermezzo in Act I. Paumgartner's version of the score came in for criticism: drastic cuts meant that whole arias, or parts of them, were excised, the resultant abridgement being a *reductio ad absurdum* of the opera's plot. Played without an intermission, the performance was too short for the opera, and too long for the audience.

The cast of the 1951 Glyndebourne production of *Idomeneo*, from left to right: Alexander Young (High Priest of Neptune), Léopold Simoneau (Idamante), Birgit Nilsson (Elettra), Richard Lewis (Idomeneo), Fritz Busch (Conductor), Oliver Messel (Designer), Carl Ebert (Producer), Michael Northern (Lighting), and Sena Jurinac (Ilia)
Sena Jurinac wrote of the production: "The 1951 Glyndebourne *Idomeneo* was, of course, the first professional performance of this *opera seria* in England, and it has always been regarded as epoch-making.... It was actually a Glyndebourne *Idomeneo*. Fritz Busch had commissioned his friend and contemporary Hans Gál to revise the work specially for this occasion, and for this house.... It proved wonderfully effective in practice. Cuts and abridgements were necessary for reasons of length, intelligibility and proportion.... The ballet was heavily cut and integrated into the chorus, Gál providing a suitable transition between them. The recitatives were performed with the utmost care and tautness, and were accompanied on the harpsichord by the young assistant conductor John Pritchard, who had also rehearsed the chorus and who took over as conductor on Busch's death."

Elettra, was said to be exaggerated, although she distinguished herself by her "tasteful costume" and by the "elevated theatrical figure" that she cut. Herr Hassloch as Idamante and Madame Wachsmuth as Ilia deserved "the audience's gratitude," it was emphasized in the report.

Editions and performances

A German libretto to *Idomeneo* was printed in Buda in 1803, and on March 31, 1804 F.S. Markt published a bilingual libretto with Italian and German words on the occasion of a concert performance of the opera in Hamburg's Concerthaus an der Kamp. Not until 1805 did the first printed score of the work appear: described as a "Drama Eroico" and entitled "Idomeneo Rè di Creta o sia Ilia e Idamante," it was published by Simrock in Bonn. A concert performance was given in the Frankfurt Schauspielhaus on Good Friday 1806, conducted by the local music director Herr Schmitt. The orchestra was reinforced by "skilled...amateurs and practiced artists from Offenbach." The Leipzig *Allgemeine musikalische Zeitung* sent along a reviewer, who expressed the hope that, following such "outstanding applause," the work might be performed in the theater. The Vienna Court Theater staged the work on

May 13, 1806 in a new German translation and revised version by Georg Friedrich Treitschke. Treitschke cut about a third of the music. The Leipzig *Allgemeine musikalische Zeitung* reported on the Vienna performance in its edition of June 11, 1806, "That Mozart's genius finds powerful and significant expression in this work, that it reveals a great profundity, a remarkable wealth and that higher characteristic, which issues directly from creative imagination alone, cannot, we think, be denied. At the same time, however, we must admit that, at the time when Mozart wrote this opera, he was still unacquainted with the theater and that he therefore often failed to write effectively. The opera was given here with so little precision and effort, the singers and orchestra fell so far short of the ideal in transforming this exceedingly difficult work of art into a perfect ensemble that we may find here, too, a reason for the scant applause which the piece received. The public was satisfied only with Herr Vogel as Idomeneus."

Idomeneo was performed at the Royal National Theater in Berlin on August 3, 1806 to mark the thirty-sixth birthday of King Friedrich Wilhelm III of Prussia. The Treitschke edition was used. The Leipzig *Allgemeine musikalische Zeitung* reported on the music, its interpretation and the performance, in its edition of August 20, 1806: "As

Bavarian State Opera, Munich, November 17, 1955
Idomeneo: Howard Vandenburg. New Munich version by Robert Heger. Producer: Heinz Arnold. Designer: Helmut Jürgens. Costumes: Rosemarie Jakameit. Conductor: Robert Heger
The winds have abated at Neptune's command, and the sea gradually becomes calm again. "Idomeneo recognizes the sea-god and pays homage to his might. Neptune looks at him darkly, then disappears menacingly into the waves." Idomeneo: "Safe on shore at last."

was to be expected, the music turned out a decent success, and in part was even impressive. The management had spared no expense in providing a number of attractive sets, and some especially magnificent costumes; ballets had been introduced in order to ensure that the opera would also attract the larger part of the general public, which would otherwise have been difficult." A concert performance of the work was given in the Frankfurt Schauspielhaus on December 25, 1806, the proceeds going towards the theater's pension fund. The audience is said to have been thin on the ground, and the performance itself tolerable. The first act was heard in a concert performance in Leipzig in December 1811, and on December 12, 1821 the Königsberg Stadttheater performed *Idomeneus, König von Kreta*.

Maurice Schlesinger published a vocal score of the opera in Paris and Berlin in 1822, the same year in which the Arras born writer Louis-Charles Caigniez prepared a French adaptation of the text for the Paris Opéra. However, the work was not taken up by the Opéra. Caigniez tightened up Varesco's action by cutting the entire Elettra subplot. Parts of *Idomeneo* were used in the pasticcio *Louis XII ou la Route de Reims* by Joseph-François Stanislas Maizony de Lauréal and Jules-Henri Vernoy de Saint-Georges, performed on June 7, 1825 in the Théâtre de

l'Odéon in Paris to mark the "Sacre de Sa Majesté Charles X." The music was arranged by the violinist and clarinetist Pierre Crémont and Alphonse Vergne, who also used parts of Mozart's *La Clemenza di Tito* in the same pasticcio.

In 1830 Richard Kiessling and Eugen Seidelmann adapted the opera for a German-language production in Breslau (modern Wrocław). Between 1830 and around 1835 vocal scores of *Idomeneo* were published by Carl Ferdinand Heckel in Mannheim and G.M. Meyer, jr. in Brunswick (Braunschweig). Also in 1835 Anton Wilhelm Florentin von Zuccalmaglio completed a textual revision of *Idomeneo* under the title *Der Hof in Melun (Agnes Sorel)*. Zuccalmaglio's version was set at the time of the Hundred Years' War between England and France which began in 1339. The text was adapted to fit Mozart's music. Many of the *recitativi secchi* were replaced by spoken dialogue.

In 1840 the Weimar Court Bookseller published a libretto for *Idomeneo*, without, however, naming the librettist. And in 1843 the Austrian writer on music Peter Lichtenthal adapted the opera in keeping with contemporary operatic taste. His changes and alterations—he cut half the numbers and reduced the action to two acts—is perhaps the most radical of all the revisions to which the work has been subjected. The Munich

Idomeneo

Salzburg Festival, July 30, 1956 (Festspielhaus) Producer: Oscar Fritz Schuh. Conductor: Karl Böhm
Caspar Neher's set designs for Act III. A constant element in Neher's sets was an irregular series of grooves in the stage floor into which pieces of scenery could be slotted. The palace architecture created a massive impression while remaining within a classical framework. The impression was enhanced by finely fluted pilasters, tall thin columns and colonnaded pavilions inserted from the back. For the appearance of Neptune and the sea monster Neher used conventional borders.

baritone, composer, and Court Opera director Leopold Lenz was commissioned by King Ludwig I of Bavaria to translate *Idomeneus, König von Kreta* into German for the Munich Court Theater. Lenz's version, said to be based "on the Italian of Alois Varesko" and to be "in keeping with the time," was first performed in the Bavarian capital on January 12, 1845. It was first and foremost a textual revision of the work, and was revived in Munich on March 13, 1862 and again on May 24, 1883. Carl Friedrich Niese adapted *Idomeneo* for the Dresden stage, where his version was first heard on January 15, 1854. He, too, was concerned with making improvements to the German text. Breslau performed the Kiessling/Seidelmann version on January 26, 1856. In 1872 the bookseller and lexicographer Hermann Mendel published a German translation of the opera. He stressed that

"the long recitatives and arias of varying worth are to blame for the tedium of 'Idomeneus'; add to them painful ritornellos and monotonous marches, and any sympathy that may have been aroused is dashed even more. The choruses, by contrast, are astonishingly beautiful ..., as are the ensembles ... and the elevating finale to the second act."

The conductor and composer Johann Nepomuk Fuchs revised *Idomeneo* for a production in Vienna on October 25, 1879. Once again, the main emphasis of the adaptation lay in the textual revisions that were made. The opera was published by Breitkopf & Härtel of Leipzig as part of the old Mozart Edition in June 1881. The text was printed in Italian and German (the latter in Niese's translation) and the edition was prepared by Count Paul von Waldersee. As he explained in the introduction, Waldersee's aim was to present the opera "in exactly the sequence and form that the individual numbers had assumed at the time of the first performance in Munich." In around 1895 Hermann Levi revised the opera for a production in Munich, his main alteration being to rewrite the *recitativi secchi* for strings. The first complete performance of *Idomeneo* in French took place on November 27, 1902 at a concert of the Paris Schola Cantorum. A staged presentation of the third act was given in Louis Laloy's translation at the Théâtre des Arts in Paris on December 12, 1912, a performance attended by Maurice Ravel, who described his impressions in the *Comoedia Illustre*: "I could not resist drawing a mental comparison between these tiny images and the beautiful scenery by M. Piot, realized by M. Mouveau, for performances of the third act of Mozart's *Idomeneo* at the Théâtre des Arts. The simple and large-scale construction of this landscape enhances, in a curious way, the proportions of this minuscule stage. In its tonality it is bold and seductive, without being unnecessarily gaudy. These are some of the finest sets that we have seen at the Théâtre des Arts."

Ernst Lewicki, Professor at the Technische Hochschule in Dresden, and a founder member, archivist, and president (in 1917) of the Dresden Mozart Society (founded in 1896) worked on an arrangement of *Idomeneo* in the years between 1902 and 1922. His adaptation, first written down between 1912 and 1916, is known to have been performed by two German theaters at least, firstly "in a version that is by no means definitive, on April 4, 1917 at Karlsruhe,

Salzburg Festival, August 18, 1962 (revival of a production first seen in the Grosses Festspielhaus in 1961)
Ilia: Pilar Lorengar. Idamante: Ernst Haefliger. Producer: Paul Hager. Designer: Stefan Hlawa. Costumes: Charlotte Flemming. Conductor: Peter Maag

"Hager achieves here a noble simplicity and silent greatness typical of Winckelmann's view of antiquity. The costumes too (Charlotte Flemming) adopt a similarly classical note. The sets by Stefan Hlawa do not quite succeed in creating the same unified impression. It is a splendid basic idea to stage the work in the spirit of a classical Greek landscape, with the sea as a dominant feature.... And the Greek columns make sense. But why ruined columns? ... And why drop scenes? A single seascape with columns would have sufficed, since the drop scenes are not followed by any radical change of scenery, but merely a rearrangement of the columns.... It is also in keeping with the spirit of the production that sea monsters do not 'appear,' but that terror simply rises up out of a darkened landscape. On the whole, then, a truly theatrical concept, filling out the width of the stage and involving many successful details, but not thought through to its logical conclusion," Kurt Nemetz-Fiedler concluded in the Salzburg *Berichte und Informationen* of July 28, 1961.

Deutsche Oper am Rhein, Düsseldorf, September 13, 1964 (revived in Duisburg on October 3, 1964)
Ilia: Elisabeth Schwarzenberg. Idamante: Andor Kaposy. Elettra: Antigone Sgourda. Idomeneo: Hermin Esser. Producer: Georg Reinhardt. Designer: Heinrich Wendel. Costumes: Inge Diettrich. Conductor: Günther Wich
Quartet from Act III (the royal gardens). Idamante: "I will go on my wanderings alone, seeking death elsewhere until I find it." Ilia: "You will have me as companion in your grief wherever you go, and where you die I too will die." Idomeneo: "Pitiless Neptune! Who, in mercy, will take my life?" Elettra (aside): "When shall I be avenged?"

Idomeneo

Cologne Opera,
September 26, 1971
Producer and designer:
Jean-Pierre Ponnelle
Finale of Act II. "The storm
breaks out anew. The Cre-
tans flee in terror, giving
expression to their fear in
singing and mime: 'Let us
run, let us fly from that
pitiless monster.'" As in all
of Ponnelle's productions,
whether in Cologne or Salzburg, Zurich or New York,
the focus of attention in
Idomeneo is Neptune.

Zurich Opera, March 23,
1980
Idomeneo: Werner Hollweg.
Idamante: Trudeliese
Schmidt. Ilia: Rachel Yakar.
Elettra: Felicity Palmer.
Arbace: Roland Hermann.
Producer and designer: Jean-
Pierre Ponnelle. Costumes:
Pet Halmen. Conductor:
Nikolaus Harnoncourt
Finale of Act II. "The form
that this *Idomeneo* takes on
stage is a strange but, in
its logical consistency, fascinating mixture of dramatic
spontaneity (in gesture and
mime, and in the musical
expressiveness of the singers
and orchestra) and a con-
scious stylization reminiscent of a Baroque court.
Ponnelle goes to great
lengths to differentiate and
'musicalize' the individual
gestures. The overall impression, however, is one of
symmetrical movement,
uncommonly effective in
its 'choreographed' routines.
In his handling of crowd
scenes he succeeds in creating magnificent stage pic-
tures which in themselves
are animated but which,
seen from afar, give an
impression of statuesque
'classicism.' What is constantly remarkable is that
on every level these formal-
ized movements and struc-
tures remain inherently
musical and music-oriented,"
commented Gerold Fierz in
Musica, 1980.

Metropolitan Opera, New York, October 14, 1982
Idomeneo: Luciano Pavarotti. Producer and designer: Jean-Pierre Ponnelle. Lighting designer: Gil Wechsler
"The issues at stake are clearly presented. The drama moves powerfully. The style chosen combines directness and romance with due formality," Andrew Porter wrote in *The New Yorker* in 1982.

under the baton of Fritz Cortelezis and with the active encouragement of Walter Steinkauler." Among those responsible for the revised text (based on Niese's German translation in the old Mozart Edition) were Lewicki himself and W. Genzmer. The second production of Lewicki's adaptation, and the one which he himself regarded as final, was heard in Dresden on March 4, 1925, when the conductor was Hermann Kutzschbach and the producer Georg Troller. In revising the opera Lewicki referred to Mozart's own plans for reworking the piece as mentioned in a letter of September 12, 1781; according to his introduction to the Dresden libretto, Lewicki hoped "to remove, as far as possible, all characteristic features of the old *opera seria,*" to bring the work closer in its content to the feelings of his own time, that is the feelings of the 1920s, and to make it "more humanly accessible."

A number of adaptations and revisions appeared in 1931 to mark the sesquicentenary of the opera's first performance. They all represented attempts to restore the work to the repertory, whatever the cost. In every case the editor's principal aim was to make the piece stageworthy in terms of theatrical practice, so that philological considerations were pushed into the background. Arthur Martin Rother, general music director in

Salzburg Festival, July 27, 1984 (Felsenreitschule)
Idamante: Trudeliese Schmidt. Ilia: Yvonne Kenny. Producer and designer: Jean-Pierre Ponnelle. Conductor: James Levine
Act I, Scene 2. As in Ponnelle's other productions of *Idomeneo,* a larger-than-life Neptune dominated the stage. In this scene Idamante promises Ilia that all the Cretans will be freed, while at the same time declaring his love for her. Idamante: "The fault is not mine, and you condemn me, my love, because I adore you."

Idomeneo

Salzburg Festival, August 2,
1976 (Kleines Festspielhaus)
Idamante: Peter Schreier,
surrounded by Cretans and
Trojans. Producer: Gustav
Rudolf Sellner. Designer:
Jörg Zimmermann. Conduc-
tor: Karl Böhm
Scene in Act I. This production, first seen in 1973, was
revised in 1976, but continued to leave a mixed impression: it was an antiquated
production dressed up with
modernistic features.

State Opera, East Berlin,
May 5, 1981
Idomeneo: Eberhard Büch-
ner. Producer: Ruth Berg-
haus. Designer: Marie-Luise
Strandt. Conductor: Peter
Schreier
Neptune warns the dilatory
king, whom the shipwrecked
sailors half encircle.

Dessau from 1927 to 1934, presented his
own version of the opera in the town on
February 19, 1931. Richard Strauss and
Lothar Wallerstein prepared a fundamental
revision of the opera for the Vienna State
opera, where it was first performed, in sets by
Alfred Roller, on April 16, 1931. An original
adaptation was made by Wilhelm Meckbach
for a production in Brunswick on May 31,
1931, when actors from the Mannheim and
Munich of 1778 and 1781 were introduced
into the action. A new German version of the

Vienna State Opera, February 21, 1987 High Priest of Neptune: Werner Hollweg. Idomeneo: Peter Schreier. Producer: Johannes Schaaf. Designer: David Fielding. Costumes: Tobias Hoheisel. Lighting Designer: Wolfgang Göbbel. Conductor: Nikolaus Harnoncourt

Scene in Act III. "Schaaf draws on every period and every style as the fancy takes him: Idamante could wear the same costume to sing Fidelio, while Ilia's court dress approaches the fashions of Mozart's own day in its Ottoman associations. Her rival Elettra wears Baroque court dress and draws a large heart on the stage with the letters E and I; when she goes into exile, large numbers of servants carry the *grande dame*'s luggage to the ship. Ilia and Idamante are at times required to adopt an equally coquettish manner, billing and cooing by the footlights like Papageno and Papagena. But alongside these inanities are a number of good ideas not too far removed from the music's eternal verities: a respectable and theatrically effective storm at sea, and a strangely distended jelly-fish-like monster recall an historical theater with its elaborate machinery, while a swaying mast and a sea-shore littered with wreckage and bodies provide an effective backdrop to Idomeneo's rescue. Neptune's statue, a splintered figurehead, gives rise to a thrilling crowd scene," Rudolf Klein wrote in the *Österreichische Musikzeitschrift*, 1987.

opera, commissioned from Ermanno Wolf-Ferrari by the Bavarian State Opera, was performed in the Residenz Theater on June 15, 1931. Mention should also be made here of a Czech translation of *Idomeneo*, published in Prague in 1931. Vittorio Gui adapted the opera for a production in Milan in 1947, and Hans Gál revised the piece for the 1951 Glyndebourne Festival. This latter production opened on June 20, 1951 and was conducted by Fritz Busch. The opera was broadcast by Hesse Radio (Frankfurt) on December 18, 1954 in a translation and radio adaptation prepared by the conductor Winfried Zillig. Zillig stressed "that thanks to the courage of theater managers this mature masterpiece is finally being restored, in the public's estimation, to the place where it rightfully belongs—in the cycle of Mozart's great operatic masterpieces." On November 17, 1955 Robert Heger conducted a new version in Munich, based on Ermanno Wolf-Ferrari's adaptation. On July 30, 1956 the Salzburg Festival performed Bernhard Paumgartner's revised version of the opera. Paumgartner took account of the Vienna alterations when revising the score. Bliss Hebert and Constance Mellen translated the opera into English in 1961, as did Lionel Salter in 1971. The Neue Mozart-Ausgabe of *Idomeneo* dates from 1972. The main section of this edition presents the opera "in the version seen and heard at the Munich premiere of January 29, 1781 ...; integrated into this main section is the 1786 Vienna revision." The first production to be staged subsequent to the publication of the Neue Mozart-Ausgabe was the one seen at the Salzburg Festival on July 26, 1973, although the edition used here was a mixture of the Munich and Vienna versions. The producer Gustav Rudolf Sellner and the conductor Karl Böhm dispensed with the closing ballet. Two other productions of note in Munich opened at the Cuvilliés Theater on July 25, 1975 and at the National Theater on February 19, 1979. The work was performed at the Zurich Opera House on March 23, 1980 in its original Munich form. A new production of *Idomeneo* was staged at the Deutsche Staatsoper in Berlin on May 5, 1981, and the Salzburg Festival again tackled the work in 1983, this time in the Felsenreitschule. A new French translation of the *dramma per musica* by Giovanni Clerico was published in Paris in 1983. The film director Johannes Schaaf staged a somewhat controversial interpretation of *Idomeneo* for Vienna in 1987.

Théâtre National de l'Opéra,
Paris, March 23, 1976
Pedrillo: Norbert Orth.
Osmin: Kurt Moll. Producer:
Günther Rennert. Designer:
Bernard Daydé. Costumes:
José Varona. Conductor:
Karl Böhm
Act II, Scene 8. Pedrillo
outwits Osmin with Cyprian
wine, offering him a large
and a small bottle. Osmin
chooses the large one, hop-
ing that Pedrillo will not
betray him and that Allah
will not see him drinking
(Duet: "Vivat Bacchus").

The Abduction from the Seraglio

Interest in German-language operas

The idea of establishing a German National Theater in Vienna was first mooted by Joseph II in 1776, when he made the Burgtheater—which until then had witnessed a series of fortunate and not so fortunate lessees—the permanent responsibility of the Court. Its first directors were the actor Johann Heinrich Friedrich Müller and the theater director from Brünn (modern Brno), Johann Heinrich Böhm. The first Singspiel to be performed in the theater under its new management was *Die Bergknappen* by Ignaz Umlauf. The idea of performing German works of music found favor not only with Joseph II but also with Viennese audiences in general. The move, none the less, represented a break with tradition on the Emperor's part. The brilliance of the Italian opera and lavish ballets disappeared, a loss which, like the reduction in the Imperial household budget, saved the state a great deal of expense. The ambitious idea of performing only German operas was soon abandoned, and the Italian *opere buffe* and French *opéra-comiques* in German translation, which entered the repertory at an early date, soon came to dominate it. In 1781 *Das Deutsche Museum* pontificated against "operettas," describing them as stiff, wooden, and marionette-like. On March 4, 1783 the German Opera Company ceased to operate, and the Italian *opera buffa* again became the focus of attention, not least because it was encouraged by the Italian kapellmeister Antonio Salieri and was demonstrably superior to the German Singspiel. Nevertheless, individual artists continued to ask for German Singspiels for their benefit performances. Certainly, the greatest and, from the standpoint of musical history, the most significant contribution to the German national Singspiel was made by Mozart with his *Abduction from the Seraglio*. "Nothing special," as Joseph II is reputed to have said about the work, could scarcely have been further from the truth.

History of the theme

The theme of Turkish sieges and Turkish wars plays a by no means unimportant role in the history of Vienna. The events of 1529, 1683-99, and 1788-92 mark three significant stages in the confrontation of the Moslem world with Western Europe. The first of these dates is determined by a religious and ideological conflict: a vast Turkish army under Soliman I overran the whole of Hungary before crossing the Austrian border and laying siege to Vienna. The House of Habsburg took upon itself the task of defending the West against the Crescent of Islam, an act of defiance which came to assume symbolic proportions. The second Siege of Vienna, which began in 1683 and ended in 1699 with the Peace of Karlowitz, when Hungary and Transylvania were ceded to Austria, and Austria thereby became a major power, was more the result of economic interests than a holy war against the infidel. The city was liberated by Imperial troops from Germany and Poland, encouraging the whole of Europe to think in terms of political solidarity and reviving thoughts of a further crusade

K.384

German Singspiel in three acts. Words by Christoph Friedrich Bretzner, adapted by Johann Gottlieb Stephanie the Younger. Begun in Vienna on July 30, 1781 and completed in Vienna at the end of May 1782. First performed in the Vienna Burgtheater, July 16, 1782. Autograph score: Acts I and III: Cracow, Biblioteka Jagiellońska; Act II: West Berlin, Staatsbibliothek Preussischer Kulturbesitz.

The Abduction from the Seraglio

Title page of an early vocal score, Mainz, 1785 (?)

Aquatint by Franz Hegi. Mozart is seen in the center of the picture, expressing violent criticism at a performance of *The Abduction from the Seraglio* in Berlin on May 19, 1789. Friedrich Rochlitz described the incident in the Berlin theater as follows: "When Mozart arrived in Berlin on the last occasion (i.e. after his second visit to Leipzig), evening was already falling. Scarcely had he alighted at the inn (on the Gendarmenmarkt at the corner of Charlottenstrasse) when he wanted to know whether any music was being performed there that evening. His interlocutor, who did not know him, replied that there was: 'The German Opera has just opened.' 'Really? What are they giving today?' 'The Abduction from the Seraglio.' 'Charming,' Mozart cried with a laugh. 'Yes,' the other man went on, 'It's a delightful piece. Composed by—what's his name?' But Mozart had already left, still in his traveling coat. He stood at the entrance to the stalls, intend-

against Islam. The names of Count Ernst Rüdiger von Starhemberg and Prince Eugen are inextricably linked with this second Turkish incursion into the Danube Monarchy. The third Turkish War, from 1788 to 1792, goes back in its origins to the Austro-Russian Alliance of 1781 in which common interests against Turkey had been emphasized. The capture of Belgrade by Baron Gideon von Laudon in 1789 confirmed the fighting strength of the Austrian Empire, which had entered the war alone.

These historical facts need to be borne in mind when we speak of the "Turkish" element in Austria. That the Moslems were popular figures on the Viennese stage—and not only here, but in the whole of Europe—goes without saying. The Turks' curious clothes and remarkable habits caught the attention of all Europeans, while the Ottomans' piratical exploits often aroused no more than caustic mockery, if not an indulgent smile. Opera librettists were somewhat cavalier in their approach to geography: no distinction was drawn between Algeria, Turkey, and Persia, and the fictional town of Ormus, a frequent setting for contemporary operas, is a classic example of the way in which "Turkey" was interpreted in the widest sense of the word. Moreover, *commedia dell'arte* had introduced into its improvised repertory the figure of the Grand Turk, while both France and the House of Habsburg had become familiar with Ottoman ideas and habits as a result of diplomatic ties.

Mozart's chronicle of composing the opera

The correspondence relating to *The Seraglio* includes not only details about the composition of the work, it also reveals the composer's critical debate with the genre of opera in general in the early 1780s.

March 16, 1781: Mozart arrives in Vienna, where, on May 9-10, he becomes involved in an argument with the prince-archbishop of Salzburg, Count Hieronymus Colloredo. On June 8 the composer breaks completely with the Salzburg Court.

April 18: Johann Gottlieb Stephanie the Younger, a member of the Burgtheater ensemble from 1769 to 1799 (his preference there was for comic roles) and the author of more than thirty stage works, expresses his wish "to give me [Mozart] a new piece and, as he says, a good one." Stephanie adapted the three-act operetta *Belmont and Constanze, or The Abduction from the Seraglio*, written by the Leipzig merchant Christoph Friedrich Bretzner and published by Carl Friedrich Schneider of Leipzig in 1781. Bretzner's text was set to music in 1781 by Johann André, the founder of the Offenbach music publishing firm that bore his name. André's version was staged by Doebbelin's ensemble in Berlin on May 25, 1781. In Bretzner's version the Pasha recognizes his son in Belmonte, whereas Stephanie focuses upon the humanitarian aspect of the work, and has the Pasha pardon the two lovers of his own free will. Bretzner availed himself of the libretto arsenal of his time: the lovers' separation and reunion, an abduction, a Turkish setting and oriental fairy-tale world, cruel Moslems, an enlightened and self-denying ruler, and a puffed-up harem guard were all part and parcel of the operas that were written before and after 1750. Closely related in their subject matter and probably Bretzner's immediate models were the anonymous French *Les Epoux esclaves ou Bastien et Bastienne à Alger*, Paris, 1755; Christoph Willibald Gluck's *La Rencontre imprévue*, Vienna, 1764; Niccolò Jommelli's *La Schiava Liberata*, Ludwigsburg, 1768; and Joseph Haydn's *L'Incontro Improvviso*, also Vienna, 1775. All of these works—and similar themes can be found from England to Italy—are textual precursors of Mozart's *Seraglio*. The composer himself had already set a similar theme to music in his Singspiel

K. 336b, later known under the title *Zaide* (see pp. 75-78). His dramatic instinct was revealed the moment he received Bretzner's libretto: "I said only that, with the exception of the long dialogues, which are easily altered, the piece was very good, but not for Vienna, where they prefer comic pieces."

April 28: Mozart asks his father for advice: should he write "a German opera" for Vienna?

May 19: "Everything is well with the opera," Wolfgang informs his father.

June 9: The "General Director of Spectacles" and Chief Chamberlain to the Viennese Court, Count Franz Xaver Wolf Orsini-Rosenberg, instructs the actor and Shakespeare translator Friedrich Ludwig Schröder "to look round for a good opera text" for Mozart.

July 30: Mozart receives the libretto for *The Abduction from the Seraglio* from Stephanie.

August 1: Mozart finds the text "very good" and explains the title and his initial thoughts on writing the work and casting it, together with his plans for a gala performance, in a letter to his father of this date: "The subject is Turkish and the title is: *Bellmont und Konstanze, oder die Verführung aus dem Serail* [Belmonte and Constanze, or The Seduction from the Seraglio].—For the Sinfonia [Over-

ing to listen to the performance unobserved. But whether inordinately pleased by the performance of certain passages, dissatisfied with some of the tempi, or dismayed by what he called the singers' superfluous flourishes—in a word, his interest was more and more intensely roused, so that he began to force his way, without noticing it, closer and closer to the orchestra, growling and grumbling the while, now in a whisper, now in a louder voice, with the result that the people around him, looking down on this small and insignificant figure in an ill-fitting overcoat, soon had reason enough to laugh at him, although Mozart himself of course remained oblivious. Finally they came to Pedrillo's aria, 'Frisch zum Kampfe, frisch zum Streite,' etc. Either the management had a faulty score or they had tried to correct what they assumed was an error, and had given a D sharp, instead of a D, to the second violin at the repeated words, 'nur ein feiger Tropf verzagt.' At this point Mozart could restrain himself no longer, and he fairly cried out, using language that was of course not known for its ornamentation: 'Damn it—why can't you play a D!' Everyone turned round, including several of the orchestral players; some of the musicians recognized him, and, like wildfire, word went round the orchestra, and from there to the stage: Mozart is here! Some of the actors, including the most admirable Madame B., who was playing Blonde, refused to return to the stage. This news was reported back to the music director and he, in his embarrassment, repeated it to Mozart, who by now had advanced to a point immediately behind him. In an instant the composer was behind the scenes: 'Madame,' he said to her, 'what nonsense is this? You have sung splendidly, quite splendidly, and so that you sing even better next time, I shall rehearse the role with you.'"

The Abduction from the Seraglio

Court Theater, Munich,
1825
Set design for Act I by
Simon Quaglio
Quaglio, who became Director of Scenic Design at the
Munich Court Theater in
1828, created a magnificent
medieval architecture with
oriental local color in his
sets for *The Abduction from
the Seraglio*.

Kärntnertortheater, Vienna,
c. 1840, but possibly as late
as 1854
Set design for "a garden"
by an unknown artist. An
exotically atmospheric, light,
and colorful picture in the
Biedermeier style.

Royal National Theater,
Berlin, 1884
Julius K. Lechner's set design for the scene "Outside
the Pasha Selim's Palace"
A grandiose design showing
the Oriental world of the
fin de siècle

ture], the chorus in the first act ['Singt dem
grossen Bassa Lieder' No. 5], and the final
chorus [the work was intended, therefore, to
end with a chorus] I shall write Turkish music
[that is, Janissary music that would give the
piece some local color]. Mlle. [Catarina]
Cavalieri, Mlle. [Therese] Teyber, M. [Johann
Ignaz Ludwig] Fischer, M. [Johann Valentin]
Adamberger, M. [Johann Ernst] Dauer, and
M. [Johann Ignaz] Walter will sing in it. I am
so pleased to be writing the piece that I have
already completed Mlle. Cavalieri's first aria
['Ach ich liebte, war so glücklich' No. 6],
Adamberger's aria ['Hier soll ich dich denn
sehen' No. 1] and the trio [for Belmonte,
Pedrillo and Osmin, 'Marsch, marsch,
marsch! trollt euch fort' No. 7] with which the
first act ends. Time is short, it is true; for it is
to be performed in mid-September; but the
circumstances connected with the time of
performance and, in general, all my other
plans have fired my enthusiasm to such an
extent that I rush to my desk with the greatest
eagerness and remain seated there with the
greatest joy."

"The Grand Duke of Russia [Paul Petrovitch, later Czar Paul I,] is coming here, and
so Stephani[e] asked me, if at all possible, to
complete the opera in this short space of time.
For the Emperor [Joseph II] and Count
Rosenberg will be here soon, and their first
question will be whether anything new is in
preparation? He will then have the satisfaction of saying that the opera by [Ignaz]
Umlauf [probably *Das Irrlicht oder Endlich
fand er sie*, words also by Bretzner], on which

he has been working for a long time, will soon
be ready, and that I am composing one
specially for the occasion—and he will certainly reckon it to my credit that I have
undertaken to write it for this purpose in so
short a time. No one but Adamberger and
Fischer knows about it yet, since Stephani[e]
asked us to say nothing till Count Rosenberg
gets back, as it could easily give rise to a
thousand different rumors. Stephani[e] does
not even want to be thought of as too good a
friend of mine, but prefers people to think
that he is doing all this because Count
Rosenberg desires it so; after all, the Count
did actually order him on his departure to
look round for a text for me."

August 10: Leopold Mozart writes to the
publishing house of Breitkopf & Son in
Leipzig: "[Wolfgang] has been asked to write
an operetta which is to be performed in
mid-September and which he has agreed to
compose because it will celebrate the arrival
of the Grand Duke of Russia."

August 22: Act I of *The Abduction from the
Seraglio* is completed.

August 29: Since the Russian Grand Duke
will not now be coming to Vienna until
November, Mozart can "write the opera at
greater leisure." He will not have it performed
before All Saints' Day, since the Viennese
aristocracy is at present in the country and
they will not be returning to the city to
resume their visits to the theater until the
month of November.

September 19: In the meantime Mozart has
performed sections of the opera to interested
parties among his private acquaintances, and
it has been greeted with exceptional acclaim.
If the piece were to prove a success in Vienna,
Mozart tells his father, he will not only be a
famous keyboard virtuoso but will also be
acknowledged as a composer.

After September 19: Mozart sends details of
his cast to Salzburg.

September 26: The composer informs his
father of a "little idea" he has had for his
work: "the opera had begun with a monologue and so I asked Herr Stephani[e] to turn
it into a little arietta ['Hier soll ich dich denn
sehen' No. 1] and then to put in a duet
['Verwünscht seist du samt deinem Liede'
No. 2] instead of making the two chatter

The Abduction from the Seraglio

Palais Garnier, Paris, December 4, 1903
Osmin: André Gresse. First performance of *The Abduction from the Seraglio* in the French version of Maurice Kufferath and Lucien Solvay. Producer: Raoul Lapissida. Designers: Marcel Jambon and Alexandre Bailly. Costumes: Charles Bianchini. Conductor: Paul Vidal
Act III, Scene 5. Osmin triumphs over the Europeans and looks forward to seeing them dragged away to be executed.

together after Osmin's short song ['Wer ein Liebchen hat gefunden' No. 2]. Since we have given the role of Osmin to Herr Fischer, who certainly has an excellent bass voice (in spite of the fact that the archbishop told me he sings too low for a bass, so that I assured him that he would sing higher next time), we must take advantage of such a singer, particularly since he has the whole of the public here on his side. But in the original libretto this Osmin had only a single short song to sing ['Wer ein Liebchen hat gefunden' No. 2], and nothing else apart from the trio ['Marsch, marsch, marsch!' No. 7] and finale ['Nie werd ich deine Huld verkennen' No. 21]. And so he has been given an aria in Act I ['Solche hergelaufne Laffen' No. 3], and will also have one in the second act [this aria was not composed]. I have given details of this aria to Herr Stephani[e];—most of the music for it had already been completed before Stephani[e] knew a word about it. I am enclosing only the beginning of it, and the end, which is bound to be effective—Osmin's anger is rendered comical by the use of the Turkish music. In working out the aria I have (in spite of the Salzburg Midas [Prince-Archbishop Colloredo]) allowed his splendid low notes to glow. Although his 'Drum beim Barte des Propheten' [from No. 3] is in the same tempo, the notes are quicker—and, as his anger keeps on increasing, there comes (at the point where his aria seems to be over) an *allegro assai*—in a completely different time and key—which is bound to be highly effective;

for just as a man in such a violent rage oversteps all the bounds of order, moderation, and propriety, and forgets himself—so the music must forget itself—but since passions, whether violent or not, must never be expressed to the point of exciting disgust, and since the music, even in the most dreadful situation, must never offend the ear but always give pleasure to the listener, in other words, must always remain music, so I have not chosen a key remote from F (the key of the aria) but rather one related to it— not the nearest, D minor, but the more remote A minor. Now Bellmont's aria in A major, 'O wie ängstlich, o wie feurig' [No. 4]. Do you know how it is expressed? His beating, lovesick heart is already indicated by 2 violins in octaves. This is the favorite aria of all who have heard it, including myself. It is written expressly for Adamberger's voice. You see the trembling—the faltering—you see his swelling breast rising—expressed by a crescendo—you hear the whispering and sighing—which is expressed by the first violins with mutes and a flute playing in unison. The Janissary chorus ['Singt dem grossen Bassa Lieder' No. 5] is all that one could wish for in a Janissary chorus. Short and cheerful;—and written entirely for the Viennese. Constanze's aria ['Ach, ich liebte, war so glücklich' No. 6] I have sacrificed somewhat to the flexible throat of Mlle. Caval[l]ieri. 'Trennung war mein banges loos. und nun schwimmt mein aug in Thränen' [Separation was my anxious fate, and now tears swim in my eyes]—I have tried to express these feelings, as far as an Italian bravura aria allows one to do so. The 'hui' [an exclamation used to make animals go faster] I have changed to 'schnell,' so that the line now runs, 'doch wie schnell schwand meine freude etc.' [but how swiftly fled my joy]: I really do not know what our German poets are thinking of;—even if they do not understand the theater, they should not make their characters speak as though addressing a herd of animals—Giddap there! 'Now for the trio ['Marsch, marsch, marsch!' No. 7], in other words, the end of the first act. Pedrillo has passed off his master as an architect, so that he has an opportunity to meet his Constanze in the garden. The Pasha has taken him into his service; Osmin, the steward, knows nothing of this, and since he is a rude and churlish fellow, and the archenemy of all strangers, he is impertinent and refuses to allow them into the garden; the first thing to be indicated is very brief, and since the words lent themselves to it, I have written the piece as an exercise in three-part writing, and done it tolerably well. But then the major key begins at once, pianissimo— it must go very quickly—and the end will be very noisy—when all's said and done, that is all one needs for the end of an act—the noisier, the better; the shorter, the better—so that the audience does not grow cold in its applause.

"Of the Overture you have only 14 bars. It is quite short and keeps changing from *forte* to *piano* and back again, with the Turkish music entering at each *forte*. It modulates through the different keys—I don't think people will fall asleep during it, even if they have not slept a wink the previous night. But here's the rub! the first act was finished over 3 weeks ago, as was one of the arias in the second act and the drunken duet [for Pedrillo and Osmin, 'Vivat Bacchus, Bacchus lebe' No. 14] (*per il Signori vieneri*) which consists entirely of my Turkish tattoo: but I cannot write any more because the whole story is now being turned on its head—and, to tell the truth, at my own insistence. At the beginning of the third act there is a charming quintet or rather finale—I'd prefer to have it at the end of the second act [the piece in question is the quartet 'Ach Belmonte, ach mein Leben' No. 16], and in order to make this possible, a great change has to be made, indeed, a whole new intrigue has to be introduced—and Stephani[e] is already up to his eyes in work, so that I shall have to be a little more patient. Everyone says rude things about Stephani[e]—and it may well be that, in my own case too, he is friendly only to my face—but, after all, he is arranging the libretto for me—and, what's more, as I want it—to the letter—and, by God, I do not ask anything more of him! Well, this is all idle chatter concerning my opera; but I cannot help it."

October 6: Mozart is angry at not being able to continue work on his opera. He claims to have written Belmonte's aria "O wie ängstlich, o wie feurig" (No. 4), Constanze's aria, "Ach ich liebte, war so glücklich" (No. 6), and the trio for Belmonte, Pedrillo, and Osmin, "Marsch, marsch, marsch!" (No. 7), in a single day and to have copied them out in a day and a half. But all this haste has been in vain, since, according to the composer, Gluck's *Iphigénie en Tauride* and *Alceste* first had to be "brought off"—"and there is still an enormous amount for the singers to learn."

October 13: Mozart gives vent to his feelings concerning the text, and opera libretti in

general, in a letter to his father: "Now for the text of the opera. As far as Stephani[e]'s work is concerned, you are right, of course. But the poetry is perfectly in keeping with the character of the stupid, boorish, spiteful Osmin. I know that the verse is not of the best—but it is so appropriate, and so much in accord with the musical ideas that were already circulating in my head, that it was bound to appeal to me; and I'll wager that, when it is performed, there will be no cause for regret. As for the poetry in the piece itself, I could really not bring myself to despise it—Belmont's aria, 'O wie ängstlich etc.' [No. 4], could scarcely be better written for music. Except for the 'hui' and 'kummer ruht in meinem schoos' [grief reposes in my bosom]—for 'grief' cannot 'rest'—even this aria is not bad, especially the first part. And I do not know—but in an opera the poetry must necessarily be the obedient daughter of the music." The question of the relative predominance of words and music has always been a popular theme for debate and has been treated in the theater in such works as Salieri's *Prima la musica e poi le parole* of 1786, Dalayrac's *Le Poète et le musicien* of 1811, and Richard Strauss's *Capriccio*, 1942.

November 3: Mozart is still waiting for Stephanie to send him further revisions, in order to be able to bring the work to a swift conclusion. He believes that "it would be a good thing if the opera were ready" and if the premiere could take place sooner rather than

Dresden State Opera, December 27, 1927
Osmin: Ivar Andrésen.
Blonde: Erna Berger
Born in Oslo in 1896, Ivar Andrésen joined the Dresden State Opera in 1925 and remained with the company until 1934. Notable above all for his Wagner roles, the Norwegian bass possessed a large, sonorous, and warmly expressive voice. Erna Berger was born in Cossebaude near Dresden in 1900 and engaged by Fritz Busch to sing at the Dresden State Opera in 1925. She moved to the Berlin State Opera in 1934, where one of the roles that Wilhelm Furtwängler asked her to sing was Constanze in *The Abduction from the Seraglio*. She had a beautiful coloratura soprano voice that radiated a mixture of virtuosity and charm, ease and warmth.

Stadttheater, Königsberg, 1932
Act I, Scene 6. Pasha Selim and Constanze arrive in a pleasure boat. The Janissaries and populace await the Pasha outside a mosque: "Sing to the mighty Pasha, resound, fiery song; and let the shore reverberate with the joyful sound of our songs!"

Salzburg Festival, August 12, 1935 (Festspielhaus)
Pedrillo: William Wernigk. Osmin: Berthold Sterneck. Producer: Herbert Graf. Designer: Oskar Strnad. Conductor: Bruno Walter Act II, Scene 8. "Vivat Bacchus, long live Bacchus, Bacchus was a fine fellow" and "Three cheers for the girls, the blondes, the brunettes."

later, since Umlauf's opera cannot be given at present because two of his singers are ill.

November 17: "Well, I have finally received something to enable me to continue work on my opera."

January 30, 1782: As a result of performances of "Gluck's great operas" *Iphigénie en Tauride, Alceste*, and *Orfeo*, and because of the many textual changes that had had to be made to the libretto, Mozart's opera has been "left behind." The premiere is now being planned for "after Easter."

May 7: Mozart plays the second act of *The Seraglio* to Countess Maria Wilhelmine Thun: she is said to be "no less satisfied with the second act than with the first."

May 30: Mozart and his "dear Constanze" dine with Countess Thun, and he plays her the third act. During this period he has the "tiresome task of correcting the score." But "I must confess that I am very much looking forward to this opera."

June 3: First rehearsal in the Burgtheater.

July 16 at 6.30 p.m: Premiere of *The Abduction from the Seraglio* in the Vienna Burgtheater.

Cast list

The cast was as follows: Constanze, Catarina Cavalieri; Blondchen, Therese Teyber; Belmonte, Johann Valentin Adamberger; Pedrillo, Johann Ernst Dauer; Osmin, Johann Ignaz Ludwig Fischer; and Bassa Selim, Dominik Jautz. Closer examination of the names of the singers involved reveals that Mozart's opera was cast from strength, and that each role was tailored to suit the artist concerned. For today's opera managements this may be a problem, since not every opera house can provide an Osmin capable of sustaining a low D for eight bars.

Catarina Cavalieri, daughter of a choir regent, was a pupil of Salieri's. She created the roles of Donna Elvira in the first Viennese performance of *Don Giovanni*, Mademoiselle

Hamburg State Opera, December 1, 1937
Belmonte: Willi Frey. Pedrillo: Peter Klein. Pasha Selim: Gerhard Bünte. Producer: Oscar Fritz Schuh. Designer: Wilhelm Reinking. Conductor: Hans Schmidt-Isserstedt

Act I, Scene 8. Pedrillo introduces Belmonte to the Pasha as "a man who has studied architecture in Italy" and who has heard of the Pasha's might and wealth. Belmonte offers to serve the Pasha as his architect.

Silberklang in *Der Schauspieldirektor*, and the Countess in the Vienna revival of *The Marriage of Figaro* on August 29, 1789. It was for her "flexible throat" that Mozart wrote the aria "Fra l'oscure ombre funeste" in *Davidde penitente* (K.469, No. 8), and the additional *scena* for Donna Elvira, "In quali eccessi .... Mi tradì quell'alma ingrata" (K.540c). The soprano is said to have been unprepossessing in appearance, but her voice combined "high and low notes with a strong chest register." Therese Teyber had been a member of the Burgtheater ensemble since the age of eighteen.

Johann Valentin Adamberger made his debut in Venice in 1762 and was engaged as a tenor at the Deutsche Singspiel-Gesellschaft in Vienna in 1780. For Adamberger, Mozart wrote the arias "Per pietà, non ricercate" (K.420), "A te, fra tanti affanni" (K.469), and "Aura, che intorno spiri" (K.431). The *Musical Almanach for Vienna and Prague* of 1796 described his voice teaching as "among the best available." Johann Ernst Dauer was a member of the Burgtheater from 1779 to his death, although he was not a member of the opera ensemble. Johann Ignaz Ludwig Fischer was a pupil of the famous *Idomeneo* tenor, Anton Raaff. Fischer, too, had an aria specially written for him by Mozart, "Alcandro lo confesso ... Non so, d'onde viene" (K. 512). Dominik Joseph Jautz is said to have specialized in playing "subsidiary roles."

Early performances

Mozart received a fee of one hundred Imperial ducats for writing *The Seraglio*, and his

The Abduction from the Seraglio

Salzburg Festival, August 7, 1939 (Stadttheater) Producer: Wolf Völker. Costumes: Ulrich Roller. Conductor: Karl Böhm Robert Kautsky's set design for Act III, Scene 1 ("Entrance to the Harem"). The *Frankfurter Zeitung* (1939, No. 403-4) wrote that *The Abduction from the Seraglio* required an intimate stage, and that this requirement had been met by renovating the Salzburg Stadttheater. "With only hours to go before the start of the performance, workmen were still hammering, painting, and polishing this jewel of a theater in white, pale gold, and crimson. All the more grateful were we then for being able to make the work's acquaintance in so suitable a setting and to enjoy its charms to the full."

librettist Stephanie was paid a similar sum. The work was performed forty-one times during the composer's lifetime, either at the Burgtheater or the Kärntnertortheater, while performances outside Vienna rapidly established the piece as its composer's most successful stage work, at least during what remained of Mozart's brief life (see p. 113). July 20: The first report on *The Abduction from the Seraglio* from the composer's own pen has not survived, although we do have a letter describing the second performance of the work on July 19: "You won't believe it, but there was an even stronger cabal yesterday than there was on the first evening. The whole of the first act was hissed. But they were unable to prevent loud shouts of bravo during the arias. And so I pinned my hopes on the closing trio ['Marsch, marsch, marsch!' No. 7], but as ill-luck would have it, Fischer [who was playing Osmin] went wrong, which made Dauer (Pedrillo) go wrong too; and Adamberger alone could not make up for everything, with the result that the whole effect was lost and, on this occasion, it was

not repeated. I was in such a rage that I was simply beside myself (as was Adamberger)—and I said at once that I would not allow the opera to be given again without a short rehearsal (for the singers) beforehand. In the second act the two duets [for Blondchen and Osmin, 'Ich gehe, doch rate ich dir' No. 9, and for Pedrillo and Osmin, 'Vivat Bacchus, Bacchus lebe' No. 14] were repeated, as they had been on the first night, and so, too, was Belmont's rondo 'wenn der freude thränen fliessen' [No. 15].

"The theater was more crowded than on the first night. The previous day it had been impossible to obtain any reserved seats either in the stalls or in the gallery, and not a single box. The opera has brought in 1,200 florins in 2 days.

"I am sending you the original score herewith, together with 2 copies of the libretto. You will find a great deal that has been cut; that is because I knew that the score would be copied here immediately—but at the same time I gave free rein to my thoughts—and before I handed it over to the copyist, I made

Salzburg Festival, August 7, 1939 (Stadttheater)
Osmin: Salvatore Baccaloni.
Blonde: Irma Beilke.
Producer: Wolf Völker.
Designer: Robert Kautsky.
Costumes: Ulrich Roller.
Conductor: Karl Böhm
Act II, Scene 1. Duet for Osmin and Blonde, "I'm going, but take my advice."
The *Frankfurter Zeitung* (1939, No. 402-4) praised the performers' and the conductor's tonal sense. "However, the knowledgeable audience that attended this performance could not abandon itself quite so confidently or enjoyably to the visual aspect of the staging. The producer, unlike the conductor, was not of course visible, but his presence was felt in every scene, 'interpreting' the outer action and thus distracting the listener from the work's inner action with its essentially musical character. The attempt to give greater emphasis to Osmin than the libretto is generally considered to justify led to an excess of detail.... A Singspiel is not a musical 'drama' nor even a 'comic opera.' It can survive on stage with somewhat less emotionalism and with much less 'business,' especially when the music speaks and 'acts' as vividly as it does here with Mozart."

various changes and cuts. It was performed just as you now have it. Here and there the trumpets and kettledrums, flutes, clarinet, and Turkish music are missing, because I could not get any paper with so many lines. They were written out on an extra sheet of paper—the copyist has presumably lost them, since he could not find them. The first act unfortunately fell into the mud (I forget where I was sending it at the time), which is why it is so dirty.

"Well, I am up to my eyes in work. I have to arrange my opera for wind instruments by a week on Sunday, otherwise someone else will get in first, and he'll take the profits, not me." The autograph score of Mozart's transcription of the opera for wind ensemble remains lost.

July 27: "My opera was given yesterday [July 26, St. Anne's Day] for the third time in honor of all the Nannerls and with the greatest applause. And the theater was again packed to the rafters, in spite of the frightful heat. It was due to be given again next Friday [July 30], but I have protested against this, since I don't want it to be flogged to death. I may say that people are crazy about this opera. And it does one good to receive such applause. I hope the original score has arrived safely. Dearest, best of fathers! I beg you, and implore you by all you hold dear in the world; give your consent to my marriage with my dear Constanze." Mozart was to marry her on August 4.

July 31: The fact that Leopold did not study the score of *The Seraglio* as soon as he received it was a source of some annoyance to Mozart: "I have today received your letter of the 26th, but a cold and indifferent letter such as I could never have expected in reply to my news of the favorable reception given to my opera. I thought (judging from my own feelings) you would scarcely be able to open the parcel for eagerness to see your son's work as soon as possible, since, far from merely pleasing, it has caused such a furore in Vienna that they refuse to hear anything else, and the theater is always teeming with people. It was given for the fourth time yesterday, and will be given again on Friday. But—you have not had the time—the whole world claims that, by boasting and criticizing, I have made enemies of the professors of music and also of other people! What world? Presumably the Salzburg world; for everyone here can see and hear enough to prove the contrary—let that be my answer to them."

August 6: *The Abduction from the Seraglio* is performed at Gluck's request: "Gluck was very complimentary to me about it."

When Bretzner heard of Stephanie's adaptation, he circulated the following protest in 1782: "A certain individual by the name of Mozart has had the audacity to misuse my drama *Belmonte and Constanze* for an opera text in Vienna. I herewith protest most solemnly against this infringement of my rights and reserve the right to take the matter

Residenz Theater, Munich, April 27, 1939 (Cuvilliés Theater)
Belmonte: Peter Anders. Constanze: Felice Hüni-Mihacsek. Blonde: Adele Kern. Pedrillo: Walther Carnuth. Pasha Selim: Odo Ruepp. Osmin: Ludwig Weber. Producer: Rudolf Hartmann. Designer: Ludwig Sievert. Conductor: Bertil Wetzelsberger
Finale. The sets have a certain oriental atmosphere, but are kept very simple, in keeping with the Singspiel. The chorus of Janissaries acclaims the Pasha: "Long live Pasha Selim! Let him be honored! Let his exalted brow be wreathed with rejoicing and renown!"

Salzburg Festival, August 3, 1955 (Landestheater)
Producer: Oscar Fritz Schuh. Designer: Caspar Neher. Conductor: Karl Böhm
Set design for the "Pasha's Garden" by Caspar Neher. Reviewing this performance in the Berlin *Tagesspiegel* of August 14, 1955, Werner Oehlmann described it as an exemplary production, "superbly matched in tone, color and gesture.... A decor of old-world flats in muted colors depicts the Pasha's garden, with a rippling blue sea in the background on which the rescue ship appears at the end, a delightful model with billowing sails lit by the rays of the moon. The acting is wholly unaffected with its Turkish Romanticism and humanitarian message, while the spoken parts that breathe the spirit of their age have been lovingly prepared, and the gestures have an uninhibitedness that wittily offsets the points of repose provided by the arias, thus avoiding the impression of rigid operatic routine."

further." And on April 21, 1783 Bretzner complained again, in a letter that appeared in the Berlin *Litteratur- und Theater-Zeitung*, that "heart-breaking and edifying little verses" were to be found in the many interpolated songs. These are the arias with which we are so familiar.

Critical reception of the opera

The first detailed review of the opera appeared in Johann Friedrich Schink's *Dramaturgische Fragmente*, published in Graz in 1782: "Bre[t]zner's comic operas are normally among the best pieces which this genre can boast, and, besides the admirable gifts that sages, angels, and gods have granted our comic and lyric stage, they are indisputably the most considerable achievement in this discipline. At least there is no want of humor or entertainment, nor of lighthearted dialogue and pleasing song. His Abduction from the Seraglio, by contrast, is very much the least significant of his lyric pieces …. Herr Bre[t]zner seems to me to have expanded his theme unnecessarily over three acts. His characters, moreover, lack attractiveness and life. Belmont's and Julia's [Constanze's] tenderness borders on the tedious, and wit and caprice limp along lamely and tiredly….

"The Abduction from the Seraglio has been taken up in Vienna to outstanding acclaim, an acclaim which it owes not to the piece itself but to the admirable music by Herr Mozard and the very fine performances by singers of the National Theater….

"The music, which works upon the human heart and upon human passion, exciting joy and sorrow, in brief, every form of emotion, and which, more than merely pleasing to the ear, is nourishment to the soul: this music is admirable in my eyes and the undeniable product of a musical genius. Judged according to this principle, Herr Mozard's music has my entire approval, and I am pleased to admit that only Benda and Glu[c]k can move and affect my heart as deeply as Herr Mozard has affected it with his delightful music…. I can say only that his declamation is correct, and his music uncommonly eloquent, being the voice of the heart and of Nature, and that he reveals a wholly accurate concept of the true purport of this finest of all the human arts.

"The singers of the local National Theater deserve our praise for having felt what they were singing, and for reproducing, from their innermost souls, all that Mozart has set; and in their case, too, all that they sang came from their hearts; and they did not merely gargle

Salzburg Marionette Theater, 1958
Costume designer: Friedl Aicher
Osmin. The Harem guard vindictively brandishes his whip: "Oh, how I shall triumph when they drag you away to be executed."

Théâtre National de l'Opéra, Paris, March 23, 1976
Producer: Günther Rennert.
Designer: Bernard Daydé.
Conductor: Karl Böhm
José Varona's costume design for Osmin, 1975

Glyndebourne Festival Opera, June 15, 1956
Pedrillo: Kevin Miller. Belmonte: Ernst Haefliger. Constanze: Mattiwilda Dobbs. Pasha Selim: Leo Bieber. Producer: Carl Ebert. Designer: Oliver Messel. Conductors: Paul Sacher and Peter Gellhorn
Act I, Scene 7. *The Abduction from the Seraglio* was given eight performances at Glyndebourne in 1956. The whole of the 1956 season at Glyndebourne was given over to Mozart's operas to mark the bicentenary of the composer's birth, with seven performances of *Idomeneo*, eight of *The Magic Flute*, eight of *Così fan tutte*, nine of *Don Giovanni*, and nine of *The Marriage of Figaro*, in addition to the eight of *The Abduction from the Seraglio*.

Salzburg Festival, July 28, 1965 (Kleines Festspielhaus)
Blonde: Reri Grist. Osmin: Fernando Corena. Producer: Giorgio Strehler. Designer: Luciano Damiani. Conductor: Zubin Mehta
Act II, Scene 8. "Strehler does away with the condescending view of a pretty-pretty 'Turkish opera,' and with the insipid jokes and pseudo-popular irrelevances with which a misunderstood tradition has so often sought to curry favor with audiences evidently regarded as immature—and all in the name of 'Singspiel.' ... His production is permeated, not to say dictated in the happiest way, by a kind of stylization for which there is no comparison in conventional operatic productions," Heinz Joachim wrote in *Die Welt* on August 4, 1965.

Dresden State Opera, September 26, 1976
Constanze: Carolyn Smith-Meyer. Pasha Selim: Werner Haseleu. Osmin: Rolf Tomaszewski. Producer: Harry Kupfer. Designer: Peter Sykora. Conductor: Herbert Blomstedt
Act I, Scene 6. The Janissaries await Pasha Selim and Constanze.

Salzburg Festival, July 29, 1980 (Kleines Festspielhaus) Osmin: Martti Talvela. Blonde: Carol Malone. Producer and designer: Filippo Sanjust. Conductor: Lorin Maazel
Set on a revolving stage, this production created a very restless effect with its frequent changes of scene. Mozart's Singspiel was turned into a glorified *dramma giocoso* lasting three and a half hours (with two intermissions). The general impression was one of overelaborate and overdeveloped sophistication.

111

Bavarian State Opera,
Munich, April 20, 1980
Pasha Selim: Thomas Holtz-
mann. Constanze: Edita
Gruberova. Producer:
August Everding. Designer:
Max Bignens. Conductor:
Bernhard Klee
Max Bignens designed a
stylized pleasure boat from
which Pasha Selim and
Constanze stepped ashore.

Salzburg Festival, July 28,
1981 (Kleines Festspielhaus)
Producer and designer:
Filippo Sanjust. Conductor:
Lorin Maazel (revival of
1980 production)
The Janissaries pay homage
to their Pasha (Frank Hoffmann).

but spoke; indeed I am convinced that Mozard's work will be performed on no other stage in Germany with such perfect feeling and acting as was the case with the National Theater here.

"It is therefore no wonder that, in spite of the faults which, because of the poet and his unwise improvement, cling to the work, The Abduction from the Seraglio has been greeted with general acclaim and continues to be greeted with such general acclaim. When composer and singers work together with such unified effort, in order to fulfill the true aim of music, our sympathies must indeed be enlisted; and where art enlists our sympathies, its impression is lasting and permanent .... "

Cramer's *Magazin der Musik*, published in Hamburg on March 27, 1783, had the follow-

ing to say about the Vienna premiere: "The Abduction from the Seraglio was produced here this year; the music for this opera was prepared by Herr Mozart the Younger. It is full of beautiful things .... It surpassed the audience's expectations, and its author's taste and ravishing new ideas were met with the loudest and most general approval."

The Abduction from the Seraglio soon became one of the most popular of all Mozart's operas in the German-speaking lands. It was performed in Prague in the fall of 1782, in Warsaw on May 8, 1783, in Bonn on June 22, 1783, in Frankfurt on August 2, 1783 (when Aloisia Lange, Mozart's first love and now his sister-in-law, sang Constanze), in Leipzig on September 25, 1783, in Warsaw again on November 25, 1783 (this time in Polish; the translator's name is not known), in

Bregenz Festival, July 19, 1980
Producer: Hans-Peter Leh- mann. Designer: Ekkehard Grübler. Conductor: Ralf Weikert
Ekkehard Grübler reduced the size of the huge floating stage by flanking it with a series of huge white stepped pyramids. In doing so he excluded Lake Bregenz and the surrounding countryside from all involvement in the action. The producer staged a naval battle before the Overture, and thus included the plot's prehistory in his production.

The Abduction from the Seraglio

Städtische Bühne, Hagen,
May 9, 1981
Osmin: Gerolf Scheder.
Blonde: Julie Kaufmann.
Producer: Manfred Schnabel.
Designer: Gabriele Jaenicke.
Conductor: Yoram David
Act II, Scene 1. Osmin:
"Don't make me use force."
Blonde: "I shall meet force
with force." Osmin (aside):
"She's the very devil! But
I'll have to give in, as sure
as I'm a Moslem; otherwise
her threats could come true."
There follows the duet, "I'm
going, but take my advice
and avoid that rascal
Pedrillo."

Komische Oper, East Berlin,
March 31, 1982
Osmin: Hans Franzen.
Belmonte: Günter Neumann.
Producer: Harry Kupfer.
Designer: Marco Arturo
Marelli. Costumes: Reinhard
Heinrich. Conductor: Rolf
Reuter
Act I, Scene 3. "Kupfer
exploits the stage space in
a paradoxical way: he makes
masterful use of the third
dimension, namely, the
height of the stage, a dimension that most stage pro-
ducers have little idea how
to handle. Right at the outset
the audience is stunned by
a sail-like curtain, which
extends into the auditorium
as far as the chandelier and
which opens to reveal a
view of Marco Arturo Ma-
relli's splendidly run-down
set (one can see why Pasha
Selim needs an architect),
with its ingenious observation platform on the garden
wall. The wall itself is posi-
tioned on a revolve, thus
enabling rapid scene changes
between inside and outside.
It combines with a perma-
nent tower to form various
structures that underline
the plot's changing moods
in a wholly inspired way,"
Stephen Hinton wrote in
Musica, 1982.

Opera House, Bremen, April 12, 1982 (Theater am Goetheplatz)
Osmin: Ilie Baciu. Blonde: Teresa Seidl. Producer: Horst Bonnet. Designer: Werner Schulz. Conductor: Peter Schneider
Act II, Scene 1. Blonde makes a fool of the furious Osmin: she was born to be free and refuses to be treated like a slave.

Opéra de Lyon, November 26, 1982
Constanze: Gianna Rolandi. Blonde: Rebecca Littig. Belmonte: Michaël Cousins. Pedrillo: Antoine David. Pasha Selim: Edgard M. Böhlke. Osmin: Kevin Langan. Producer: Georges Lavaudant. Designer: Jean-Pierre Ponnelle. Conductor: Claire Gilsault
Vaudeville in Act III: "Never will I forget your benevolence; forever shall I sing your praises."

Staatstheater, Kassel,
April 6, 1986
Pedrillo: Edgar Schäfer.
Blonde: Martha Sharp. Constanze: Yoko Kamahora.
Belmonte: Alexander
Stevenson. Producer: Peter
Mussbach. Designer: Johannes Schütz. Conductor:
Christian Fröhlich
Act II, Scene 9. "What
Mussbach presents on stage
here is not the usual noble
Constanze, chivalrous
Belmonte, chocolate-box
Blondchen, cheerful Pedrillo,
grumbling Osmin, and magnanimous Pasha; but characters perverted by power
and impotence, their passions acted out on a rectangular stage jutting obliquely
into the auditorium, with
triangular surfaces in front
of and behind the orchestra
pit, which divides them diagonally. Radiant and insistently luminous rainbow
colors and transparent
scrims, in addition to mysteriously black-clad figures,
who are almost always on
stage, creeping around and
preoccupied with various
props (Osmin's tree, Pedrillo's ladder, and so on) create
an atmosphere of magic,
unease, and oppression,"
according to Vera Lumpe
in *Musica*, 1986.

Mannheim on April 18, 1784, in Karlsruhe on
October 16, 1784, in Cologne on October 24,
1784, in Salzburg (by Ludwig Schmidt's
company) on November 17, 1784, and in
Dresden on January 12, 1785. The last-
mentioned of these performances was described in the *Magazin der Sächsischen Geschichte* (Dresden 1785) as follows: "In
January the local Theater Company [under
the direction of Pasquale Bondini] performed: ... on the 12th an operetta, by Bretzner, The Abduction from the Seraglio, composed by Mozart, which met with general
approval, although somewhat ponderously
set, and which was most entertaining thanks
to Günther's caricature (as Osmin) and Mme.
Günther's playful acting. Herr [Friedrich
Franz] Hurka as Belmont sang well, with
feeling and often brilliantly, so that we will-
ingly overlooked his somewhat unpracticed
acting."

On October 22, 1789 the Frankfurt *Dramaturgische Blätter* published the following
piece: "Herr von Knigge says of Mozart's
music to this opera that, in general, it does
not leave behind the impression that one
would expect of it as a genuine work of art.
This is not the case with us at least, since we
have seen the piece on frequent occasions
and with ever renewed delight. It may be that
the orchestra in Brunswick is unable to play
Mozart's difficult music in the correct manner, or that the necessary number of instruments was lacking, or that, in judging the
music, the audience there was of a different
opinion from ours. Criticism has been leveled
against the way in which this composition

Royal Opera House, Covent Garden, November 9, 1987 Osmin: Kurt Moll. Belmonte: Deon van der Walt. Producer: Elijah Moshinsky. Designers: Sidney Nolan and Timothy O'Brien. Costumes: Timothy O'Brien. Conductor: Georg Solti
Covent Garden's 1987 staging of *The Abduction from the Seraglio* was the work's first airing in the house since Sir Thomas Beecham had conducted it there in 1938. "Mr Moshinsky stressed the theatricality of the work both in his direction and in the designs.... A false proscenium, an extension of that of the opera house itself, and a chandelier framed the action; floats strengthened the impression of a stage within a stage. Mr O'Brien's naturalistic permanent set of an orchard outside a crumbling Levantine palace (any passing architect would certainly have been welcome) was in turn framed by Sir Sidney's abstract, strongly coloured and very beautiful front- and back-cloths," Rodney Milnes wrote in *Opera* magazine (January 1988).

now and again combines the serious with the comic: but I do not understand why one should wish to deny the musician an advantage that is granted to the poet? Modulations away from the tonic enhance the sense of multiplicity and liveliness, only they must not occur too frequently, or be too starkly contrasted."

The opera was translated into Dutch in 1797 (by Gerrit Brender à Brandis, Amsterdam), into French in 1798 (by Pierre-Louis Moline for a performance on September 26, 1798), into Russian in 1810 (by Semen Kuvichinsky for a performance in Moscow on February 8, 1810), into Danish in 1813 (by Niels Thoroup Bruun for a performance in Copenhagen on April 1, 1813), into Swedish in 1814 (by Martin Altén for a performance in Stockholm on September 21, 1814), into English in 1827 (by William Dimond, with additional arias by Christopher Kramer for a performance at Covent Garden, London, on November 24, 1827), into Czech in 1829 (by Josef Jungmann for a performance in Prague on November 8, 1829), into French in 1857 and again in 1859 (by Charles Destrais and Prosper Pascal respectively, the latter for a performance at the Théâtre Lyrique in Paris on May 11, 1859), into English in 1881 (by Josiah Pittman for a production at Covent Garden), into Hungarian in 1882 (by an unknown translator for a production in Budapest on March 21, 1882), into Greek in 1889, into Danish in 1897 (by Salomon Levysohn, who based his translation on Bruun's), into French in 1901 (by Maurice Kufferath and

Louis Solvay; the Italian recitatives by Sir Julius Benedict were arranged by Paul Vidal), into Hungarian in 1913 (by Sándor Hevesi), into Croatian in 1922, into Swedish in 1924 (by Arvid Petersen in Stockholm), into Lettish in 1924, into Finnish in 1926, into Rumanian in 1927, into Spanish in 1928 (by Joaquim Pena), into Bulgarian in 1928, into Slovenian in 1929 (by Franjo Bučar for a performance in Ljubljana on November 20, 1929), into Hebrew in 1935 (by Zwi Israel), into Danish in 1936 (by Mogens Dam in Copenhagen), into English about 1938 (dialogue by Albert Stressel and musical numbers by Robert Lawrence), again into English in 1952 (by Edward J. Dent, London), into Italian in 1952 (by Rinaldo Küfferle, Milan), into Norwegian in 1957 (by Tor Holmen, Oslo), into English in 1960 (by Robert Pack and Marjorie Lelash, London), in 1962 (by Ruth and Thomas Hawkes, London, and by John W. Bloch, New York), in 1968 (by Raymond Walker and William Beaumont, London), in 1971 (twice; firstly by Edmund Tracey [dialogue] and Anne Wood [musical numbers], and secondly by Lionel Salter), and about 1972 (by Gustave Motta and Richard Murphy), and into French in 1978 (by Gérard Gubisch in Paris). The first vocal score of *The Abduction from the Seraglio* was arranged by Abbé Starck and published as early as 1785 by Schott of Mainz. The first printed full score (in German and French, and full of mistakes) was published in 1813 by Simrock of Bonn. The old Mozart Edition brought out the work in August 1882, the Neue Mozart-Ausgabe in 1982.

◁
Salzburg Festival, July 27, 1987 (Kleines Festspielhaus) Belmonte: Deon van der Walt. Osmin: Kurt Rydl. Producer: Johannes Schaaf. Designer: Andreas Reinhard. Costumes: Peter Pabst. Conductor: Horst Stein
The action enfolds between two bare walls that hem in the actors. The Pasha appears in a larger-than-life boat. The sea is visible in the background, with small ships sailing around on its surface.

L'Oca del Cairo

K. 422

Dramma giocoso per musica by Gianbattista Varesco. Composed in Salzburg (?) and Vienna during the second half of 1783. Autograph score: Staatsbibliothek Preussischer Kulturbesitz in West Berlin.

Mozart's comments on the libretto

Mozart wrote to his father from Vienna on December 21, 1782 to inform Leopold that the Court Theater Intendant Count Franz Xaver Wolf von Orsini-Rosenberg had invited him to write an Italian opera. In the same letter he goes on to report that he has already ordered the latest "opere buffe texts" from Italy, but has not yet received them. Other individuals who were asked to look out for a suitable libretto in Italy include Ignaz Joachim Hagenauer, the founder of the Trieste branch of his father's famous business concern, Pietro Lugiati, who had commissioned Saverio dalla Rosa to paint Mozart's portrait in oils, and the composer Luigi Gatti, who was in the service of the Salzburg court from 1782 onward.

Mozart wanted a good libretto: "I've looked through at least 100 libretti—probably more," he wrote to his father on May 7, 1783, "but I've hardly found a single one that I could be satisfied with; at any rate a lot of changes would have to be made to it here and there. And even if a poet were to undertake to do so, it would probably be easier for him to write a completely new libretto. Something new, after all, is always to be preferred. We've a certain abate [sic] da Ponte here as poet. He's a tremendous amount to do at present, revising pieces for the theater, and—per obligo—he has to write an entirely new libretto for Salieri [*Il Ricco d'un Giorno*, first performed at the Burgtheater in Vienna on December 6, 1783]. He won't have finished it for another two months. After that he's promised to write a new one for me; but who knows whether he can keep his word, or whether he intends to! You know of course that these Italian gentlemen are always very civil to your face!—enough, we know them!—If he's in league with Salieri, I'll never get anything out of him as long as I live—much as I'd like to appear before the public in an Italian opera. And so, I'd like to think that—unless Varesco is still annoyed with us over the Munich opera [*Idomeneo*]—he might write me a new libretto for seven characters. Basta; you'll know best whether this can be done; in the mean time he could jot down his ideas. And we can then work them out together in Salzburg. The most essential thing is that it is genuinely *comic* as a whole, and, if possible, it ought to include two equally good women's roles. One of them would have to be *seria*, but the other *mezzo carattere*—but both roles must be equally good. However, the third female role can be entirely *buffa* in character, just as all the male characters can be, if necessary. If you think that anything can be achieved with Varesco, I'd suggest that you have a word with him about it as soon as possible. You don't need to tell him that I'll be coming myself in July, otherwise he'll not do a stroke of work. I'd prefer to receive a part of it while I'm still in Vienna. He'd certainly get 4 to 500 fl. out of it, since it's the custom here to pay the poet the receipts of every third performance."

Since Da Ponte was working for Salieri, Mozart turned once again to his *Idomeneo* librettist, Gianbattista Varesco, with whom he had already experienced considerable difficulties in 1780-81. His reason for turning to

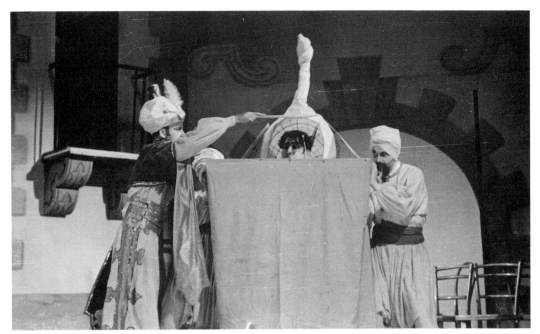

Stadttheater, Salzburg, August 22, 1936
Designer: Willi Bahner. Although performed during the 1936 Salzburg Festival, this production did not figure in the official program. Disguised as a goose, Biondello is concealed in the tower.

Varesco again was presumably because the latter delivered the goods on time, and because the composer wanted to strike while the iron was still hot by following up *The Abduction from the Seraglio* with a successful *opera buffa*. On May 21, 1783 he asked his father to "keep on" reminding Varesco: "the comic element must be uppermost in importance, for I know the taste of the Viennese." As for Varesco's scenario and plan, Mozart had the following to say in a letter to his father dated June 21, 1783: "I like his plan very much. I must speak to Rosenberg at once and make sure the poet is paid. But the fact that Herr Varesco feels doubts about the opera's *incontro* [reception] is something that I find deeply and personally insulting. I can assure him that his libretto will certainly not find favor if the music isn't good. The music, after all, is the most important thing about an opera; and so, if it is to find favor (and if, in consequence, he hopes to be paid), he will have to alter things and recast them as much and as often as I wish, and he mustn't allow his own ideas to guide him, since he doesn't have the slightest practical experience or knowledge of the theater. You could even give him to understand that, in the main, it doesn't much matter whether he wants to do the opera or not. I now know his plan; and, as a result, anyone else can do it as well as he can; and what's more, I'm expecting today four of the latest and best opera libretti from Italy.... So there is still time."

Mozart does not seem to have been altogether satisfied with Varesco's work, and even at this stage was still searching for an alternative and better librettist. On July 5, we find him writing from Vienna to inform his father: "The advice which you gave me concerning the opera was one I had already given myself. But since I prefer to work slowly and deliberately, I thought I could not begin too soon. An Italian poet here has now brought me a libretto which I may use if he's prepared to tailor it to suit my own ideas on the subject ... P.S: this does not mean that you should stop pressing Varesco, who knows whether I shall like the Italian poet's opera?"

Perhaps Mozart worked on the libretto with Varesco during his visit to Salzburg from the end of July to October 27, 1783. If so, the composition of *L'Oca del Cairo* may have been begun during this period.

On December 6, 1783 we find Wolfgang writing to his father: "Now for something else. Only three more arias to go, and I'll have finished the first act of my opera. The *buffa* aria ['Siano pronte alle gran nozze'], the quartet ['S'oggi, oh Dei'], and the finale ['Su via, putti, presto'] are cause for the greatest satisfaction, and I'm actually looking forward to them [that is, hearing them performed]. And so I'd be sorry if I'd written such music in vain, in other words, if what is indispensably necessary doesn't happen. Neither you, nor Abate Varesco, nor I have reflected on how unfortunate it would be for the opera—indeed, it would cause it to fail altogether—if neither of the two leading women was to appear on stage until the very last

119

moment, but were left instead to wander round the bulwarks or ramparts of the fortress. I've enough confidence in the audience to think that they'll remain patient for the first act— but they'll not be able to last out for a second act, it's out of the question. It was only in Linz that this thought occurred to me [the Mozarts had stopped off in Linz on their way back from Salzburg]. And so there's no alternative but to have some of the scenes in the second act take place in the fortress (Camera della fortezza.) This scene can be arranged in such a way that Don Pippo orders the goose to be brought into the fortress; and then the stage can represent the room in the fortress where Celidora and Lavina are being held. Pantea enters with the goose. Biondello crawls out of it. They hear Don Pipo [sic] coming. Biondello becomes a goose again. A good quintet could be inserted at this point, which will be all the more comic in that the goose will join in too. For the rest, I have to say that my only reason for not objecting to this whole goose story was because two people with more insight and judgment than myself could not find anything to object to in it; I mean you and Varesco. But there's still time to think of other solutions. Biondello once vowed that he'd get inside the tower; how he sets about doing so, whether he gets inside by means of an imitation goose or by some other ruse is all the same. I should have thought that the scene could be made much more comical and natural if Biondello were to remain in human form. For example, the news that Biondello has thrown himself into the sea in his despair at no longer being able to enter the fortress could be brought in right at the beginning of the second act. He could then disguise himself as a Turk or whatever, and introduce Pantea as his slave (as a Mooress, of course). Don Pippo is willing to buy the slave for his bride. As a result, the slave-dealer and the Mooress are allowed into the fortress in order to be inspected. In this way, Pantea has an opportunity to bully her husband, and to hurl a thousand insults at him: and she'll get a better part, for the more comic an Italian opera, the better. May I ask you, therefore, to make my views known to Herr Abate Varesco, and tell him to get on with it. I've been working flat out recently. Indeed, I'd have finished the whole of the first act if I'd not needed to alter the words in some of the arias; but please don't tell him this for the moment."

Mozart, then, found fault with Varesco's text and demanded further changes to the words and plot. He finally abandoned *L'Oca del Cairo* on February 10, 1784: "I've no thought of giving it at present. I've things to write at present that are bringing in money right now, but which won't do so later. The opera will always bring in money; and besides, the more time you take, the better the result. Herr Varesco's verse smacks too much of haste!—I hope that he'll realize this himself in time;—that's why I want to see the opera as a whole (tell him just to jot his ideas down on paper)—only then can we raise fundamental objections;—but for God's sake let's not be hasty!—If you were to hear what, for my own part, I have already written, you'd agree with me that it doesn't deserve to be spoilt!—And it's so easy to do!—and happens so often. The music I've completed is lying on my desk, and sleeping soundly. Among all the operas that may be performed before mine is finished, no one will think up a single idea like mine, I'll bet!"

Characters and résumé of the plot

Don Pippo, Marquis of Ripasecca, in love with Lavina (bass); Donna Pantea (known as Sandra), wife of Don Pippo but believed by him to be dead (silent role); Celidora, their only daughter, destined in marriage for Count Lionetto di Casavuota but in love with Biondello (soprano); Biondello, a rich nobleman from Ripasecca (tenor); Calandrino, Donna Pantea's nephew, Biondello's friend, and Lavina's lover (tenor); Lavina, Celidora's companion (soprano); Chichibio, Don Pippo's majordomo, in love with Auretta (bass); Auretta, Donna Pantea's chambermaid (soprano). Hairdressers, a tailor, a shoemaker, sailors and landing crew, market crier, townspeople, Don Pippo's court dignitaries, servants of Biondello and Calandrino, and soldiers (palace guard). The action takes place in Ripasecca, the Marquis's maritime capital.

A number of events have already taken place before the curtain rises: Don Pippo, a conceited, arrogant, and irascible marquis has repudiated his wife and believes her to be dead, whereas she is in fact living in secret on the opposite shoreline. He hates Biondello, not least for loving his daughter Celidora, whom he intends shall marry Count Lionetto di Casavuota. For his own part, Pippo has his eye on Celidora's companion, Lavina, who in turn has an understanding with Pantea's nephew, Biondello's friend, Calandrino. Pippo keeps both girls carefully hidden away in a fortified stronghold. So confident is he that he has promised his daughter to Biondello if the latter can gain entry to the tower within the space of a year. Calandrino had thereupon made a life-size imitation goose, operated by a person concealed inside it. The plan is for Pantea, disguised as a Mooress, to present this marvel to Don Pippo: the conspirators hope that Pippo will then show the goose to the girls in the tower, thereby enabling Biondello to gain access to their place of concealment. In return Calandrino will receive Lavina's hand in marriage.

ACT I.   The opera begins a year to the day after the wager was first agreed. Count Lionetto has been invited to attend the wedding of Don Pippo and Lavina. Calandrino rushes in to report that a storm has prevented Pantea from coming. He and Biondello decide to build a bridge in order to gain entry to the tower where their lovers are being held. The chambermaid Auretta and her lover, the majordomo Chichibio, will be bribed into removing Don Pippo's clothes, thus preventing him from leaving the house. Biondello and Calandrino begin building the bridge, and strike up a conversation with the girls in the tower. Auretta and Chichibio having failed to keep Don Pippo indoors, the latter appears on the scene, and puts an end to all further work on the bridge.

ACT II.   In spite of the storm, Pantea has managed to reach land with her goose. Disguised as a Mooress, she causes something of a sensation at the annual fair with the imitation animal. Chichibio tells Don Pippo all about it. The latter invites Pantea to his palace. She explains that the goose has lost its voice during the storm, but that it will regain the use of it if allowed to eat a certain herb that grows in a secluded garden. Without a moment's hesitation Don Pippo has Pantea and her goose ushered into the fortress garden, where he intends to show them off to the two girls who have been watching the fair from the tower window. An argument ensues which Biondello joins in, and the scene ends in general tumult, with Don Pippo trying in vain to restore order. Pantea conceals Biondello in the goose and goes into the tower. Calandrino tells Don Pippo that, in his despair, Biondello has set out to sea in the teeth of the storm, a fabrication which Auretta tearfully corroborates. Delighted at the news, Don Pippo joins the wedding procession and makes his way to the tower, where the two girls are standing at the window, exchanging pleasantries with the goose, much to the amusement of a crowd of onlookers. The wedding is due to take place immediately after Lionetto's arrival, but news arrives that the latter has cried off. In spite of this setback, Don Pippo offers Lavina his hand, at which point Pantea confronts him as her true self. The goose begins to speak, and Biondello emerges from it, to remind Don Pippo of his promise. The Marquis is forced to put on a brave face, and the three couples embrace.

Editions and performances

The Neue Mozart-Ausgabe took up the work in 1960 but reproduced only drafts for six numbers from Act I, together with a recitative from Scene 8, a handful of sketches, and a fragment of the aria "Siano pronte alle gran nozze." In the early 1960s Andreas Holschneider discovered the complete score of this aria in Bergamo, in a transcription by Johann Simon Mayr.

There has been no shortage of attemps to adapt the piece for the stage. Victor Wilder reworked it for a production at the Fantaisies-Parisiennes on June 6, 1867; it was also seen at the Friedrich Wilhelmstädter Theater in Berlin on October 4, 1867 in a translation by Thuiskon Hauptner; and a third production followed at Vienna's Carltheater on April 15, 1868. Diego Valeri completed the work in 1936, using a German text by Adolf Krücke; the music was reconstructed and orchestrated by Virgilio Mortari, and the piece was performed that same year in the Salzburg Stadttheater and the Vienna Opera Studio, with sets by Willi Bahner. In 1952 Hans Erismann wrote a three-act opera *Don Pedros Heimkehr* (Don Pedro's Return) with words by Oskar Wälterlin and Werner Gallusser, who in turn based their libretto on Varesco's text. In 1965 August Schmidt-Lindner published an orchestral reconstruction, with words adapted from Varesco's original by Willi Wöhler and translated into German. An overture was provided by the G major Symphony K.318, while the fragmentary aria "Müsst' ich auch durch tausend Drachen" (K.435 [416b]) was adapted to suit Varesco's text and pressed into service as the opening chorus. Schmidt-Lindner's adaptation was staged by the Freiburg Opera Studio in Nuremberg on May 17, 1982.

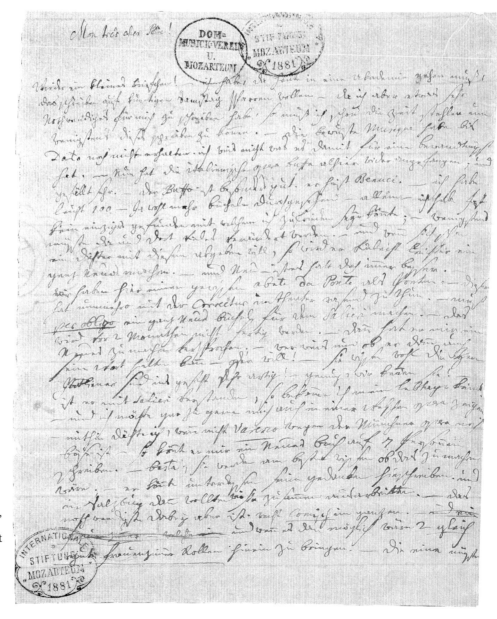

Autograph letter from Mozart to his father, May 7, 1783
This letter contains the first mention of Lorenzo Da Pónte, whom Mozart hoped would provide him with a new libretto.

Lo Sposo Deluso
ossia La Rivalità di Tre Donne per un Solo Amante

Résumé of the plot and cast list

Mozart's *Lo Sposo Deluso ossia La Rivalità di Tre Donne per un Solo Amante* (The Deceived Husband, or The Rivalry of Three Women over One Lover) was probably written in Salzburg and Vienna (?) during the second half of 1783. It is unfinished, and only the overture, a quartet "Ah, ah, che ridere!" and a trio "Che accidenti" are performable.

The plot of this *opera buffa* is as follows: the wealthy and romantically inclined but elderly Bocconio (called Sempronio by Mozart) hopes to marry proud Eugenia (Emilia) from Rome, but his plans are frustrated by a series of intrigues. Bocconio's rival is the officer Don Asdrubale (Annibale), who is also the object of amatory attentions on the part of both Bocconio's niece Bettina (Laurina) and a singer and dancer by the name of Metilde. Bocconio is perpetually led around by the nose, while Asdrubale is for ever being courted for his affections. To these characters can be added the misogynist Pulcherio (Fernando) and Gervasio (Geronzio).

It is not entirely clear who wrote the libretto to *Lo Sposo Deluso*. We know, however, that this was not the first of Mozart's collaborations with Lorenzo Da Ponte. The composer had been introduced to Da Ponte in the spring of 1783, and on May 7 we find him writing to tell his father that the librettist had promised him a new text. On July 5, 1783 Mozart then went on to report that he was

intending to start on an "opera." "An Italian poet here has now brought me a libretto which I may take up if he tailors it to suit my own ideas on the matter." Mozart may have been attracted most of all by the *buffo* role of Bocconio but also by the fact that the characters were all well delineated, thus guaranteeing that the result would be a viable dramatic creation. Why did he not complete the work?

Lo Sposo Deluso was not a *scrittura* or commissioned piece. Mozart had chosen the subject himself and was soon bound to realize that he had no chance of getting the work performed. The extent to which he was anxious to tailor particular roles to certain well-known singers currently engaged in Vienna is clear from a detailed list of names which has survived from this time: Bocconio was to have been sung by Francesco Benucci, Mozart's first Figaro; Eugenia by Ann Storace, his first Susanna; Asdrubale by Stefano Mandini, his first Count; Bettina by Catarina Cavalieri, his first Constanze; Metilde by Therese Teyber, his first Blondchen; and Pulcherio by Francesco Bussani, his first Don Basilio.

Structure of the opera

The Overture and Introduction (a quartet for Bettina, Don Asdrubale, Pulcherio, and Bocconio) form a single number, the vocal section being a rondo-like repeat of the first

K. 430 (424a)

**Opera buffa in two acts. Words by ?
Autograph score (draft): Cracow, Biblioteka Jagiellónska.**

symphonic *allegro*. The whole complex is written in the Italian *buffo* style, with fanfares, slides, chuckling orchestral motifs, and Italian grandiloquence. The hero of the quartet is the highly-strung Bocconio, as much in love as ever before.

Quartet

PULCHERIO

Ah, ah, che ridere! Voi siete sposo?

Haha, it's laughable, so you're betrothed?

BOCCONIO

Che c'è da ridere? quale stupor?
Le freccie amabili del Dio bendato

What is so laughable? Why so surprised?
Blind Cupid's arrows of love have transfixed

M'hanno ferito, piagato il cor.

And wounded a heart for so long despised.

PULCHERIO

Povera giovane! Scusate, amico!
Uno sposo antico ritroverà.

The poor little girl! Forgive me, my friend!
An ancient old fossil is all she will get.

BOCCONIO (with irony)

Seguiti, seguiti, ch'è verità!

Go on then, go on; it is true what you say.

BETTINA, ASDRUBALE (looking at Bocconio)

Cervel più stolido, nò, non si dà!

A stupider person I've never yet met.

PULCHERIO

Povera giovane, mi fa pietà!

The poor little girl! She'll fade clean away!

BOCCONIO (to Pulcherio)

Ma lei mi secca; che cosa vuole?

How you annoy me! What is it you're after?

Lei spieghi altrove le sue parole;

Be off with you now! No more of this laugther!

Con più chiarezza s'ha da parlar?

I trust after all that I make myself clear?

PULCHERIO (noticing a clock on the dressing table, with a smile)

Bell'orologio! bello, bellissimo!
E quest'annello è pur ricchissimo:

What a beautiful clock, the finest I've seen!
And this ring too! Exquisite! And priceless I ween:

Sarà di Francia, così mi par.

I'd say it was French, or so 'twould appear.

BOCCONIO

O Francia o Tunesi lo lasci stare.

French or Tunisian, take your hands off it.

(aside)

Costui qua venne per criticare.

At my private expense he's come here to profit.

E già la bile saltar mi far.

I can feel that my bile is beginning to rise.

PULCHERIO (averted by a servant)

Signor, correte subito.
La sposa arriva già!

Be quick. Signor!
Your bride is here!

BOCCONIO (to the servants)

Finitele, sbrigatevi,
I miei brillanti qua!

Enough! No more!
My diamonds dear!

124

Catarina Cavalieri was to
have sung Bettina in *Lo
Sposo Deluso*. Silhouette by
Hieronymus Löschenkohl,
Vienna 1785

Lo Sposo Deluso

ASDRUBALE

Signor, io parlo chiaro:	Signor, I'll tell you plainly:
Se più civil non siete,	Unless you curb your anger,
La sposo annoiarete,	Your bride will die of languor
Disordine vi sarà.	There'll be all hell to pay.

BOCCONIO

Andate tutti al diavolo!	The devil take the lot of you!
Presto la spada qua!	Go fetch my sword without delay!

BETTINA

Se or ora non mi date	Unless I get a husband
Lo sposo a genio mio,	In answer to my prayer,
Gran chiasso, signor zio,	Your bride had best beware
La sposa troverà.	Of getting divorcée.

BOCCONIO

Nipote del Demonio,	You daughter of Beelzebub,
Presto la spada qua!	Go fetch my sword without delay!

PULCHERIO

Se voi non la finite,	Unless you stop delaying,
Se voi non vi sbrigate,	Unless you're somewhat fleeter
Se incontro non le andate,	And go at once to meet her,
La sposa griderà!	She'll start causing an affray!

BOCCONIO

Che seccature orribili!	How terribly vexatious!
Uomini incivilissimi!	These men are so uncivil,
Servi maledettissimi!	And the servants stand and snivel!
Presto la spada qua!	Go fetch my sword without delay!

BETTINA, ASDRUBALE, PULCHERIO

Cervel più stolido, nò, non si dà!	A stupider person I've never yet met!

(Exeunt omnes, with the exception of Bocconio and Asdrubale.)

Trio

The trio for Eugenia, Asdrubale, and Bocconio presupposes the following developments: Eugenia, thinking that Asdrubale is dead, collapses in a chair in a faint. Bocconio hurries away in search of smelling salts. Hoping to marry Eugenia but believing her unfaithful, Asdrubale heaps reproaches on her head. Before Eugenia has a chance to explain herself, Bocconio returns. It is at this point that the trio begins. In it Mozart gives expression to the different emotions felt by each of the three characters: the threatened tragedy soon turns, fittingly enough, to tragicomedy.

BOCCONIO (aside)

Che accidenti! che tragedia!	What a misfortune! It couldn't be worse!
Son confuso ... cosa fò?	My brain is befuddled: call for a nurse!

ASDRUBALE (aside)

Perdo il senno ... sono perplesso	I'm losing my senses: what shall I do?
E risolvermi non so!	Her words have confused me: can they be true?

BOCCONIO (aside)

Sta a veder, ch'io dormo adesso
E sognandomene sto.

I bet I shall wake in a moment to find
That all that has happened's a dream of some
kind.

EUGENIA (aside)

Vive ancora e morto egl'era?

Asdrubale alive? I thought he was dead.

ASDRUBALE (aside)

Il mio amor da lei che spera?

What hope can my love place in all she has
said?

BOCCONIO (aside)

Se viene lei poi questo qua!

Eugenia's here, and now *he* is here too!

EUGENIA, ASDRUBALE

Tetro orror il cor mi serra,

My heart is oppressed by the blackest of
fear

Già lo sento palpitar!

And the sound of its beating is only too
clear!

BOCCONIO

Una sincope m'afferra
Qui non v'è che replicar.

My head is beginning to spin like a top!
I keep on repeating myself: I must stop!

EUGENIA, ASDRUBALE, BOCCONIO

Crudo amore, stelle irate,
Perchè mai così spietate?
Questa pena è troppo barbara,
Quest'è troppa crudeltà!

Why persecute me, cruel love?
Why punish me, you stars above?
This pain is more than I can bear;
Such cruelty is hardly fair.

Editions and performances

The draft of the full score of *Lo Sposo Deluso* was published in the old Mozart Edition in November 1882, but has not yet been edited for the Neue Mozart-Ausgabe. Individual numbers from the opera are often performed in the concert hall. Constanze Mozart twice sang the part of Eugenia at public performances of the trio (No. 4).

Kärntnertortheater, Vienna,
August 28, 1858
Costume designs by Giro-
lamo Franceschini: (clock-
wise from top left) Aloisia
Lange, née Weber, Emanuel
Schikaneder, a theater ser-
vant, Wolfgang Amadeus
Mozart

128

Der Schauspieldirektor

Origins of the opera

Der Schauspieldirektor (The Impresario) is a *pièce d'occasion*. Mozart was obliged to take on the task of writing the work in order to avoid being forgotten as an opera composer. His last operatic success had been four years previously, when *The Abduction from the Seraglio* had first been heard in Vienna. The composer's immediate reason for writing *Der Schauspieldirektor* was a reception held by Joseph II in the Orangery at Schönbrunn on February 7, 1786. The Orangery was an imposing structure, much admired in its day, 183 meters long, 10 meters wide, and 9 meters high; it was heated from a space beneath it to which entry was gained by means of two trapdoors let into the floor of the hall. Wood fuel warmed cast-iron tiles that ran round the circumference of the hall, in addition to being located in the heating cavity itself. The tiles retained their heat for two days, so that there was no risk of visitors being frozen. A detailed report on the reception was carried by the *Wiener Zeitung* of February 8, 1786:

"On Tuesday last His Majesty the Emperor held a reception for Their Excellencies the Governor-Generals of the Imperial and Royal Netherlands and a gathering of the local aristocracy. Invitations had also been sent to forty persons of rank including the aforementioned Prince Stanisław Poniatowski, all of whom had chosen ladies to escort and who, together with His Majesty the Emperor and Her Serene Highness the Archduchess [Marie] Christina, were driven in pairs in barouches and closed carriages to Schönbrunn, leaving the Hofburg here at 3 o'clock, and alighting together at the Orangery, which had been most spendidly and elegantly laid out for a midday repast to welcome these distinguished visitors. The table beneath the Orangery trees was most agreeably bedecked with indigenous and exotic blooms, blossoms, and fruits. While His Majesty partook of the repast with his august visitors from home and abroad, the sound of wind instruments was to be heard, played by the musicians of the Imperial and Royal Chamber. [Probably individual numbers from Antonio Salieri's *opera buffa La Grotta di Trofonio* were performed.] The tables having been removed, a new play with arias entitled *The Impresario*, specially composed for the reception, was performed by the actors of the Imperial and Royal National Theater, on a stage erected at one end of the Orangery. At its conclusion an *opera buffa* entitled *Prima la Musica e poi le Parole*, also newly written for the occasion, was performed by the company of Court Opera Singers on the Italian stage erected at the other end of the Orangery. During which the Orangery was most splendidly lit by numerous candles in chandeliers and plates. It was after 9 o'clock before the whole company returned to town in the same order as before, each carriage accompanied by two grooms carrying torches."

What these distinguished visitors saw were exemplary highlights from burlesque, spoken drama, and opera. What was being satirized was the institution of German strolling players with their high level of vocal achievement, and the Italian cult of the *prima*

K.486
Comedy with music in one act, words by Gottlieb Stephanie the Younger. Begun in Vienna on January 18, completed in Vienna on February 3, 1786. First performed in the Orangery at Schönbrunn (Vienna) on February 7, 1786. Autograph score: New York, Pierpont Morgan Library.

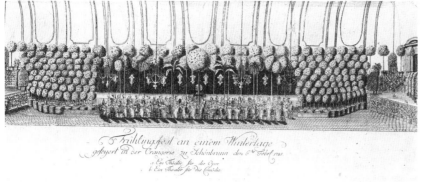

Frühlingsfest an einem Winterlage gefeyert in der Orangerie zu Schönbrunn den 6.ᵗᵉⁿ Febof 1785.
a Ein Theater für die Oper.
b Ein Theater für die Comödie.

Even the Overture enters into the spirit of this lighthearted piece. Primadonna-ish and soubrettish elements run through the work, as do *buffo* and parodistic features. The world of the theater is already open to the listener in the 240-bar *presto* Overture, scored for two flutes, two oboes, two clarinets, two bassoons, two horns, two trumpets, kettledrums, and strings. It is noteworthy that the Overture goes beyond what one would normally expect in a one-act work. Mozart described the piece as a "sinfonia" and endowed it with all the elements of a classical symphony. The Overture to *Der Schauspieldirektor* can stand comparison with that of *The Marriage of Figaro*. The two overtures were written within the space of two or three months: in both of them Mozart offers an impressive display of the compositional skills that were available to him in his "opera year" of 1786.

donna, themes which had already been treated in *Il Teatro alla Moda*, in Venice about 1721 by Benedetto Marcello, and which were especially popular in France through the celebrated comedies of Charles-Simon Favart.

The libretto of Salieri's *Prima la Musica e poi le Parole* was by the experienced librettist Giambattista Casti. It contains a satire on Mozart's own librettist, Lorenzo Da Ponte, who — understandably — was far from pleased to find himself thus parodied, describing Casti's text as "an inferior fabrication, lacking in wit, characters, and commensurate content."

Joseph II paid 1,000 gulden for the reception; Mozart's fee was 50 gulden, Salieri's 100, or about $1,100 and $2,200 respectively, at today's rate of exchange. The disparity in the fee paid to the two composers begs the question as to whether Mozart's piece was in some way inferior to Salieri's. The answer is that Mozart had written only five musical numbers: in other words, it was not a complete opera that he had provided. Salieri, by contrast, had written an entire *opera buffa*, with all that that entailed in terms of operatic spectacle.

Structure of the opera

There have been countless attempts to rewrite Mozart's *Der Schauspieldirektor* and to adapt the text to suit particular periods and circumstances, but the piece has never enjoyed a lasting theatrical success. Its mediocre text will probably always prevent the piece from being treated as a self-contained unity. Nonetheless, Mozart's *musical* contribution to the 1786 Schönbrunn reception deserves to survive by virtue of the composer's masterly portrayal of the typical figures who make up the acting profession and its theatrical presentation of theater life.

Cast list and résumé of the plot

Frank, the impresario (Johann Gottlieb Stephanie the Younger); Eiler, a banker (Johann Franz Hieronymus Brockmann); Buff, an actor (bass; Joseph Lange, Mozart's brother-in-law); Herz, an actor (Joseph Weidmann); Madame Pfeil, an actress (Johanna Sacco); Madame Krone, an actress (Maria Anna Adamberger); Madame Vogelsang, an actress (Anna Maria Stephanie); Monsieur Vogelsang, a singer (tenor; Valentin Adamberger); Madame Herz, a singer (soprano; Aloisia Lange); Mademoiselle Silberklang, a singer (soprano; Catarina Cavalieri).

The impresario Frank is busy assembling a company of strolling players. The actor Buff, an experienced man of the theater, advises him to engage a large number of actors, but to ensure that they are cheap. In his choice of plays he should avoid being exclusive, but strive instead to cater for audience's tastes. The financial side of the undertaking is to be entrusted to the banker Eiler, although one of the latter's conditions is that his lady friend Madame Pfeil be taken on as a member of the company. A series of actors and singers demonstrate their abilities. The two rival prima donnas sing a number apiece, Madame Herz performing the arietta "Da schlägt die Abschiedsstunde," Mademoiselle Silberklang (who makes it clear to the impresario that he must "doubtless" know her "par renommée") a short rondo, "Bester Jüngling! Mit Ent-

Inside the Orangery at Schönbrunn. "Spring Festival on a winter's day, celebrated in the Orangery at Schönbrunn on the 6th of February 1785." Engraving by Hieronymus Löschenkohl, Vienna 1785

zücken nehm' ich deine Liebe an," in order that he may judge their abilities for himself. An argument breaks out over the question of the actors' wages, each of them claiming he deserves something better. In a trio for Madame Herz, Mademoiselle Silberklang, and Monsieur Vogelsang, "Ich bin die erste Sängerin," Mademoiselle Silberklang insists on her own preeminent reputation. In the absence of any agreement among the singers, Frank is on the point of abandoning his plans to form a company. The singers reach an agreement. In a closing chorus, "Jeder Künstler strebt nach Ehre," they all observe that a work of art can prosper only if everyone has a share in it; the public must decide who is best.

Editions and performances

Since *Der Schauspieldirektor* is too short to provide a whole evening's entertainment, it has often been incorporated into other works as a play within a play. In 1796, for example, it was interpolated into *L'Impresario in Angustie* by Domenico Cimarosa, the original words being adapted for the occasion by Goethe's brother-in-law Christian August Vulpius. Emanuel Schikaneder staged a production of K.486 in Vienna's Freihaustheater auf der Wieden on August 5, 1797. In 1809 the work was heard in St. Petersberg in Russian; and on February 20, 1814 a new German version was performed at the Theater an der Wien under the supervision of the composer, singer, and choirmaster Matthäus Stegmayer. In addition to Mozart's one-act work, the audience on this occasion was also regaled, *inter alia*, with pieces by Karl Ditters von Dittersdorf. In 1824 Wilhelm Ehlers arranged the piece for the Königstadt Theater in Berlin (music by Mozart and Cimarosa); and on April 25, 1846 Louis Schneider's version received its first performance at the Royal Opera in Berlin. Schneider brought Mozart himself on to the stage and interpolated three of the composer's lieder, together with the trio "Liebes Mandel, wo in's Bandel", K.441. This version was used by the Leipzig Stadttheater on April 3, 1852 and by the Not Theater in Pest in 1864. The Théâtre des Bouffes Parisiens performed the piece on May 20, 1856 under the title *L'Impresario*: the new text was by Léon Battu and Ludovic Halévy. Vienna's Kärntnertortheater presented the work on August 28, 1858 with costumes by Girolamo

Franceschini. In 1872 Oswald Mutze of Leipzig published a free adaptation of Stephanie's text by Alfred von Wolzogen; and five years later William Grist produced an English adaptation under the title *The Manager*, first performed at London's Crystal Palace on September 14, 1877. The Kroll Opera in Berlin took up the piece on May 22, 1896; Rudolph Genée followed in Schneider's footsteps in revising the work in 1906 as a Singspiel entitled *Der Kapellmeister*; and in around 1916 Henry Edward Krehbiel wrote *Hoodwinking the Impresario or The Wiles of a Prima Donna*. Anton Rudolph's one-act Singspiel *Mozart in Prag* in 1917 used music from *Der Schauspieldirektor, Lo Sposo Deluso*, etc. Lajos Boldogh translated the piece into Hungarian for a production in Budapest in 1924, a Czech version was published in Brünn (modern Brno) in 1928, and in 1936 Friedrich Gessner revised the text for performances in Berlin. Also during the 1930s Cornelis Bronsgeest adapted K.486 for Berlin Radio, and in 1940 Hans Stieber devised a new framework and new dialogue for the piece. In 1953 Eric Blom published a translation and free adaptation under the title *An Operatic Squabble or The Impresario Perplexed*, and in 1955 Hubert Marischka and Bruno Hardt-Warden presented *Drei Küsse: ein Liebesmärchen in sieben Bildern, unter Zugrundelegung des Einakters Der Schauspieldirektor* (Three Kisses: A Love Story in Seven Scenes Based on the One-Act Drama *Der Schauspieldirektor*). Bernnard Paumgartner revised the work for the Salzburg Landestheater in 1958; this production, which opened on January 25, 1958, was designed by Gustav Vargo.

The full score was engraved and published in Leipzig in December 1883 as part of the old Mozart Edition. The Neue Mozart-Ausgabe edition dates from 1958.

Tokyo, February 21, 1987 Mozart's comedy was transferred to a present-day setting and performed as part of a double bill with Domenico Cimarosa's *Il Maestro di Cappella*. The orchestra was placed on stage.

Salzburg Festival, August
2, 1970 (Kleines Festspielhaus)
Susanna: Reri Grist. Figaro:
Geraint Evans. Producer:
Günther Rennert. Designer:
Rudolf Heinrich. Conductor:
Karl Böhm
Revival of the 1966 production. "With Rennert the
audience is on safe ground.
He is a sensitive and tech-
nically incorruptible producer. A Rennert *Figaro* is
always a well-oiled af-
fair—how often can he
have produced it? But that's
the problem: it's *too* well-
oiled. Rennert's response
to masterpieces of this order
is always an objective cool-
ness that rules out any sense
of spontaneity.... Heinrich
brings the opera back closer
to Beaumarchais by stress-
ing its socio-critical impact.
What he offers is not just
the scene in question but
also fragments of the surrounding scenes. In this
way, Figaro's social status,
and the Count's insidious
designs on Susanna are
revealed in a flash, since
Heinrich shows us the servants' quarters as a poky
run-down hovel with numerous doors and a single large
window through which its
occupants can be observed,"
Alfons Neukirchen wrote
in the *Düsseldorfer Nachrichten* of August 10, 1966.

The Marriage of Figaro

History of the libretto

In an article entitled "Figaro" and published in *Romanische Forschungen* in 1942, the Romance scholar Eduard von Jan prefaced his remarks with the following observation: "It was Beaumarchais who created the character of Figaro. In a trilogy comprising two comedies, *Le Barbier de Séville* and *Le Mariage de Figaro*, and a *comédie larmoyante, La Mère coupable*, he breathed theatrical life into a dramatic figure who has become as archetypal a character as Falstaff or Mephistopheles, and whose name has entered the vocabulary of almost every European language." Pierre-Augustin Caron de Beaumarchais wrote the five-act *comédie, La Folle Journée ou Le Mariage de Figaro*, between 1776 and 1781, although the piece was already completed in outline by 1778.

The play was accepted by the Comédie-Française on September 29, 1781, but it was not to receive its first public performance until April 27, 1784. During these three years the work was the object of heated discussion in French theatrical circles. In November 1781 the Empress Catherine II took an interest in the new comedy, instructing her General Director of Spectacles Bibikov to obtain the performing rights to the work. Beaumarchais, however, wanted the premiere to take place in Paris, not in Russia, and, in order to meet the Empress halfway, he read his play to the Russian Crown Prince, Grand Duke Paul, who was staying in Paris in 1781 under the pseudonym "Count of the North." This reading caused such a stir that the famous guest and his wife requested a public performance of the work, but the Commissioner of Police in Paris, Jean-Claude-Pierre Le Noir, refused his consent, arguing that the comedy was nothing short of scandalous and an affront to religion, morality, parliament, and virtue itself. As a result of indiscretions on the part of the censor's office, the comedy was read aloud at a number of evening performances at Versailles, and from that time onward Beaumarchais' play was the talk of the town and a source of public scandal.

Beaumarchais began to make changes to the piece, but the alterations were superficial and did not affect the more offensive sections of the play. The scene of action was moved from France to Spain, and the characters acquired Spanish local color. Once again the work was submitted to the censor. In the meantime Beaumarchais had been frequenting the *salons*, reading his new opus to high-ranking individuals in order to win their sympathies. More than that, he had Chérubini's romance "Mon coursier hors d'haleine" (II,4) printed; the nobility and bourgeoisie were soon singing it to the tune of "Marlbrough s'en va-t'en guerre." By now, however, the censor and journalist Jean-Baptiste Suard had again refused the play a licence. And yet only a few months later the Comédie-Française was instructed to begin rehearsing the piece. The order had no doubt come about at the instigation of the Comte d'Artois, the brother of Louis XVI. The premiere was announced for June 13, 1783 in the Menus-Plaisirs, but a sudden change of heart persuaded the King to prevent the performance from going ahead. Public opinion felt this as an affront, and individual safety could no

K.492

Opera buffa in four acts. Words by Lorenzo Da Ponte. Begun in Vienna in October 1785. Completed (and dated) Vienna, April 29, 1786. First performed in the Vienna Burgtheater on May 1, 1786. Autograph score: Acts I and II: East Berlin, Deutsche Staatsbibliothek; Acts III and IV: Cracow, Biblioteka Jagiellońska.

The Marriage of Figaro

longer be guaranteed. In September 1783, during a visit to the Château de Gennevilliers, the Duc de Fronsac asked his host, the Marquis Louis Philippe Rigaud de Vaudreuil, a notable political figure of the day, to arrange for a performance of the play to take place. The audience was to include the Comte d'Artois and his retinue. The first private performance of the play thus took place on September 26, 1783: it was given by the Comédiens Français before an audience of three hundred guests. The Comte d'Artois and Duchesse Yolande de Polignac, a close friend of Marie Antoinette's, ensured that Beaumarchais' play met with gratifying success. Approaches were made to various ministers and censors, and these, together with Louis XVI's final consent, made it possible for the first public performance to go ahead on April 27, 1784. The aristocracy's intellectual sport sowed the seeds for Beaumarchais' worldwide success.

An unexpurgated setting of Beaumarchais' play was not possible in Vienna. The city's theater censor was the senior civil servant Franz Carl Hägelin. He had taken up his appointment at the Imperial and Royal Court of Vienna in 1770, and in 1795 reported on his duties in a 58-page treatise *Hochlöbliches Directorium in politicis et cameralibus* (Highly Estimable Directory in Politics and Finances). In the section entitled "Defects of Dialogue Affecting the State," he writes that "regents, figures in authority, and entire classes, more especially the upper classes" should not be "impugned, satirized, or made to appear ridiculous." Criticism of foreign rulers was forbidden on principle. It was Joseph II's policy as a diplomat to avoid disparaging religion and morality, and to ensure that the state and foreign princes were not insulted; intellectual liberalism was not to be politically disadvantageous to him. As a result, Beaumarchais' *Mariage de Figaro* was removed from the Viennese repertory after only a short time.

According to Da Ponte, it was Mozart himself who suggested Beaumarchais' play as the subject for an opera. This raises the question whether the composer intended setting the entire play, including its political content, and whether, by doing so, he was aiming a blow at his former employer, the prince-archbishop of Salzburg, or whether he thought he was complying with Joseph II's enlightened ideas and thus hoping to receive a suitable appointment at the Viennese Court.

Da Ponte saw that his hour had come: it was he who was entrusted with the task of adapting Beaumarchais' box-office hit for Vienna. In his preface to the libretto he defends himself against well-informed readers who missed the political essence and explosiveness of the original: "The time prescribed by custom for dramatic performances, a certain fixed number of characters as is generally to be found in such works, and diverse other sensible considerations, necessary in respect of morality, place, and spectators, are the reason why I did not so much translate this admirable comedy as imitate it, or rather merely prepare an abstract of it."

What this means is simply that Da Ponte was conscious of the fact that, because of its politically explosive nature, he could not put Beaumarchais' play on the stage as it stood, but that he had to comply with the theatrical regulations imposed by the censor's office, take account of conditions in Vienna, and, in addition, write for a more or less aristocratic and bourgeois audience.

The main difference between Da Ponte's libretto and Beaumarchais' comedy lies in the fact that Da Ponte has eradicated the element of political satire. In this way he has turned *Le Mariage de Figaro* into a witty social comedy in which the subterranean rumblings of the approaching Revolution can be heard only in the distance. Although Da Ponte sticks close to his source, retaining its train of thought and the order of its scenes, he emphasizes the bourgeois element by underlining the individuality and will to achieve of the two servants. The dramaturgy of libretto-writing required him to tighten up the action, pare down the dialogue, create new, self-contained numbers, reproduce emotional reflexes, and cut passages that were not germane to the action.

One of the reasons for avoiding political satire was no doubt Da Ponte's respect for Joseph II. "I know, but since I was writing an opera (*dramma per musica*) and not a comedy. I had to omit many scenes and cut others considerably. In doing so I cut everything that might offend good taste or public decency and that might be inappropriate in a theater in which His Sovereign Majesty is present."

That political subjects are unsuited to musical treatment does not necessarily follow, as the French opera repertory gives ample proof. In the case of Mozart's *Marriage of Figaro*, the suppression of all political ideology was strictly speaking unnecessary.

Twelve scenes from Beaumarchais' *The Marriage of Figaro*. Etching by Daniel Nikolaus Chodowiecki, 1785

Voila votre baiser Monsieur; je n'ai
plus rein a Vous.
La folle journée ou le Mariage de Figaro.
Acte V. Scene 1re.

D. Chodowiecki del. et Sc.

... et je vois........ Ah!
Acte Ire. sc. 9.

Auprés d'une fontaine
Que mon coeur, mon coeur a de peine.
Acte II. sc. 4.

Tués donc ce mechant Page.
Acte II. sc. 17.

Délicieuxe créature!
Acte III. sc. 9.

Dieu c'est lui!
Acte III. sc. 16.

Ah! ce baiser—là m'a été bien loin!
Acte IV. sc. 4.

Il vous rend chaste et pure aux
mains de votre époux.
Acte IV. sc. 9.

Tout ça pourtant m'a couté un fier
baiser sur la joüe.
Acte V. sc. 1re.

Suzon, Suzon, Suzon, que tu me
donnes de tourmens.
Acte V. sc. 3.

A quoi bon? nous n'avons rien a lire.
Acte V. sc. 7.

Il n'y a qu'un pardon, bien genereux.
Acte V. sc. derniere.

The Marriage of Figaro

Pierre-Augustin Caron de
Beaumarchais. Oil painting
by Jean-Marc Nattier,
c. 1760

Lorenzo Da Ponte. Engrav-
ing by Michele Pekenino
after Nathaniel Rogers,
New York, c. 1820.
The Piedmontese architect
and engraver Michele Pekenino lived in New York in
1820 and in Philadelphia
in 1821-22.

Another reason may be adduced here and that is Mozart's lack of interest in politics. Of primary concern to the composer was not society in general but a more purely human dimension. The individual fascinated him as a human personality, not as the product of material circumstances. Mozart was any-thing but a *homo politicus*. The "state" was of even less concern to him than society, and political ideas and views belonged, as far as he was concerned, in the realm of abstract thinking. Political principles were a matter of indifference to him, he was aware only of the people who embodied them. In his letters he neither anticipates nor mentions the begin-ning of the French Revolution; and there is never a word pertaining to "liberté, égalité, fraternité."

Of course, the political picture of the time plays a major part in *The Marriage of Figaro*, more so, perhaps, than in any of his other operas. But the political picture of the time is not the main point; it is merely the outer form in which the interplay of the individual char-acters is reflected. Mozart was not attempt-ing to write a moralizing work, nor to cham-pion an ethical or political trend. His aim was merely a human comedy in the spirit of his age. Beaumarchais, by contrast, wished to reflect upon the regime of pre-revolutionary France, with all its problems.

That is why Beaumarchais' *Le Mariage de Figaro* gives the impression of being tied to its age, whereas Mozart's *Marriage of Figaro* is timeless. Mozart is not interested in poli-tics, and not concerned with appealing to reason or being witty. His aim is to create characters who stand before us freed from all the contingencies of a particular setting. Da Ponte restores Figaro to the ranks of the servant classes from which Beaumarchais had raised him. But Mozart does not allow the character to become a political dissident, nor even a mischievous *buffo* servant, but creates instead a living figure free from stereotype. And the same is true of the other characters: they are not the mouthpieces of specific qualities and ideas but living figures of flesh and blood.

The Marriage of Figaro occupied Mozart, essentially, from mid-October 1785 to April 29, 1786. According to Da Ponte, the two men worked hand in hand, so that as soon as a scene was finished in the libretto, Mozart would set it to music.

On November 3, 1785 Leopold Mozart wrote to his daughter, Maria Anna (Nannerl) in St. Gilgen, to report that Mozart had said "something about a new opera": "I dare say we shall hear about it!" This is the first mention of *The Marriage of Figaro* in the Mozart family correspondence; no detailed reports have survived in the letters that passed between father and son. On Novem-ber 11, 1785 Leopold wrote to tell his daughter that Wolfgang had honored him with only twelve lines: "He says he is sorry, but he is up to his eyes in work and has to finish the Marriage of Figaro." This is the first time the opera is mentioned by name. On November 18 Leopold again reminds Nannerl of her brother's new opera. And on April 28, 1786 he writes to St. Gilgen: "Your brother's opera, The Marriage of Figaro, is being performed for the first time today, the 28th. It will be a feather in Wolfgang's cap if it succeeds, because I know he has incredibly powerful cabals against him. Salieri and all his hangers-on will again try to move heaven and earth. Herr and Madame Duschek said that your brother had so many cabals against him because of the very great reputation which his exceptional talent and ability have won him."

Cast list for the premiere

In the event, the first performance of *The Marriage of Figaro* took place not on April 28 but on May 1, 1786 in Vienna's Burgtheater. The cast was as follows: Almaviva, Stefano Mandini (baritone); Countess Almaviva, Luisa Laschi-Mombelli (soprano); Susanna, betrothed to Figaro, Ann Storace (soprano); Figaro, Francesco Benucci (bass); Cherubino, Count Almaviva's principal page, Dorothea Bussani, née Sardi (soprano); Marcellina, Maria Mandini, née Piccinelli (soprano); Bartolo, physician in Seville, Francesco Bussani (bass); Basilio, music teacher, Michael O'Kelly (tenor); Don Curzio, judge, Michael O'Kelly; Barbarina, Antonio's daughter, Anna Gottlieb (soprano); Antonio, the Count's gardener and Susanna's uncle, Francesco Bussani. In terms of the singers, this was the best possible cast that Vienna could offer at the time.

Mozart's fee for the composition was 450 gulden, Da Ponte's 200. For 500 gulden a family in Vienna could live comfortably for a year.

The Marriage of Figaro was performed nine times in 1786, on May 1, 3, 8, and 24, July 4, August 28, September 22 (23?), November 15, and December 18. Mozart conducted the first three performances, and the remainder were conducted from the harpsichord by the twenty-year-old Joseph Weigl.

The *Figaro* craze

The President of the Vienna Court Accounting Office, Count Johann Karl Zinzendorf,

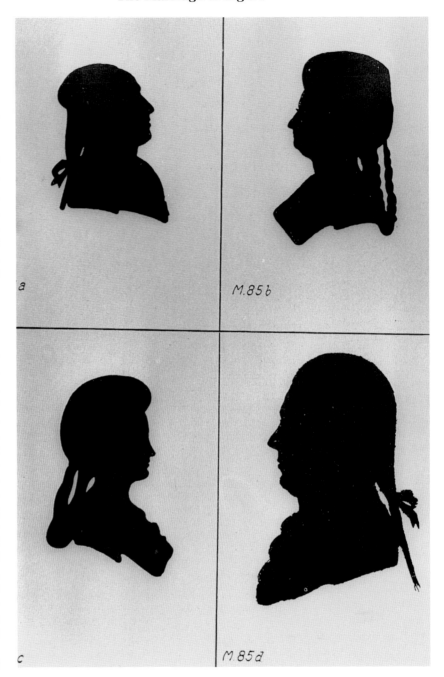

found *The Marriage of Figaro* boring. The *Wiener Zeitung* of May 3 gave little space to the premiere, praising the two women Laschi and Bussani, but not discussing Mozart's music in any detail. On July 11 the *Wiener Realzeitung* discussed the work more fully: "Herr Mozart's music was generally admired by connoisseurs even at its first performance, the only exception being those whose self-love and pride does not permit them to find something good in a work that they themselves did not write. The audience, it must be said (and this is often true of audiences), did not rightly know what to make of the work at

Paolo Stefano Mandini, the first Count Almaviva; Luisa Laschi-Mombelli, the first Countess; Maria Mandini, née Piccinelli, the first Marcellina; Francesco Bussani, the first Bartolo and Antonio. Silhouettes by Hieronymus Löschenkohl, Vienna 1785

Electoral Court Theater, Kassel, 1825
Friedrich Christian Beuther's set design for Act III, "A Reception Hall." Beuther trained under Giorgio Fuentes in Frankfurt am Main and was highly regarded as a scene painter in his day. He moved to Weimar in 1818, probably at Goethe's instigation, and in 1825 settled in Kassel on a permanent footing. His sets are distinguished by their resplendently painted architectures.

first. Many a cry of bravo by unprejudiced connoisseurs was to be heard, but boisterous and ill-mannered louts in the upper part of the house burst their hired lungs deafening the singers and spectators with their shouts of 'shh' and 'psst'; and in consequence opinions were divided at the end of the piece. It is, moreover, true that the first performance did not pass off as well as it might have, since the music is very difficult. But now that repeated performances have taken place, the listener who refused to concede that Herr Mozart's music was a masterpiece of art would clearly have to admit his allegiance to the cabal or else that he had no taste. It contains so many things of beauty, and such a wealth of ideas which can issue only from the wellspring of a born genius. It has pleased a handful of newpaper reporters to claim that Herr Mozart's opera was not liked. It is easy to guess what kind of person these correspondents must be ...."

At the end of 1786 and beginning of 1787 Prague was caught up in a real *Figaro* craze. The Prague writer Anton Daniel Breicha wrote a poem in homage of the composer, *To Mozart on the Occasion of the Performance of the Opera "The Marriage of Figaro,"* and on January 15, 1787 Mozart wrote to one of his closest friends, Emilian Gottfried von Jacquin, to confide that, "I looked on with the greatest pleasure while all these people leapt around in sincere delight at the music of my Figaro, arranged for nothing but contredanses and allemandes; for here they talk about nothing but Figaro; nothing is played, sung or whistled but Figaro: no opera draws the crowds but Figaro, always Figaro; it is certainly a great honor for me." And he added a postscript to the letter: "On Wednesday [January 17] I shall see and hear Figaro here, if I have not become blind and deaf before then.—Perhaps I shall become so only after the opera—."

Two copper engravings by Johann Heinrich Ramberg, engraved by Carl Büscher and reproduced from *Orphea Taschenbuch für 1827*. Ramberg made a name for himself not only as an etcher and copperplate engraver but also as a painter in oils and watercolors. He shows a lively sense of humor and satire, and was influenced chiefly by "unacademic" English draughtsmanship and, more especially, by caricature. Following the death of Daniel Chodowiecki in 1801, Ramberg became the most sought-after illustrator in Germany.

On January 22 Mozart himself conducted a performance of *The Marriage of Figaro* in Prague. The composer Vincenz Maschek published a vocal score of the opera, and Johann Baptist Kucharz, the local organist and kapellmeister at the Prague Opera from 1791 to 1800, prepared a piano score of the opera, while the Abbé Georg Joseph Vogler adapted the opera for quintet; a further, anonymous, arrangement for wind instruments was also published.

In August 1789 Mozart wrote to his wife in Baden near Vienna, "I shall be sailing off tomorrow morning at 5 o'clock—if it were not simply for the pleasure of seeing you and holding you in my arms, I should delay driving out to see you, because they are soon going to be performing Figaro, for which I have to make a few alterations, in consequence of which my presence will be required at the rehearsals." The first rehearsal for the new production of *The Marriage of Figaro* was held in the Burgtheater on August 19, 1789, and the premiere was fixed for the 29th. Two new numbers had been written for Adriana Ferrarese del Bene, who was singing Susanna, firstly a rondo "Al desio, di chi t'adora" (K.577), and, secondly, the aria "Un moto di gioia mi sento" (K.579), with words probably by Lorenzo Da Ponte. *The Marriage of Figaro* was performed ten more times in 1789, on August 31, September 2, 11, 19,

October 3, 9, 24, and November 5, 13, and 27. The performances in Vienna and Prague were followed by productions in Donaueschingen (September 23, 1787), Monza (fall 1787), Lübeck (May 18, 1788), Leipzig (August 3, 1788), Graz (August 9, 1788), and Frankfurt am Main (October 11, 1788). The earliest German translations were by Michael Held, private secretary to the Prince von Fürstenberg, by the Kammersänger Franz Walter of Donaueschingen, by Philippine Eregine (dialogue) and Baron Adolf von Knigge (arias), and by Christian August Vulpius. The opera was not always praised unequivocally by critics, who complained that the music, while containing beautiful passages, was characterized by overfamiliar ideas and phrases. The libretto was frequently dismissed as a feeble dramatic product. A new German translation was prepared in 1798 by Carl Lippert for a production in Frankfurt am Main. Countless other translations have followed down to the present day.

Set designs and stagings

The first full score of the opera was published by Imbault of Paris in around 1795, and a full score with Italian and French words was produced by Le Magasin de Musique in around 1810. The edition published by Nico-

Costume-Bild zur Theaterzeitung. № 63

Eine Scene aus Figaros Hochzeit.

Wien; im Bureau der Theaterzeitung; Rauhensteingasse № 926

Salon der Gräfin.

50

laus Simrock in Bonn and Cologne in 1819 shows considerable divergencies from the original; the arias and ensembles were underlaid with Italian, German, and French text, the recitatives with only Italian words. These first editions were reprinted by Jacques-Joseph Frey and Charles-Simon Richault in Paris at some date after 1820. A full score in French and Italian, with arbitrary omissions and alterations by Castil-Blaze, was printed in Paris about 1821 by La Lyre moderne. The old Mozart Edition published the opera in November 1879. The work was reedited on the basis of the autograph score by Hermann Abert (published by Eulenburg of Leipzig and Vienna about 1920), by Adolphe Boschot (Durand & Cie of Paris in 1938), and by Georg Schünemann and Kurt Soldan (for Peters of Leipzig in 1941). Ludwig Finscher was responsible for the two-volume edition of the opera published by the Neue Mozart-Ausgabe in 1973.

No illustrations have survived of the premiere and early performances of *The Marriage of Figaro*, but only silhouettes and engravings of the principal performers. The nineteenth century saw the work as realistic, idealistic, classicistic, and romantic. The designs by Friedrich Christian Beuther for the Electoral Court Theater in Kassel in 1825 were classical in inspiration: the reception room in Act III is inspired by a classicistic ideal of art of the kind that Beuther will have learned from his Italian mentor Giorgio Fuentes in Frankfurt in the years about 1800 and which he adapted for Goethe at the Weimar Court Theater. Beuther's designs are highly symmetrical and reveal a meticulous handling of perspective, although the delicate colors of the walls and ceiling give the reception room a romantic touch. Sets and characters are illustrated in numerous nineteenth-century journals and magazines. Eight witty, original, and erotic prints based on the work of Johann Heinrich Ramberg were reproduced in the *Orphea* Manual of 1827.

In a supplement to Volume 26 of Adolf Bäuerle's *Allgemeine Theaterzeitung* of November 26, 1838, there is a colored steel engraving by Karl Mahlknecht based on a drawing by Josef Hasslwander, depicting Wilhelmine Marie von Hasselt as Cherubino and Jenny Lutzer as Susanna. It is striking that there were no uniform costumes, and that the sets for *The Marriage of Figaro* were also used in other works. For example, Brioschi's set design for Act II, the Countess's boudoir, at the Vienna Court Opera, was also used in

Le Postillon de Lonjumeau by Adolphe Adam, while his "French garden," first seen at the Vienna Court Opera in 1866, also appeared in *Lucia di Lammermoor* by Gaetano Donizetti. Of importance for critical responses to *The Marriage of Figaro* are thirty pen-and-ink drawings by Moritz von Schwind in which "Figaro's wedding procession" unfolds before the spectator's eye. Schwind also designed the new Vienna Opera House, built between 1861 and 1869, for the foyer of

which he created fourteen murals, one of which depicts *The Marriage of Figaro*. A pencil drawing has caught the dance scene in the third act: two women and two men dance a fandango, festively bedecked with ribbons, while one of the couples accompanies the other on the guitar and tambourine.

Theaters were springing up all over Europe at the end of the nineteenth century. In order to avoid having to build their own expensive scenery, opera houses had re-

Kärntnertortheater, Vienna, 1838
Karl Mahlknecht: Wilhelmine Marie von Hasselt as Cherubino and Jenny Lutzer as Susanna. Colored steel engraving after a drawing by Josef Hasslwander. Published as a supplement to Adolf Bäuerle's *Allgemeine Theaterzeitung*, No. 236, Vienna, November 26, 1838

Vienna Court Opera, second half of nineteenth century. Set design for Act II, "The Countess's Boudoir," "painted by Herr Brioschi." This set was also used in Adolphe Charles Adam's *Le Postillon de Lonjumeau.*

Cherubin: „Neue Freuden, neue Schmerzen toben jetzt in meinem Herzen; ja, ich bebe, ich bebe, ich zittre p."

Graf } „Ach, das arme Mädchen zittert!
Basilio } Wie das Herzchen im Busen pocht!"

Marzelline }
Basilio } „Gnädiger Herr, von ihren Händen fordern wir Gerechtigkeit."
Bartolo }

Graf: „So lang' hab ich geschmachtet, ohn' Hoffnung dich geliebt!"
Susanne: „Die wird gar leicht verachtet, die sich zu bald ergibt!"

Susanna: „Nun soll ich?"
Gräfin (Dictirt:) „Wenn die sanften Abendlüfte über unsre Fluren weh'n, wollen wir durch süsse Düfte in den stillen Garten geh'n."

Figaro: „Ach, öffnet eure Augen, blinde bethörte Männer! Und sehet, wie das Weibervolk euch durch Bezaub'rung täuscht!"

The dance scene ("Fandango") in Act III, crayon drawing by Moritz von Schwind as a sketch for a fresco in the new Vienna Opera House, 1866

Gustav Kölle: Opera Types, Berlin 1882
Born in Breslau, the painter and graphic artist Gustav Kölle caricatured figures from operatic literature in his book *Opern-Typen*. His reputation in Berlin rested chiefly upon crayon drawings of humoristic content.

Stadttheater, Hamburg, 1894
Franz Gruber's set design
for Act III

course to theater studios that sold and distributed sets and costumes according to certain standard designs. Ostentation and plush were in demand, with audiences of Makart's time wanting to rediscover their own surroundings in the theater. Franz Gruber's designs for the reception room in Act III of *The Marriage of Figaro* realized by the local theater studio of Franz Gruber & Co. in 1894 for the Hamburg Stadttheater were very much in keeping with this demand. A vast room, in shades of brown, ocher, and green, was structured around pillars, statues, mirrors, vases, and flights of stairs, affording a view of the garden at the rear, the focal point of which was an obelisk. Magnificent floral decorations with palms rounded off the resplendent picture. Other designs that belong to this same tradition of stage design include Johann Kautsky's reception room for a production at the Kassel Royal Theater in 1895, Wilhelm Krüger's park for the Hamburg Stadttheater in 1889, and the sets by Francesco Angelo Rottonara for Act II in a production at the Cologne Stadttheater in

1901. The years around the turn of the century were marked by the fundamental theater reforms associated with the names of Adolphe Appia and Edward Gordon Craig. The producer was now becoming a figure of greater importance, and the production, scenery, and costumes began to take on individual features. Of particular interest here is the production of *The Marriage of Figaro* seen at the Vienna Volksoper in 1905; produced by Rainer Simons and conducted by Alexander von Zemlinsky, it was notable above all for the costumes of Heinrich Lefler. Lefler did not emphasize the idea of beauty or elegance, but produced designs for characters who were eccentric and comical. Basilio, in a red cloak, was a Rigoletto figure, while the gardener Antonio clutched a bunch of flowers and a bobble hat, his harelip giving him the appearance of permanent inebriation; Dr. Bartolo was a fat and raucous little old man with a walking stick and small metal-rimmed glasses, in comic contrast to Marcellina, a self-important housekeeper who dressed like a young girl but whose face was covered in

Vienna Volksoper, 1905
Producer: Rainer Simons.
Conductor: Alexander von
Zemlinsky
Heinrich Lefler's costume
designs. Lefler was a member of the progressive Hagenbund. On August 1, 1900
he was elected "Head of
Design, Artistic Adviser,
and Costume Designer" at
the Court Opera, and was
instrumental in helping Art
Nouveau achieve its victory
over heroic and academic
art.

The Marriage of Figaro

Berlin, c. 1910
Basil Crage's costume design
for the Countess
Crage's designs were realized by the Berlin Theater
Studio of Baruch, who
distributed them in turn to
interested opera houses.
They followed contemporary
fashions in style.

warts. Her sense of "dignity" was underlined
by her enormous hat, a crucifix around her
neck, and a prayerbook in her hand. Gustav
Mahler ended his Mozart cycle at the Vienna
Court Opera with a production of *The Marriage of Figaro* in 1906. He commissioned a
new translation from Max Kalbeck, and tam-
pered with the recitatives to the extent of
adding a trial scene with his own *recitativo
accompagnato*. The scenery, by Alfred Roller,
was dominated by monumental pillars. Roller
accentuated the work's element of social
criticism in his costume designs, creating
realistic types of the kind that are also to be
found in *Der Rosenkavalier*. The influence of
Lefler is unmistakable here. In order to
ensure the smooth running of the production,
he used a revolving stage, which had first
been deployed in Munich in 1896 in a produc-

tion of *Don Giovanni* designed by Karl
August Lautenschläger. The costume designs created by the English designer Basil
Crage for a production in Berlin in around
1910 are entirely in keeping with the fashion
of the day with their love of luxury and feeling
of decadence. The Countess, rigged up to
look like a character from an Art Nouveau
revue, wears a long dress and has a feather in
her hat.

Opulent reception rooms were designed
around 1910 by Georg Hacker for the Düsseldorf Stadttheater, by Erich Hartwig for the
Bremen Stadttheater, and by Michael Dammers for the Koblenz Stadttheater. Georg
Daubner's park for a production at the Strasbourg Stadttheater in 1911 was notable for
the symmetrical arrangement of its pavilions,
trees, and alcoved hedges, through which the
Almavivas' house could be seen in the distance. A magnificent false proscenium and
colorful costumes characterized the designs
by Bernhard Pankok for a production of the
opera at the Royal Court Theater in Stuttgart
in 1912. The sets' basic colors were white,
gold, and green, light colors that revealed a
Rococo atmosphere.

The 1920s were particularly fond of experimentation, with architecture, painting, sculp-
ture, film, and theater all at the apogee of
their respective styles. Stylistic forms were
mixed and revealed the influence of expressionism, constructivism, and the Neue Sachlichkeit; (left-wing) innovation was found side
by side with classical influences; and lavish
spectacle did not exclude a fondness for
symbolism on the operatic stage. Ludwig
Sievert simplified his designs for the Frankfurt am Main Opera House in 1924. The
room in Act I was almost devoid of props and
notable for its light, bright colors. The production, directed by Lothar Wallerstein and
conducted by Clemens Krauss, concentrated
upon the purely human aspect of Mozart's
opera buffa. Bright colors also typified the
sets designed by Hans Strohbach for the
Städtische Bühnen in Cologne in 1925.
Strohbach was also the producer on this
occasion; the conductor was Eugen Szenkar.

Pastel shades were preferred by Eduard
Löffler for the National Theater in Mannheim
and by Leo Pasetti for the Residenz Theater
in Munich. In contrast to these designs was
the constructivist unit set designed for a
revolving stage which Gustav Singer built for
the Oberhausen Stadttheater in 1928. (With
its cubist and curving shapes, this design for
an all-purpose set was never realized.) An

Stadttheater, Düsseldorf, c. 1910
Georg Hacker's set design for Act III. Born in Dessau in 1865, Hacker studied scene-painting with Max Brückner in Coburg. When Brückner's studios closed down, Hacker moved to Strasbourg to teach decorative art and in 1896 was engaged by the Stadttheater in Düsseldorf. Hacker's decorative style was influenced by landscape painting. His festival decorations for the Rhineland Goethe Society met with considerable acclaim.

Stadttheater, Strasbourg, 1911
Producer: Wilhelm Maurenbrecher. Conductor: Hans Pfitzner
Georg Daubner's set design for Act IV, "The Castle Garden." Born in Berlin, Daubner studied scene-painting with Heinrich Lefler in his hometown before being appointed to the Strasbourg School of Art and Craft in 1890. In 1902 he became head of the Theater Design Studio at the Strasbourg Stadttheater, where he was joined in 1910 by Hans Pfitzner as the new director of opera. Pfitzner's years in Strasbourg from 1910 to the end of the First World War were a high point in his career: in addition to conducting and composing, he also produced operas and was active as a writer.

Salzburg Festival,
August 16, 1922
Producers: Harry Stangen-
berg and Hans Breuer.
Conductor: Franz Schalk
Alfred Roller's set design
for Act I, an "Anteroom."
Roller's sets were also used
in 1925, 1927, 1930-39,
1941, and 1947.

influential production of *The Marriage of Figaro* was seen in 1931 at the Berlin Staatsoper am Platz der Republik (a branch of the Staatsoper, which played in the Kroll Theater from 1927 to 1931). The producer, Gustaf Gründgens, laid emphasis upon perfect ensemble (the conductor was Otto Klemperer), while the sets by Teo Otto, constructed on a revolving stage, were realistically modern, a reaction against Rococo splendor, with whitewashed walls edged in black and a somber-hued park with dull green trees.

Ostentation and opulent sets characterize productions of the opera after 1933. The Dresden production of December 7, 1934, directed by Hans Strohbach, designed by Gustav Mahnke, conducted by Karl Böhm and with costumes by Leonhart Fanto, was notable for its lavishness and use of the finest materials. The Rococo world was seen as a mirror of the current political system. A new production first seen in Hamburg on January 17, 1940, directed by Oscar Fritz Schuh and designed by Wilhelm Reinking, was equally monumental in its stylization. The first act took place before a vast backdrop depicting a garden, Susanna's bedchamber having been tranferred outside and enclosed with huge

screens; Figaro held part of a bed in his hand, and Susanna—as befitted any good German housewife—sat at a sewing table.

During the last years of the War and in the post-war period, the tendency was for somewhat sparsely furnished sets that made up for their lack of means with often highly inventive ideas. One thinks here of Walter Gandolf (Baden-Baden 1944), Cäsar Klein (Lübeck 1945-46), and Robert Pudlich (Düsseldorf 1947). The 1950 production by Walter Felsenstein for the Komische Oper in Berlin, designed by Josef Fenneker and conducted by Hans Löwlein, was modeled on Beaumarchais' original, and emphasized the political and revolutionary aspect of the work with its class struggle. Fenneker's Baroque mansion housed a moribund aristocratic society, while Susanna's bedchamer was enclosed within a grand but dilapidated building. A timeless setting was created by Rolf Christiansen for the Städtische Bühnen in Freiburg im Breisgau in 1951. The acting area was framed by a huge iron grille, creating a cage in which the various scenes of the *opera buffa* were enacted. For the 1952 Salzburg Festival Stefan Hlawa provided an abstractly angular set that had to be constructed against an

imaginary background. The producer on this occasion was Herbert Graf and the conductor Rudolf Moralt. Parts of a bed stood in an alcove, while the remaining props comprised a chair, a chest, and a large table; an exit to the right led off into the garden. For Oscar Fritz Schuh's 1956 Salzburg production (conducted by Karl Böhm), Caspar Neher designed a realistic park for Act IV with pavilions and trelliswork. The set depicted a maze suitable for lovers and for a histrionic game of mistaken identity. For the 1957 Salzburg Festival Ita Maximowna (who also designed the costumes) provided a long and very deep room for Act III, pillars and large doors focusing the spectator's eyes on the garden at the farther end of the gallery. (The producer was Günther Rennert and the conductor again Karl Böhm.) The 1962 production (directed by Gustav Rudolf Sellner, conducted by Heinz Wallberg and Bernhard Conz, and with costumes and sets by Michael Raffaeli) had an abstract park in black and white with touches of gold, a combination which lent itself to chiaroscuro effects. For the 1966 production by Günther Rennert (again conducted by Karl Böhm), Rudolf Heinrich provided realistic sets and costumes: Act I, for example, was an angular and

Royal Court Theater, Stuttgart, 1912
Producer: Emil Gerhäuser, Conductor: Erich Brand Bernhard Pankok's costume designs for Basilio, Figaro, and Susanna. Born in Münster (Westphalia) in 1872, Pankok was active as a painter (especially of portraits), designer, architect, sculptor, and graphic artist. He moved to Stuttgart in 1902, and in 1913 became director of the city's School of Applied Arts.

147

The Marriage of Figaro

Frankfurt Opera, 1924.
Producer: Lothar Waller-
stein. Conductor: Clemens
Krauss
Ludwig Sievert's set design
for Act III. Born in Hanover
in 1887, Sievert studied at
the School of Applied Arts
in Aachen. He was active
as a scene-painter from
1904 until 1912, when he
became artistic director of
the *Werkstätten für
Bühnenkunst* in Munich.
In 1918 he was engaged
by the Frankfurt Opera. His
set designs follow the stylistic developments of his
day. Especially important
are the sets he designed for
Mozart's operas and which
offer new solutions to staging these works.

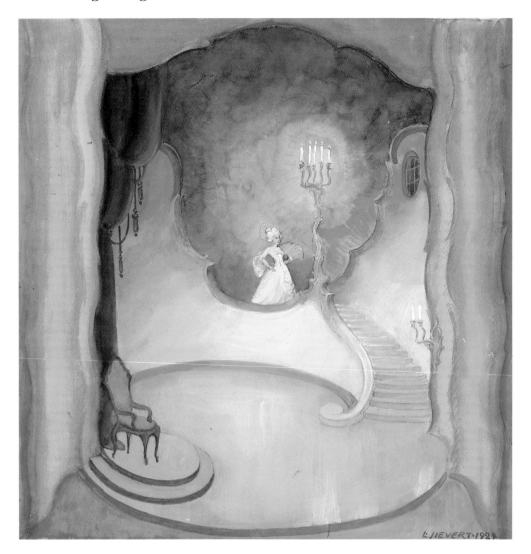

Residenztheater, Munich,
June 29, 1927
Producer: Kurt Barré.
Conductors: Hans Knap-
pertsbusch and Egon Pollak
Leo Pasetti's design for
Act IV

148

Nationaltheater, Mannheim, 1930
Producer: Richard Hein. Conductors: Erich Ortmann and Eugen Jochum
Eduard Löffler's portfolio on the opera, showing the Count and Countess

Staatsoper am Platz der Republik (Kroll Opera), Berlin, January 25, 1931 Producer: Gustaf Gründgens. Conductor: Otto Klemperer Teo Otto's design for Act IV. Otto was set-designer and head of design at the Prussian State Theaters from 1927 to 1933. He said of his sets, "Naturalism can be as good a device as it is bad as a program. Abstractionism can be as equally good a device as it can be fatal as a program."

Dresden State Opera,
December 7, 1934
Producer: Hans Strohbach.
Costumes: Leonhart Fanto.
Conductor: Karl Böhm
Adolf Mahnke's set design
for Act IV. Born in Berlin
in 1891, Adolf Mahnke
began his career as a
lithographer, painter, and
architect. He studied with
Professor Lütkemeyer in
Coburg, and in 1933 was
appointed head of design
at the Dresden State Opera,
where the intendant was
Alfred Reucker and the
general music director was
Fritz Busch. Mahnke's de-
signs were highly impres-
sionistic in style and owed
their effects above all to
their use of light.

Dresden State Opera,
December 7, 1934
The Count: Mathieu Ahlers-
meyer. Susanna: Maria
Cebotari. Figaro: Paul
Schöffler. Producer: Hans
Strohbach. Designer: Adolf
Mahnke. Costumes: Leon-
hart Fanto. Conductor:
Karl Böhm
A comparison between
Mahnke's design and its
realization shows that an
additional colonnade has
been added in the middle,
and that the steps have been
turned into a bench and
extended in width.

Hamburg State Opera, January 17, 1940
Figaro: Johannes Drath. Producer: Oscar Fritz Schuh. Designer: Wilhelm Reinking

Reinking's sets are rationally structured, and the acting area is geometrically laid out. He preferred to work with fixed elements with which he filled the space available. The painterly and decorative element took second place.

Bavarian State Opera, Munich, April 27, 1940
Susanna: Adele Kern. Count Almaviva: Walter Höfermeyer. Figaro: Heinrich Rehkemper. Marcellina: Luise Willer. Bartolo: Odo Ruepp. Countess Almaviva: Felice Hüni-Mihacsek. Producer: Rudolf Hartmann. Designer: Ludwig Sievert. Conductor: Clemens Krauss

Finale of Act III. According to Da Ponte, "During the duet, Susanna kneels at the Count's feet, tugs at his coat and shows him the note; then, in sight of the audience, she puts her hand to her head while slipping the note to the Count, who appears to be straightening her hat. The Count quickly conceals the letter. Susanna rises to her feet and curtseys. Figaro receives her hand from the Count and together they dance a fandango; Marcellina gets up a moment later and Bartolo receives her from the Countess's hand. The Count goes to one side and takes out the note, behaving as he does so like someone who has just pricked his finger. He squeezes it, sucks it etc., and, discovering that the letter was sealed with a pin, throws the pin away with the words, 'How typical of a woman.'"

Teatro Municipal, Rio de
Janeiro, 1942
Producer: Hermann Geiger-
Torel. Conductor: Eugen
Szenkar
Eduard Löffler's set design
for Act IV

shabby partitioned area with numerous doors
leading off to the staircase in Act III. Each of
the scenes included fragments of the scenes
on either side of it. The 1972 production,
conducted by Herbert von Karajan, and
directed and designed by Jean-Pierre Ponnelle, aims at producing a contrastive effect
in black and white, while elements of the park
are taken over from Act III.

Augsburg's production of *The Marriage of
Figaro*, designed by Hans-Ulrich Schmückle,
caused a sensation when first seen in 1962.
Schmückle dispensed with a realistic space:
his stage was an architectural skeleton with
transparent walls on which was projected a
photomontage of erotic masterpieces from
the Renaissance to the Baroque. The producer, Karl Bauer, emphasized the frivolous
element in the plot. A scandal was inevitable,
the prosecuting attorney's office was called
in, and a series of articles appeared under the
title "The Obscene Figaro," with statements
by Arno Assmann, Werner Egk, Helmut
Heinrichs, Rolf Liebermann, Ludwig Marcuse, Siegfried Melchinger, Hermann Mostar, Carl Orff, and the district attorneys Dr.
Fritz Bauer and Dr. Ernst Buchholz. In spite
of the alleged obscenity of the production,
performances of the work were allowed to go
ahead. Robert Stahl's designs for his 1964
production in Osnabrück were notable for
their gentle colors. Sophia Schroeck's design
for Figaro's costume for the Städtische
Bühnen in Cologne in 1965 shows a revolutionary and rebellious servant in a demon-
strative pose. Rudolf Heinrich's designs for
the 1967 Munich production (directed by
Günther Rennert and conducted by Joseph
Keilberth) investigated the collapse of the
feudal regime: the castle looked scruffy, the
reception room was sober and simple in
design. In the mist-enshrouded park the

Salzburg Festival, August 5, 1942 (Festspielhaus) Countess: Helena Braun. Susanna: Irma Beilke. Producer: Walter Felsenstein. Designer: Stefan Hlawa. Conductor: Clemens Krauss This is one of the first color photographs to be taken of the Salzburg Festival. "Hlawa created a fixed framework for all four acts, using a deep rectangular hall whose walls were covered with bright murals reminiscent of Gobelin tapestries and whose ceiling was graced by a large fresco," Karl Heinz Ruppel wrote in the *Kölnische Zeitung* of September 2, 1942. "Two chandeliers hung down into the room, while two others were suspended over the orchestra and lit up during the Overture and last-act finale; the orchestra itself was drawn into the stage area, so to speak, by means of screen-like structures placed at either side of the proscenium arch. The different locations for the individual acts were created by positioning various objects within this 'box,' including walls, steps, balustrades with delicate trelliswork, gracefully ornamented door frames, and elegant little pavilions—a harmonious collection of Rococo architectural elements that structured the scene not according to illusionistic laws, but rather according to the laws of a purely decorative composition."

The Marriage of Figaro

Fisk University, Nashville,
Tennessee, April 1946
Amateur performance given
by black students at Fisk
University

Metropolitan Opera, New
York, November 17, 1951
Cherubino: Mildred Miller.
Figaro: Cesare Siepi.
Producer: Herbert Graf.
Designer: Jonel Jorgulesco.
Costumes: Ladislav Czettel.
Conductor: Fritz Reiner
This production was first
seen at the Met on February
20, 1940, when the cast
had included Elisabeth Reth-
berg, Risë Stevens, and Ezio
Pinza. Mildred Miller's ap-
pearance in the 1951 revival
marked her Metropolitan
debut.

Städtische Bühnen, Freiburg im Breisgau, 1951
Producer: Reinhard Lehmann. Conductor: Heinz Dressel
Rolf Christiansen's set design for Act III. Christiansen emphasized the depth of the reception hall above all, creating a space that resembled a cage.

Glyndebourne Festival Opera, June 13, 1958
Figaro: Geraint Evans. Producer: Carl Ebert, Designer: Oliver Messel. Conductor: Hans Schmidt-Isserstedt
Figaro was one of Sir Geraint Evans's star roles. Although he played the part as a *buffo* character, he was also able to extract an element of social criticism from it.

Deutsche Oper am Rhein, Düsseldorf, March 21, 1963
Producer: Wolfgang Liebeneiner. Designer: Heinz Ludwig. Costumes: Edith Szewczuk. Conductor: Fritz Zaun. Program illustration by Elly Ohms-Quennet. The artist studied at the School of Applied Arts in Hamburg and at the Academy of Art in Munich, before going on to design sets and costumes for opera, theater, and ballet productions in Duisburg, Hanover, Stuttgart, Lille, Ghent, Antwerp, Prague, Krefeld, Münster, Düsseldorf, Helsinki, Munich (Bavarian State Opera), Kassel, and Frankfurt am Main. Since 1944 she has been active as a freelance painter.

The Marriage of Figaro

Opéra-Comique, Paris,
January 31, 1964
Georges Wakhevitch's cur-
tain for the opera. It depicts
all the stage properties from
the opera within a picturesque framework. Wakhe-
vitch's designs were first
seen during the 1963-64
season. Until 1970 it was
customary at the Opéra-
Comique to perform *The
Marriage of Figaro* with
Mozart's arias interspersed
with spoken dialogue from
Beaumarchais' play.

Städtische Bühnen, Cologne,
1965
Producer: Hans Neugebauer.
Designer: Walter Gondolf.
Conductor: István Kertész
Sophia Schroeck's costume
design for Figaro. Figaro
appears here as a class-
conscious and rebellious
servant who opposes the
nobility.

Opéra Royal, Versailles,
March 30, 1973, and
Théâtre National de l'Opéra,
Paris, April 7, 1973
Producer: Giorgio Strehler.
Conductor: Georg Solti
Ezio Frigerio's costume
design for the Countess

◁
Opéra Royal, Versailles,
March 30, 1973, and
Théâtre National de l'Opéra,
Paris, April 7, 1973
Producer: Giorgio Strehler.
Conductor: Georg Solti
Set design by Ezio Frigerio

157

Salzburg Festival, August 11, 1979 (Grosses Festspielhaus)
Producer and designer: Jean-Pierre Ponnelle. Conductors: Bernhard Klee and Herbert von Karajan
Finale of Act III. A highly mannered production first seen on July 26, 1972, when it was conducted by Herbert von Karajan. Over the years the producer has made innumerable changes to his original conception.

Stuttgart State Opera (Grosses Haus), July 12, 1983
Producer: Peter Zadek.
Designers: Johannes Grützke and Barbara Naujok.
Conductor: Dennis Russell Davies
Johannes Grützke's costume designs for Figaro, the Countess and Marcellina. Figaro was sung by Karl-Friedrich Dürr, the Countess by Raili Viljakainen, and Marcellina by Milagro Vargas. Under the heading "The Oblique Style! Why?" Johannes

Grützke wrote in the program that, "The Oblique Style is not crooked but diagonal. It is straight after its own fashion. It has a special characteristic: it expresses striving. Its sense of striving does not lead directly upward or, indeed, anywhere at all, rather does it lead intentionally away from itself. The Oblique Style is expressive: it reveals itself. It does not laugh, since its very existence is a source of torment. It does not look good, since it is in

flight, plunging headlong! (And we feel no pity.)
"We do not use the Oblique Style, the Oblique Style is simply there. It complains, and we leave it to complain. "Is the Oblique Style asking us something? "Should we be beating our breasts? Is the Oblique Style inviting us to confess? Is the Oblique Style a Cassandra? "We do not hear anything—because we ourselves are part of the Oblique Style."

The Marriage of Figaro

Opéra National de Belgique, Brussels, November 7, 1984
Figaro: Marcel Vanaud. Susanna: Hildegard Heichele. Producer: Willy Decker. Designers: Claudia Doderer and Achim Freyer. Conductor: Friedemann Layer
For this opening scene Da Ponte specified "an incompletely furnished room with an armchair in the middle. Figaro with a ruler in his hand, Susanna standing in front of a mirror, trying on a hat decorated with flowers."

actors had to fight their way round thick branches. Every character became a type, revealing his or her social status and attitude, and the same was true of such additional characters as a farm hand, coachman, hairdresser, scribe, and stable lad. Götz Friedrich produced the opera in Bremen in 1968 in the spirit of the student revolts of that year, but he also gave due weight to the theme of love in all its manifold guises. Karl-Ernst Herrmann's sets for this production were sober to be point of seeming fragmentary. The same may be said of Gaby Frey's designs for Wolf Völker's Heidelberg production (conducted by Kurt Brass), which were equally sober and cool. Dark red sections of trees and boughs were drawn across the inner stage in Act IV, suggesting a park by the simplest of means.

A widely discussed production of the opera was staged by the Stuttgart Opera in 1983. The producer was Peter Zadek, the designer Johannes Grützke, and the conductor Dennis Russell Davies. Thomas Körner, Klaus Peter Kehr, and Zadek "translated" Da Ponte's text into modern German, transferring the action to our own century, sprinkling the text liberally with slang expressions and reducing the dialogue to the level of the language of present-day students and schoolchildren. Zadek saw *The Marriage of Figaro* as a social

satire intensified to the pitch of a grotesque social caricature. For a normal opera audience the characters must have seemed decidedly curious: Susanna, brashly sexy in an off-the-shoulder minidress, was seen sleeping with the Countess, who looked a slut in her underskirt, knocking back cocktails and chewing gum. Figaro, flabbergasted by all that he saw, was shown as a servile figure, in tails and gym shoes, fond of his hipflask, a fat old man, stupidly cunning and down-at-heel. The Count, in hunting pink, morning coat, or suspenders, was seen in Act IV chasing the womenfolk like some Spanish *torero*, clearly having lost all interest in his wife. Marcellina was an overdressed battle-ax, Dr. Bartolo, complete with club-foot, puffed up with self-importance, looking not a little like Quasimodo. Cherubino was seen as a well-dressed gigolo who enlisted in the army in a blue and white Ludwig II uniform evidently with the aim of forgetting women's love and indulging in certain other inclinations. Antonio was completely degenerate.

Two hundred years of *Figaro* productions reveal a colorful range of interpretations, attesting to the piece's vitality. In honor of the work an exhibition devoted to Figaro and his intellectual world was held in 1986 in the house where Mozart was born.

San Francisco Opera, September 6, 1986
Susanna: Gianna Rolandi.
The Countess: Kiri Te Kanawa. Producer: John Copley. Designer: Zack Brown.
Conductor: Jeffrey Tate
The Countess and Susanna watch the lovesick Cherubino (Susan Quittmeyer).

San Francisco Opera,
November 21, 1984
Producer: John Copley.
Designer: Toni Businger.
Conductor: Myung-Whun
Chung
Wolfgang Brendel in the
title role sings the so-called
"Champagne Aria," bidding
Leporello: "Now prepare a
great feast until the wine
makes their heads reel."

162

Il Dissoluto Punito
o sia *Il Don Giovanni*

Sources of the story

The three-act play *El Burlador de Sevilla y Convidado de Piedra* (The Playboy of Seville and the Stone Guest) by Tirso de Molina (Fray Gabriel Téllez), frist performed in Madrid around 1624 by the Compañia Roque de Figueroa and published in 1630, marked the stage debut of Don Juan: with him one of the archetypal characters of western Christian civilization entered European consciousness. He is the epitome of the modern age, an expansive type who is determined to enjoy the world, immeasurably self-aware, defiant of all forms of authority, and opposed to all higher order. Tirso de Molina, a member of the Ordo Beatae Mariae de Mercede Redemptoris Captivorum, knew the practices and malpractices of his day and saw in the figure of Don Juan a rebel against God and human society. He wrote a Baroque *Lehrstück* in which the obstinate sinner is visited by divine judgment. Almost all later plays and operas on the subject have been based on Tirso's tale.

The subject was a popular one in seventeenth-century Italy, where the *commedia dell'arte* turned him into a figure of theatrical spectacle, with a servant figure at his side who provided the principal focus of the audience's attention. As a result, the leading male part in Mozart's *Don Giovanni* is not Don Giovanni but Leporello. In France the theme was popularized above all by the *Dom Juan ou Le Festin de Pierre* by Molière, first performed in the Paris Palais Royal in 1665. Molière conjures up a picture of his age and criticizes society. England, Germany, Holland, and Austria soon appropriated the subject matter for themselves, and the operatic stage showed a similar fascination with the theme. Mozart's *Don Giovanni* is the culmination of all these adaptations, many of which would not have seen the light of day in the nineteenth and twentieth centuries if it had not been for Mozart's own operatic setting of the work.

The 1787 Venice carnival witnessed the first performance in the city's Teatro S. Moisè of *Il Don Giovanni ossia Il Convitato di Pietra*, music by Giuseppe Gazzaniga and words by Giovanni Bertati. Mozart's librettist, Lorenzo Da Ponte, drew on Bertati's text as the source of his own adaptation. How this came about is revealed by Da Ponte in his memoirs: "But I thought that it was again time to reanimate my poetic vein .... Mozart, [Vicente] Martini [Martin y Soler], and Salieri gave me the best opportunity to do so, since they simultaneously all demanded a text of me .... I considered whether I could satisfy all three composers at once and write three libretti instantaneously. Salieri was not wanting an original text from me. He had written the opera *Tarare* for Paris [first performed at the Académie Royale de Musique on June 8, 1787] and wanted to Italianize both the characters and the music, so that he asked me to provide a free rendering. Mozart and Martini left the choice entirely to me. For Mozart I chose Don Giovanni, a theme which appealed to him enormously, and for Martini the Tree of Diana [*L'Arbore di Diana*, first performed in the Vienna Burgtheater on October 1, 1787]. In working on Don Giovanni I shall think of Dante's Hell."

K.527

Dramma giocoso in two acts. Words by Lorenzo Da Ponte. Begun in Vienna, probably in March 1787. Completed (and dated) Prague, October 28, 1787. First performed in Prague's National Theater on October 29, 1787. Autograph score: Paris, Bibliothèque Nationale, Département de la Musique.

Don Giovanni

Composing the opera

Mozart was in Prague when, around February 8, 1787, he received a commission from the impresario Pasquale Bondini to write an opera for the forthcoming season. It was to be *Don Giovanni*. The composer began work on the score in Vienna in March 1787. On October 1 he and his wife Constanze set off for Prague, where the premiere of the new work had been fixed for the 14th. They arrived on the 4th and put up at the inn *Zu den drei Löwen*, but also stayed for a time in the Villa Bertramka, the country seat of the Duschek family in the suburb of Smichov. Da Ponte arrived in Prague on or before the 8th, and stayed at the inn *Zum Platteis*, opposite the *Drei Löwen*. On the day planned for the premiere of *Don Giovanni*, Mozart's *Marriage of Figaro* was performed instead. The composer wrote to Gottfried von Jacquin in Vienna on the 15th:

"Dearest friend,
You will probably think that my opera is already over by now—but—you are a little mistaken; firstly, the theater personnel here are not as skilled as those in Vienna when it comes to rehearsing such an opera in so short a time. Secondly, I found on my arrival that so few preparations and arrangements had been made that it would have been simply impossible to have performed it yesterday, the 14th ... Don Giovanni has now been fixed for the 24th;—the 21st: it had been fixed for the 24th but a singer who has fallen ill has caused a new delay; since the company is so small, the impresario is in a constant state of anxiety and has to spare his people as much as possible, lest some unexpected indisposition plunge him into the most critical of critical situations and prevent him from giving any show at all! That is why everything is delayed here, since the singers (being lazy) refuse to rehearse on opera days, and the manager (being anxious and afraid) will not force them .... Next Monday, the 29th, the opera will be performed for the first time ...."

The premiere was destined to be a brilliant success. During the next hundred years it was performed 532 times in Prague, 491 times in Berlin and 472 times in Vienna.

Cast list and critical reception of the opera

The cast was as follows: Don Giovanni, a young and extremely licentious nobleman, Luigi Bassi (baritone); the Commendatore, Giuseppe Lolli (bass); Donna Anna, his daughter, promised in marriage to Don Ottavio, Teresa Saporiti (soprano); Don Ottavio, Antonio Baglioni (tenor); Donna Elvira, a lady from Burgos, abandoned by Don Giovanni, Catarina Micelli (soprano); Leporello, Don Giovanni's servant, Felice Ponziani (bass); Masetto, in love with Zerlina, Giuseppe Lolli; Zerlina, a country girl, Teresa Bondini (soprano).

On November 3, 1787 the *Prager Oberpostamtszeitung* carried the following report: "On Monday the 29th the Italian Opera performed Maestro Mozard's eagerly awaited opera Don Giovani [sic] or the Stone Banquet. Connoisseurs and musicians say that nothing to equal it has ever been seen before in Prague. Herr Mozard himself conducted and when he entered the orchestra, he was greeted by three cheers, which were repeated when he left the same. The opera, we must add, is uncommonly difficult to perform, but, notwithstanding this fact, there was general admiration for an excellent performance after so short a rehearsal period. Everyone, on stage and in the orchestra, gave of their best, thanking and rewarding Mozart with their excellent performances. Considerable costs

Medardus Thoenert: "Don Giovanni in Count Nostiz's National Theater," Prague 1787. Luigi Bassi as Don Giovanni

were incurred as a result of the several choruses and sets, the latter resplendently prepared by Herr Guardasoni. The extraordinary crowd of spectators bears witness to the general acclaim."

The opera was repeated on November 3, a benefit performance for the composer, and on the 4th Mozart wrote to Gottfried von Jacquin: "My opera D. Giovanni had its first performance on the 29th Oct., and met with the loudest acclaim .... Perhaps it will be performed in Vienna. I hope so." On December 19 we read in a letter from Mozart to his sister, "That I wrote D. Juan in Prague, and that it met with unprecedented acclaim, you perhaps know already, but that His Maj. the Emperor has taken me into his service you will perhaps not know." (Mozart was appointed Kammerkomponist to the Imperial and Royal Court on December 6-7 at an annual salary of 800 gulden.)

No playbills have survived from the Prague premiere: a playbill published in 1887 was merely based on the 1787 one. On the other hand, an engraving by Medardus Thoenert *has* survived, showing Luigi Bassi singing the Serenade in Act II, Scene 3. It appears from this that the scenery was straightforward, late Baroque in style with Rococo elements. It shows a street with a column, with Donna Elvira's house on the right. The Prague stage, with its relatively poor acoustics, was 10 meters wide, around 20 meters deep, and 8 1/2 meters high. The stage was divided into seven horizontal sections, with two traps between the second and third of them. Backdrops were hung from the seventh of them. On April 24, 1788 Mozart noted in his private catalogue, "An aria for the opera Don Giovanni. In G major. For M. Morella: Dalla sua pace etc." On April 28: "A duet for the opera Don Giovanni. For Mme. Mombelli and Sig. Benucci, in C major. Per quelle tue Manine etc." and "Scena for the said opera for Mlle. Cavallieri. Recit. In quali Eccessi etc. Aria.—Mi tradi quell'alma ingrata." On May 7 the opera was performed, together with these additional numbers, in the Vienna Burgtheater. The cast on this occasion was: Francesco Albertarelli (Don Giovanni), Aloisia Lange (Donna Anna), Catarina Cavalieri (Donna Elvira), Francesco Morella (Don Ottavio), Francesco Benucci (Leporello), Francesco Bussani (Commendatore, Masetto), Luisa Laschi-Mombelli (Zerlina).

Count Johann Karl Zinzendorf attended the Vienna premiere and found Mozart's

music "pleasant and varied." The composer was paid a fee of 225 gulden for writing the music, while Da Ponte's fee was 100 gulden. Contemporaries found the opera too learned, and Joseph II wrote to his Intendant Count Orsini-Rosenberg to complain that Mozart's music was too hard to sing.

Leipzig heard *Don Giovanni* in Italian as early as June 15, 1788, when it was performed by a visiting company from Prague. The playbill described the work as "a large-scale Singspiel." Joseph II attended a performance of the opera on December 15, 1788, the last time the work was performed in Vienna during the composer's lifetime.

The first performance of the work in German translation was given in Mainz on March 13, 1789. The translator was the Mainz theater poet Heinrich Gottlieb Schmieder. The Frankfurt *Dramaturgische Blätter* reported, "A great deal of pomp and noise for the multitude; insipid, tasteless stuff for the educated section of the public. And the music, although grand and harmonic, is more difficult and more elaborate than it is pleasing and popular." A performance in Frankfurt on May 3, 1789, presented by the Mainz Electoral National Theater, was reviewed as follows by the *Dramaturgische Blätter*: "A tale to suit the Pharisee's taste, to which Mozart's glorious—if occasionally overrefined—music is as suited as Raphael's manner is to the ideas of a Teniers or Callot. Notwithstanding the fact that the entire piece is a monkish farce, I must confess that the scene in the graveyard filled me with terror. Mozart seems to have learned the language of

Don Giovanni. Alabaster relief, 1787
The relief depicts Don Giovanni and the Commendatore in the graveyard (II,12). The Commendatore is shown standing on a gravestone, not on horseback as described in the libretto. Leporello's absence is noteworthy.

Don Giovanni

Vienna, c. 1810
Angelo Quaglio's design for the graveyard scene. A Romantic view of the work dominated by the Commendatore's equestrian statue

Milan, Teatro alla Scala, March 13, 1816
Set design for the "Garden" by Alessandro Sanquirico and Giovanni Perigo. The first performance of *Don Giovanni* at La Scala, Milan, was given on October 17, 1814. It was an indifferent performance and the critics were divided. The opera was revived in the same theater in 1816, 1825, 1836, 1871, and 1881: its success varied depending on the casts and productions seen in any one year.

ghosts from Shakesper [!]. It was a dull and eerie sepulchral tone which seemed to issue from within the earth, as though the shades of departed souls had walked abroad." The Mannheim production, first seen on September 27, 1789 in a German translation by Christian Gottlob Neefe with the title *The Rake Punish'd, or The Pitcher Goes Often To The Well But Is Broken At Last*, showed a classicistic graveyard symmetrical in design. The statue of the Commendatore was at the front of the stage, with skulls to the left and right on the graveyard walls. The churchyard nestled beneath a blue firmament. The opera was performed in Hamburg on October 27, 1789 in a German translation by Friedrich Ludwig Schröder. *Schinks Dramaturgische Monate*, published in Schwerin (modern Szczecin) in 1790, claimed that Mozart had attempted to glorify the absurdities of the Spanish original with his music. "Don Juan combines all that is senseless, eccentric, contradictory, and unnatural, and whatever else may qualify a poetical monstrosity of a human being as an operatic hero. It is the maddest, most nonsensical figment of a confused Spanish imagination. The most dissolute, abject, and wicked of men, whose life is an uninterrupted sequence of infamy, seduction, and murder. A hypocrite who mocks religion, a licentious rake and arrant knave, a cheat and a fop; the most malicious and spiteful of beasts, a rogue without conscience or honor." For this "typically Italian operatic theme" the composer had written "such uno-

peratic, beautiful, great, and noble music." In Munich the work was banned for a time in 1791, not until August 7 did the Elector Karl Theodor release the opera for performance. The music was found to be extraordinarily popular in the Bavarian capital, only the text being dismissed as fatuous. The sets were designed by Angelo Quaglio. Mozart himself conducted a gala performance of *Don Giovanni* in Prague on September 2, 1791, when the Emperor Leopold II was probably present. "The spacious theater," the *Prager Oberpostamtszeitung* reported on September 6, "can hold several thousand persons, and yet it was packed full, and the route which Their Majesties followed was crowded with people." That same year—the year of his death—Mozart put his name to a vocal score of the opera, published by Schott in Mainz and prepared by Karl Zulehner.

A new German translation was made by Christian Heinrich Spiess for a performance at the Freihaustheater auf der Wieden in Vienna on November 5, 1792. A new and enlarged vocal score, revised on the basis of Schröder's textual revisions, was made by Neefe and published by Nicolaus Simrock of Bonn in 1797. The tenor Carl Friedrich Lippert translated *Don Giovanni* for the Vienna Kärntnertortheater on December 11, 1798, and a German translation by Friedrich Rochlitz, redolent of a bourgeois spirit and teeming with alterations and distortions, appeared in 1801. This translation was still being used by the majority of German-speak-

Leporello sings his Catalogue Aria to Donna Elvira. Pen-and-ink drawing after Horace Vernet, 1819

Académie Royale de Musique, Paris, first quarter of the nineteenth century Costume design for Carlo Zuchelli as Don Juan, with a description of the costume by Auguste Garnerey

Don Giovanni

Mr. Harley as Leporello.
Engraving published
by J. Bailey of London,
April 1, 1828

Antonio Tamburini as Don
Giovanni. Born in Faenza
on March 23, 1800, Tam-
burini made his debut in
Cento at the age of 18,
before appearing in Pia-
cenza, Naples, Livorno, and
Turin. He was engaged to
sing at La Scala in 1822,
and was also heard in
Trieste, Vienna, Rome, Naples, Venice, and Palermo
during the 1820s. He sang
at the Théâtre Italien in
Paris for the first time in
1832. He performed the
title role in *Don Giovanni*
in 1834, and was also heard
as Count Almaviva in *The
Marriage of Figaro*. Many
of Donizetti's baritone roles
were created by Tamburini.
His warm and flexible voice
had a range of two octaves
(*F-f'*). Tamburini died in
Nice on November 8, 1876.

M.ʳ HARLEY as LEPORELLO, VALET to DON GIOVANNI in that Piece

ing theaters as late as the middle of the
nineteenth century. The full score was published in the same year by Breitkopf & Härtel
in Leipzig. The title page shows the Commendatore seizing hold of Don Giovanni as he
attempts to flee. A French adaptation of the
piece was performed at the Paris Opéra on
September 17, 1805, in an arrangement by
Henri Joseph Thuring and Denis Baillot (text)
and Christian Kalkbrenner (music). The performance was attended by the Empress Joséphine. This version was performed twenty-
eight times between 1805 and January 27,
1807.

Nineteenth-century productions

After 1800 the work was set either in the
German Middle Ages or in Spain. Production
designs for a Munich performance in 1810
show monumental graves with the Commendatore's tombstone at their center. The background is filled with a neo-Gothic church. The
cemetery scene also figures in an aquatint
engraving in August Eberhard Müller's vocal
score of 1810-11, which shows the Commendatore on horseback, together with Leporello
and Don Giovanni. Leporello can be seen
reading out the words, "Vengeance awaits my
murderer here."

Wilhelm Ehlers, who sang Don Giovanni at
the Vienna Court Opera, was to be seen in a
triumphant posture singing the so-called
Champagne Aria in 1807, while Friedrich

Haberkorn, who took the part of the protagonist at the German Opera in Amsterdam, is
depicted wearing a plumed hat and carrying a
rapier. About 1820 designers started to work
with scenic effects, creating wide and expansive spaces and turning the work into a
Romantic opera. The sets by Norbert Bittner
for the Vienna Kärntnertortheater in 1817,
based on designs by Antonio de Pian, were
somber in color. Heinrich Blume sang the
part of Don Giovanni at the Royal Opera
House in Berlin in 1830, when Julius
Schoppe depicted him holding a candelabrum
and turning away from the Commendatore in
terror. And Franz Wild's performance at the
Kärntnertortheater in 1833 was captured by
Andreas Geiger, who portrayed the singer in
a radiant attitude, holding a plumed hat in
his hand and singing his Champagne Aria.
Detailed stage directions have survived from
the Paris performances of 1834. The French
adaptation by Castil-Blaze and Emile Deschamps opened at the Académie Royale de
Musique on March 10 and divided the work
into five acts. The aim of the production was
to introduce Mozart to French audiences, and
in order to make *Don Juan* more stageworthy,
new sets were built, including new scenes and
new stage directions which went far beyond
anything intended by Da Ponte. After the
Commendatore's death, for example, people
issued from the neighboring houses, creating
a crowd scene and producing an effective
tableau. The action was clearly set in Burgos,
Da Ponte's non-specific "città della Spagna"

being spelled out by the arrangers. The librettist's "sala" at the beginning of the second-act finale was transformed into a glittering banquet. Numerous dancers and servants filled the stage, Elvira appeared as a nun, and advanced on Don Giovanni and the women surrounding him. The opera ended with Don Giovanni's descent into hell, a piece of stage business accompanied by the "Dies irae" from Mozart's Requiem K.626 and underlined by a symphony by Castil-Blaze. The confrontation between Don Giovanni and the Commendatore was staged as follows: Don Giovanni snatches up his rapier from the couch, seizes a candelabrum, and leaves the room through a door on the right. When he returns, he throws his rapier aside, lighting the way for the Commendatore's statue which follows him. At the Commendatore's first word, he drops the candelabrum. Dancers, musicians, and servants throw themselves to the ground, and the lights go out. Dense mists envelop the stage. Only Don Giovanni, the Commendatore, and Leporello remain standing at the center of the mists. Don Giovanni's downfall is played out in the park of his castle. Skeletons rise up out of the darkness of the night, and girls clad in white appear at the back of the stage. Virgins lower a coffin to the ground from which Donna Anna rises up. Don Giovanni tries to flee in his demented state, but meets the Commendatore, who thrusts him aside into an open grave which the damned souls have dug for "their brother." The Commendatore's statue becomes rooted in the park.

For a performance at the new Vienna Court Opera on May 25, 1869 Carlo Brioschi created a magnificent banqueting hall decorated with flowers, pilasters, and caryatids. The set was dominated by a huge flight of stairs leading off into spacious corridors. At the beginning of the second act, the spectator saw a street with a neo-Gothic church in the background. Brioschi reveals an evident trend toward spacious designs. He created oriental forms reminiscent of Klingsor's magic garden in Wagner's *Parsifal*. The Orient and Arabia came to symbolize sensuality. Wilhelm Gropius's ballroom, designed for a production in Berlin on April 4, 1870, is similarly spacious in its impact, with three other rooms receding into the distance; heavy portieres and a coffered ceiling add to the impression of heaviness. Don Giovanni's descent into hell was realistically depicted: two devils bore the sinner aloft and cast him down into the refining fires of Purgatory.

Also from 1870 are a series of wash drawings by Moritz von Schwind depicting scenes from *Don Giovanni*.

For a production in Frankfurt on October 20, 1880 Waldemar Knoll designed sets which were bombastic and somber in style. In February of that year the work had been published in the old Mozart Edition. Numerous theaters staged *Don Giovanni* in 1887 to mark the centenary of the opera's first production. The Kammersänger Theodor Reichmann sang the title role at the Salzburg Music Festival on August 20 and 22, 1887. Contemporary illustrations show him confident of victory, with a plumed hat in his hand.

Fin de siècle staging

Karl August Lautenschläger designed the sets for the 1896 Munich production, when a revolving stage was used for the first time in an opera production. Lautenschläger's monumental and colorful revolve measured 16 meters across, and the four sets for Act I and five for Act II were already in place, so that scene-changes were avoided. All the sets, moreover, were three-dimensional, rather than painted flats, as had always been the case previously. Francisco d'Andrade came to be seen as the quintessential Don Gio-

Académie Royale de Musique, Paris, March 10, 1834 (Salle Le Peletier) Adolphe Nourrit (tenor) as Don Giovanni. Nourrit was also in charge of the production, for which he used the five-act French version by Castil-Blaze and Emile Deschamps. He had made his debut as Pylades in Gluck's *Iphigénie en Tauride* at the Académie Royale de Musique in 1821. He had a large operatic repertory, and also introduced a number of Schubert's Lieder to France.

Don Giovanni

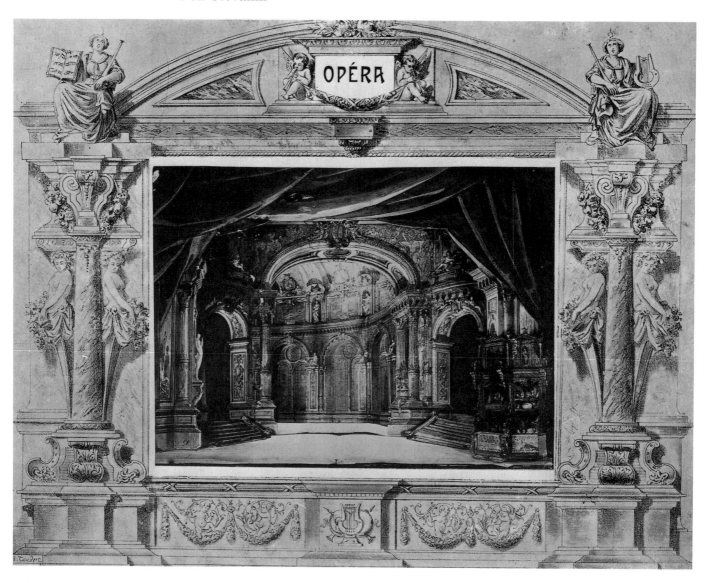

Théâtre Impérial de l'Opéra, Paris, April 2, 1866
Set designs by Charles Cambon, Joseph Thierry, Edouard-Désiré-Joseph Despléchin, Auguste Rubé, Philippe Chaperon, Jean-Baptiste Lavastre, and Joseph L. Chéret. Costumes: Alfred Albert. Conductor: Georges Hainl.
Act V, first and second tableau: Don Juan's banquet hall and apotheosis. Set designed by Jean-Baptiste Lavastre and Edouard-Désiré-Joseph Despléchin. Romantic view of *Don Giovanni*, first seen in Paris in a mutilated version on September 17, 1805, and restaged in the Salle Le Peletier on March 10, 1834, when Mozart's score was adapted.

vanni. He was painted by Max Slevogt in 1901. Slevogt shows a victorious and radiant hero, wearing a plumed hat on his head and carrying a rapier in his right hand. Slevogt's sets for a production in Dresden in 1924 represented "an exemplary embodiment of Don Giovanni's immense love of life." "That is why I have given preference to an overflowing Baroque style, but a style which I myself invented in order to keep the whole as timeless as possible."

A new chapter in stage designs was inaugurated by Alfred Roller. Born in Brünn (modern Brno), Roller was a painter, architect, and cofounder of the Vienna Secession. He designed the sets for the Vienna production of *Don Giovanni* conducted by Gustav Mahler on December 21, 1905. He used rostrums and three-dimensional sets at the sides of the stage, and exploited the medium of light. He bridged the gulf between stage and auditorium by means of door panels and towers; and he broke with realistic sets, preferring a stylized stage picture. Critics were divided in their reaction to Roller's work. In the *Illustriertes Wiener Extrablatt* of December 22, 1905, Hans Liebstoeckl wrote, "Scenery! Scenery! Fetch high towers with embrasures! Milky ways! Bright red trees! Mystifying courtyards! Darkrooms! Ocher castles! Lines, angles, contrasts, clashes of color! Out with discordant geniality! It is getting worse and worse! Because it is done out of method, out of principle. Not out of humor or a diabolical delight in making people laugh. No: these decorators are now mystics, 'latterday Christians,' or something similar. 'Europeans.' As though 'European' were some sort of discovery, or even something to their credit. Good old Schikaneder once played an extremely unseemly joke on 'Don Juan' by adding three extra characters,

Théâtre Impérial de l'Opéra, Paris, April 2, 1866 (Above left) Act II, first tableau: Don Juan's park and castle. Set designed by Joseph L. Chéret. (Above right) Act III, first tableau: A Street in Burgos. Set designed by Charles Cambon.

(Center left) Act III, second tableau: The Ruins. Set designed by Jean-Baptiste Lavastre and Edouard-Désiré-Joseph Despléchin. (Center right) Act IV, first tableau: Donna Anna's apartments. Set designed by Charles Cambon. (Below) In this scene, designed by Edouard-Désiré-Joseph Despléchin, the Commendatore thrust Don Giovanni into a pit from which he was raised aloft by "damned souls."

Don Giovanni

Vienna Court Opera,
May 25, 1869
Carlo Brioschi's set design
for Act II, Scene 1: "Street,"
part of a grandiose Spanish
city (Seville) created by the
artist

Théâtre National de l'Opéra,
October 8, 1902
Set design for the "Cemetery
Scene." This Romantic set
had been in use since 1866.
The conductor at this—the
341st—performance of *Don
Giovanni* at the Paris Opéra
was Paul Vidal; the title
role was sung by Francisque
Delmas, and André Gresse
was Leporello.

Mme. Kalna as Donna Anna. Undated studio portrait, c. 1900

Max Slevogt: "The Champagne Aria." Francisco d'Andrade as Don Giovanni, 1902. Stuttgart, Staatsgalerie
D'Andrade's Don Giovanni exuded an overwhelming love of life. He gave guest performances in Germany from the 1890s onward, and was able to persuade the major opera houses to revert to the original Italian text. The Portuguese baritone inspired the Impressionist painter Max Slevogt to undertake three portraits of Don Giovanni: the so-called "White Don Giovanni" (reproduced here), in which Mozart's titular hero is seen standing alone, his right hand held aloft, the embodiment of radiantly triumphant high spirits; the "Black Don Giovanni" of 1906, recoiling from the Commendatore's ghostly white hand; and the so-called "Red Don Giovanni" of 1912, depicting the protagonist with half-drawn sword in the cemetery scene.

Académie Nationale de Musique, Paris, October 8, 1902
Marguerite Carrère-Xanrof as Zerlina, a role she first sang in 1897

Lilli Lehmann as Donna Anna. Oil portrait by Hans Volkmer
Lilli Lehmann, a well-known interpreter of both Wagnerian and Mozartian roles, taught for a time at the Salzburg Mozarteum. In her book *Meine Gesangskunst* (first published in Germany in 1902 and translated into English as *How to Sing*), she examined the problems of voice production. During her operatic career, which ended in Vienna in 1910, she sang more than 170 different roles.

Don Giovanni

Dresden State Theater, 1924
Producer: Alois Mora. Conductor: Fritz Busch Max Slevogt's set design for "A Square in Seville." The artist emphasized the opera's *giocoso* element, insisting on "the immense joviality and flexibility of a hero who uses every situation, whether good or bad, as a means of entertaining and amusing himself, a man who, conscious of this immense vitality, is not discouraged by any custom or by any law.... He is a man who strives for dominance a man who torments others, playing with them and yet binding both men and women to him through his compelling and effervescent high spirits! ... In Don Giovanni we see the energy that makes life worth living."

an examining magistrate, a tradesman, and a hermit. What is this joke when compared with the earnestness, grandeur, and grande toilette which Professor Roller wears to murder—one might almost say, make fun of—a work of art that is more than a hundred years old! English theater! Old English theater! Just as it was in Munich! That was his basic idea. Alas."

In the *Neues Wiener Journal* of December 22, 1905, Max Graf wrote that, "'A modern artist's fantasies on Don Juan' is how one is tempted to describe the backdrops and artistic use of light and color. Don Juan in terms of brilliant red rose bushes, an arcaded villa on a high hill, red rugs in the banqueting hall, garlands, servants, and musicians dressed in red, the gaudy red of damask wall hangings and the gold of the tableware. Don Juan in terms of enchanting nocturnal atmospheres, Mediterranean moonlit nights inviting amorous trysts and serenades, cypresses towering out of distant darkness, deep-blue starlit nights, gleaming balustrades, rose bushes, palaces .... The Commendatore in terms of a graveyard whose walls and tombstones gleam in the moon's white light, while giant cypresses sway in the background. The Com-

mendatore as a huge equestrian statue, an armed man with a marshal's baton in his hand, riding on a heavy Andalusian horse. Never have such an artist's fantasies been seen on the stage, such an autonomous and often entirely free invention of themes in color and light, themes that derive from the music." If, on the other hand, we look at the designs by Verch and Flotow for the Vienna Volksoper in 1906, we can see how conventional their *Don Giovanni* was in its Rococo borrowings. How violent a contrast!

A more abstract design was created by Bernhard Pankok for the Royal Court Theater in Stuttgart in 1909; the producer on this occasion was Emil Gerhäuser and the conductor Max von Schillings. Ludwig Sievert denaturalized the work for a production in Freiburg in 1913, offering a transition between Art Nouveau and Expressionism. Art nouveau elements are also seen in the designs by Adalbert Franz Seligmann, intended for the 1914 Salzburg Music Festival but abandoned on the outbreak of the First World War. A project by Ernst Stern for the Grosses Schauspielhaus in Berlin in 1919 set great store by monumentality and ostentation in its design.

Modern productions

The Berlin architect Hans Poelzig, who was asked to design a Festival Theater for Salzburg (the plans came to nothing), designed the sets for a production of *Don Giovanni* first seen at the Berlin Opera House on February 8, 1923. His basic idea was to "associate architecture with vegetation, in other words, to structure trees as ornamental contours and to spray out architecture, allowing it to move within the lines of Mozart's music." That same year Oskar Strnad designed sets for Paris, Salzburg, and Vienna, all of which were enclosed within a Baroque framework. As he wrote of his work, "Space as such becomes active ..., through their corporeality street, room, lamp, stairs, trees, and rocks live in the same space and in the same light as the actor. They move forward as he moves forward and disappear when he disappears. They adopt the same spatial dimension and are only important as long as they are active, becoming unimportant the moment they no longer contribute to the action .... The stage should not feign a closed spatial dimension in a pictorial sense. It is itself space." The designs by Hans Wildermann for a production in Dortmund in 1924 and by Leo Pasetti for the 1925 Munich production (produced by Max Hofmüller and conducted by Karl Böhm) were notable for their colorfulness. The influence of the Bauhaus is clearly apparent in the sets designed by Ewald Dülberg for Wiesbaden in 1925 and for the Berlin Staatsoper am Platz der Republik (Krolloper) in 1928. Ludwig Sievert used sinuous and undulating curves for a production at the Städtische Bühnen in Frankfurt am Main in 1926, and rounded forms were also favored by Helene Gliewe, who designed the sets for a production of *Don Giovanni* first seen in Mönchengladbach-Rhydt during the 1930-31 season. Sievert retained his fondness for rounded outlines from his Frankfurt am Main production of 1933-34. The Prague production of 1934 was notable for its use of a revolve with a column at the center dominated by a cross. The sets were supported by this column for each of the individual scenes. Emil Pirchan created expressionist sets for a production of *Don Giovanni* in Vienna at the end of the 1930s. Clemens Holzmeister twice designed productions of *Don Giovanni* for the Salzburg Festival. For the Kleines Festspielhaus in 1950 he chose a revolving stage which he combined with movable pieces of scenery

suspended from the flies and depicting architectural motifs. The revolving stage contained a second revolve, and was surrounded by an outer and an inner circular stage. Each section of the stage could be moved independently of the others, and sets constructed on one section did not encroach on the other sections. By dividing up the revolve into three sections and by combining it with drops, scene changes were quickly and easily carried out. Holzmeister's designs were historicist in approach, based as they were upon a realistic portrayal of architectural detail. Architectonic principles recur again and again in his conception, but never in the same form twice. One thinks here of the colossal columns of rustic ashlars with lion's heads holding huge iron rings in their mouths. They

Stadttheater, Breslau, 1925
Producer: Heinz Tietjen.
Conductor: Ernst Mehlich
Costume design for the
Commendatore by Günter
Hirschel-Protsch

175

Don Giovanni

Metropolitan Opera, New York, November 29, 1929
Josef Urban's set design for Act II, Scene 2: "Outside Donna Elvira's House."
With over fifty successful designs to his credit between 1917 and his death in 1933, the Vienna-born artist Josef Urban dominated Giulio Gatti-Casazza's period of management at the Met.

Teatro alla Scala, Milan, December 19, 1929
Producer: Giovacchino Forzano. Designers: Antonio Rovescalli and Santori. Costumes: Casa d'Arte Caramba Studio photograph of Mariano Stabile as Don Giovanni. The Sicilian baritone was a first-rate singing actor with a bright but poorly produced voice of limited compass. As Don Giovanni he was said to be a "dangerous seducer."

Teatro alla Scala, Milan, December 19, 1929
Producer: Giovacchino Forzano. Designers: Antonio Rovescalli and Santori. Costumes: Casa d'Arte Caramba Salvatore Baccaloni as Leporello. The Roman bass was a convincing Leporello, not least because of his gift for comedy and mime. His voice, according to one critic, smelt of "garlic and olive oil." Baccaloni was a great actor and a skilled diseur, able to reduce an audience to laughter with astonishing ease.

176

State Opera "Unter den Linden," Berlin, February 8, 1923
Producer: Franz Ludwig Hörth. Conductor: Egon Pollak
Hans Poelzig's set design for the "Banquet Hall." According to Karl Scheffler, writing in *Kunst und Künstler* (Vol. 22, No. 7, 1923), "The operatic characters move around in conventional theater costumes between gigantic fairy-tale ornaments, and look embarrassingly odd. When the singers stand in front of huge ornamental branches, or when the chorus sings in front of eccentric Rococo pediments, the individual character is simply swallowed up by gigantic arabesques that shimmer as though with Bengal lights. Larger-than-life Gargantuan figures might feel at home in these grotto-like halls; Wagner's theatricality would be better suited to such brutally pervasive Expressionist romanticism; and this cinematic fantasticism might be better applied to the dissonant racket of certain ultramodernists; but Mozart demands a lighter touch, more tender hearts, and a nobler imagination. Poelzig's talented exuberance is not without its impressive features, as witness his great banquet hall and the sets for the final scene, but ultimately this only makes matters worse.... However liberally Poelzig showers the spectator with his massive and frothy Rococo ornaments, they remain painted cardboard as before, daubed with aniline dyes and lit by harshly contrasting color wheels."

generally have the character of an imposing portal, delimiting and framing. Loggias are used, either arranged in a semicircle to form a street scene or, placed together, to create the ballroom in Don Giovanni's castle. For his 1953 production in the Felsenreitschule, Holzmeister decided to create an entire town on stage. He had already chalked up a considerable success with his "Faust town" in 1933. The individual scenes were laid out like a fan on a simultaneous stage, with the action beginning at the left-hand side, outside the Commendatore's palazzo, and leading through the town to end in Don Giovanni's castle. The center of the stage was taken up with the cemetery and statue of the Commendatore. To the left there were additional municipal reminiscences, including a town-gate, church, perron, and Donna Elvira's house, while the right-hand side of the stage was entirely given over to Don Giovanni's castle.

In 1960 Teo Otto was entrusted with the task of designing the sets for a production of

Staatsoper am Platz der Republik (Krolloper), Berlin, January 11, 1928
Producer and designer: Otto Klemperer
Ewald Dülberg's set design for the "Banquet Hall"

Don Giovanni

Nationaltheater, Prague, June 17, 1934
Producer: Josef Turnau. Designer: Vlastislav Hofmann. Conductors: Otakar Ostrčil and František Škor. The set seen here is the first section of a revolving stage. Hofmann's set-pieces were heavy in style and influenced by Henry Moore, while the decor as a whole was marked by a mixture of Expressionism and Symbolism.

Salzburg Festival, 1934
Producer: Karl Heinz Martin. Designer: Oskar Strnad. Conductor: Bruno Walter Virgilio Lazzari as Leporello and Ezio Pinza as Don Giovanni (I,15). Born in Rome in 1892, Ezio Pinza was the *basso cantante supremo* of his generation, a Don Giovanni of natural elegance with a voice of rare tonal beauty and great brilliance. The Cairo newspaper *La Liberté* reviewed the Salzburg production in its edition of November 18, 1934: "By working fastidiously and choosing only the very best, it was Bruno Walter's dream to seek out and discover Mozart's original ideas.... Walter had a hand-picked team. His Don Giovanni was indeed a happy find: tall, slender, nimble, a lively glance, laughter on his lips, which all too often parted to reveal beautiful but cruel teeth—the hero possessed all the physical qualities needed for the role, coupled with a beautiful voice, refined and sonorous: the famous rondo was performed with such exhilarating ardor that it elicited a cry of admiration from the auditorium. The name of this baritone is Ezio Pinza. As Don Giovanni's protagonist, Virgilio Lazzari presented a comic Leporello—an honest man who displayed his vocal and artistic qualities to the full in his 'Catalogue Aria.'"

Don Giovanni in the new Grosses Festspielhaus in Salzburg. Otto had the following to say about his ideas: "Setting out from the realization that *Don Giovanni* is not a work that can be rationally understood, I used a pictorial world of a visionary kind. It was the first time this has been done. By 'visionary' I do not mean something surreal, but something that distorts reality and makes it unfamiliar." Otto created a bizarre architecture of vaguely delineated structural forms. Vertical lines predominated. The sets were assembled out of slender pillars, with lancet-shaped windows, tapering to a point. Everything was pressed closely together, dovetailed into place, bizarre and fantastical. What Otto showed the spectator was more of an idea than a reality, the framework of a town devoid of monumental structures. The basic colors were reddish brown and dark red. The cemetery was no more than a vision, with fragments of stairs, obelisks, burial chambers, and towers dominating the background. The center of the stage was kept free for the Commendatore, who appeared to rule over this city of the dead.

The Glyndebourne Festival has always staged Mozart's operas with particular care, and *Don Giovanni* has been subjected to repeated new productions there. John Piper was responsible for the decor of the 1951 production, and Ita Maximowna designed elaborate sets for the 1960 Festival. It was Emanuele Luzzati's turn in 1967 to design a new production, while John Bury created the sets for Peter Hall's 1977 production, bringing the action forward to the time of Goya. For many years Covent Garden was proud to

Städtische Bühnen, Frankfurt am Main, 1926 Producer: Lothar Wallerstein. Conductor: Clemens Krauss
Ludwig Sievert's costume designs for the "three masked revelers"

179

Don Giovanni

Glyndebourne Festival Opera, May 29, 1936
Producer: Carl Ebert.
Designer: Hamish Wilson.
Conductor: Fritz Busch.
Hein Heckroth's costume design for Donna Anna. *Don Giovanni* received ten performances at Glyndebourne in 1936. Heckroth, who was born in Giessen in 1901, worked for Frankfurt in 1922, for Münster (Westphalia) from 1924 to 1926, and for Essen from 1928 to 1933. He left Germany in 1933, emigrating first to France and then to England, where he designed many productions. In 1955 he again worked for the Städtische Bühnen, Frankfurt. Heckroth favored sumptuous and exuberant designs which reveal the influence not only of Impressionism, but more especially of Surrealism.

Glyndebourne Festival Opera, May 29, 1936
Producer: Carl Ebert.
Designer: Hamish Wilson.
Conductor: Fritz Busch.
Hein Heckroth's costume design for Leporello. The part of Leporello was sung by Salvatore Baccaloni.

Glyndebourne Festival Opera, 1948 (guest performance at the Edinburgh Festival)
Masetto: Ian Wallace. Zerlina: Hilde Güden? (the part was sung at some performances by Ann Ayars). Donna Anna: Ljuba Welitsch. Don Ottavio: Richard Lewis. Donna Elvira: Christina Carroll. Don Giovanni: Paolo Silveri. Producer: Carl Ebert. Designer: Hamish Wilson. Costumes: Hein Heckroth. Conductor: Rafael Kubelik
Finale of Act I. Ebert grouped the characters according to their social status: Masetto/Zerlina—Donna Anna/Don Ottavio—Donna Elvira/(and with his back to her) Don Giovanni.

Don Giovanni

Glyndebourne Festival
Opera, May 29, 1936
Producer: Carl Ebert.
Costumes: Hein Heckroth.
Conductor: Fritz Busch
Hamish Wilson's design for
"A Street in Seville." It was
not the *giocoso* element that
was emphasized here:
Wilson's oppressively heavy
sets pointed implacably
toward the downfall of the
eponymous hero.

Stavovské divadlo, Prague,
October 25, 1937
Producer: Ludek Mandaus.
Designer: Frantisek Muzika.
Conductor: Václav Talich
Sets for Act II. Muzika's
sets combined imaginative
and constructivist elements.
He created a balance be-
tween reality and irreality,
and between grotesquerie
and madness, which he concealed behind the mask of
classical forms. His *Don
Giovanni* was one of the
last pre-war productions in
Prague to be influenced by
the European Surrealist
movement.

181

Don Giovanni

Festival International de Musique d'Aix-en-Provence, July 1949 (Théâtre National de l'Opéra, Paris, 1949) Producer: Jean Meyer. Conductor: Hans Rosbaud Design for the "Banquet Hall" by Cassandre (Adolphe Mouron). "I do not think that the unusual, rigorous constraints imposed by this theater—a kind of vast, open-air 'magic lantern'—inhibited me in any way in designing these sets. Once these constraints had been laid down and accepted, the resultant economy of means demanded a discipline that was bound to favor a simple and obvious solution. It was this sense of *obviousness* which I felt I should explore by ignoring the picturesque and surprise elements that the work contains, for this alone possesses that primordial quality to which every theater set must tend: the quality of being *perceived* and *forgotten* in one and the same moment," Cassandre wrote in 1957.

Festival International de Musique d'Aix-en-Provence, July 1949 (Théâtre National de l'Opéra, Paris, 1949) Producer: Jean Meyer. Conductor: Hans Rosbaud Costume design for Leporello and Don Giovanni by Cassandre (Adolphe Mouron).
Best known perhaps as the designer of a series of world-famous posters during the 1920s and 1930s, Cassandre also designed typography as well as creating the sets and costumes for numerous stage plays, ballets, and operas. In 1949 he was commissioned to design the open-air theater for the festival at Aix-en-Provence. His designs for *Don Giovanni* remained in the repertory for twenty-five years.

Don Giovanni

Glyndebourne Festival
Opera, July 11, 1951
Producer: Carl Ebert. Conductors: Fritz Busch and
John Pritchard
John Piper's design for the
"cemetery." Describing Piper's sombre designs for
this production, John Julius
Norwich wrote that, "no
one who saw it will ever
forget his dark, brooding
Don Giovanni.... For all its
brilliance and its humour,
Don Giovanni remains a
tragedy, the only one Mozart
ever wrote; never, I think,
have we been made more
conscious of the fact."

Städtische Bühnen,
Frankfurt am Main, 1952
Producer: Walter Jacob.
Conductor: Georg Solti
Wolfgang Znamenacek's
set design for Act II,
Scene 2: "Outside Donna
Elvira's House."
After training at the Cologne
Werkschule from 1931 to
1933, Wolfgang Znamenacek
worked for a number of
German theaters. His design
sketches were executed in
gouache and borrowed from
various expressive styles,
including Biedermeier,
Edvard Munch, and Surreal-
ism, depending on the piece
he was designing.

183

Don Giovanni

Salzburg Festival, July 27, 1953 (Felsenreitschule)
Producer: Herbert Graf.
Conductor: Wilhelm Furt-
wängler
Set design by Clemens Holzmeister. As for his *Faust*
(1933), Holzmeister designed
a simultaneous set depicting
an entire town strung out
along the Felsenreitschule
stage.

Metropolitan Opera, New
York, December 10, 1953
Charles Elson's design for
the "Cemetery," Act II, Scene
11. Da Ponte demanded "a
walled cemetery with various
equestrian statues, including
a statue of the Commenda-
tore." Elson's set was dominated by a statue of the
Commendatore.

Don Giovanni

Metropolitan Opera, New York, October 31, 1957
Donna Anna: Teresa Stich-Randall. Don Ottavio: Léopold Simoneau. Don Giovanni: Cesare Siepi. Donna Elvira: Lucine Amara. Producer: Herbert Graf. Designer: Eugene Berman. Conductor: Karl Böhm
Karl Böhm made his Met debut conducting this production.

Glyndebourne Festival Opera, July 1, 1960
Masetto: Leonardo Monreale. Zerlina: Mirella Freni. Donna Elvira: Ilva Ligabue. Leporello: Geraint Evans. Donna Anna: Joan Sutherland. Don Ottavio: Richard Lewis. Producer: Günther Rennert. Designer: Ita Maximowna. Conductors: John Pritchard and Peter Gellhorn
Act II, Scene 7. Maximowna followed Da Ponte's instructions for a "dark hall on the ground floor of Donna Anna's house, with three doors."

Don Giovanni

Royal Opera House, Covent Garden, London, February 23, 1965 Producer and designer: Franco Zeffirelli. Conductor: Rudolf Kempe. Revival of a production first seen on February 9, 1962 when the conductor was Georg Solti Michael Langdon as the Commendatore. A member of the Covent Garden ensemble from 1948 until his retirement in 1977, Michael Langdon brought luster to the most varied roles. His most famous interpretation was Baron Ochs in Richard Strauss's *Der Rosenkavalier*, a part which he studied with Alfred Jerger in Vienna and sang over a hundred times, including many continental productions.

Glyndebourne Festival Opera, July 2, 1967 Producer: Franco Enriquez. Designer: Emanuele Luzzati. Conductor: John Pritchard Paolo Montarsolo as Leporello. Born in 1926, Montarsolo is an effective actor, a man of the theater who impresses through his comic brio. But his singing always remains dramatic and expressive, even in the comic situations in which Leporello typically finds himself.

Royal Opera House, Covent Garden, London, July 8, 1967 Leporello: Geraint Evans. Don Giovanni: Tito Gobbi. Producer and designer: Franco Zeffirelli. Conductor: Colin Davis Born in Pontypridd (Wales) in 1922, Geraint Evans made his Covent Garden debut in 1948. He was a born actor, and his great strength lay in his ability to play with words and textual nuances; the art of characterization and singing were perfectly matched. Figaro and Leporello were two of Evans's star roles. Tito Gobbi was born in Bassano del Grappa in 1913 and, like Evans, was a singer noted for his vocal and verbal subtlety. Tonal beauty and characterful gestures complemented his stage presence.

186

Don Giovanni

Salzburg Festival,
August 3, 1960
Producer: Oscar Fritz
Schuh. Conductor: Herbert
von Karajan
Teo Otto's set design, "Out-
side the Gates of Seville."

"Lorenzo da Ponte ... left a
note to the effect that he
worked on the libretto of
Don Giovanni at night, while
thinking of Dante's *Inferno*.
Teo Otto must likewise
have been thinking of hell.
His magnificent sets are
visions of infernal might.
At the back of an almost
empty stage—a flight of
stairs to the left, and a lower
flight with a balcony to the
right—the outline of a town
towers up threateningly, its
spires and pointed gables
recalling the angular shapes
of paintings by Graham
Sutherland. The changing
backdrops appear to be
coated with plaster of Paris.
Sinister collages rise up
from broad bases seemingly
two-dimensional in spite of
being worked in mezzo
relievo. Mythic images haunt
the spectator: a pale necro-
polis built of human bones
for the cemetery scene, a
fragmented Tower of Babel
symbolizing the hero's hub-
ris, and an archaic relievo
wall lit in such a way that,
..., it resembled the tym-
panum of a medieval cathedral door. These masking
flats were lit so that the
walls glowed from within,
appearing to burn or to fade
into the night," according
to Rolf Michaelis in the
Stuttgarter Zeitung on
August 5, 1960.

Salzburg Marionette
Theater, 1966
Producer: Wolf-Dieter
Ludwig. Designer: Günther
Schneider-Siemssen.
Costumes: Ronny Reiter.
Puppet heads: Josef Magnus
Act II, Scene 15. Don Gio-
vanni descends into hell. In
the background are Donna
Elvira, Donna Anna, and
the Commendatore.

Don Giovanni

Glyndebourne Festival Opera, July 2, 1967 Producer: Franco Enriquez. Conductor: John Pritchard Emanuele Luzzati's design for the "Cemetery" (II, 11). This set was also used for the supper scene. John Warrack wrote that, "Emanuele Luzzati's sets skilfully support this final transformation, though I find his usual device of revolving floats limiting, and their messy prettiness ultimately inarticulate about the drama.... The dresses, particularly Anna's variations on the colours of mourning, are much more effective."

perform Franco Zeffirelli's sensuously romantic production that was premiered there on February 9, 1962.

The numerous new productions of *Don Giovanni* which have been staged since 1960 are marked above all by a stylistic pluralism. The individual element has been highlighted, and the *dramma giocoso* brought up to date, interpreted ironically, subjected to a Brechtian alienation effect or psychologized. The hero has been seen as psychically ill or as an aging seducer. His inner conflict has found expression in the sets around him. In Bremen in 1985 the Commendatore did not appear as an actual statue in the final scene, but a larger-than-life figure was projected onto a gauze. In the 1978 Darmstadt production women projected onto the scrim drove Don Giovanni to distraction. In Heidelberg in 1978 and Stuttgart in 1984 the hero died of heart failure. An even more extreme solution was adopted in Bonn in 1983: Masetto entered, disguised as the Commendatore, causing Don Giovanni to die of shock. Writers on the subject have seen Don Giovanni as

an unscrupulous sexual offender, but also as "Brother Hitler." The 1969 Amsterdam production saw him as the henchman of American imperialism, while Kassel in 1981 set the piece inside a huge stylized human brain. But in some productions the hero has survived: in Ludwigsburg in 1977 he handed out the music for the final sextet, and in Bremerhaven, too, he reappeared in the *scena ultima*, wearing a modern summer suit and leafing through a newspaper. The women's movement has also taken a critical look at *Don Giovanni*: a Mexican theater company with the name Compagnie Divas A.C. Mexico has toured the world with a show entitled *Donna Giovanni*. The piece is played entirely by women and Don Giovanni is not a man but merely a state of mind.

To mark the bicentenary of the opera's first production, Mozart and Don Giovanni were the subject of exhibitions in 1987 both in the house in Salzburg where the composer was born and in the city where the *dramma giocoso* had first seen the light of day in 1787.

188

LEPORELLO

Glyndebourne Festival
Opera, July 2, 1967
Producer: Franco Enriquez.
Conductor: John Pritchard.
Emanuele Luzzati's costume
design for Leporello. Reviewing the Glyndebourne pro-
duction in *Opera* magazine
(Festival edition, 1967),
John Warrack wrote, "This
is a swift and dynamic *Giovanni*, sharply contrasting
with the vaulted Romantic
mystery of Zeffirelli's Covent
Garden version. It is filled
with a sense of heady danger, of living on the edge
of disaster: it is a production
which the overture for once
genuinely introduces, with
its sense of retribution loom-
ing over total abandon to
la libertà."

Don Giovanni

Salzburg Festival, July 26, 1968 (Grosses Festspielhaus) Leporello: Geraint Evans. Don Giovanni: Nicolai Ghiaurov. Donna Elvira: Teresa Zylis-Gara. Producer and conductor: Herbert von Karajan. Designer: Günther Schneider-Siemssen. Costumes: Georges Wakhevitch Klaus Adam headed his review in the Zurich *Die Tat* of August 5, 1968 "Eight Characters in Search of A Director": "No one expects that, as a producer, Karajan will provide a brilliant solution to the problem of this opera's seductively multifaceted nature, a problem, after all, which has already forced men like Felsenstein, Rennert, and Schuh to recognize their limitations. But it is not enough to stage *Don Giovanni* guided only by self-confidence. Karajan turns it into a monstrous cinemascope film...; the clash between the physical and the metaphysical falls by the wayside, and what unfolds is a fashion parade (the Spanish peasants disport themselves in the clothes of counts and countesses) staged, as far as possible, in contradiction of the work's inherent logic. Musical ideas such as whipping up the stretta that ends the first act are countered on stage by insipidly lifeless tableaux.... Some of the audience found Günther Schneider-Siemssen's cluttered sets 'lovely,' while Georges Wakhevitch's orgy of opulent costumes was said to be 'marvellous.' And the maestro of course was 'out of this world.' All those for whom the Salzburg Festival is synonymous with the highest quality can but protest in a loud voice. But no doubt in vain."

Royal Opera House, Covent Garden, London, June 11, 1976
Don Giovanni: Ruggero Raimondi. Producer: John Copley. Designer: Stefanos Lazaridis. Conductor: Colin Davis. Revival of a new production first seen on April 18, 1973

190

Don Giovanni

Born in Bologna in 1941, Ruggero Raimondi is one of the top international opera stars, known above all for his incarnation of Don Giovanni, a part in which he sang under Lorin Maazel in Joseph Losey's film of the opera. According to David Hamilton in *The Metropolitan Opera Encyclopedia*, Raimondi is "the leading Italian basso cantante of his generation, with an imposing stage presence to match his smooth and powerful voice."

Glyndebourne Festival Opera, June 2, 1978
Donna Elvira: Rosario Andrade. Leporello: Stafford Dean. Don Giovanni: Brent Ellis. Producer: Peter Hall. Designer: John Bury. Conductors: Kenneth Montgomery and Nicholas Braithwaite
Act I, Scene 5. "Where can I find the traitor who took my love in vain?" Don Giovanni unwittingly hears himself indicted.

Salzburg Festival, August 1, 1978 (Kleines Festspielhaus)
Leporello: Walter Berry. Donna Anna: Anna Tomowa-Sintow. Don Ottavio: Peter Schreier. Donna Elvira: Teresa Zylis-Gara. Don Giovanni: Sherrill Milnes. Producer and designer: Jean-Pierre Ponnelle. Conductor: Karl Böhm
In Ponnelle's production there was no descent into hell: Don Giovanni succumbed to a heart attack. This was a grandiose production. Many of the musical numbers were performed like concert arias in front of a drop curtain.

Don Giovanni

Grand Théâtre, Geneva, September 13, 1980
Leporello: Stafford Dean. Don Giovanni: Ruggero Raimondi. Producer: Maurice Béjart. Designer: Thierry Bosquet. Conductors: Horst Stein and Reinhard Peters

According to Béjart, "The entire piece is like a perpetual, never-ending race, involving the constant movement of beings, elements, streets, and objects in a labyrinth in which everything is eternally changing. It's like a labyrinth in which Don Giovanni can continue his cheerful existence, far removed from any philosophical considerations that might transform him into the archangel of some revolution. Don Giovanni is no rabble-rouser, because he is unhappy. He pays no heed to obstacles, but circumvents them. Perpetually on the move, he attempts to enjoy life—but enjoyment means not seeing reality, it means the opposite of self-improvement. He wants neither law nor order; he does not rebel against reality: only when reality begins to annoy him does he get down to business; when one door refuses to open, he looks for another one—he continues to pace through the labyrinth."

Royal Opera House, Covent Garden, London, July 6, 1981
Producer: Peter Wood. Designer: William Dudley. Conductor: Colin Davis
David Walker's 1980 costume design for Richard Van Allan as Leporello. The production met with widespread criticism, not least because it was felt that the singers were forced to put up with a great many unnecessary and unmusical ideas inflicted on them by the producer.

Don Giovanni

Staatstheater, Kassel, 1981
Producer: Peter P. Pachl.
Designer: Dietrich Schoras.
Conductor: Alexander
Sander

"Our set represents an abstract model of the human brain," Dietrich Schoras wrote in the Kassel program. "External stimuli are perceived through the eyes and ears and transmitted along nerves to individual parts of the brain (visual memory, cerebral hemisphere, cerebellum, thalamus) where they are processed. On stage, the eye is replaced by a video camera that transmits images to the visual memory. In its individual stages this theatrical conception (brain, thought, or time machine) seeks to steer its hero's fantastical world into the future. Perceived as part of a dialectical relationship with the ordered world, the fantastical is intended to function as a structural element in some vision of the future. The fantastic element in *Don Giovanni* is not identical with dreams or psychological interpretations, because, if it were, neither the Utopian nor the fantastic element would stand a chance. Rather it implies ambiguity. The dull presence of the animal in man. Ambiguity lodges in the evolutionary transitions between animal and man, nature and man, and between machine and man. Don Giovanni is in search of the new man, and of a new world. He is at odds with society. But he insists upon reality as the basis for his actions."

Hungarian State Opera, Budapest, October 24, 1982
Don Giovanni: György Melis.
Donna Elvira: Mária Sudlik.
Don Ottavio: Dénes Gulyás.
Donna Anna: Julia Kukely.
Producer: Yuri Lyubimov.
Designer: Dávid Borowski.
Conductor: Iván Fischer
Da Ponte's "brilliantly lit hall, prepared for feasting and dancing" is seen here enclosed in a wooden barn. As is evident from the illustration, the orchestra was placed on stage for this production.

193

Don Giovanni

Salzburg Easter Festival, April 11, 1987
Zerlina: Kathleen Battle. Don Giovanni: Samuel Ramey. Donna Anna: Anna Tomowa-Sintow. Don Ottavio: Gösta Winbergh. Donna Elvira: Julia Varady. Leporello: Ferruccio Furlanetto. Masetto: Alexander Malta. Producer: Michael Hampe. Designer: Mauro Pagano. Conductor: Herbert von Karajan

This production was taken over by the Salzburg Festival in the summer of 1987. In his program note for the 1987 Easter Festival, Michael Hampe asks the question whether the Grosses Festspielhaus in Salzburg is suitable for *Don Giovanni*, given the fact that Mozart preferred small theaters for his operas. Hampe conceives of the Grosses Festspielhaus not as a huge and static space, but as an undefined space "in which different sized rooms could be variously realized from one extreme to another. If it were possible to play with this space in a musical and dynamic way, so to speak, and adapt the size of the stage to suit each musico-dramatic situation, it might be possible to develop a conception of space which would always reflect the conflicting dramaturgical and musical elements—*buffa* and *seria*, aria and ensemble, and mythological and realistic plot levels. Were this the case, then the Grosses Festspielhaus would enable us to achieve something that is not possible in other houses because of their space limitations, namely a 'partnership' between the stage space and the music, rather like a film camera whose image can expand to take in a long shot, or contract to allow for a close-up."

Hamburg State Opera, September 17, 1987
Leporello: Gilles Cachemaille. Donna Elvira: Roberta Alexander. Producer and designer: Marco Arturo Marelli. Costumes: Dagmar Niefind. Conductor: Peter Schreier
"Leporello is just as much a representative of the lower classes as his master represents the aristocracy," Attila Csampai wrote in the Hamburg program. "They are both chained to each other through being uprooted and through being outsiders. Leporello is the ordinary man's Don Giovanni, just as Don Giovanni is in a certain sense the Leporello or drop-out among the princes.... The extent to which he can empathize with Don Giovanni ... is clearly and convincingly demonstrated in the Catalogue Aria..., so that we can no longer be certain which are his own feelings and which are his master's."

Opéra National de Belgique, Brussels, October 2, 1984 (Théâtre Royal de la Monnaie)
Zerlina: Patricia Schuman. Masetto: Marcel Vanaud. Producer and designer: Karl-Ernst Herrmann. Conductor: Sylvain Cambreling
Herrmann transported the characters from the *tiers état* into the world of the *commedia dell'arte*.

Opéra National de Belgique, Brussels, October 2, 1984 (Théâtre Royal de la Monnaie)
Don Giovanni: José van Dam. The Commendatore: Pierre Thau. Producer and Designer: Karl-Ernst Herrmann. Conductor: Sylvain Cambreling
Scene in Act II. Karl-Ernst Herrmann linked together the individual scenes using magnificent curtains painted in designs reminiscent of Piero della Francesca and Giovanni Battista Tiepolo. Naples and Venice are clearly recognizable. Don Giovanni's costume is initially pastel pink but gradually grows stronger in color. By the finale it is fiery red, recalling paintings by Velázquez.

Teatro alla Scala, Milan, December 7, 1987
Don Giovanni: Thomas Allen. Zerlina: Susanne Mentzer. Producer: Giorgio Strehler. Designer: Ezio Frigerio. Costumes: Franca Squarciapino. Conductor: Riccardo Muti
Described as the production of the century, Strehler's staging of *Don Giovanni* transferred the work to the late Baroque. The producer exploited all the effects of the Baroque theater, creating dramatic and aesthetic effects by means of a cleverly thought-out lighting plot in which color values and moods played a major part. On a formal level, Strehler stuck close to Mozart's score and turned it into great theater. The designer, Ezio Frigerio, created a majestic space entirely in keeping with Strehler's production concept; and the colorful, elegant costumes of Franca Squarciapino fitted well into this luxurious framework.

Così fan tutte
o sia La Scuola degli Amanti

A mysterious commission

None of Mozart's operas has been so misunderstood and so variously interpreted as *Così fan tutte*. We are admirably informed about the genesis of the operas that Mozart wrote for Italy (*Mitridate, Rè di Ponte, Ascanio in Alba*, and *Lucio Silla*), and are fortunate in having a series of letters relating to *Idomeneo* and *The Abduction from the Seraglio* in which the composer describes his working methods. But virtually no documents have survived relating to *Così fan tutte*.

In December 1789 we find Mozart writing to Michael Puchberg, his "most honorable friend and fellow member" (fellow Freemason), to report that the following month he would be receiving 200 ducats for *Così fan tutte* from the Burgtheater management, and asking whether Puchberg could lend him 400 gulden (about 70 ducats) until then in order to rescue his friend "from the greatest embarrassment." Mozart promises that "by that time you will have the money back in full and with many thanks .... Once more I beg you," Mozart goes on in the same letter, "rescue me just this once from my desperate situation, and as soon as I get the money for the opera [*Così fan tutte*], you will have the entire sum of 400 gulden back for certain." Although he had invited Puchberg to visit him at his home on December 30, 1789, he now has to cancel that arrangement, saying that he has too much work. "But I invite you (and you alone) to come along on Thursday [New Year's Eve 1789] at 10 in the morning for a short rehearsal of my opera; only you [Puchberg] and [Joseph] Haydn have been invited."

And on January 20, 1790 Mozart informs his "dearest friend" Puchberg, "We are having the first instrumental rehearsal in the theater tomorrow. Haydn will be coming with me—if your business allows you to do so, and if you care to attend the rehearsal, all you need do is to be kind enough to come here at 10 o'clock tomorrow morning, and we shall all go there together." This is all that we know of the origins of *Così fan tutte*. When Mozart began work on the score we do not know. But he must have devoted the greater part of 1789 to the task of writing out the opera. The autograph score runs to 587 written pages (316 folios), together with a handful of sketches. (How many sketches have been lost or found their way into the wastepaper basket?) In his private catalogue, the so-called "Verzeichnüss aller meiner Werke," Mozart made the following entry for January 1790: "Così fan tutte: o sia la scuola degli amanti. Opera buffa in 2 Atti, pezzi di musica.—Attori. Signore. Ferraresi del Bene, Villeneuve e Bussani. Signori Calvesi, Benucci e Bussani." (Thus Do All Women Behave; or The School for Lovers. Opera buffa in 2 acts, musical numbers.—Singers. Mmes. Ferraresi del Bene, Villeneuve, and Bussani. MM. Calvesi, Benucci, and Busani.) The singers named here by Mozart (they were the Viennese opera stars of their day) were the ones who sang in the first performance of the opera, given in "the Imperial and Royal National Court Theater next to the [Hof]Burg" in Vienna on January 26, 1790.

To this day we still do not know who commissioned the opera from Mozart. The composer's biographer Franz Xaver Niemetschek appears to have been the origin of one

Salzburg Festival, August 6, 1976 (Kleines Festspielhaus) Fiordiligi: Gundula Janowitz. Guglielmo: Hermann Prey. Don Alfonso: Rolando Panerai. Ferrando: Peter Schreier. Dorabella: Brigitte Fassbaender. Producer: Günther Rennert. Designer: Ita Maximowna. Conductor: Karl Böhm (Revival of the 1972 production)

K. 588

Opera buffa in two acts. Words by Lorenzo Da Ponte. Completed in Vienna in January 1790. First performed at the Vienna Burgtheater on January 26, 1790. Autograph score: Act I: Cracow, Biblioteka Jagiellońska; Act II: West Berlin, Staatsbibliothek Preussischer Kulturbesitz.

Così fan tutte

Vienna Court Opera, late nineteenth century Johann Kautsky's set design for the "Garden Salon." Johann Kautsky joined the staff of the Vienna Court Opera in 1863. He was born in Prague and had trained as a landscape artist. In 1883, together with Carlo Brioschi and Hermann Burghard, he succeeded relatively easily in replacing gaslight on stage by modern electric lighting.

particular myth in this repect. In his *Life of the Imperial and Royal Kapellmeister Wolfgang Gottlieb Mozart, Based Upon Original Sources*, published in Prague in 1798, he remarks, "In the month of December in the Year of Our Lord 1789, Mozart wrote the comic Italian Singspiel 'Così fan tutte or The School of Lovers'; it is a source of general wonderment that so great a mind could have sunk to the depths of squandering his divinely sweet melodies on so wretched a fabrication. It was not in his power to decline the commission, for he was expressly enjoined to set this text." Like Mozart's later biographer, Georg Nikolaus Nissen, Niemetschek does not name the person who is said to have commissioned the opera. The rumor that it was Joseph II goes back to the theater journalist Friedrich Heinse, who wrote in his *Traveler's Tales and Scenes from Theatrical Life, together with Loose Leaves from a Dramatist's Journal*, published in Leipzig in 1837, "But I would only draw your attention to the fact that, in his biography of Mozart, von Nissen is not entirely clear in observing that it was Joseph II who expressly commissioned the composition of this very libretto from Mozart. According to rumor, an incident that had actually occurred in Vienna between two officers and their lovers and which was similar to the plot of the libretto, offered the Emperor an opportunity of honoring his court poet Guemara [presumably Heinse is thinking of Giovanni de Gamerra, although the latter did not become theater poet in Vienna until after Joseph II's death] with a commission to turn this piece of gossip

into a *dramma giococo da mettersi in musica* [burlesque drama to be set to music]."

Among the folios which contain a daily record of the letters issued by the Emperor, most of which he dictated, there are no reports relating to the theater from the years 1789 and 1790. In these two years (which also witnessed the war with Turkey) the state of Joseph II's health had deteriorated to the point where he was no longer able to leave his sickroom. It seems unlikely that he would have commissioned an opera by word of mouth. In his monograph *Da Ponte's "Così fan tutte,"* Kurt Kramer has sought to show that, in writing *Così fan tutte*, Da Ponte was parading his humanistic education and drawing upon the traditions of European culture.

Mozart's cast list for the first performance

Francesca Gabriel[l]i, known by the name of Adriana Ferraresi del Bene, hailed from Ferrara and created the part of Fiordiligi. She had made her debut on October 13, 1788 in Vincente Martin y Soler's *L'Arbore di Diana*, in which she sang the title role. She remained a member of the Burgtheater ensemble until 1791, and sang the part of Susanna in the Vienna production of *The Marriage of Figaro* on August 29, 1789. In the *dramma giocoso. Le Trame Deluse ovvero I Raggiri Scoperti* by Domenico Cimarosa (first performed in the Teatro Nuovo in Naples during the summer of 1786), Mozart found Maddalena Allegrante, a pupil of Ignaz Holzbauer, much better than Ferraresi. "The little aria [K.579] which I wrote for Ferraresi ought to please people provided she is capable is singing it in an artless manner, which I very much doubt. She herself liked it a lot," Mozart wrote to his wife on August 19, 1789.

The role of Dorabella was created by Louise Villeneuve, first heard at the Burgtheater on June 27, 1789 when she had sung the part of Amor in *L'Arbore di Diana*; her engagement there lasted until 1790. Mozart wrote three concert arias for her, "Alma grande e nobil core" (K.578), "Chi sà, chi sà, qual sia" (K.582), and "Vado, ma dove? oh Dei" (K.583).

Dorothea Bussani, had married the bass singer Francesco Bussani (see below) on March 20, 1786. She was Mozart's first Despina, having already sung the part of Cherubino in the premiere of *The Marriage of*

Figaro on May 1, 1786. She was a permanent member of the Burgtheater ensemble from 1786 to 1794, returning as a guest performer between August and October 1796. The tenor Vincenzo Calvesi, who sang the part of Ferrando, was a member of the Burgtheater (with a few interruptions) from 1785 to 1794. He made his debut with the company on April 20, 1785, singing the part of Sandrino in Giovanni Paisiello's *Il Rè Teodoro in Venezia*. He also sang the tenor part in Mozart's quartet "Dite almeno, in che mancai" (K.479) and in the trio "Mandina amabile" (K.480).

The composer was on friendly terms with his first Guglielmo, Francesco Benucci, who had also been his first Figaro and who sang the part of Leporello in the first Vienna production of *Don Giovanni* on May 7, 1788. It was Benucci whom Mozart had in mind when planning the part of Bocconio in *Lo Sposo Deluso*, and it was also for Benucci that the composer wrote the aria "Rivolgete a lui sguardo" (K.584), intended to be interpolated into *Così fan tutte*. Benucci made his debut at the Burgtheater on April 23, 1783, when he sang Blasio in Salieri's *La Scuola de' Gelosi*. He remained loyal to the company until 1795.

Mozart had a very positive opinion of Benucci, as is clear from a letter to his father, written from Vienna on May 7, 1783: "Well, the Italian opera buffa has started again here; and is very popular.—The buffo is particularly good. He is called Benuci."

Francesco Bussani, born in Rome in 1743, was Mozart's choice for Don Alfonso. He, too, was far from unknown to the composer, who wrote the bass part in the quartet "Dite almeno, in che mancai" (K.479) specially for his voice. He also sang Bartolo and Antonio in the first performances of *The Marriage of Figaro*, and the Commendatore and Masetto in the first Vienna production of *Don Giovanni*. Bussani had begun his career at the Burgtheater on April 22, 1783 in a performance of Salieri's *La Scuola de' Gelosi*, in which he sang the part of Lumaca. He remained a member of the company until 1794.

The theater in which *Così fan tutte* was first performed, the old Burgtheater, was by no means excessively large. It was long and narrow, with a depth of 44 meters and a width of 15. The main acting area was some

Vienna Court Opera, late nineteenth century
Set design for the "Coffee-House Garden" by Anton Brioschi. Anton Brioschi succeeded his father Carlo as head of the theater design studio at the Vienna Court Opera in 1885. He is generally regarded as the finest theatrical representative of Hans Makart's decorative historical style.

Così fan tutte

Nationaltheater, Munich, June 9, 1928
Producer: Josef Geis.
Conductor: Hans Knappertsbusch
Costume design for Fiordiligi and Dorabella by Leo Pasetti

Nationaltheater, Munich, November 21, 1941.
Producer: Rudolf Hartmann.
Designer: Rochus Gliese.
Conductor: Clemens Krauss Fiordiligi, sung by Viorica Ursuleac, was dressed either in outdoor attire or widow's weeds. As both costumes were from the same pattern, it was evident that the mourning clothes were intended as a mask. The opera was sung in Georg Schünemann's German translation.

12.60 meters deep, with an 8-meter deep rear stage. In 1790 the theater could accommodate around 1,350 persons and had a centrally fired heating system that ensured agreeable temperatures even in winter.

There were ten performances of *Così fan tutte* at the Burgtheater between January and August 1790, after which the *opera buffa* disappeared from Vienna until 1794.

What the first-night audience thought of Mozart's opera is not known. Count Karl von Zinzendorf, who attended the performance on January 26, found Mozart's music "charming" and described Da Ponte's original text as "assez amusant." The *Wiener Zeitung* of January 30, 1790 merely observed: "Last Wednesday the 16th [*recte* the 26th] inst. a new comic Singspiel in two acts entitled *Così fan tutte, o sia: la Scuola degli Amanti* was performed for the first time in the Imperial and Royal National Court Theater. The poem is by Abbate da Ponte, the poet of the Italian Singspiel at the Imperial and Royal Court Theater, and the music by Herr Wolfgang Mozart, kapellmeister in effective service to H.M. the Emperor." It must be remarked, however, that the Vienna press never wrote detailed reviews of Mozart's operas, or indeed of any opera premieres of the time, in contrast to the Paris *Mercure de France,* for example, which regularly carried "Mémoires secrets."

Contemporary reception of the opera

Music lovers in Mozart's own day could get to know *Così fan tutte* only incompletely. The Vienna publishing firm of Artaria & Co. announced a vocal score of the duet for Dorabella and Guglielmo, "Il core vi dono, bell'idol mio" (No. 23), a mere three weeks after the premiere, in other words, on February 20, 1790. The Overture and Nos. 4 (the duet for Fiordiligi and Dorabella, "Ah guarda sorella"), 7 (duettino for Ferrando and Guglielmo, "Al fato dan legge quegli occhi"), 8 (the chorus, "Bella vita militar"), 15 (Guglielmo's aria, "Non siate ritrosi"), 19 (Despina's aria, "Una donna a quindici anni"), 20 (the duet for Fiordiligi and Dorabella, "Prenderò quel brunettino"), 23 (the duet for Dorabella and Guglielmo, "Il core vi dono, bell'idol mio"), and 28 (Dorabella's aria, "E amore un ladroncello") were published in 1790 by Artaria & Co. in an arrangement for voice and keyboard as part of the series *Raccolta d'arie* (Nos. 56-66). Karl Zulehner edited the first vocal score in around 1796. It was published in Mainz by Schott. The *Répertoire International des Sources Musicales* (RISM) does not list a copy of this edition. The first vocal score to contain a German translation (by Christoph Friedrich Bretzner) is still in use today: "Così FAN TUTTE. / o sia / la scuola degli amanti. / WOMEN'S FAITHFUL-

Städtische Bühnen, Frankfurt am Main, March 28, 1928. Producer: Lothar Wallerstein. Designer: Ludwig Sievert. Conductor: Clemens Krauss

Ludwig Sievert's set design for the "Garden" (1926). Theodor W. Adorno reviewed the 1928 production in *Die Musik* (May 1928): "The Frankfurt Opera continues to hold back in performing contemporary works that might provoke discussion. But can one even talk of 'holding back?' There has not been a single novelty recently; with the exception of a not entirely happy, although very lively, new production of *The Gypsy Baron*, all we have had has been a *Così fan tutte*, given, it must be admitted, in a very well-prepared production, with most charming scenery by Sievert, some nice ideas by Wallerstein, and well-chosen tempi by Clemens Krauss. It will not do to ascribe this work's lack of popularity to the flaccid transparency of its plot, to an extension (in the logical sense) which is musical rather than theatrical, or to a lack of musical contrast in this opera for six singers; for all of this ought to be neutralized by the perfection of the music, whose form is fully self-contained in the painful distance of the late work. We should rather ask ourselves whether it is not precisely this perfection that frightens people away from a work in whose limpid mirror the listener recognizes himself as mortal; the opera lacks a certain element of low life, lacks a Papageno or a Leporello to atone for the grief of its spiritualization through the reflex of reality. In this way *Così fan tutte* does not live, but lasts; yet it will always be a source of renewed astonishment, and no one can pass by this monument unchanged, even if its language be written in hieroglyphics."

NESS. / or / The Girls are from Flanders. / A comic opera in 2 acts / by W.A. Mozart. / Vocal score / by C[hristian] G[ottlob] Neefe. / N[icolaus] Simrock in Bonn 1799. / 208 p. qu-4°.

The first full score did not appear until 1810. It was published in Leipzig by Breitkopf & Härtel and contained a reprint of Bretzner's text by way of an introduction (the music itself was underlaid with German and Italian words), together with *secco* recitatives. Not until after 1820 did the Paris publisher J. Frey bring out a full score of *Così fan tutte* in his *Collection des Opéras de Mozart* (No. 6). Full scores that adopted a critical approach to the source material were published by Breitkopf & Härtel in 1871 (edited by Julius Rietz, the revised edition included complete secco recitatives, and Italian and German words); by the same firm in January 1881 (the old Mozart Edition); and by Peters of Leipzig in 1941 (edited by Georg Schünemann on the basis of the Urtext). The Neue Mozart-Ausgabe will reflect the latest state of research and contain all the surviving sketches and drafts.

In March 1790 the *Journal des Luxus und der Moden* observed that its reviewer was again able to announce "an admirable work by Mozart." "As for the music," the announcement went on, "I believe that it is enough to say that it is by Mozart."

Even by the year of Mozart's death there were frequent remarks of a negative kind concerning Da Ponte's libretto. When the actor, theater manager and writer Friedrich Ludwig Schröder read the first German translation of the opera by Heinrich Gottlieb Schmieder and Carl David Stegmann, prepared for performances in Frankfurt am Main and published under the title *Love and Temptation or That's What Girls Are Like*, he noted in his diary on April 28, 1791, "That's what they are all like, a Singspiel with music by Mozart is a wretched affair that debases women; it cannot possibly find favor with female audiences and in consequence will not be successful." The Berlin *Annalen des Theaters* of May 1791 adopted a similar tack: "May 1. Love and Temptation, a wretched, Italian product with the sublime and virile music of a Mozart."

An anonymous arranger adapted *Così fan tutte* as a German Singspiel for the Electoral Saxon Court Theater in Dresden, where it was first produced on October 5, 1791. He chose the title, *They are All as Bad as Each Other, or The School for Lovers. A Burlesque*

201

Così fan tutte

Städtische Bühne, Posen,
1942
Paul Haferung's drop curtain
for *Così fan tutte*

Singspiel for the Electoral Saxon Theater.
Eleven of the work's thirty musical numbers
were omitted, and Don Alfonso was placed
firmly in the limelight.

Frankfurt performed *Love and Temptation*
in 1791 in Stegmann's translation, and
Amsterdam followed suit the same year,
presenting the opera under the title *That's
What Girls Are Like.* A further translation
was published in Prague in 1791-92 under
the title, *One Woman Just Like the Next, or
The School for Lovers. Adapted as a German
Singspiel for the National Theater By Wenzel
Mihule, a man of means in Prague.* Berlin
performed the opera on August 3, 1792 using
Mihule's title. The *Journal des Luxus und der
Moden* wrote of the Berlin performances, "It
is truly a matter for regret that our best
composers so often squander their talent and
their time on such pitiful subjects. The present Singspiel is the silliest thing in the world,
and audiences will attend performances of it
only out of consideration for the admirable
music which it contains."

Throughout the 1790s translators contin-
ued to devise new titles for the opera. *That's
How All Girls Behave* was heard in Hanover
on October 10, 1792, *That's How Each of
Them Behaves* in Passau on January 3, 1793,
The Wager or Girls' Cunning and Love in
Mannheim on May 12, 1793, and *That's How
They All Behave or The School of Love*

(translated by Karl Ludwig Giesecke) in
Vienna on August 14, 1794. Vocal numbers
from *The School for Lovers or One Woman
Just Like The Next* were published in Augsburg in 1794. That same year a *dramma
giocoso per musica, Gli Amanti Folletti* (The
Love-Stick Polgergeists) was performed in
the Electoral Theater in Dresden. It was a
pasticcio based on Mozart's operas, in which
the text was radically altered.

Christoph Friedrich Bretzner's *Women's
Faithfulness or The Girls are from Flanders*
(even as late as Goethe's time Flanders was a
synonym for fickleness and infidelity), first
performed in Leipzig in 1794, marked the
beginning of a second wave of translations
which pointed the way ahead for many theaters in the years that followed, not least
because Bretzner's text was used in the vocal
score of the opera published by Nicolaus
Simrock of Bonn in 1799. Bretzner gave the
women German names (Julie, Charlotte, and
Nannchen), and turned Guglielmo into Wilhelm. Later versions invented the education-
alist Altberg (Don Alfonso) and Lieutenants
Steinfeld (Ferrando) and Walling (Guglielmo).
A striking feature of Bretzner's translation is
its moralizing tone and toning down of Da
Ponte's delineation of his characters' emotional states. The scene of action is transferred from southern Naples to more northerly
climes and to a "garden on the banks of a

Redoutensaal, Vienna, 1943
Producer: Oscar Fritz
Schuh. Conductor: Karl
Böhm
Caspar Neher's set design
for Act I. During the war,
opera performances in
Vienna were given in the
city's Redoutensaal until
the fall of 1944 when "total
war" was declared and all
the theaters were closed.

navigable river." In his introduction to the libretto Bretzner acknowledged the superior merit of Mozart's music: "The charming and admirable music of this masterpiece by the immortal Mozart, and the extraordinary acclaim that greeted this opera during two whole summers in the Italian theater here, persuaded me to adapt the same for the German stage, and I am certain that, if well performed, the music will be universally popular. Of course, I recall having read that it has already been given in German in a number of places, without leaving any great impression: but either the translation was far too pitiful or the performance itself was to blame.

"The listener should not be deterred if the impression made by the first performance does not come up to the expectations that he had had of the piece; he should listen to it several times, and I am convinced that, once he has grown a little more familiar with the beauties of the music, he will not be able to hear enough of it. In revising the work, I have allowed myself a few divergencies and cuts such as I considered necessary if the piece is to appear in a German guise.

"I flatter myself, moreover, that connoisseurs who are aware of the difficulties of adapting a German text to Mozart's music, will judge my work indulgently."

A second version by Bretzner, this time in four acts and entitled *The Wager or Girls' Cunning and Love*, was performed in Stuttgart on May 16, 1796.

Così fan tutte—One Woman Just Like The Next or The School for Lovers was presented in Wäser's Theater in Breslau (modern Wrocław) on January 16, 1795, *The Wager or Girls' Cunning and Love* in Stuttgart on May 16, 1796, *The Wager or Women's Faithfulness Is Not Faithfulness* in Munich in May 1795, and *The Wager or Girls' Cunning and Love* (Bretzner's four-act revision) in Hamburg's Theater beim Gänsemarkt on July 6, 1796. *That's How They All Are, All Of Them*, translated by Goethe's brother-in-law, the writer Christian August Vulpius, was performed in Weimar on January 10, 1797. Frau Goethe begged her son to send her the revised version of the text. In a letter to him in Weimar, dated May 15, 1797, she wrote, "The opera Cosa van Tutti [!] or That's how they all behave—is said to have gained so much in Weimar through the revised text—for the one we have here is dreadful—it is this revised one which Herr Bernhardt asks you to obtain—all the expense of copying it out and whatever other costs are incurred—these will be refunded with the greatest thanks."

That *Così fan tutte* failed to appeal to German audiences was a matter of regret for the writer on music Johann Friedrich Rochlitz, who complained in the Leipzig *Allge-*

Così fan tutte

Metropolitan Opera, New York, December 28, 1951
Ferrando: Richard Tucker.
Don Alfonso: John Brownlee.
Guglielmo: Frank Guarrera.
Producer: Alfred Lunt.
Designer: Rolf Gérard.
Conductor: Fritz Stiedry
Da Ponte's coffeehouse has been transformed into an *osteria* in the Neapolitan docklands.

meine musikalische Zeitung in 1801: "It is much to be deplored that the piece has not been seen to its best advantage on German stages. German audiences everywhere no doubt have too much gravity and too little levity for this kind of comedy, and most of our singers, male and female, are too inexperienced as actors and, above all, too little sophisticated, too little given to waggish humor and roguish behavior for the genre of Italian burlesque as it is pushed to the extremes that are demanded here."

Nineteenth-century performances

At the beginning of the nineteenth century the Vienna Theater in der Leopoldstadt gave Bretzner's two-act version a new and eye-catching title, *The Two Aunts from Milan or The Masquerades*. This version was first performed on July 1, 1802.

Throughout the nineteenth century, reviewers returned to the improbability and triviality of the plot. It seemed too lacking in logic, encouraging writers to provide a better motivated intrigue. The *Fidelio* poet Georg Friedrich Treitschke supplied a new translation for the Vienna Burgtheater, first performed there on September 19, 1804 under the title *Girls' Faithfulness*. A revised version of this text was performed on January 20,

1814 at the Theater an der Wien; *The Magic Test or That's What They Are All Like* was the title of this new two-act Romantic Opera. Magic elements in the style of Vienna's suburban theaters characterize the action. Alfonso appears as a magician, wearing a doctor's hood. Having entered into a wager with the two officers, he invests their engagement rings with magic powers so that their wearer can change shape. Alfonso also has an accomplice in the shape of the jinni Celerio, who repeatedly slips into the role of the chambermaid Rosina (Despina) and seeks to influence the two girls. A chorus of jinn has the power to transform the magician's ill-lit chamber into a magnificent hall where the girls are seduced into being unfaithful. The entire emphasis here is upon theatrical effect, and what had once been a finely balanced interplay of head and heart, of love, loyalty, and disloyalty, and of rational and emotional responses is completely upset.

Johann Gottlieb's Rhode's *The Girls' Revenge* (Breslau, April 10, 1806), Johann Baptist Krebs's *Girls Will Be Girls* (Stuttgart, January 7, 1817), Carl Alexander Herklots's *The Insidious Wager* (Berlin, March 25, 1820), Karl von Holtei's *That's How They All Behave* (Berlin, December 29, 1825) and Johann Daniel Anton's *The Guerillas* (Mainz, October 11, 1838) were not destined to enjoy any lasting success, and not even their translations contributed to a more positive attitude toward the work or helped to ensure a lasting place for it in the repertory.

The fact that music can express comicality in all its nuances, and that *Così fan tutte* contains an expression of the most delightful irony was confirmed by E.T.A. Hoffmann in his *Serapionsbrüder* of 1819-21. However, among the writers and composers who condemned the text were Ludwig van Beethoven, Ernst Ortlepp, Alexander Dmitryevich Ulïbïshev, Richard Wagner, and Eduard Hanslick. In May 1825 Beethoven told Ludwig Rellstab, "I could not write operas like *Don Juan* and *Così fan tutte*. I have an aversion to such things. I could not have chosen such subjects, for I find them too frivolous." In 1841 Ernst Ortlepp devoted a whole chapter to *Così fan tutte* in his book *Grand Instrumental and Vocal Concert. A Musical Anthology*, published by Franz Heinrich Köhler in Stuttgart. He argues, among other things, that "One can find neither plan nor arrangement in this piece, and it would be difficult to judge it as a work of art. It is a collection of individual beauties, the majority of which are characterized by a cheerful and willful mood. Youthful energy and luxurious fullness blossom forth in it. The wealth of melodies is inexhaustible. In this respect it has much in common with Figaro, except that in this latter work the mood of cheerful good humor achieves a far higher level."

The Russian writer on music, Alexander Dmitryevich Ulïbïshev, a passionate admirer of Mozart, wrote in the German edition of his *Nouvelle Biographie de Mozart* in 1847, "In order to appreciate the music of this opera and to judge its beauties and relative imperfections, we must first speak of a text which is so inferior as to be beneath all criticism. We may begin by remarking that in this piling up of platitudes there is not a single moment which might give rise to laughter. It is not in the least comical—it is stupidity pure and simple. Mozart ... did of necessity what Italian composers do out of habit and method. He treated the text in a cursory manner and appeared at times to forget it entirely. The music does not always chime in with the spirit of the situations or with the feelings of the characters on stage, but never does it formally give the lie to them." And Richard Wagner, who, it must be remembered, was his own librettist, found it impossible to give the text his approval. In *Opera and Drama* of 1851 he reflects, "How little did this most richly talented of all musicians understand

the work of art of our modern musicmakers, a work which involves the erection of glittering gilded towers on a stale and unworthy basis, and which commits them to playing the role of the rapt and inspired composer when the poetry is all hollow and empty .... Oh, how deep is my love and respect for Mozart precisely because it was *not* possible for him to invent music for *Titus* like that of *Don Giovanni* and for *Così fan tutte* like that of *Figaro*: how shamefully would this have dishonored the music!"

Eduard Hanslick, the feared Viennese critic, wrote a damning indictment of the libretto following a performance of *Così fan tutte* in the Austrian capital: "Could a more fatuous demand be made on the audience's implicit faith than the permanent state of

Opéra-Comique, Paris, March 30, 1952
Producer: Georges Hirsch.
Designer: Romain Erté.
Conductor: Georges Sébastian
Romain Erté's costume design for Fiordiligi. The part of Fiordiligi was sung by Jacqueline Brumaire at this performance.

205

Così fan tutte

Salzburg Festival, July 31, 1953 (Residenz)
Ferrando: Anton Dermota.
Don Alfonso: Paul Schöffler.
Guglielmo: Erich Kunz.
Producer: Oscar Fritz Schuh. Designer: Caspar Neher. Conductor: Karl Böhm

From a musical point of view, this economically staged production of *Così fan tutte* was one of the Salzburg Festival's great occasions. Emmanuel Buenzod reviewed the performance of August 29, 1953 in the *Gazette de Lausanne*: "So perfect an architectural layout of the scene of action, distinguished as it is by spaciousness as well as intimacy, was acclaimed by the audience as a matter of course.... At the back of the stage, four chandeliers shimmer with exquisite light. At the front are two light silvery metal couches and two chairs of an equally sobre design. In the midst of this unbelievably simplified set, this bewitching fairy-tale piece is performed for us, without the least detail being altered in any way, but solely through the magic charm of the music and the acting of the performers."

Glyndebourne Festival Opera, August 31, 1954 (guest appearance at the Edinburgh Festival)
Ferrando: Richard Lewis.
Don Alfonso: Sesto Bruscantini. Guglielmo: Geraint Evans. Producer: Carl Ebert. Designer: Rolf Gérard. Costumes: Rosemary Vercoe. Conductor: Vittorio Gui
Gérard set Da Ponte's coffeehouse by the seaside. The three protagonists drink wine instead of coffee and seal their wager with alcohol.

Salzburg Festival, July 27, 1960 (Landestheater) Producer: Günther Rennert. Designer: Leni Bauer-Ecsy. Conductor: Karl Böhm Set design for Act I. The cast for this production was Elisabeth Schwarzkopf (Fiordiligi), Christa Ludwig (Dorabella), Hermann Prey (Guglielmo), Waldemar Kmentt (Ferrando), Graziella Sciutti (Despina), and Karl Dönch (Don Alfonso).

blindness shown by the two heroines, who do not recognize their lovers in spite of having been on the most intimate terms with them barely a quarter of an hour previously, and who, when their own chambermaid appears in a full-bottomed wig, take her first as a doctor and then as a notary? Da Ponte's libretto is witless and offensive, precisely because the two men succeed in deceiving their lovers and making them unfaithful within the space of very few hours. The forgiveness that finally covers up for the act of betrayal of these two foolish women ... is even more offensive than the earlier impertinences with which this libretto teems."

If one surveys the period between 1791 and, say, the middle of the nineteenth century, the result is a colorful range of versions of the opera, some of which were of supraregional significance, some of only local importance. After 1850 few versions had any determining influence on the theaters of the day. The scholarly debate over Mozart, encouraged by the 1856 centenary celebrations, began to bear fruit during the second half of the nineteenth century. Among the works that deserve to be mentioned here pride of place goes to the biography of Mozart by Otto Jahn, together with the old Mozart Edition of *Così fan tutte*. It is against this scholarly background that the translations by Carl Friedrich Niese (Dresden, September 19, 1856) and Eduard Devrient (*That's How They All Behave*, Karlsruhe, September 9, 1860; recitatives arranged by Wilhelm Kalliwoda) must be seen. A lapse, albeit well-intentioned, was the pasticcio *Winzer und Sänger* by Johann Peter Lyser, published in his Mozart Album of 1856. It was staged at the Tivoli, Hamburg, on June 2, 1856, and, in addition to music from *Così fan tutte*, it contained three numbers from the opera *Idomeneo*.

The performance of *Così fan tutte* that Gustav Mahler conducted at the Vienna Court Opera on October 4, 1900 is of interest from a musical point of view. He cut a number of arias in Act II, which he introduced with the finale from the Divertimento in B flat (K.287). He also rewrote some of the transitions, but always with material from *Così fan tutte*. Also unusual for Vienna was the fact that the prose dialogue was replaced by *recitativi secchi*, which Mahler accompan-

Così fan tutte

Scottish Opera, Edinburgh,
May 31, 1967.
Dorabella: Janet Baker,
Fiordiligi: Elizabeth Harwood. Producer: Anthony
Besch. Designer: John Stoddart. Conductor: Alexander
Gibson
Stoddart designed a painted
garden for the second scene
of Act I, but did not locate
it, as Da Ponte prescribes,
at the edge of the sea.

ied from the keyboard. The costumes for this production were designed by Heinrich Lefler, and the sets were painted by Anton Brioschi. Mahler himself directed. The work was performed on a revolving stage made out of thirty wooden sections. Rapid scene changes were possible as a result of this technical innovation.

Hedwig von Friedländer-Abel wrote of the new production in the *Montags-Revue* of October 8, 1900, "In *Così fan tutte* one revels in the most authentic Rococo. Everything carved out to the daintiest degree, like something by Watteau or Greuze. The Court Opera has succeeded in conjuring up the spirit of that time and breathing life into the strange little people of ages ago. The intentional affectedness of these little ladies and men was emphasized with particular felicity. Fiordiligi and Dorabella, the twofold brides, revealed a delightful affectation, as, indeed, did Guglielmo and Ferrando. The mincing Despina was equally indisputably a figure straight out of the eighteenth century, just like scheming old Don Alfonso."

An entirely new text, prepared on the basis of *La Dama Duende* by the Spanish dramatist Pedro Calderón de la Barca, was made by the baritone singer and writer on music, Karl Scheidemantel. Entitled *Dame Kobold*, this version was launched in Dresden on June 6, 1909.

Non-German-speaking countries also took up *Così fan tutte*, although the work enjoyed a more modest success here. Trieste first heard the work in June 1797 in the original language, while other early performances in Italy include ones in Milan (La Scala, September 19, 1807), Turin (fall of 1814), and Naples (Carnival of 1815). Barcelona presented the work as early as November 4, 1798, and in Copenhagen the opera opened on October 19, 1798 under the title *Veddemaalet eller Elskernes Skole*, translated by Adam Gottlob Thoroup.

The first performance of *Così fan tutte* on French soil took place in the Théâtre de l'Impératrice at the Odéon on January 28, 1809. Da Ponte's text was revised and prefaced by the following motto, written by L. Pignotti and placed on the title page of the libretto: "Ladies, I do not know whether this book tells the truth; but I know full well that evil or foolish men do a grave injustice to

Salzburg Festival, July 28, 1969 (Kleines Festspielhaus) Don Alfonso: Walter Berry. Ferrando: Lajos Kozma. Guglielmo: Tom Krause. Fiordiligi: Anneliese Rothenberger. Dorabella: Rosalind Elias. Producer and designer: Jean-Pierre Ponnelle. Conductor: Seiji Ozawa

Ponnelle's production stressed a Baroque playfulness which nonetheless breathed a certain Romanticism. The scenery suggests a southern, Mediterranean setting, with the outline of a town visible against the cyclorama. The basic structure of the set is provided by a series of false prosceniums consisting of finely woven trelliswork with vine-like ornaments for the luxuriant vegetation of the garden scenes, while the trelliswork is replaced by masonry for the indoor scenes. Symmetry is created by benches, ornamental vases, and herms. The central perspective is dominated by fountains, *amoretti*, and gateways.

wise women because of one or two other women. They presume to give them a bad reputation, as though they were tiny butterflies for all to catch. But if it were ever to prove that the greater part of your fair sex were really so fickle and wayward, what praise should we then have to lavish upon those whom you single out from the common herd as seeking virtue and wit?"

It is interesting that the character of Don Alfonso was made more prominent in Paris: he was accorded two scenes to himself, no doubt because the part had been upgraded for the famous bass singer Barilli. The fourth scene of Act II aimed at being particularly topical with its allusions to Parisian women. Indeed, sections of the text were in French, presumably in order to achieve greater intelligibility. The arranger sought to address the local audience in an ironical vein and took a well-aimed shot at the specious virtues of Parisian women. Don Alfonso was given the following text to sing: (Recitative) "Victory is at hand, I am certain that this pleasant surprise will create an impression. I understand women and know from experience that you have to deal kindly, skillfully, and, above

all, gently with them. If you show yourself kind and unassuming, they will sooner or later not be able to resist you. (Aria) If, head-over-heels in love, you offer women your heart, they lower their eyes, conceal themselves, say no, and act the prude. But do not fear their stern demeanor, in vain they pretend to be bashful, whether they be free or whether their heart belongs to another, they are always pleased to be courted. My dear ladies, keep calm, I beg you, I speak only of the women of Italy, Greece, and India. As God is my witness, the charming Parisians are utterly different. They are loyal and tempting, and they never deceive their lovers, their steadfastness is as one with their charm. If they have once bestowed their heart on a man, and if another then demands their love, they lower their eyes, conceal themselves, say no: our hearts belong to another, they say, your entreaties are all in vain. Ever chaste and spotless, they never fall into temptation. In the whole wide world you can find no such women."

Little remained of Mozart's *Così fan tutte* at these 1809 performances in Paris. The most striking vocal numbers, including those

209

Così fan tutte

Salzburg Festival, July 27, 1972 (Kleines Festspielhaus)
Producer: Günther Rennert.
Conductor: Karl Böhm
Ita Maximowna's design for Fiordiligi's costume in Scenes 2 and 3. The design expresses a sense of serene harmony tinged with irony and also with a touch of resignation. Rennert and Maximowna were very much of one mind on this point.

which depict the lovers' frame of mind (Nos. 11, 14 and 17), the beginning of the girls' decision to devote their attentions to the other partner (No. 20) and Dorabella's and Guglielmo's confession of love (No. 23), were all cut. In this way the work's entire charm was lost, and an action enriched by deeply felt musical numbers was reduced to the level of a silly comedy with musical extras. It looks as though the psychology of Mozart's opera was completely alien to the French arranger. In

consequence the first French Così fan tutte remained sadly deficient and failed to inspire its audience. The Paris Opéra showed no further interest in the work throughout the rest of the nineteenth century.

An attempt to stage the work in 1816 in a French translation entitled *The Neapolitan Lovers* was similarly unsuccessful. The arranger Antoine-Francois Le Bailly de Saint-Paulin did not want Così fan tutte to be regarded as a pasticcio, but intended the piece to redound exclusively to Mozart's honor. The music was to be retained, but the course of the action had to be altered to become a satire of the fair sex. This attempt to present Così fan tutte in the language of the country concerned misfired, and the adaptation again remained a musical torso. Of interest is the fact that in Act II, Scene 4 Emilie (Fiordiligi) and Isabelle (Dorabella) learn from Delphine (Despina) that the whole affair is a charade, and that their lovers are planning to disguise themselves. In this way Delphine destroys the entire charm of the plot; in this version both the women and men know that it is all no more than a comedy. There can be no question here of any real exchange of roles, and the main thrust of Da Ponte's text has been missed.

The opera was staged in a three-act version at the Grand Théâtre de Lyon on March 1, 1823. The text was arranged and edited by Castil-Blaze who enlivened the plot by supplementing Mozart's music with individual num-

Vienna State Opera, May 22, 1975
Producer: Otto Schenk.
Designer: Jürgen Rose.
Conductor: Karl Böhm
Jürgen Rose designed grandiose sets for this Vienna production of the work. For each scene—the illustration shows his design for Scene 1—he created a different set, each of which was naturalistic and fully developed.

bers by Cimarosa, Paer, Rossini, Pavesi, Generali, and Steibelt. The title of this farrago was *Les Folies Amoureuses*. Another version was seen at the Théâtre Lyrique in Paris on March 31, 1863, this time under the title *Love's Heartache*. Text and music were revised and arranged by the dramatists Jules Barbier and Michel Carré. They conceived the piece as a four-act French opera, cutting all the recitatives and replacing them with spoken dialogue. The musical numbers were grouped together in an arbitrary fashion, and additional pieces were introduced from Mozart's instrumental music, including the third movement of the B flat major Symphony K.319, the seventh movement of the Posthorn Serenade (K.320), the third movement of the G minor Symphony (K.550), and the second movement of the B flat major Quartet (K.458).

London saw *Così fan tutte* on May 9, 1811. The performance was given in Italian in the Haymarket Theatre. An English version with the title *Tit for Tat; or the Tables Turned* was performed at the Lyceum Theatre on July 29, 1828. The first performance of *Così fan tutte*

at the Metropolitan Opera, New York, was on March 22, 1922.

The revival of Mozart's score

Not until the twentieth century was *Così fan tutte* rediscovered in its original form. An essential part in this rediscovery was played by Richard Strauss, Clemens Krauss, and Karl Böhm. A new production of the work was given by the Vienna State Opera on November 23, 1929, directed by Lothar Wallerstein, conducted by Clemens Krauss and designed by Ludwig Sievert. The theater historian Heinz Kindermann recalls the occasion: "With Sievert's help, Wallerstein had moved a kind of miniature stage onto the huge stage of the State Opera House. Rapid scene changes of the kind that had persuaded Mahler to introduce a revolving stage to the Vienna Opera, were achieved by Wallerstein and Sievert having the beginning and end of each vocal number sung in front of a curtain. While this was going on, the sets would be quickly and invisibly changed .... The match-

Hamburg State Opera, December 7, 1975 Producer: Götz Friedrich. Conductor: Aldo Ceccato. Toni Businger's costume design for Dorabella

Salzburg Festival, August 6, 1976 (Kleines Festspielhaus) Producer: Günther Rennert. Designer: Ita Maximowna. Conductor: Karl Böhm Don Alfonso (Rolando Panerai) persuades Despina (Reri Grist) to introduce two smart young men to her mistresses. He promises her twenty *scudi* if the ploy works.

Così fan tutte

Deutsche Oper am Rhein, Düsseldorf, July 1, 1976
Producer: Georg Reinhardt.
Costumes: Inge Diettrich.
Conductor: Friedemann Layer
Ruodi Barth's set design for the "Pavilion"

Stadttheater, Würzburg, October 5, 1978
Producer: Wolfram Dehmel.
Costumes: Anke Behrens.
Conductor: Max Klink
Ernst Masson's design for a "Garden." Da Ponte prescribes "a garden at the edge of the sea" for Act I, Scene 4; a "small ornamental garden with two grassy banks at either side" for the finale to Act I; and "a garden overlooking the seashore, with grassy banks and two small stone tables" for Act II, Scene 4.

212

Così fan tutte

Städtische Bühnen, Freiburg im Breisgau, April 28, 1978
Producer: Ulrich Melchinger.
Conductor: Klauspeter Seibel
Thomas Richter-Forgách's set model. The two enormous sculptures symbolize the male and female elements.

Ulm Theater, January 28, 1979
Producer: Cornel Franz.
Designer: Rüdiger Tamschick. Conductor: Friedrich Pleyer
Set model, "open doors of a room looking out onto the beach." "Anyone who is involved with *Così fan tutte* is struck by the fact that the superficial action is not tied to any fixed space. What takes place inside a room could equally well happen in a garden or on a terrace. The space is defined simply by the way in which the six characters act. Two groups confront each other: those who know about the wager (Don Alfonso, Ferrando, and Guglielmo), and those who know a little (Despina) or nothing (Fiordiligi and Dorabella). Those who know nothing about it believe themselves safe and well-protected. They live in a space that shields them from all injustice. But this space provides only the illusion of protection. It is invaded by an intrigue that Don Alfonso has set in motion to teach the girls and their male friends a lesson in the spirit of the Enlightenment. He wants to disabuse them of their sentimental naïveté and beat some sense into them. At the same time the mechanics of the intrigue need to be visible. In other words, doors: doors afford protection against the outside world, and doors allow the outside world to enter unhindered. By Act II, the doors have become superfluous and now simply stand around as stage properties recalling a lost time when the characters were 'protected,'" Cornel Franz wrote in the Ulm program.

Così fan tutte

Salzburg Festival, July 28, 1982 (Kleines Festspielhaus) Fiordiligi: Margaret Marshall. Dorabella: Agnes Baltsa. Producer: Michael Hampe. Designer: Mauro Pagano. Conductor: Riccardo Muti
Scene in Act I. "Everything necessary for this experiment—the scene of action and the plot—could be dreamed up on the empty stage with all the requisite wealth of mood and atmosphere, all the truthfulness of human relationships—and yet remain a recognizable event that has a purpose to it, the consequence of a wager which, if needs be, can be interfered with. In this way the action can develop on several levels. One character can depict another one if the course of the action invites him to do so, or, conversely, he may step outside the action and comment upon it. Stage properties can move imperceptibly from one level to another, small interruptions can reflect the progress of the action, consciousness of the game that is being played on the basis of the wager can be maintained without impairing the credibility of a situation or of a relationship. And, finally, an experiment that is otherwise heading for disaster can be broken off from outside, and the participants can rediscover themselves on an empty stage, as though waking from a dream. Perhaps Mozart's and Da Ponte's playful concern with a thesis and its antithesis may be realized in this way and resolved through the music," Michael Hampe wrote in his program note.

ing harmony that existed between Krauss's conducting and Wallerstein's production, including the light pastel shades that Sievert chose for his highly imaginative sets and costumes, created a wholly convincing impression in the parallelism of gaiety and a simultaneous hovering on the brink of a precipice, a parallelism of irony and a deeper significance that could easily slip into melancholy, a parallelism, finally, between sweeping momentum and demarcation .... In contrast to Roller's static and stylized secessionist designs of 1920, Sievert's waywardly emotional sets gave Wallerstein the opportunity to elaborate this psychological correspondence between music, gesture, and facial expressions and thus to enhance the overall optical impression. In doing so Wallerstein arrived at a new stage in the history of the evolution of productions of *Così fan tutte*."

Numerous producers have wrestled with *Così fan tutte* during the last fifty years and written about their experiences. Rudolf Hartmann wrote of a Munich performance in 1937, "The sets ... were designed by Ludwig Sievert. *Così* after all is the opera in which the structuring law of symmetry is exaggerated to the point where it resolves itself. And it was this law of symmetry that was symbolized in Sievert's stage picture in a wholly discreet and delightful way. His sets can be regarded very much as a classic example of

the way that music may be transformed into something visual, dominated as they were by the harmony of charming arabesques. The pavilion-like bowers, dainty dressing tables, the flirtatious garden swing set the tone of artful overrefinement, but also added a note of tender sentimentality. And against this shimmering background the comedy of disloyalty—but also the comedy of Mozart's music—could unfold with equal validity in keeping with the overall atmosphere .... In their acting the characters retained the most elegant composure, avoiding all exaggeration; and even in the scenes where the men are disguised they observed a certain 'nonsensical dignity.'" Günther Rennert commented on his Salzburg production in 1972: "It is a question of achieving a synthesis between the *opera buffa* tradition, in other words, the typology of character and plot, on the one hand, and, on the other, the psychological and individually determining emotional factors. The task of the producer is to perform an unique balancing act between marionette theater and humanity, between parody and reality, between thoughtlessness and melancholy, between frivolity and psychological law—between playfulness and earnestness. An overemphasis upon one or other of these many components can coarsen a performance, making it farcically superficial, or else simplify it to the point where it

214

becomes bitterly ironical, embarrassing, and defamatory."

András Fricsay said of his 1974 Frankfurt production, "In Fiordiligi and Ferrando, and Dorabella and Guglielmo, four partners come into conflict who actually suit each other rather better, since they largely correspond in character and temperament. The experience of this different understanding as something that they have in common and which is a form of being in love is the basis for their experience of infidelity which the partners can no longer hide behind. As a result the meaning of the ending is changed: the semi-rational, semi-conciliatory happy ending of Da Ponte and Mozart appears as a concession to contemporary taste, a concession which conceals a provocation. If Fiordiligi and Ferrando secretly hold out their hands while the reunited couples exchange a kiss of recon-

ciliation, it becomes clear that their newly acquired feelings will have an explosive impact on their present relationships."

For his 1975 Hamburg production Götz Friedrich provided the following program note: "Mozart's humane irony in *Così fan tutte* teaches us a naïve pleasure in playing, exposes the all-too-human in people, shows us laughter in the midst of tears, tells us not to take things too seriously and yet not to underestimate the dangers that lie in jest. In this way Mozart creates the rare model of a music theater in *Così fan tutte*, a theater in which truth emerges only through playing, not through borrowing from realities outside this piece and outside this theater." And the Kassel program booklet of 1977 includes the following remark by Peter Windgassen: "The 'bare stage' around the music box is intended as a symbol of reality, disillusionment, of

Salzburg Festival, July 28, 1982 (Kleines Festspielhaus) Producer: Michael Hampe. Conductor: Riccardo Muti Mauro Pagano's set design for Act I

215

Così fan tutte

Opéra de Lyon, March 17, 1983
Fiordiligi: Michèle Lagrange.
Dorabella: Magali Damonte.
Guglielmo: François Le Roux. Ferrando: Leonard Pezzino. Don Alfonso: Pierre-Yves Le Maigat.
Producer: Guy Coutance.
Designer: Yannis Kokkos.
Conductor: Serge Baudo
Ferrando and Guglielmo take their leave of their lovers, who are comforted by Don Alfonso.

Dresden State Opera, May 23, 1983
(main auditorium)
Fiordiligi: Ana Pusar. Guglielmo: Andreas Scheibner.
Ferrando: Armin Ude.
Dorabella: Elisabeth Wilke.
Producer: Joachim Herz.
Designer: Bernhard Schröter. Conductor: Hans Vonk.
Text revised by Joachim Herz.
"First things first: *Così fan tutte* does not take place today. It is a period piece from the past, and it reflects, in the most delightful way possible, an epidemic of the time: sentimentalism.... The outcome of this painful explanation of events is that 'ideals,' or what were considered as such, are revealed as a convention and as a social requirement, and that they are not rooted in human nature: the ideals in question are the irreplaceability of the young men and the inviolability of their brides. The men have discovered that they have set fire to their own homes, and they have all learned that life is far more confused than they had thought," Joachim Herz wrote in his program note.

San Francisco Opera, Summer Festival 1983 (June 23, 1983)
Dorabella: Tatiana Troyanos. Guglielmo: Tom Krause. Producer and designer: Jean-Pierre Ponnelle. Conductor: Andrew Meltzer
Disguised as an Albanian, Guglielmo sues for the hand of his fiancée's sister, Dorabella.

Così fan tutte

Komische Oper, East Berlin, April 13, 1984
Producer: Harry Kupfer. Designer: Reinhard Zimmermann. Costumes: Eleonore Kleiber. Conductor: Joachim Willert
During the Overture, Don Alfonso (Werner Haseleu) stands in front of a large transparent tent, the key figure in the drama that ensues. The auditorium is reproduced on stage, mirroring the audience.

Zurich Opera, February 26, 1986
Despina: Julia Hamari. Fiordiligi: Lucia Popp. Guglielmo: Thomas Hampson. Dorabella: Ann Murray. Ferrando: Gösta Winbergh. Don Alfonso: Claudio Nicolai. Producer and designer: Jean-Pierre Ponnelle. Costumes: Pet Halmen. Conductor: Nikolaus Harnoncourt
Scene in Act I. "Many years ago Ponnelle was one of those producers who were uncompromising in directing our attention to the bitter unfathomableness of operatic subjects, especially those that are concerned with love and with the risks to which it is exposed. All the more surprising is it, therefore, to discover in Zurich that in this of all operas he has emphasized the work's farcical element. He dresses Guglielmo and Ferrando in Turkish costumes. This may be seen as a concession to the kind of masquerade that Mozart seems to have been crazy about all his life. But given the work's thematic context, this emphasis upon fancy dress and the slapstick that is bound up with it was bound to make the two women seem foolishly naïve. As so often with Ponnelle's earlier productions, this staging of *Così fan tutte* conveyed the impression that his preference was for a brilliant stage spectacle," Dieter Rexroth wrote in *Musica*, 1986.

sobering, painful truth." Michael Hampe expresses his ideas as follows in the 1982 Salzburg Festival program: "There is an empty stage—a proscenium, a few flats, a backdrop—neutral, a vacuum waiting to be filled. It could set the scene for Mozart's and Da Ponte's psychological experiment which, elegantly and discursively presented, simultaneously shows how questionable it is to conduct such experiments on human beings, inasmuch as the living individual is more than the rational sum of his parts."

Richard Strauss gave a special place to *Così fan tutte*: "If all were well with our opera houses, *Così fan tutte* should now at least be granted a special place in the repertory of all German theaters, a place which it has always deserved. But how many such places are standing empty, even today?"

Opéra National de Belgique, Brussels, October 28, 1984
Don Alfonso: Claudio Nicolai. Despina: Elzbieta Szmytka. Guglielmo: Marcel Vanaud. Ferrando: Jerome Pruett. Fiordiligi: Barbara Madra. Dorabella: Patricia Schuman. Producer: Luc Bondy. Designer: Karl-Ernst Herrmann. Costumes: Jorge Jara. Conductor: Michael Schønwandt
"A panoramic backcloth, 190 meters long and 11 meters high, moves along a complicated system of rollers.... reminiscent of the huge theatrical machines of the Baroque age, and it turns this Brussels *Così fan tutte* into a constantly moving picture show in which the Gulf of Naples appears at one moment with tiny islands dotted with temples reflected in its surface, only to be replaced at the next moment by a Rococo grove. Changes of lighting make the scenery appear alternately veiled in thundery darkness, suffused in moonlight, or bathed in glistening sunshine.... The characters are the playthings of love, exposed to a visible aging process, while the comedy pursues its pitiless course, running the gamut of inconstant feelings, a course which nature herself appears to keep in working order like the mechanism of a clock" (*Der Spiegel*, No. 1, 1985).

The Magic Flute

Origins of the opera

More has been written about *Don Giovanni* and *The Magic Flute* than about any other Mozart opera. If one sifts through all that has been said about *The Magic Flute*, the story that emerges is of a genesis lacking, in many cases, in concrete details, a tale largely devoted to legends and hypotheses, and a variety of interpretations relating to the intellectual and ideological background of the work, but with the main emphasis frequently placed on the element of Freemasonry.

It is not known what concrete circumstances led to the composition of *The Magic Flute*, since no documents have survived that would throw light on the question of the fee that Mozart received, on details of who commissioned the work, or on facts relating to the opera's rehearsal period. To learn more about the origins of the opera, we need to go back to Salzburg in 1780-81 and to the figure of Emanuel Schikaneder. Born in the Lower Bavarian town of Straubing on September 1, 1751 (he died in Vienna on September 21, 1812), Schikaneder brought his 34-strong theater company to Salzburg between September 1780 and the Shrovetide festival of 1781. With the prince-archbishop's consent they performed at the Salzburg Theater, where they enjoyed a great success, many of their performances being sold out. The Mozart family was among the regular audience at Schikaneder's performances. A bond of friendship sprang up between Mozart and Schikaneder, and the Mozarts were given free tickets for Schikaneder's performances. From 1784 to 1786 Schikaneder was an actor and impresario in Vienna. It was here, in the Kärntnertortheater on November 5, 1784, that the Schikaneder-Kumpf troupe performed Mozart's *Abduction from the Seraglio* in the presence of Joseph II. Schikaneder moved to Vienna in the spring of 1789, and in the July of that year he opened the 1000-seat Freihaustheater with a performance of the comic opera *Der dumme Anton im Gebirge oder Die zween Anton*, music by Benedikt Schak and Franz Xaver Gerl. The repertory was made up for the most part of magic operas. In November 1789 he performed the Romantic comic opera *Oberon, König der Elfen*, with words by the actor, jurist and mineralogist Karl Ludwig Giesecke and music by Paul Wranitzky. This work is generally regarded as the forerunner of *The Magic Flute*.

Mozart attended a performance of *Oberon*, at Schikaneder's Freihaustheater on June 1, 1790. On June 2 he wrote to his wife, "Yesterday I was at the second part of Cosa rara [by Vicente Martin y Soler], but I do not like it as much as the Antons." A piece from the first of the six *Anton* comedies inspired Mozart to compose his keyboard variations on the song "Ein Weib ist das herrlichste Ding" (K.613) in March 1791. It was probably at the end of August 1790 that he instrumented (and perhaps also composed) the duet "Nun, liebes Weibchen, ziehst mit mir" (K.625 [592a]) for Schikaneder's and Schak's heroic comic opera *Der Stein der Weisen oder Die Zauberinsel*.

Throughout 1790 and 1791 Mozart had regular dealings with members of Schikaneder's ensemble, and was on friendly terms

Salzburg Festival, July 28, 1978 (Felsenreitschule) Papageno: Christian Boesch. Producer and designer: Jean-Pierre Ponnelle. Conductor: James Levine
This production ran from 1978 to 1986. According to Schikaneder's stage directions, "Papageno comes down the pathway with a large birdcage on his back; it towers over his head and contains various birds; he is also holding some Pan pipes in both hands, and he plays them and sings."

K. 620

A German Opera in two acts. Words by Emanuel Schikaneder. Begun in Vienna, probably in the spring of 1791. Dated July 1791 (Overture and Priests' March [No. 9] September 28, 1791). First performed at Vienna's Freihaustheater auf der Wieden, September 30, 1791. Autograph score: East Berlin, Deutsche Staatsbibliothek.

The Magic Flute

Theater an der Wieden, Johann Baptist Henneberg. At the first performance on September 30 the cast was as follows: Sarastro, Franz Xaver Gerl (bass); Tamino, Benedikt Schak (tenor); Speaker, Herr Winter (bass); First Priest, Herr Schikaneder the Elder (bass); Second Priest, Johann Michael Kistler (tenor); Third Priest, Herr Christian Hieronymus Moll (speaking role); Queen of Night, Josepha Hofer (soprano); Pamina, her daughter, Anna Gottlieb (soprano); First Lady, Mlle. Klöpfer (soprano); Second Lady, Mlle. Hofmann (soprano); Third Lady, Elisabeth Schak (soprano); Papageno, Emanuel Schikaneder (bass); An Old Woman (Papagena), Barbara Gerl (soprano); Monostatos, a Moor, Johann Joseph Nouseul (tenor); First Slave, Karl Ludwig Giesecke (speaking role); Second Slave, Wilhelm Frasel (speaking role); Third Slave, Herr Starke (speaking role).

The libretto, "illustrated by two engravings ... in which Herr Schikaneder is shewn in the role of Papageno wearing his actual costume," was published at 30 kreutzers by "the Vienna Masonic Printer and Engraver Ignaz Alberti." Mozart conducted the premiere "out of his high regard for the kind and venerable public and out of friendship for the author of the piece."

Mozart attended a performance of *The Magic Flute* on October 7, 1791 and afterwards wrote to his wife, "Dearest, most beloved little wife, I have just returned from the opera; it was as full as ever. The duet 'Mann und Weib etc.' [No. 7] and the glockenspiel in Act I were repeated as usual, as was the boys' trio [No. 16] in Act II—but what gives me most pleasure is the silent approval! You can see how much this opera continues to improve." And on October 8-9 he told his wife, "Although Saturday (being post-day) is always a bad day, the opera was performed to a full house, with the usual applause and encores; it will be given again tomorrow .... But for Papageno's aria with the glockenspiel ['Ein Mädchen oder Weibchen'] I went behind the scenes, because I felt such a desire to play it myself today. Just for fun, at the point where Schikaneder has a long pause, I played an arpeggio—which made him jump—so that he looked into the wings and saw me. The second time round I did nothing—but he stopped, refusing to go on—I guessed what he was thinking and played another chord—at which he struck the glockenspiel and said 'shut up'—then everyone laughed—I think that it was only

View of the Freyung in Vienna, with a so-called Hanswurst Theater. Hanswurst was a comic figure from the German-speaking popular theater who survives in the figure of Schikaneder's Papageno. Copper engraving by Johann Adam Delsenbach based on a drawing by Josef Emanuel Fischer von Erlach, 1719.

with his business associate Joseph von Bauernfeld.

It was probably in the spring of 1791 that Mozart began composing *The Magic Flute*, although the plan and individual sketches may well predate this. By mid-April 1791 he was working on the score in earnest, On June 4 (?) his wife went to Baden near Vienna for a course of spa treatment. On the 7th Mozart dined with Schikaneder, and on the 11th he wrote to Constanze, "Out of sheer boredom I wrote an aria for the opera [*The Magic Flute*] today—I was up at half past four." On July 2 Mozart again dined with Schikaneder, and wrote to his wife the same day, "Please tell that idiotic child Süssmayer [Franz Xaver Süssmayr] to send me my score of the first act, from the introduction to the finale, so that I can orchestrate it." Süssmayr, who was staying with Constanze in Baden, had to copy out Mozart's score since the singers needed it for rehearsals. Mozart presumably began orchestrating the score on July 3 and by the end of the month had virtually completed the entire work. The only pieces missing were the Priests' March (No. 9) and the Overture, which were not written until two days before the premiere.

On August 28 Mozart arrived in Prague for a gala performance of *Don Giovanni* planned for September 2, followed by the premiere of *La Clemenza di Tito* four days later.

Cast list for the premiere

The rehearsals of *The Magic Flute* were taken by the young kapellmeister at the

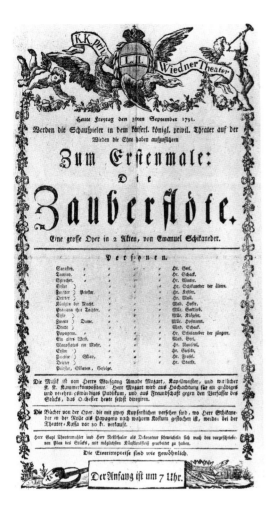

Playbill for the first performance of *The Magic Flute* in the Theater auf der Wieden, September 30, 1791. Schikaneder's elder brother Urban was a member of the theater ensemble, as were Josepha Hofer, Mozart's sister-in-law, Anna Gottlieb, and Karl Ludwig Giesecke. Mozart himself conducted only the first two performances; during the weeks that followed the opera was given almost every day.

Emanuel Schikaneder as Papageno. Copper engraving by Ignaz Alberti, a Freemason who printed the earliest libretto for *The Magic Flute* in Vienna in 1791. The engraving should not be seen as a portrait of Schikaneder, although it clearly shows his costume as Papageno.

Salvatortheater, Munich, 1793
Giuseppe Quaglio created thirteen designs for the Salvatortheater on Munich's Salvatorplatz. His contemporaries regarded him as the inventor of three-point perspective, although this device had already been known to the Galli-Bibiena school, after which it had fallen into oblivion. The Queen of Night enters in Act I with two black horses, holding their reins in her hand. The stage floor is covered with spherical clouds, while narrow columns linked together by tendrils in rows create a series of exits and entrances. Quaglio's design was criticized for the fact that the columns standing on the spherical clouds were felt to fly in the face of all engineering and architectonic principles.

223

The Magic Flute

Städtisches Theater, Leipzig, January 25, 1793
The Leipzig *vedutisto*, draughtsman, etcher, color engraver, and watercolorist Carl Benjamin Schwarz, who was also curator of the Winkler Collection and a member of Friedrich Seconda's chartered *Deutsche Gesellschaft*, designed the sets for the Leipzig performance of *The Magic Flute*. The scene reproduced here is "Sarastro's Temple of the Sun" (II, 30).

because of this joke that many people realized he was not playing the instrument himself."

The *Musikalisches Wochenblatt*, published in Berlin on December 10 (?), 1791, carried the following report: "Vienna, October 9. The new 'machine comedy,' *The Magic Flute*, with music by our kapellmeister Mozart, is being given at great expense and with magnificent stage settings, but it has not met with the hoped-for acclaim since the content and the language of the piece are far too inferior."

On October 13, Mozart traveled to Perchtoldsdorf with his brother-in-law Franz de Paula Hofer in order to collect his son Carl; that evening the two of them, together with Mozart's mother-in-law, Frau Maria Cäcilia Weber, attended a performance of *The Magic Flute*. Also present, at his invitation, were the Vienna Court kapellmeister Antonio Salieri and the singer Catarina Cavalieri. On the 14th he wrote to inform his wife Constanze, "At 6 o'clock I called in the carriage for Salieri and Cavalieri, and drove them to my box—then I hurried off to fetch Mamma and Carl ..., how much they enjoyed not only my music, but also the book and everything else. He [Salieri] listened and watched most attentively, and from the sinfonia [Overture] to the final chorus there was not a single piece that did not elicit a 'bravo' or a 'bello' from him. They could not thank me enough for my kindness. They had in any case intended to go to the opera yesterday .... After the theater

I drove them home and dined with Carl at Hofer's."

There were twenty-four performances of *The Magic Flute* during October alone, all of them sold out. The *Wiener Zeitung* of November 5 carried the following advertisement: "The Magic Flute, Opera by Herr Mozart, kapellmeister in Actual Service to His Majesty the Emperor, from which various pieces, suitable for singing at the clavier, may be obtained from Lausch's music bookshop." Fragments of an early vocal score have survived by Joseph Heidenreich. And on November 23 the same newspaper advertized: "Artaria & Comp., Fancy Stationer on the Kohlmarkt, is offering the following new publications: Mozart, Duet 'Bey Männern welche Liebe fühlen' arranged for keyboard from the new opera *The Magic Flute*, 20 kreutzers. Aria: 'In diesen heil'gen Hallen' arranged for keyboard from the same opera, 20 kreutzers." On December 4, the day before Mozart's death, his pupil Ignaz von Seyfried reported that Mozart had whispered the following words to his wife: "Quiet! Quiet! Hofer [The Queen of Night] is singing her high F;—your sister-in-law is now singing her second aria, 'Der Hölle Rache'; how powerfully she hits the B flat and holds on to it: 'Hört! hört! hört! der Mutter Schwur!'" The *Allgemeines Theaterjournal*, published in Frankfurt am Main and Mainz in 1792, included the following report on *The Magic*

Ducal Court Theater, Weimar, January 16, 1794 Johann Wolfgang von Goethe produced a series of set designs for the Weimar production; the one reproduced here is the "entry of the Queen of Night." Goethe was director of the Weimar Theater from 1791 to 1816, and during that period opera was well represented. *The Magic Flute* received 82 performances under his administration (*Don Giovanni* was given 68 performances, *The Abduction from the Seraglio* 49, *Così fan tutte* 33, *La Clemenza di Tito* 28, and *The Marriage of Figaro* 20). Picking up where Schikaneder had left off, Goethe planned a sequel to *The Magic Flute* during the 1790s, but the work remained a fragment. It was intended as a symbolic continuation of Schikaneder's plot, using the same characters and including spoken dialogue, songs, arias, ensembles, a number of choruses, instrumental music, mime, etc. The fragment contains numerous instructions to the composer. Additional scenes were planned, including a battle of spirits involving meteors and comets. One scene was rewritten in 1826 and used in the Euphorion episode in *Faust Part II*.

Flute: "We must at least say this to Herr Schikaneder's credit, that he spares no expense on his newly rehearsed pieces, and that, where necessary, he has new stage settings and costumes prepared. The cost of presenting Mozart's final opera, *The Magic Flute*—Mozart's swansong—is said to have amounted to 5,000 florins, but he more than makes up for his loss by appealing to the senses of those who come to the theater wanting to see rather than feel, by offering them beautiful stage settings and elaborate costumes, and by sparing no expense; for only in this way, and by making economies on so many other new pieces, can the director repeat a piece and more than make good his losses."

King Friedrich Wilhelm II of Prussia expressed the wish to see *The Magic Flute* performed at the National Theater in Berlin in 1792. He invited the director of the theater, Professor Johann Jakob Engel, to write a report on the work, which the latter submitted on March 8, 1792: "The Singspiel *The Magic Flute* which Your Majesty most graciously deigned to despatch to me yesterday for my examination was already familiar to me through reports from Vienna and Prague: its reputation was that of a piece with the finest and most varied stage settings and transformations, a performance of which requires a theater of considerable size, so that it is certainly not suited to the narrow confines of the National Theater here. Having read the text in detail, I find this first impression confirmed beyond all expectation. The author appears to have had no other purpose than to create all conceivable difficulties for the stage-machinist and set-designer, so that a work has come into being whose entire merit lies in its being a joy to behold. At all events, an audience unfamiliar with certain mysteries and unable to penetrate the dark and heavy veil of allegory will certainly not be able to derive any interest from it. I regret that so great a composer as Mozart was obliged to squander his talent on so thankless, mystical and untheatrical a subject." The king recommended *The Magic Flute* to Engel again in May 1792, but once more he went unheard. Not until May 12, 1794 was the opera staged in Berlin.

Even today *The Magic Flute* remains one of the most popular pieces in the operatic repertory. Schikaneder was able to announce the hundredth performance of the opera on November 23, 1792, by October 22, 1795 he had chalked up two hundred performances, and by January 1, 1798 three hundred. Prague was the next city after Vienna to hear the work, where it was performed on October 25, 1792. An Italian version, *Il Flauto Magico*, translated by Giovanni de Gamerra and with recitatives by the Bohemian organist and composer Johann Baptist Kucharz, was performed in the city during the 1794 carnival;

The Magic Flute

Six colored engravings of scenes from *The Magic Flute* by Josef and Peter Schaffer, published between January and July 1795 in the Brünn monthly magazine *Allgemeines Europäisches Journal*. Act I, Scene 3: In the foreground is the giant serpent, hacked into three pieces, with Tamino to the left and Papageno to the right; the Three Ladies are standing in the middle.

Act I, Scene 15: Grove with entrances to the Temples of Wisdom, Reason, and Nature. It is striking that Tamino is holding his flute the wrong way round.

Act I, Scene 18: Sarastro enters on a carriage drawn by six lions. He has a young, beardless face and wears an ermine coat; his long hair hangs down from under a pointed cap. His retinue consists of men wearing turbans and dressed in the Turkish fashion. Papageno is on the right at the front, with Pamina on the left. She is wearing an elegant dress of puffed material.

Act II, Scene 14: A landscape garden with a lake and a circular temple facing the open countryside is the scene for the test of silence.

Act II, Scene 25: Vaults inside the pyramids. A priest leads Papagena and Papageno away.

Act II, Scene 28: Trial by fire and water. The stage directions contained in the libretto have been closely followed here: "The scene changes to two great mountains; in one of them is a waterfall from which the sounds of water roaring and foaming can be heard: the other spits out fire; each mountain has a grille with holes in it, through which the fire and water can be seen; where the fire is burning, the backcloth must be bright red, and where the water is, a black mist lies. The sets are rocks, each of which is closed off by an iron door. Tamino is lightly dressed, without sandals."

and a Czech version by Adalbert Nejedlý, Antonín Jaroslaw Puchmayer, and Šébastián Hněwkowský was published there in the same year. The opera was performed in Josef Krasoslaw Chmelenský's Czech translation on January 11, 1829. A later performance in Czech on December 5, 1874 used a new translation by Johann Böhm.

During the course of 1793 the opera was performed in German in Augsburg (January 21), Leipzig (January 25), Passau (January 31), Budapest (March 3), Graz (May 29), Brünn (June, given by the Karl Hain Society), Bad Godesberg near Bonn (June), Munich (July 11), Warsaw (July 27), Dresden (August 7), Frankfurt am Main (August 16), Linz (August 25), and Hamburg (November 15; the two-hundredth performance was given there on November 2, 1836). Berlin did not hear the opera until May 12, 1794. The five-hundredth performance of the work was celebrated there on September 3, 1905. A sequel to *The Magic Flute*, a heroic comic opera entitled *The Labyrinth or The Battle with the Elements*, with music by Peter von Winter, was produced by Schikaneder in Vienna on June 12, 1798. The Vienna Court Theater first performed *The Magic Flute* on February 24, 1801 and by November 18, 1893 had recorded four hundred performances of the work. It was first heard in Amsterdam, in a Dutch translation by Jan Coenraad Meyer, on April 3, 1799; a Russian production followed in Moscow in 1801, the same year in which a French adaptation, *Les Mystères d'Isis*, was heard at the Paris Opéra. The text was by Etienne Morel de Chédeville and the music by Ludwig Wenzel Lachnith. The production opened on August 20, 1801. A new French translation by Charles Nuitter and Adolphe Beaumont was performed at the Théâtre Lyrique on February 23, 1865; and a third adaptation, by Alexandre Bisson and Paul Ferrier, was seen at the Opéra-Comique on May 31, 1909. A version prepared by Jacques-Gabriel Prod'homme and Jules Kienlin for a production in Brussels in 1912 was presented by the Paris Opéra on December 22, 1922.

The opera was performed in Warsaw in a Polish translation by Wojciech Boguslawski on January 29, 1802, while London first heard the work, in Gamerra's Italian translation, on June 6, 1811, when it was presented in the Haymarket Theatre. Covent Garden performed the work in German on May 27, 1833, and on May 10, 1838 the Drury Lane Theatre performed *The Magic Flute* in an

adaptation by James Robinson Planché. A new English translation by Edward J. Dent was given in Cambridge on December 1, 1911. The opera was heard in Swedish on May 30, 1812, when Hermann Anders Kullberg's translation was performed in Stockholm; and in Danish (Act II only) on March 23, 1816, in a translation prepared for the Copenhagen Royal Theater by Niels Thoroup Bruun. La Scala, Milan, took the work into its repertory on April 15, 1816, but the piece was not revived there until May 12, 1923. New York heard its first *Magic Flute* on April 17, 1833, in an adaptation by Charles Edward Horn. Anders Törneroos translated the opera into Finnish in 1877 (Helsinki, January 12), and Johann Böhm into Hungarian the same year (Budapest, February 17). It was sung in Flemish in Antwerp on March 14, 1896, in Croatian in Zagreb on February 18, 1899 (the translator on this occasion was August Harambašič), in Lettish in Riga on November 28, 1923, in Slovenian in Ljubljana on December 22, 1927, and in Bulgarian in Sofia on May 1, 1931 (in a translation by B. Danovsky). In April 1912 a performance took place in front of the Egyptian pyramids.

The first vocal score of *The Magic Flute* was published, number by number, by the Musikalisches Magazin in der Unteren Breunerstrasse No. 1152 (and 1158) in Vienna in 1791-92, but the first full score did not appear until 1814. It was published in Bonn by Nicolaus Simrock and contained both Italian and German text. The opera was included in the old Mozart Edition in July 1879, and in the Neue Mozart-Ausgabe in 1970.

Production designs throughout the history of the opera

Schikaneder's Freihaustheater was a stone-built structure with a tiled roof. It was 30 meters deep by 15 meters wide, while the stage itself measured 10 meters wide by 12 meters deep. The proscenium opening was at least 9 meters by 4. In Knüppel's *Intimate Letters on the Characteristics of Vienna*, the following details are given concerning the Theater auf der Wieden: "The interior of the house is well equipped, the machines on stage well placed so that major transformations may be carried out." Schikaneder shortened the stage by adding a backdrop behind which he could change the old

In diesen heiligen Hallen

Der Hölle Rache kocht, in meinen Herzen!

Ein Jüngling schön und liebevoll.

zum Ziele führt dich diese Bahn.

Tamino mein, o welch ein Glück!

Pamina mein, o welch ein Glück!

Die Zunge bindet Eid und Pflicht.

bewahret euch vor Weibertücken.

Pa-pa Pa-pa Pa-pa-geno!

Der Vogelfaenger bin ja haysa lustig hopsasa!

Mond, verstecke dich dazu!

Welcher wandert diese Strassen?

sets while a new scene was being played in front of it. In this way he alternated scenes on a "deep" stage with ones on a "short" stage, deploying the entire theatrical apparatus of Baroque stagecraft, including flying machines, conjuring tricks, lions, monkeys, snakes, and resplendent processions. Familiar motifs such as a room, columned hall, courtyard, garden, palace, temple, dungeon, and grottoes formed the basic elements of the sets for the work. The stage scenery was painted by the theater's scene-painters Gayl and Resslthaler. The orchestra comprised 35 musicians (5 first violins, 4 second violins, 4 violas, 3 cellos, 3 double basses, and wind). The original sets from the first production have not survived, but six sets from one of the early stagings of the work, engraved by the brothers Josef and Peter Schaffer, were published in the *Allgemeines Europäisches Journal* in Brünn (modern Brno) in 1795.

The Munich production of 1793 was the first time that *The Magic Flute* was presented on a large-scale stage, when it was introduced to the world of court theaters and staged in the tradition of that well-known family of Italian architects Galli-Bibbiena. The sets were designed by Giuseppe Quaglio, who, together with Lorenzo Quaglio, had created the sets for *Idomeneo* in 1781. Quaglio's designs combine Baroque and Rococo elements, being both decorative and elegant.

Goethe's brother-in-law Christian August Vulpius adapted *The Magic Flute* for a production in Weimar on January 16, 1794, altering the wording of the spoken dialogue and also changing certain details of the staging. For example, Tamino was not pursued by a snake, but by a dragon. The Three Ladies did not kill the dragon, but drove it back into its cave. No illustrations have survived to show what the Weimar production looked like, although there is a water color in Schloss Tiefurt by Georg Melchior Kraus, the director of the Weimar scenery workshop. It depicts the costumes worn by singers during a performance in Weimar in 1794. The style is midway between Baroque

Twelve costume designs for *The Magic Flute* by Johann Baptist Klein of Leipzig, c. 1793

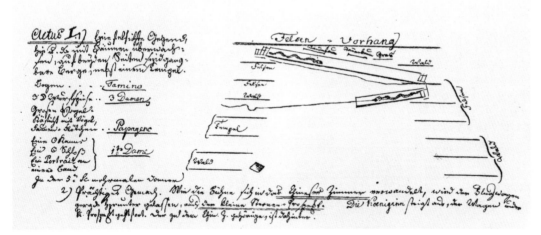

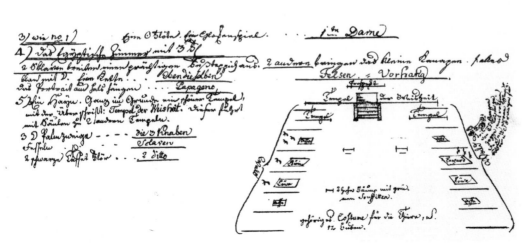

Grand Ducal Court and National Theater, Mannheim, March 29, 1794
At the end of the eighteenth century the Mannheim Theater was noted above all for the picturesque effectiveness of its painted flats. The ledger of the Mannheim prompter Trinkle gives us a good insight into the theater's basic equipment. The actor and writer August Wilhelm Iffland staged *The Magic Flute* in Mannheim on March 29, 1794. Reproduced here are two sketches of the stage area from the ledger: a) the path taken by the serpent, and b) the position of the animals.

229

The Magic Flute

Kärntnertortheater, Vienna, 1812
Costume design for the Queen of Night by Philipp von Stubenrauch. The Queen of Night was sung by Therese Rosenbaum, a pupil of Antonio Salieri's and a daughter of the Court kapellmeister Leopold Florian Gassmann who, in his day, had himself taught Salieri. It was Gassmann who, in 1766, brought Salieri from Venice to Vienna. A libretto for this performance describing *The Magic Flute* as "a grand opera" was published by Johann Baptist Wallishausser of Vienna in 1812.

Teatro alla Scala, Milan, April 15, 1816
Filippo Pistrucci created the costume designs for the first performance of *The Magic Flute* in Italy. They were colored by Vincenzo Batelli and Raniero Fanfani. The scene reproduced here shows Monostatos (Filippo Ricci) and Pamina (Teresa Belloc) wearing the Egyptian Look.

and Romanticism. Tamino appears in a heroic baroque costume, Sarastro in a classically inspired robe, the Three Boys in white tunics. Papageno's costume is modeled on the engraving in the Vienna libretto.

Schikaneder himself restaged the opera in Vienna on November 24, 1798, when Vincenzo Sacchetti created twelve magnificent sets for him. For the Kärntnertortheater, Lorenzo Sacchetti, brother of the foregoing, painted new sets for a production that opened on February 24, 1801. A design depicting the appearance of the Queen of Night shows only clouds, in the middle of which a large crescent moon is suspended, with the Queen of Night standing in the crescent and leaning on a staff. Her classical costume is complemented by a large mantle, crown, and veil. The Paris production of *Les Mystères d'Isis* was set in the ancient Egyptian city of Memphis, thereby subscribing to the contemporary view of Egypt. Bonaparte's Egyptian campaign of 1798-99 was still fresh in the minds of all Frenchmen, who fondly recalled their hero's victory over the Mamluks at the Pyramids and his capture of Cairo. The text was completely rewritten, and far-reaching changes were made. Tamino was not pursued by a serpent, but driven back by flames leaping up out of the ground. Engulfed by fire, he sees the underworld opening up at his feet. Losing his reason, he calls on the gods and believes his end is at hand. The flames suffocate him, and he faints. The Three

Ladies extinguish the fire. The Paris costumes were almost all in white, only Papageno appeared wearing a red costume.

The sets designed by Karl Friedrich Schinkel for a production at the Royal National Theater in Berlin on January 18, 1816 have since become famous. Schinkel combined cool classicism with Romantic ideas, and also used a contre-jour technique. He demanded that the sets be given a "soul" in harmony with the work that was to be performed. It is to the architect and landscape painter Schinkel that we owe an Egyptian *Flute* in which historical architectural forms were structured in a severely frontal and symmetrical style. Sarastro's temple, halls and gardens were inspired by the originals in Luxor and Philae. The palace of the Queen of Night rose up over a fissured rock, its three wings supported by lion-like mythological beasts. Behind the palace Schinkel's famous backdrop spread its starry vault. Before the Queen of Night appeared, the rock and palace vanished, and the entire stage was spanned by a dark blue expanse of stars, while clouds settled on the floor of the stage. The Queen of Night was seen enthroned on a sickle moon in the center of the stage. The three temples combined to form a single, low-built structure with three wings. The forest of palm trees was a narrow gorge in the midst of a fantastical forest, with a mountain lake visible in the distance. The ordeal by fire and water was enacted in a temple hall designed in the

Egyptian style and enclosing a walled pool. The walls of the pool were broken up by grottoes which afforded a glimpse of the sea of flames. The final scene was dominated by a statue of the god Osiris framed by temple buildings. All the structures were engraved with hieroglyphs, and the most important ornament was a winged disk of the sun.

Friedrich Christian Beuther designed new sets for a production in Weimar in 1818. He worked with chiaroscuro effects and used perspective to create a neutral and theatrical view of Egypt. Monumentalism in an archaeologically accurate milieu, of the kind demanded by Goethe, was achieved by means of obelisks, groups of sphinxes, florid capitals and relief decoration showing Egyptian motifs of every description.

Simon Quaglio designed *The Magic Flute* for Munich in 1818 and 1839. His first set of designs may be described as Romantically classicistic, his second as fantastical and neo-Gothic. Quaglio was familiar with Egyptian architecture and created archaeological historicizing structures which often departed from Schikaneder's staging instructions. Egyptian motifs were combined with fantastical fairy-tale elements. A sphinx and pyramid at the back of the stage set the scene for the Queen of Night's empire and localized the action in Egypt, while other sets similarly borrowed elements of Egyptian culture.

Antonio de Pian designed the sets for a new production at the Vienna Kärntnertortheater in 1818. De Pian worked with heavy arches and stark contrasts of light, borrowing freely from Revolutionary architecture. Flats and backdrop formed a unified system of axes that was typical of the nineteenth century as a whole. De Pian was strongly influenced by the architectural engravings of Giambattista Piranesi, and space and light formed a single unity for him.

On August 16, 1818 the Vienna Theater in der Leopoldstadt presented a farce *The Travestied Magic Flute*, words by Karl Meisel and music by Wenzel Müller. Ferdinand Raimund appeared in the role of Wastl.

Production designs throughout the second half of the nineteenth century are notable for their delight in visual images and movement. The new Vienna Court Opera staged *The Magic Flute* on September 1, 1869 in designs by Josef Hoffmann that were large and spacious. Hoffmann's qualifications were chiefly in the area of historical landscape painting, so that he achieved an added sense of depth in the staging of the opening scene, for example,

by using branches, tops of palm trees, agaves, and other tropical plants. The invention of gas lighting meant that sets no longer needed to be sharply outlined: contours dissolved and flowed into each other in an impressionistic manner. Hoffmann's sets were modified in 1906 at Gustav Mahler's bidding. Under Alfred Roller's influence, Francesco Angelo Rottonara made only sparing use of decorative elements in the "magnificent chamber" seen in Act I, Scene 6. Anton Brioschi altered the sets for Act I, Scene 15 so that the deep grove into which the temples disappeared was now replaced by a temple frontage with three doors. The "magnificent Egyptian room" in Act I, Scene 19 was designed by Roller and painted by Brioschi. It was made of heavy, unstructured sections of a wall. The architecture of the designs was indebted to the Secessionist style and may be described as archaically Greek.

A new perspective in set design was opened up by Heinrich Lefler and Josef Urban. Their 1909 production of *The Magic Flute* in Dresden was characterized by towers and ashlars and by a total absence of Egyptian motifs; its economical use of ornament was typical of the Secessionist style. The trials in Act II were played without a break, thanks to the use of moving transformations. In 1913 Bernhard Pankok planned to set *The Magic Flute* in a golden framework and to ensure that all the transformations took place with the speed of lightning, but the outbreak

In 1816, under the direction of the theater manager Count Karl Friedrich Moritz Paul von Brühl, the Berlin artist Johann Heinrich Stürmer designed a series of costume sketches for *The Magic Flute* characterized by their historical authenticity and by their rejection of decorative splendor.

The Magic Flute

Royal Playhouse and Opera House, Berlin, January 18, 1816
Design for the "Entry of the Queen of Night" by Karl Friedrich Schinkel. In the preface to his *Dekorationen auf den beiden kgl. Theaters unter der Generalintendatur des Herrn Grafen Brühl* (Decorations for the Two Royal Theaters under the General Administration of Count Brühl) (Berlin 1819), Schinkel expressed his views on the interrelationship between sets and costumes: "The management here assumes as a basic principle that in the case of each decoration the characteristic element will emerge above all else; indeed, it would not be unreasonable to say that a correct costume must go with the decorations.... A thorough knowledge of the general and specific history of architecture of all ages and nations, the greatest skill and precision in perspective, even a knowledge of archaeology, an exact knowledge of every branch of painting, principally landscape painting and true local color, indeed, even of botany, etc., so that the appropriate forms of trees, plants, rocks, and mountains can be given to each country: these are the essential requirements of what a theater designer must be like."

of the First World War prevented the production from being staged. For his Mannheim production of *The Magic Flute* in 1916 (directed by Carl Hagemann and conducted by Wilhelm Furtwängler), Ludwig Sievert dispensed with all historical associations. Hagemann staged the opera as a "German fairy tale." Instead of creating realistic landscapes, Sievert, whose work was highly decorative, designed luxuriant plants and fantastic flowers, giving the Queen of Night blue and purple colors, while Sarastro's realm was assigned yellow and white. Only the instinctual world of Papageno was colorfully arranged. Hans Wildermann designed three-dimensional sets for Breslau (modern Wrocław) in 1927, but decided against relief effects. He set great store by a neutral stage on which transformations were achieved by the use of light. Equally neutral was the basic color of gray, which can assume any shade under certain lighting conditions. The Greek set-designer Panos Aravantinos transferred Mozart's opera to an imaginary realm, combining numerous oriental stylistic elements and using the full height of the stage, for a production of *The Magic Flute* first seen at Berlin's Theater Unter den Linden on April 28, 1928. For the 1928 Salzburg Festi-

val Oskar Strnad created an architectonically neutral stage consisting of a stepped pyramid, with a fixed oval proscenium passepartout as a Baroque motif. The basic moods of individual scenes were changed by means of a series of drops in different colors from the brightest white to the darkest blue, painted to look like clouds and suspended one behind the other. As with Schinkel, sun symbolism was dominant. For a production at the Berlin Staatsoper am Platz der Republik (Krolloper) in November 1929 Ewald Dülberg created an abstract space without any decorative element. Wilhelm Reinking, known as an objective realist, devised a mixture of oriental and hellenistic stylistic elements for a production in Hamburg in 1940, combining them with Roman arcades and Greek colonnaded rotundas.

The sets designed after the Second World War are not indebted to any one style. For his 1949 production in the Felsenreitschule in Salzburg, Caspar Neher integrated the orchestra pit into the acting area, creating complex structure in keeping with the shape of the space. Columns and pediments underlined the oriental forms that were entwined with decorative garlands, and colonnades and loggias were used to vary the manner of exits

Royal Playhouse and Opera House, Berlin, January 18, 1816

Karl Friedrich Schinkel's set design for the "Temple of the Sun." "The 'Temple of the Sun' (II, 30) is no more than a rough approximation of Schikaneder's ideas. To the left and right are two flats with figures kneeling and praying. Together with the entablature above them, these flats form a portal through which one can see into the inner courtyard of the temple. The courtyard (painted on the backdrop) is bounded at the sides by four temple buildings, but closed off at the back by three huge terraces on which distant buildings, obelisks, enormous flights of stairs, and hanging gardens can be seen. At the very top is a pyramid, its summit disappearing into the clouds. In the center of the courtyard, flanked by sphinx-lined avenues, is a colossal representation of the sun god, towering even higher than the terraces and surmounted by a radiant, serrated nimbus—the sun—which is assumed to be the sole, central source of light. Everything is painted in blurred shades of red and yellow, with harsh, grayish blue shadows. In no other design by Schinkel is the pervasive influence of architectonic design as strong as it is here. Apart from the strikingly megalomaniac trait which is typical of revolutionary architecture in general, all the motives used here may be traced back to ideas which Schinkel was to realize sooner or later," Wolfram Skalicki wrote in *Maske und Kothurn*, 1956.

and entrances. Oliver Messel combined Egyptian and Classical styles in his production for Glyndebourne in 1956. Oskar Kokoschka, who designed *The Magic Flute* for Salzburg in 1955 and for Geneva in 1964, worked with light and space and used expressive colors, creating a large, open, colorful set for the Felsenreitschule in which the fairy-tale, mythic element of the opera was emphasized. He wrote of his Salzburg production: "The Magic Flute should not be Egyptianized, and the sets should not be stylized in a historical, much less 'modern' sense; for in this way only the skeleton of the piece would be visible, its life would be drained away. The Felsenreitschule in Salzburg is a special case, since it is not possible to make any structural alterations, or to increase or remove elements during the performance, but this very fact necessitates the attempt to illustrate the individual scene changes by means of lighting, blackouts, and colored light." In a letter of April 23, 1955 he expressed his views on the character of Papageno: "Papageno is, and always will be, a materialistically orientated, sharp, sweet-toothed, bibulous clown, a figure from the Viennese popular theater, a conventional everyday person of the kind who still existed during the Biedermeier period, bow-ing and scraping at anything unexpected, at the 'great men of the world,' and at the unnatural and eerie events that are beyond his imagination."

Thirteen colored allegories were designed by Marc Chagall for the Met's staging of this opera in New York in 1967. Brightly colored and emblematic allusions to the scene of action merge with Chagall's fantastical dreamworld. His detailed symbolism allows him to create a mythical world which combines human and animal shapes with plant-like forms, fantastic landscapes and elemental representations.

A laser effect was used by Josef Svoboda for the 1970 Munich production by Günther Rennert. In a neutral space he worked with symbolic signs and colored light. For the 1977 Hamburg State Opera production, the Viennese fantastic realist Ernst Fuchs brought his bizarre pictorial language to bear on the world of Papageno, creating a realm of rank and luxuriant vegetation, while Sarastro's realm was based on steps and columns. The designs that David Hockney created for the 1978 Glyndebourne Festival were those of a Pop artist: familiar images such as the temple, Baroque garden, Egyptian columns and pyramids, fire and water, and the repre-

Royal Playhouse and Opera House, Berlin, January 18, 1816
Karl Friedrich Schinkel's set design for the "Garden." "Schinkel transferred this scene to the banks of the Nile and in doing so influenced productions right down to our own day. Even the obligatory Sphinx must date back to Schinkel's solution. The foreground is separated from the river-bank by a stone wall with kneeling figures holding flowerpots. The backcloth depicts the Nile at high tide, a silent expanse lying in the moonlight. In the middle of the river is an island over which a gigantic Sphinx soars, its base also serving as a temple. The doorway and steps, together with the adjacent palms, give an idea of its scale. Behind the Sphinx is a vast expanse of sky stretching as far as the horizon, and in it are suspended remarkable white fleecy clouds and a small (transparent?) moon. The balustrade and Temple of the Sphinx are grayish brown in color, while the sky is a dull grayish blue," according to Wolfram Skalicki in *Maske und Kothurn*, 1956.

Grand Ducal Court Theater, Weimar, 1818
Friedrich Christian Beuther's set design for the "forecourt of the Temple of Isis." Johann Wolfgang von Goethe appointed Beuther to the Weimar Theater in 1815. In his *Tag- und Jahreshefte* he wrote of Beuther as follows: "It was a most opportune appointment that brought the scene-painter Friedrich Beuther to Weimar, for he is an admirable artist, trained in the school of Giorgio Fuentes, and has successfully used perspective to give endless depth to our tiny stage, diversifying it through characterful architecture, and making it highly agreeable through his sense of taste and elegance. Every kind of style has been subjected to his scenographic skill, and he has studied Egyptian and old German architecture at the Weimar Library, giving the pieces which demand these styles a wholly new aspect and a unique splendor."

sentation of the sun were stylized in the manner of Cubist Pop Art and treated like picture-book illustrations. Strong, even harsh, colors dominated the stage picture.

The Magic Flute was made into a film in 1975 by Ingmar Bergman. The film was produced, in a free Swedish translation, to mark the fiftieth anniversary of Swedish Radio. It was made in a Swedish film studio in which the inside of the Drottningholm Court Theater was reconstructed in original detail. Special exhibitions devoted to *The Magic Flute* where held in 1928 in the house in

which Mozart was born in Salzburg, in 1979 in the Max Reinhardt Research Institute in Salzburg ("From the Salzburg Buffoon to the Worldwide Success of *The Magic Flute*"), and in 1985 in the Palazzo della Permanente in Milan ("Intorno al Flauto magico").

The Salzburg productions of *The Magic Flute* in 1967, 1974, and 1978 may be seen as paradigms of production styles during the 1960s and 1970s, and may be described, respectively, as manneristic, machinistic, and unencoded. The 1967 production was by Oscar Fritz Schuh, the 1974 production by

Kärntnertortheater, Vienna, 1818
Set model by Antonio de Pian, reconstructed on the basis of set designs in Vienna's Kärntnertortheater from 1815.
The Venetian designer Antonio de Pian was appointed "Decorateur der k.k. Oberst Hoftheater-Direction" in 1816, and between then and mid-century he designed a vast number of Romantic sets, generally exotic in character.

Kärntnertortheater, Vienna, 1822
Costume design for Sarastro by Moritz Michael Daffinger. It was as Sarastro in this production that Johann Nestroy made his operatic debut on August 24, 1822. From 1823 to 1825 he was contracted to the German Theater in Amsterdam, after which he sang in Brünn, Graz, Pressburg, Lemberg, and Vienna. With his engagement at the Theater an der Wien in 1831 came the beginning of his career as a comedian and dramatist. He was manager of the Vienna Carlstheater from 1854 to 1860 and spent the final years of his life in Graz. He is best known for his magic plays that are indebted to the tradition of the Old Viennese popular theater.

The Magic Flute

Grand Ducal Court Theater, Mannheim, 1834
Joseph Mühldorfer's set design for the "Egyptian Temple Road." This was a standard design and was used in other stage works besides *The Magic Flute*.

Vienna Court Opera, September 1, 1869
Josef Hoffmann's set design for the "Hall of Silence." This production was first seen during Franz von Dingelstedt's three-year intendancy at the Vienna Court Opera (1867-70), and during that time it received 25 performances, making it the most often performed opera in the new house on the Ringstrasse. Wolfram Skalicki describes the gray wash drawing: "An Egyptian columned hall runs from left to right along an acutely angled diagonal. The ground-plan attached to the reverse of the design shows that the hall dissolved into a system of flats. Between the columns a brightly lit hall can be seen, with further temple halls beyond it. The entire layout suggests that Hoffmann used the illustration of an Egyptian temple as his model."

The Magic Flute

Vienna Court Opera, 1874
Franz Gaul's design for the
final apotheosis

Giorgio Strehler; both took place in the Grosses Festspielhaus. Both Schuh and Strehler were assisted by designers who were responsible for the sets and costumes, namely Teo Otto and Luciano Damiani. Both teams were confronted by the task of filling a stage which is not easily adaptable to the scale of Mozart's operas. For the 1978 production Jean-Pierre Ponnelle, appearing as both producer and designer, moved the work to the Felsenreitschule. As early as 1921 Schuh had written in the *Communications of the Salzburg Festival Patrons*, expressing his support for the view that *The Magic Flute* was a fairy-tale mystery. Thus his 1967 staging was predominantly a drama of ideas enacted in the empires of the sun and moon; the action was motivated by ideas, not people, and as a result was transformed into visual images; the symbolic world of the elemental and tellurian was intended to allow the imagination completely free play. Within this framework the individual characters became no more than a decorative element. The victorious forces of light were confronted with the nocturnal realm of daemonic powers. Schuh did not seek to interpret *The Magic Flute* through the roots of suburban Viennese comedy, but staged the work as an example of large-scale world theater. In doing so he deprived the Papageno scenes of their good-natured humor, relegating this earth-bound

character to the edge of the action and having his scenes played out on a side stage. In addition, a number of cuts were made in these scenes. While Schikaneder offers fairy-tale elements, solemn symbolism, farce, magic theater, and Singspiel, Schuh overstylized the action, stylizing even the naïveté of the animals, and emphasizing the operatic, symbolic, and Masonic elements in the work, so that, thanks to Teo Otto's massive sets, it was turned into a larger-than-life spectacular show in gold and silver, weighted down with sculptural ambitions and small-scale craft objects. The wide-screen stage of the Grosses Festspielhaus was made even wider by opening the slats at either side and having flanking plexiglass columns jutting into the orchestra stalls, so that the audience was drawn into the action. The producer was not always successful in focusing attention on the individual singers.

The symbolism of numbers and sequences was evident even during the Overture. The safety curtain, effectively lit, parted to reveal a solid barrier made up of four sections of a wall, which, in the course of the work, could be used as an onstage curtain or as a backdrop for brief scenes and thus facilitate rapid scene-changes. The ellipse for the first scene symbolized an open mountain landscape (only rarely was the full depth of the stage used). Schuh was consistent in applying

Vienna Court Opera, June 1, 1906
Alfred Roller's set design for "Pamina's Scene." *The Magic Flute* was performed as part of a Mozart cycle organized by Gustav Mahler in 1906 to mark the sesquicentennial of the composer's birth. "The series of gala performances of newly staged Mozart operas came full circle yesterday with a performance of *The Magic Flute*. After Hoffmann we now have Roller. After Roller there will be someone else. Perhaps every age needs its own picture books, its own fairy tales and, on stage, its own moons. Roller's moons are distinguished by their poetry and their size; but they rise and then suddenly come to a standstill as though in astonishment. The same is true of the streaks of light that herald the new dawn in *Tristan*. A false aesthetic. A moon that does not move will never destroy the illusion. But once the moon begins its journey across the heavens, we become realistically attuned and demand the logical consequence of its continuing movement. But there is a beautiful, fairy-tale moon in the bower scene, modeled on Schwind, in which Monostatos importunes the sleeping Pamina; and it makes sense to use steps in the scene outside the three temples.... What was new on this occasion seemed not merely new but also good and harmonically suited to the music," Robert Hirschfeld wrote in the *Wiener Zeitung* of June 2, 1906.

his basic concept of a drama of ideas to the work as a whole, logic and density of detail, together with an admirably clear delivery of the text, contributing much to his overall approach. But absurdities were also to be found, as in the first of the Queen of Night's arias, where five larger-than-life men in armor provided a guard of honor.

The sets impressed by virtue of their use of matt shades of gold and silver, and of corresponding shades of yellow, brown, and blue. Brilliant white stood out effectively against an amorphously dark gray-green. The size of the stage influenced the sets, while a sumptuous and fantastical wealth of visual images was channeled into freely stylized forms, communicating a sheen of relative coldness. Sarastro's realm was decorated with colossal zoetropes, large sun disks, stylized laurel branches with gold and silver leaves, allegorical figures with cosmic associations, and unfamiliar shellwork designs. The rocky landscape was a dark and magic creation, a cosmic laboratory at the back of which writhed a bluish snake, more dragon-like than serpentine in its rhythmic contortions. Pamina's chamber was adorned with a white filigree couch; the three temples in the grove (in the first-act finale) had three strangely luminescent doors reminiscent of old archiepiscopal treasures. The subterranean vaults of the temple in which the trials by fire and water took place were hung with rotating mobiles and golden outlines. The animals were larger-than-life: lolloping lions, comical apes, stilt-legged herons were rich in design. Tamino wore oriental silk trousers and an exotic headdress, Pamina an Eastern gown with an Indian red mark on her forehead. Saratro was shaved bald, and the priests moved around in yellow soutanes as though at some Platonic symposion. The Queen of Night sported metallic breasts, and both she and her Three Ladies wore mythical costumes. The Three Ladies, however, were dressed in a smart and discreet light gray, rather than the black that is so often seen. Monostatos appeared in exotic livery.

In Giorgio Strehler's production a fairy tale for adults unfolded against a brightly shining surface that, like a mirror, reflected a picture of humankind. A vast tent was suspended over the stage of the Grosses Festspielhaus, 30 meters wide and 23 meters deep, producing its own transformational dramaturgy by creating mountains, temples and monumental statues and causing forests of palm trees to appear and vanish. The acting area was strung with thin vertical wires along which huge flats ran ceaselessly up and down between the trap and the flies. In this way the scene could be changed in seconds. Strehler aimed at creating a modern equivalent of eighteenth-century theatrical

The Magic Flute

Metropolitan Opera,
New York, November 23,
1912
In the 1912 Metropolitan
Opera production, designed
by Johann Kautsky, Sarastro
(Edward Lankow) entered
on an elephant. The Amer-
ican critic William James
Henderson described it as
"without question the finest
spectacle.... the lyric drama
has known here."

Metropolitan Opera,
New York, November 23,
1912
Georg Heil's costume design
for Papageno.
Giulio Gatti-Casazza, manager of the Met from 1908
until 1935, brought over
designers from Europe.

Württemberg State Theater,
Stuttgart, August 31, 1919
(Grosses Haus)
Producer: Franz Ludwig
Hörth. Designer: Bernhard
Pankok. Conductor: Fritz

Busch.
Bernhard Pankok's costume
design for Monostatos.
His aim with this production
was to set *The Magic Flute*
within a golden frame. Franz
Ludwig Hörth described the
technical advantages of this
system as follows: "At best,
there are some fourteen
scene changes that have to
be mastered with the speed
of lightning; the more primitive the stage machinery
in question, the simpler
these changes have to be
designed. Things have been
made easier during recent
years by having a neutral,
three-dimensional structure
erected behind the proscenium, an extension, as it
were, of the proscenium
arch, which remains in position throughout every scene.
Behind it, painted backcloths
or small three-dimensional
set pieces can then provide
the characteristic features
of the individual scenes."

Städtische Bühnen, Frankfurt am Main, 1921 Producer: Ernst Lert. Conductor: Eugen Szenkar Ludwig Sievert's design for the trial by fire and water. In his book *Mozart auf dem Theater* (Leipzig 1918), Ernst Lert writes as follows on *The Magic Flute*, "We have ignored all Egyptology of the kind that has dominated the work since Goethe's Weimar production, and we have ignored the work's spectacular aspects, nor have we played artistically with modernizations or ideas borrowed from literature and the arts and crafts. We prefer to stick close to the first performance and to Goethe's idea for staging the work. The costumes conform to this histrionic approach. The bird costumes of the animal group are unmissable.... Tamino as a Javanese prince can wear clothes reminiscent of Indian fairy tales. The Queen of Night group is threatening in its silvery black splendor and its costumes are somewhat Greek in their cut. The Three Ladies are first seen wearing hunting costumes, like Baroque Dianas, since spears do not go well with formal dress. Only when they return heavily veiled to they wear court dress."

Théâtre National de l'Opéra, Paris, December 22, 1922 Tamino: Edmond Rambaud. Pamina: Gabrielle Ritter-Ciampi. The Queen of Night: Marguerite Monsy. Sarastro: Albert Huberty. Papageno: Jean Aquistapace. Producer: Pierre Chéreau. Sets based on designs by Jacques Drésa. Conductor: Reynaldo Hahn
The Magic Flute received its first performance in the Palais Garnier on December 22, 1922. It was the 129th new production at the Paris Opéra. The French version was the work of Jacques-Gabriel Prod'homme and Jules Kienlin.

241

The Magic Flute

Stadttheater, Hamburg, 1927 Leopold Sachse's set design for "Sarastro and Priests" (II, 1). Schikaneder's stage direction reads, "The stage represents a forest of palms; all the trees are silvery, with leaves of gold. Eighteen seats of leaves; on each of the seats there stands a pyramid and a large black horn mounted in gold. In the center is the largest pyramid and also the tallest trees. Sarastro and the other priests enter at a solemn pace, each bearing a palm branch in his hand. A March with wind instruments accompanies the procession."

Stadttheater, Hamburg, 1927 Carl Keller's set design for Act I, Scene 9, "An Egyptian Room." Emanuel Schikaneder wrote of this scene, "The stage is transformed into a magnificent Egyptian room."

242

The Magic Flute

Salzburg Festival,
August 18, 1928
(Festspielhaus)
Producer: Lothar Waller-
stein. Conductor: Franz
Schalk
Design for "The Three
Temples" (I, 15) by Oskar
Strnad. The production was
much criticized by the press,
who complained that the
scene-changes took nearly
as long as the musical numbers and that the style of
the production, far from
being unified, combined
archaic and modern elements
in a somewhat naïve fashion.
The costumes, by contrast,
were delightful and sufficiently colorful to compen-
sate for the primitiveness
of the sets.

Staatsoper am Platz der
Republik (Krolloper), Berlin,
November 10, 1929
Producer and designer:
Ewald Dülberg. Conductor:
Otto Klemperer
Set design for "The Three
Temples" (I, 15). Ewald
Dülberg shows himself here
to be a prominent represen-
tative of the Neue Sachlich-
keit movement.

The Magic Flute

Metropolitan Opera,
New York, December 11,
1941 (performances given
in English)
Pamina: Jarmila Novotná.
Sarastro: Alexander Kipnis.
Producer: Herbert Graf.
Designer: Richard Rychtarik.
Conductor: Bruno Walter
Jarmila Novotná emigrated
to the United States in 1939
and sang at the Met until
1956. She had an irresistible
charisma on stage, and she
also enjoyed a notable film
career. Alexander Kipnis
was a member of the Met
ensemble from 1940 to
1946. He had previously
sung in Salzburg and Bay-
reuth. Thanks to his beautiful and expressive bass
voice he was able to invest
the part of Sarastro with
richly resplendent emotion.

Salzburg Festival, 1949-52
(premiered in the Felsenreitschule on July 27, 1949)
Producer: Oscar Fritz
Schuh. Conductor: Wilhelm
Furtwängler
The sets and costumes were
designed by Caspar Neher.
He worked with numerous
sketches from which the
definitive design eventually
crystallized. As is clear from
the sketches, the artist simplified the scenery in the
process of working out the
design. His initial idea was
for two acting levels, but
in the end he settled for
one. The sketch reproduced
here shows the second courtyard leading to the Temple
of Trials.

Salzburg Festival, August 2, 1955 (and 1956; Felsenreit-schule)
Producer: Herbert Graf.
Designer: Oskar Kokoschka.
Conductor: Georg Solti
Costume design for Papageno, incorporating a self-portrait of the artist

Glyndebourne Festival
Opera, July 19, 1956
Tamino: Ernst Haefliger.
Monostatos: Kevin Miller.
Sarastro: Drago Bernadič.
Pamina: Pilar Lorengar.
Papageno: Geraint Evans.
Members of the Glynde-
bourne Festival Chorus.
Producer: Carl Ebert.
Designer: Oliver Messel.
Conductor: Vittorio Gui
Oliver Messel's sets were
a mixture of Egyptian and
classical Roman styles.

Metropolitan Opera,
New York, February 23,
1956 (performances given
in English)
Producer: Herbert Graf.
Designer: Harry Horner.
Conductor: Bruno Walter
Tamino (Brian Sullivan)
and an assortment of ani-
mals. For this scene (Act I,
Scene 15) Schikaneder noted
that, as soon as Tamino
begins to play, "wild animals
of every description enter
in order to listen to him."

246

machinery and at reviving the primitive machine theater of the baroque age, a theater which knew no budgetary limitations. Nonetheless, the machinery did not all function properly, and nineteen days of technical rehearsals were still not enough to get things right. As a result a great deal remained incomplete, whereas a production that had been rehearsed for so many months ought to have worked right down to the very last detail. The world of fairy-tale fantasy and the work's philosophical and metaphysical aspect which the producer had wanted to bring out fell by the wayside, since the technical problems meant that too few rehearsals were used for working with the singers, who had no physical contact on the huge stage. As one critic commented, Papageno jumped around like an oversized piece of popcorn in an oversized pan.

Let us stay with the overdrawn figure of Papageno: Strehler invested him with *commedia dell'arte* elements, in spite of the fact that the work is a *German* Singspiel; he was stripped of his feathery costume, and rigged out instead in a hat and cloak adorned with

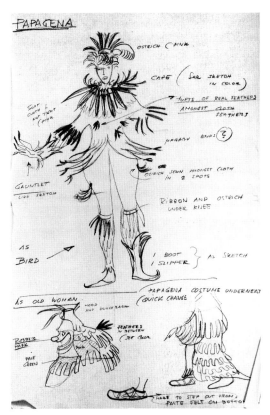

Metropolitan Opera, New York, 1956
Costume design and detailed sketches for Papagena (work copy) by Harry Horner

Metropolitan Opera, New York, c. 1956
Bruno Walter, one of the most distinguished Mozart conductors of his day, is seen here rehearsing *The Magic Flute* with Brian Sullivan (Tamino) and Theodor Uppman (Papageno). In April 1955, while living in Beverly Hills, Walter wrote an essay entitled *Vom Mozart der Zauberflöte*, in which he confessed: "And so I believe that in this final, immortal opera of Mozart's I come closest to the man himself and that I hear his first private confession, nay, the *only* confession that allows us a proper glimpse into the depths of his heart. Just as Shakespeare, after the lifelong anonymity of a dramatist who remains concealed behind the characters of his stage works, finally appears before us in the figure of Prospero in one of his final dramas, *The Tempest*, so I believe that, in *The Magic Flute*, I am confronted by the human personality of Mozart himself. And just as he acquaints us with his ideas on human greatness, wisdom, and closeness to God through his invention of the figure of Sarastro, so we can recognize Mozart himself and his heartfelt striving for a higher humanity in the figure of Tamino, a figure who is drawn towards Sarastro's realm so irresistibly that he submits to all the trials that he is required to undergo if he is to be admitted to that higher world."

247

Komische Oper, East Berlin, February 25, 1954 Tamino: Richard Holm. Producer: Walter Felsenstein. Designer: Rudolf Heinrich. Conductor: Meinhard von Zallinger. According to Schikaneder, the Three Boys arrive in a "flying machine covered in roses."

feathers. Papageno was basically a Truffaldino acrobat with all the wit and charm of a Berliner. As Arlecchino he gorged himself on spaghetti at a lavishly spread table jokingly crying out "Mamma mia, quel servizio!" His aria "Ein Mädchen oder Weibchen" was a dream, which he recounted lying on his back. His partner Papagena was basically a wellbred lady with a feather hat, a Columbine figure from the *commedia dell'arte.* Both characters lacked warmth and sincerity, uprooted as they were from their place of origin, the Viennese suburban theater. Papageno was even allowed to play with the stage machinery. Three times he flew through the air in an air-borne gondola, although, according to Schikaneder, only the Three Boys are entitled to use this form of transport. He was also robbed of his glockenspiel, only Tamino being allowed to play his flute.

Sarastro entered the temple of the sun like some Assyrian potentate astride a golden carriage drawn by six lions. During the chorus "O Isis und Osiris" his priests strolled across the width of the stage, juggling with illuminated building bricks that were piled up to the right and left of the stage. (Schikaneder had asked for a transparent pyramid the size of a lantern.) The spectator was greeted by an empty stage in Strehler's production. Rocks to the right and left in the shape of animals, a steep mountainside and the serpent appeared as though from a magic box during the 39-bar orchestral prelude. The wounded snake con-

tinued to run in a straight line, but in three separate sections.

With its prodigious technical and financial extravagance, Strehler's total domination over the production drove the music into the background. He cut Schikaneder's text and turned the opera into a monster spectacle—Pamina, for example, was held prisoner beneath the belly of a huge Babylonian lion. The constant movement up and down, the world of images that floated in, however fascinating, diverted attention from the music, and the visual gags could be appreciated only at the expense of the aural impression.

Damiani's stage was a conglomerate of Greek, Egyptian, and Oriental elements on the Baroque model. Schinkel's classicistically Romantic versions of the temple and sky were redefined for the modern theater. The theater in general was interpreted as the *teatro all'italiana,* as a theater of wondrous events and magic (shimmering silver mountains, iridescent blue-green grottoes, and painted forests of palm trees). The actors were dwarfed by the lion reliefs, made of expanded polystyrene and measuring 9 meters long and 4.5 meters high, while the Queen of Night was visible only as a miniature figurine from the back rows of the stalls.

In his 1978 production Jean-Pierre Ponnelle gave equal and proper weight to the work's disparate elements as an Oriental fairy tale, a Singspiel derived from the popular Viennese theater of the time, a Masonic myth, a spectacle using stage machines, and a piece of moral didacticism. His characters were men and women of flesh and blood, rather than mere abstract creations. A unity of imagination and intellect was the predominant mood, allowing the textual meaning and music to triumph and hinting discreetly at the opera's symbolism. Ponnelle took as his guide the text of the Neue Mozart-Ausgabe—traditional cuts were opened up—and he produced the opera from the full score, granting primacy to the music and handling the singers in a thoroughly naturalistic way. He filled the space of the Felsenreitschule with highly elaborate stage machines, creating a picturesque landscape in the spirit of the eighteenth century and setting the work in the time of Joseph II. The priests, wearing wigs and long white cloaks over their black court dress, were real people from the eighteenth century, while the Three Boys were Rococo children in their white powdered wigs and black frock coats. The sets depicted a

Tyl Theater, Prague, 1961
Producer: Václav Kašlík.
Conductor: Jaroslav
Krombholč.
Josef Svoboda's basic structure for *The Magic Flute*.
Svoboda studied architecture
in Prague and since 1951
has been chief designer and
technical director at the
National Theater complex
in Prague. In developing
the concept of the "psycho-
plastic stage" he has worked
chiefly with mechanical and
electronic devices, including
light. According to Henning
Rischbieter, "He realizes
spaces, structures, and low-
voltage light walls that are
invented (and therefore
abstract), and divorced from
all historical and local associations. His theater is the
embodiment of illusion-
ism—using the technological
means of today and
tomorrow."

Salzburg Festival, July 26,
1967 (Grosses Festspielhaus)
Pamina: Helen Donath. The
Three Boys: Monique Lo-
basà, Ileana Cotrubas, and
Dwyla Donohue-Schmeiser.
Producer: Oscar Fritz
Schuh. Designer: Teo Otto.
Conductor: Wolfgang
Sawallisch
"We paid special attention
to the fusion of the two
apparently contradictory
worlds of the Queen of
Night and of Sarastro, treat-
ing one as the mirror image
of the other.... We placed
our set in a dream world
accentuated visually by a
profusion of architectural
styles and plants, together
with a labyrinthine world
that combined the coldness
of metal with the transparency of glass," Oscar Fritz
Schuh wrote in 1977.

The Magic Flute

Metropolitan Opera, New York, February 19, 1967 Producer: Günther Rennert. Conductor: Josef Krips Set design by Marc Chagall. In an article published in the 1967 Met program book under the title "'The Flute' from Schinkel to Chagall," Rennert wrote that he had first met Chagall in 1964. By that date he had been producing *The Magic Flute* for some twenty years. He discussed the subject matter with the artist, and explained the well-known theatrical characters and situations. They also spoke of the opposition between good and evil which, in keeping with Masonic thought, is expressed in the opposition between night and day. Chagall and Rennert decided to use a stage with movable side sections and walls, flying machines, and curtains. They conceived of *The Magic Flute* not as a fairy tale with music but as a fairy tale that embraces every aspect of human, animal, and vegetable existence such as grief and joy, war and peace, good and evil. The whole of the modern universe was to be represented in all its creative colors and expressive force. In this way, unsuspected possibilities were opened up to Chagall. Every painterly element, every symbol, every color and shape received its own precise significance—Masonic symbols were merely hinted at. "We attempted to avoid a doctrinaire symbolism at all costs."

Bavarian State Opera, Munich, July 14, 1970 Producer: Günther Rennert. Costumes: Erich Kondrak and Anneliese Corrodi. Conductors: Rafael Kubelik and Matthias Kuntzsch

Josef Svoboda's set design, "Circles." "What we *weren't* aiming for was an Egyptian decor or a divine Oriental ritual," Günther Rennert and Josef Svoboda wrote in the Munich program, "but nor did we want a production dominated by the visual symbols of Freemasonry, no classicistic architecture, no colorful fairy tale for children, nor, finally, a retreat into Schikaneder. Musically and thematically, a work like *The Magic Flute* offers us nowadays the chance to use stage spaces which, anonymously, as it were, may consist only of light and color. The mystery of initiation and purification, or, psychologically speaking, the process of individuation that two people undergo in the course of the work, may well be seen as the dramaturgical axis on which the piece turns, and it must therefore be the center of attention. There is no need, however, for a traditional staging. Color and lighting (such as the use of lasers during the central 'trials by fire and water') can be used to create three-dimensional light spaces, thus enabling the visual wealth of the work to conjure up the images and symbols of the mythological parable by means of a process of association."

bleak landscape with rocky prominences, mossy banks and the ruins of a classical civilization between which Sarastro's Masonic temple would rise up solemnly and Papageno's popular Viennese street theater would spring up out of the ground, while the trees themselves came to life. The arcades of the cliff-face, firmly integrated into the overall design, concealed the secrets of Sarastro's empire and opened to disclose the sun and its radiating beams; here, too, the vast circular night sky of the Queen of Night was eerily and enchantingly projected; and here, finally, the serpent was seen, winding its way endlessly over half the hillside, its head so huge as to conceal the Three Ladies.

Papageno, a child of nature wearing Tyrolean suspenders over his feathered costume, entered his realm turning somersaults. A natural landscape, with a backdrop depicting the local countryside painted in a naively primitive style, rose up out of the trap. The birdcatcher was alternately moody and fearful, happy and playful, rejecting the bans that were placed on him, behaving like Schikaneder, speaking in an uninhibited Viennese dialect, fully aware of the fun that is part of the

popular Viennese theater, and catching the birds that were handed to him on poles as he stood on his stage within a stage. Ponnelle gave Papageno an uncommonly lively profile, turning him into the central figure of his interpretation.

The Queen of Night appeared against a web of ten thousand tiny electric bulbs arranged in three concentric galactic rings and depicting a bluishly glittering sea of stars. She did not remain on high, but descended to ground level to negotiate with Tamino for her opening aria.

A sophisticated lighting plot allowed the mood to be constantly changed: Sarastro, for example, entered surrounded by glittering golden theater lions, gleaming sunbeams issuing from the arcades and depicting his empire. The ordeal of fire and water led the lovers through the arcades into a world of dreams created by light. In order to facilitate the most surprising transformations, the arcades of the cliff-face were covered with stone-colored blinds, while the stage floor was closed off by seven traps allowing temples, magic tables, and so on to be transported.

The Magic Flute

Salzburg Festival, July 26, 1974 (Grosses Festspielhaus) Tamino: René Kollo. Papageno: Hermann Prey. The Three Boys: Soloists of the Tölz Boys' Choir. Producer: Giorgio Strehler. Designer: Luciano Damiani. Conductor: Herbert von Karajan
Schikaneder: "The Three Boys enter on a flying machine covered with roses. In the center is a table already beautifully laid. One of the Boys carries the flute, another the bells."
Strehler wrote of his production: "I should like to convey an idea of the form that influenced the theater at the time when *The Magic Flute* was written, by which I mean the magic of theatrical machines.... I have laid great emphasis upon the story, on the fairy tale, which I see as a kind of archetypal fairy tale, the fairy tale to beat all fairy tales. *The Magic Flute* is rescued childhood, eternal childhood. If *The Magic Flute* is correctly staged, it grants us entry to this archetypal fairy tale and to the roots of our childhood. One of the most important things that can be achieved through *The Magic Flute* is to be reminded of our lost childhood."

Glyndebourne Festival Opera, May 28, 1978 Papageno: Benjamin Luxon. Tamino: Leo Goeke. The Three Ladies: Mani Mekler, Patricia Parker, and Nucci Condò. Producer: John Cox. Designer: David Hockney. Conductor: Andrew Davis
This production was taken over by San Francisco Opera on September 19, 1987, when the cast included David Malis as Papageno, Francisco Araiza as Tamino, and Deborah Voigt, Kathryn Cowdrick, and Judith Christin as The Three Ladies. The conductor was Friedemann Layer
The First Lady removes the padlock from Papageno's mouth, so that he can continue his idle chattering.
"If we could give such liars all / A lock their slander to restrain."

Bavarian State Opera, Munich, October 30, 1978
Producer: August Everding.
Conductor: Wolfgang Sawallisch
Jürgen Rose's design for the "old" Papagena (as a stone statue) and the "ideal" one

Cuvilliés Theater, Munich, November 18, 1978
Producer: August Everding.
Conductor: Wolfgang Sawallisch
Jürgen Rose's set design for "Papageno's House" in *The Labyrinth, Or The Battle with the Elements. The Magic Flute: Part Two*, words by Emanuel Schikaneder, music by Peter von Winter
First performed in Vienna on June 12, 1797, this piece draws on the same characters as Mozart's *Magic Flute*. Winter used elements of *opera seria* and *opera buffa* in his two-act heroic comic opera, but the influence of German Singspiel, *tragédie lyrique*, and *opéra-comique* is also in evidence.

253

The Magic Flute

Glyndebourne Festival
Opera, May 28, 1978
Producer: John Cox.
Conductor: Andrew Davis
Set designs by David Hockney.
In their book *Designing
The Magic Flute*, Martin
Friedman and David Hock-
ney discuss the artist's conception of the work. Having
studied the history of *The
Magic Flute* in detail, Hockney came to the conclusion
that there was no question
of choosing any fixed historical period. What he
wanted instead were exotic
forms from various historical
periods, a decision which
led him to study the works
of Paolo Uccello, Giotto,
and Schinkel. Sarastro's
realm was originally in-
tended as an ideal space,
but in the event Hockney
decided in favor of a geo-
metric solution. Since the
Glyndebourne stage is relatively small and does not
allow major scene changes,
he worked with illusionistic
drop curtains in order to
maintain a variety of acting
levels. To these were added
smaller elements such as
rocks, obelisks, and classical
columns that were placed
in front of the drop curtains.
Hockney argued that *The
Magic Flute* represents the
progress from chaos to
order, and he designed his
sets accordingly. For Act I
he created a mountainous
promontory in the realm of
the Queen of Night, and a
multicolored room in Sarastro's palace. The entrance
to the priests' domain was
marked off by three narrow
temples. In Act II we saw
a grove of trees, the temple
courtyard, the temple garden,
the temple hall, a vault, and
two spectacular natural
phenomena, a huge wall of
fire and a larger-than-life
waterfall. The opera ended
with an epiphany: glistening
sunbeams filled the whole
of the stage.

Staatstheater, Dresden,
April 27, 1979
Producer: Harry Kupfer.
Designer: Peter Sykora
Conductor: Siegfried Kurz
Peter Sykora's design sketch
for Scenes 1 and 2. "Why
not surround *The Magic
Flute* with a ruin and place
the most beautiful of all
literary fairy tales in the
ruins of an opera house?
Why not play Mozart's
immortal music in front of,
and on top of, a pile of rubble? Certainly, no wars are
waged in *The Magic Flute*;
human dwellings are not
reduced to rubble, and temples of the mind are not
turned to ashes. But the
fairy tale can be read as a
story that describes how a
new world is built. This
new world is still in a state
of feud with the old one,
but it will rise above its
predecessor's ruins. If we
take account of the fact
that it is not geographic
barriers that divide people
in *The Magic Flute*, but
that each living person carries within his breast the
barrier between good and
evil, then it becomes clear
that a threat to human existence lurks behind any series
of actions. This threat spr-
ings from the life-or-death
struggle between the Queen
of Night and the band of
initiates," Eberhard Schmidt
wrote in the Dresden
program.

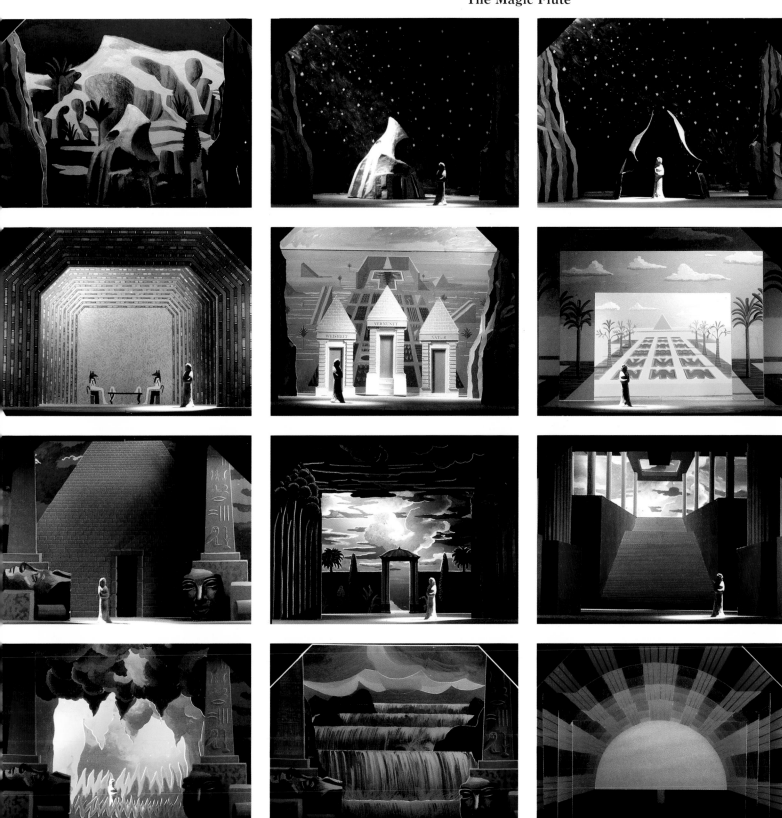

The Magic Flute

Hamburg State Opera, May 20, 1982
Papagena: Marianne Hirsti.
Papageno: Mikael Melbye.
Producer and designer: Achim Freyer. Conductor: Christoph von Dohnányi
"Achim Freyer is a pupil of Brecht who seeks in the theater a field of operation for his painting, an art in which he symbolically expresses human resistance to fossilized customs and constraints. In the case of *The Magic Flute*, he set out from Plato's *Symposium* in which the latter had advanced the theory that there had originally been three sexes. But because the androgynous hermaphrodites, whose breast and back formed a complete circle, had become too powerful for the gods, they were cut into halves, a scene which Freyer portrays in a prelude played out in the opera house foyer. Here he introduces a component that is typical of his work, namely the desire to emphasize the artificiality of the operatic genre and to stress its unreal, surreal form. Tamino, Pamina, the wild animals, people wearing masks that could be touched, Tamino's search for his other half—all this begins in the foyer, from where the hero is led through the auditorium and onto the stage, where he faints at the sight of the evil serpent and dreams of his fantastic journey into the realm of the Temple of the Sun." Thus wrote S. Matuschek in *Das Opernglas*, October 1984.

Hessisches Staatstheater, Wiesbaden, January 29, 1983
Tamino: Dean Schoff. Monostatos: Hubert Delamboye. Sarastro: Georg-Emil Crasnaru. Pamina: Cheryl Studer. Producer: Nikolaus Lehnhoff. Designer: Suzan Pitt. Conductor: Siegfried Köhler
Born in Kansas City, the American artist Suzan Pitt designed colorful costumes and sets for this Wiesbaden staging of the work, into which she introduced a cheerful element of Pop Art.

256

Bregenz Festival, July 24,
1985 (Lake Stage)
Producer: Jérôme Savary.
Designer: Michel Lebois.
Costumes: Michel Dusserrat.
Lighting Designer: Alain
Poisson. Conductor: Theo-
dor Guschlbauer
"Everything moves, every-
thing revolves, on the left
the volcano of evil, on the
right the oasis of good, everywhere there are spitting
fires, sulphurous clouds,
trapdoors opening and closing, flying machines hovering high in the air, fabulous
creatures swimming in from
below across the lake, and
at the end Savary even succeeds in staging what Schikaneder had added to the
end of his work as a hitherto
unrealizable stage direction:
'The stage is transformed
into a sun.' Into a sun which
also explodes," Gotthard
Böhm wrote in *Die Bühne*
in August 1985.

Komische Oper, East Berlin, March 30, 1986
Pamina: Beatrice Niehoff.
Papageno: Maartern Flipse.
Producer: Harry Kupfer.
Designer: Hans Schavernoch. Costumes: Eleonore Kleiber. Conductor: Rolf Reuter

"And there is a deep meaning to the fact that, even before becoming acquainted with the misogynous doctrine of the initiated brotherhood, we hear one of the most remarkable love duets in the whole history of opera sung by Papageno and Pamina. Here are two people, one of whom (Pamina) thinks of the concrete object of her affection, while the other (Papageno) thinks only of the imaginary object of his desire, who come together for a duet about love, as though it were they themselves who ought to sink into each other's arms. The words of this duet, 'A man who feels the pangs of love, he will not lack a gentle heart,' sound very much like a programmatic rejoinder to the view advanced by the brotherhood of priests, a rejoinder that culminates in the splendid formulation, 'In man and wife, in wife and man, twixt men and gods the gulf doth span,'" Eberhard Schmidt wrote in the Berlin program.

Vienna State Opera, March 19, 1988
Three Boys: Soloists from the Vienna Boys' Choir.
Producer: Otto Schenk.
Designer: Yannis Kokkos.
Conductor: Nikolaus Harnoncourt
Yannis Kokkos designed a highly imaginative staging of the work. When asked whether he had ever felt *The Magic Flute* to be a "German opera," Harnoncourt replied, "rather a Viennese one.... *The Magic Flute* is so typically Viennese for me, I see it as part of a typically Viennese tradition of dialogue that includes writers like Raimund and Nestroy, I even think of *Fidelio* as part of this sequence, in other words, people would probably have said 'German' at that time, since Viennese was something quite different." (Quoted in the program booklet.)

Grand Théâtre, Geneva, October 29, 1987
Producer: Benno Besson.
Designer: Jean-Marc Stehlé.
Conductor: Jeffrey Tate
Born in French-speaking Switzerland, Benno Besson spent many years in Berlin as a successful and famous producer with the Berliner Ensemble, before making his debut as an opera producer with this production of *The Magic Flute*.

Opéra National de Belgique, Brussels, June 16, 1982
Vitellia: Christiane Eda-Pierre. Annius: Daphne Evangelatos. Servilia: Christine Barbaux. Sextus: Alicia Nafé. Titus: Stuart Burrows. Publius: Jules Bastin. Producer and designer: Karl-Ernst Herrmann. Conductor: Sylvain Cambreling
Herrmann created an abstract space for *La Clemenza di Tito*, using the space to probe the drama's psychological depth.

La Clemenza di Tito

The historical figure

The Roman Emperor Titus Flavius Sabinus Vespasianus is an enigmatic and rather dubious shady character from first-century Roman history. He began his career as military tribune in Germania and Britain, and from A.D. 67 assisted his father Vespasian in suppressing the Jewish rebellion. From April to September 70 we find him besieging the city of Jerusalem. Following his return to Rome he was appointed praetorian prefect in 71 and censor in 73-74; he held the office of consul on no fewer than seven occasions. Vespasian had doubts about Titus's suitability as his successor: his son was fond of oriental harem life, he maintained a household of eunuchs and dancers, and he had a Jewish mistress, Berenice. He was seen as a latter-day Nero. These apprehensions were not fulfilled, however. On his father's death he assumed the rule of state and showed self-discipline, clemency, and liberality. During his reign Pompeii and Herculaneum were destroyed when Vesuvius erupted on August 24, 79, and a major fire and pestilence broke out in Rome in 80. He offered generous support to all who had suffered, and financed a rebuilding program from his own purse. He showered gifts on the populace, paying for festivities and gladiatorial games. He became popular through his proverbial clemency, and according to Suetonius no one was executed during his reign. His liberality was praised by contemporaries and Suetonius apostrophized him as "amor et deliciae generis humani." A man of great beauty ("corporis dotes"), Titus had an excellent memory, was devoted to the fine arts, a skilled fencer and horseman, and an eloquent orator in Latin and Greek.

The basic text of Mozart's *La Clemenza di Tito* is by the Imperial Court poet Pietro Metastasio and dates from 1734. It was first set by Antonio Caldara and performed on November 4, 1734 in the presence of their "augustissimi sovrani" at the large Vienna Court Theater. It is very much the ideal court opera, the opera of enlightened absolutism. Metastasio's text was set at least 45 times between 1734 and 1839. Only one of these settings, that of Mozart, makes substantial changes to the existent text (see below). From Seneca's time onwards the most distinguished imperial virtue was *clementia*, a virtue which the Austrian royal house claimed for itself and which as *clementia austriaca* assumed the force of a proverbial expression. Karl VI, the last of the old Habsburgs but the first German Habsburg for two centuries, reigned over large sections of Italy, and his Italian subjects called him "Cesare," regarding him as successor to the Roman imperatores. His name day, which Karl VI celebrated on November 4, 1734, was really no reason to pay tribute to a victorious military commander. The War of the Polish Succession had broken out in 1733, involving the whole of Europe, and the Imperial troops suffered a decisive defeat in northern Italy on July 29, 1734.

Voltaire, more than anyone else, helped to popularize Metastasio's work through the praise which he lavished on it. Titus he described as "an eternal lesson to all kings and a delight to all mankind, worthy of a

K. 621

Opera seria in two acts. Words by Caterino Mazzolà after Pietro Metastasio. Begun in Vienna, probably in mid-July 1791 (Vitellia's rondo "Non più di fiori" [No. 23] was written before April 26, 1791). Dated Prague, September 5, 1791. First performed in the Prague National Theater on September 6, 1791. Autograph score: West Berlin, Staatsbibliothek Preussischer Kulturbesitz.

La Clemenza di Tito

Engraved title page of the vocal score: LA CLEMENZA DI TITO / Opera seria / Del Sign. W.A. Mozart / Aggiustata per il Piano Forte / DEL SIGN. A[ugust] E[berhard] MÜLLER / In HAMBURGO PRESSO GÜNTHER E BÖHME / (before 1795). The illustration shows the contrite Sextus before the Roman Senate.

Corneille when he does not declaim and of a Racine when he is not weak."

Metastasio's text was revised for Mozart by the Saxon court poet Caterino Mazzolà, who made various changes, and turned the piece into a "vera opera" by the following artistic means: he cut the text by about a third and removed virtually the whole of Metastasio's second act, since it contained a subplot irrelevant to the main action. Arias and ensembles often resulted from taking existing recitatives and arias and either rewriting them or turning them into verse. Mazzolà shortened Metastasio's recitatives, since closed musical forms were more important for him and Mozart. What is essential is expressed, what is peripheral is cut. Metastasio's basic dramatic principle, the succession of recitative and aria, was broken down and replaced by a sequence of recitative/aria/ensemble with extended finale. Mazzolà made Metastasio's schematicism less rigid, replacing his 25 arias and 4 choruses by 11 arias, 3 duets, 3 trios, 1 quintet, 1 sextet, and 5 choruses. In Mozart's opera the character of the various figures is expressed less by the text than by the music. Mazzolà tightens up the action in order to give the protagonists a clearer profile and to deploy them contrapuntally. He creates two great finales (as was usual at the time), both of which aim at being impressive and spectacular (the first act ends with the burning of the Capitol). Metastasio, by contrast, ended Acts I and II with an aria, and Act III with a chorus. If drama and plot require it, Mozart cuts exit arias, and passes directly into the next scene (No. 23 into

No. 24). In doing so he disregards one of the structural principles of the Metastasian libretto, in addition to robbing the individual singer of any potential applause. Only the theatrical effectiveness of the piece is important to Mozart.

Mazzolà and Mozart extended *opera seria* to the very limits of its possibilities, and in their ensemble technique are already some distance removed from the prototype of the genre. In his music, too, Mozart has eliminated the ballast of the traditional *opera seria*. The sweeping ritornellos have disappeared, the forms have become more concise, the arias are limited to shortened da capos, and the instrumentation is as transparent as in his symphonic works. Mazzolà and Mozart have overcome the limitations of the Metastasian libretto and created a new form of libretto which gives the music more scope.

Origins of the opera

La Clemenza di Tito was commissioned by the Bohemian Estates to mark the coronation celebrations of Leopold II as king of Bohemia. The theme was tailored to suit the new ruler's qualities: during his twenty-five-year rule of Tuscany, Leopold had created a model state of European enlightenment, pursuing an effective policy of neutrality, abolishing torture and the death penalty, and moderating the punishments enshrined in Joseph's Civil Code. He concluded the war with Turkey on August 4, 1791 by signing the Peace of Sistova, and was given the honorary title of "Il Rè Pastore." In speeches and epigrams on Leopold's death there are repeated allusions to the figure of Titus, who had become the symbol of supranational Austrian culture in the eighteenth century. To quote Suetonius, Titus and Leopold became "amor et deliciae generis humani."

The contract requiring an effective festival opera to be written for these celebrations was concluded on July 8, 1791 between the theater manager Domenico Guardasoni and the Bohemian Estates. It emerges from the contract that the Estates were chiefly concerned to engage famous singers—the composer was a matter of indifference to them—and to ensure a magnificent spectacle. It appears to have been Guardasoni alone who chose Mozart. The claim put about by the Bohemian writer and professor of philosophy, Franz Xaver Niemetschek, and frequently repeated ever since, that Mozart

Nationaltheater, Frankfurt am Main, August 22, 1799 Giorgio Fuentes's set design for a "Square in the Vicinity of the Capitol." Fuentes made a name for himself with his spacious and openly classicistic approach to architectonic scene-painting. Goethe, who tried to lure him to Weimar, required his own set designers to produce light painted flats in the style of Fuentes, insisting that they should be varied but that they should also express magnificence, sublimity, and nobility. The *Allgemeine musikalische Zeitung* described the Frankfurt production in its edition of October 16, 1799: "The magnificence with which this opera was given surpassed my own expectations and those of everyone else. Of special note was a phenomenon otherwise found only rarely, whereby good taste and magnificence went hand in hand. Scenery, costumes, and stage properties—in a word, everything down to the very last detail was planned and executed with the greatest precision on the basis of ancient Roman models. All that was required was for the spectator to pay close attention and he was transported back to the days of ancient Rome. The music, at least in retrospect, went so perfectly that we were not aware of a single error, be it ever so small. Of course even here, as with every theater, a number of the roles could have been better cast."

completed *La Clemenza di Tito* "in the short space of eighteen days in Prague," has been called into question by writers on music. It seems more logical to argue that Mozart heard of his commission soon after Guardasoni had signed the contract with the Bohemian Estates, so that he would have had about eight weeks in which to write the opera. It must nonetheless be admitted that Mozart did not hear of the definitive cast in Prague until the middle of August, which means that he wrote the greater part of the opera in three weeks.

Original casting and staging

Mozart's private "Verzeichnüss" contains the following entry: "The 5th of September. [1791] – Performed in Prague on the 6th of September. / La Clemenza di Tito. opera Seria in Due Atti. per l'incoro- / nazione di sua Maestà l'imperatore Leopoldo II – ridotta à / vera opera dal Sig:re Mazzolà. Poeta di sua A: S: l'Elettore di / Sassonia. Atrici: – Sig:ra Marchetti fantozi. – Sig:ra Antonini. Attori. Sig:re Bedini. Sig:ra Carolina Perini / da Uomo / Sig:re Baglioni. Sig:re Campi. – e Cori. – 24 Pezzi. –" (La Clemenza di Tito. Opera seria in two acts. For the coronation of His Majesty the Emperor Leopold II. – Adapted as a *vera opera* by Signore Mazzolà,

poet to His Highness the Elector of Saxony. Actresses: Signora Marchetti Fantozzi, Signora Antonini. Actors: Signore Bedini, Signora Carolina Perini as a man, Signore Baglioni, Signore Campi. And choruses. 24 numbers.")

The singers at the premiere were therefore: Titus Vespasianus, Roman Emperor, Antonio Baglioni (tenor); Vitellia, daughter of the Emperor Vitellius, Maria Marchetti-Fantozzi (soprano); Servilia, Sextus's sister, in love with Annius, Signora Antonini (soprano); Sextus, friend of Titus and in love with Vitellia, Carolina Perini (soprano); Annius, friend of Sextus and in love with Servilia, Domenico Bedini (male soprano); Publius, prefect of the Praetorian Guard, Gaetano Campi (bass).

Antonio Baglioni is already familiar to us as the first Don Ottavio in Mozart's *Don Giovanni*. Maria Marchetti-Fantozzi, had married the tenor Fantozzi in 1788, sang in Naples and Milan, and had enjoyed a successful career in Italy. She is said to have had a full and beautiful voice, to have declaimed well and to have been a good actress, in addition to being good-looking. From Prague she went to Venice in 1791, and later to Berlin. Of Gaetano Campi, a *buffo* bass, we know only that he was a good singer "whose voice is pure, bright, and penetrating, able to

La Clemenza di Tito

National Theater, Frankfurt
am Main, August 22, 1799
Giorgio Fuentes's design
for a "palace with two flights
of stairs leading up to it"

National Theater, Frankfurt
am Main, August 22, 1799
Giorgio Fuentes's design
for "part of a palace with
countryside in the
background"

Teatro alla Scala, Milan, December 26, 1818
Alessandro Sanquirico's design for "Atrio del tempio di Giove Statore." The first Italian production of this opera had taken place two years earlier, on December 26, 1816, at the small Teatro Rè in Milan, when the work had enjoyed a considerable success. The *Allgemeine musikalische Zeitung* of March 5, 1817 commented, "Herr Tramezzani, tenor, sang Sextus, and since we must thank him for having allowed us to hear this glorious opera for the first time in Milan, twenty-five years on, we shall forbear to mention that the role of Sextus belongs to the soprano voice; rather do we admire Herr T. in this same role, and admire him, moreover, as an excellent singer and actor at one and the same time, and as someone who at certain moments in this opera is unsurpassable. Herr [Domenico] Ronconi looked quite good as Titus, and earned a good deal of applause for himself. That worthy young singer Mlle. [Emilia] Bonini also made a valiant attempt at the role of Vitellia.... The decorations by Herr [Giovanni] Pedroni were attractive enough, but we missed the chief decoration—the burning of the Capitol, which was simply hinted at in a very vague way by the rapid appearance and disappearance of a flame; but the music of the first-act finale speaks far too eloquently for us to need the assistance of our eyes to understand what is happening." The production at La Scala two years later was reviewed in the *Allgemeine musikalische Zeitung* of February 10, 1819, but the report was rather more negative in tone.

Stadttheater, Mainz, October 8, 1933
Final tableau of a gala performance held to celebrate the centenary of the Mainz Stadttheater

articulate the most difficult passagework with ease and possessing a thoroughly agreeable tone. He also has the merit of never exceeding his own limitations. His acting is truly funny and never exaggerated, which is why he never entirely pleases our standees." Unfortunately, nothing is known of the other singers, since no register of Guardasoni's troupe has survived.

The sets for the first three scenes (Vitellia's apartments, the Roman Forum, and the Imperial Apartment on the Palatine Hill) were created by Pietro Travaglia, who was employed in the service of Prince Anton von Esterházy. The fourth scene, and presumably also the closing scenes, were designed by Herr Preisig of Koblenz. The new costumes, opulent and graceful, were by Cherubino Babbini of Mantua.

Résumé of the plot

ACT I.   Rooms in Vitellia's house. The young Roman patrician Sextus (Sesto) loves Vitellia, daughter of the deposed Emperor Vitellius. Since Titus has not chosen Vitellia as his wife, in spite of her legitimate claim to the throne, she agrees to marry Sextus, but only on condition that he murder the Emperor. Sextus is prepared to perform the deed although he is Titus's friend and confidant. Another of Sextus's friends, Annius, reports that Titus has dismissed his mistress Berenice. He begs Sextus to help him gain the Emperor's consent to his betrothal to Servilia (Sextus's sister). Sextus agrees to the marriage. The scene changes to a part of the Roman Forum with triumphal arches, obelisks and trophies. To the sounds of loud jubilation the people of Roman welcome Titus to the Forum. He thanks them, but gives them to understand that he sees it as his highest duty to support the needy and to perform good deeds. He informs Sextus of his decision to marry Servilia. When Annius reports this news to his lover, she again assures him of her loyalty. The third scene takes place in the Emperor's gardens on the Palatine Hill. Servilia comes to visit Titus and to confess that her hand is already promised to Annius. Titus generously renounces her in favor of his friend Annius. Incensed at the news that Servilia is to be made Empress, Vitellia orders Sextus to begin the conspiracy without further delay and to comply with her cruel demand. Publius, the captain of the Praetorian Guard, informs Vitellia that Titus is now resolved to ask for her hand in marriage. The scene changes to the Capitol. In her dismay, Vitellia hurries away to find Titus. The conspirators have set fire to the Capitol, causing fear and panic among the populace. Publius is concerned for the Emperor's safety. Distraught, Sextus announces that Titus has fallen by a traitor's hand. Vitellia succeeds in preventing him from accusing himself of the deed.

ACT II.   A pleasant retreat in the Emperor's garden on the Palatine Hill. Sextus confesses his guilt to Annius. The latter advises him not to flee but to entrust himself to the Emperor's clemency, since Titus has not after all perished in the conspiracy. Meanwhile, however, Sextus has been betrayed by Lentulus, the leader of the conspirators. Publius enters, disarms Sextus, and leads him away. The scene changes to a large audience chamber where Roman citizens and ambassadors from foreign countries are assembled. They give thanks for the Emperor's lucky escape. For his own part, Titus shows himself moved by the populace's love and affection. Sextus has confessed to his crime and been sentenced to death by the Senate. The Emperor has still to confirm the sentence. Annius manages to convince Titus that he should listen to Sextus once more. Ashamed of what he has done, Sextus is led into the Emperor's presence. He does not dare to ask for mercy, but begs his forgiveness, that he may die more easily. Sextus is led away, leaving Titus to brood on his manner of government. He would rather be seen as a just and lenient ruler than as a tyrant: Sextus's fate is decided. Servilia is able to convince Vitellia that, in order for Sextus to be pardoned, she must confess to her own complicity. The final scene unfolds in a magnificent square outside the amphitheater in which traitors are torn apart by wild beasts. Vitellia throws herself at Titus's feet, admitting her guilt as instigator of the conspiracy. Titus finally forgives his enemies and shows leniency toward Sextus, Vitellia and all the conspirators. They all entreat the gods to grant a long life to this kindhearted ruler.

The gala premiere of *La Clemenza di Tito* began at 7 o'clock on September 6, 1791. According to Johann Debrois' *Urkunde über die vollzogene Krönung ... Leopold des Zweiten*, published in Prague in 1818, "The usual theater guard was doubled, a division of

carabineers occupied the appropriate positions, and the fire services made additional arrangements. Their Majesties the King and Queen, together with the royal family, honored the National Theater with their presence and were received with loud rejoicing. The theater was as full as could be, without giving rise to a crush, and, out of Prague's well-known obligingness, the first seats were made over to the visitors."

Attended exclusively by the highest social circles, the premiere was not fated to enjoy a brilliant success. The Emperor and Empress arrived late for the opera, and the Empress Maria Louisa is said to have described Mozart's work as "porcheria tedesca" (German filth). Her remark, however, is not attested by contemporary sources but derives from secondary sources of the nineteenth century. Nor is it easy to explain the coarseness of such an expression on the lips of an empress. It is striking that although Leopold II did not receive Mozart in Prague, he had granted him an audience in Florence in 1770, when he was Grand Duke of Tuscany.

The audience had lasted "a good quarter of an hour," according to Leopold Mozart's letter to his wife of April 3, 1770, and the Grand Duke was "uncommonly kind, and asked at once about Nannerl. He said that his wife was most anxious to hear Wolfg." Could it be that her "anxiousness" to hear Mozart had evaporated during the intervening twenty-one years?

A handful of reports have survived describing the premiere of *La Clemenza di Tito*. In the *Krönungsjournal für Prag*, edited by Johann Friedrich Ernst Albrecht or, more probably, by Sophie Albrecht, we read:

"Festivities of the Gentlemen Estates
On the 6th, being coronation day, and in order to celebrate this day for His Majesty, the Estates gave a newly composed opera, the text of which, though based upon Metastasio's Italian, had been adapted by Herr Mazzola, the theater poet in Dresden. The composition is by the famous Mozart, and does him honor, although he did not have much time to write it and was, moreover, afflicted by an

Nationaltheater, Munich, June 20, 1936
Producer: Kurt Barré.
Conductor: Wilhelm Sieben
Leo Pasetti's set design for the "Forum Romanum." Born in Russia in 1892, Pasetti was descended from the Italian set designer and architect Carlo Pasetti (1613-1679). He began his career in Munich, collaborating on the review *Die elf Scharfrichter*, after which he became artistic adviser to the *Münchner Kammerspiele*. He did sterling service as head of design at the Nationaltheater, the Residenztheater, and the Prinzregententheater. His set designs are dominated by a painterly element, and his use of light is particularly suggestive. His "Forum Romanum" is notable above all for its spatial depth.

La Clemenza di Tito

Salzburg Festival,
August 10, 1949
(Landestheater)
Titus: Julius Patzak. Vitellia:
Hilde Zadek. Sextus: Marta
Rohs. Producer: Hans Curjel.
Designer: Hans Erni. Conductor: Josef Krips
The sets by the Lucerne artist Hans Erni are notable for their clear architectonic structuring. The central feature is the huge cylindrical shape of an amphitheater rising straight up. The street leading into the arena breaks up the walls with its shadow effect, while the perspective created by upright structures is used to enhance the sense of depth. Hans Erni's work gives particular emphasis to "space," employing light and shade to invest it with constantly changing dimensions.

number of people, but one can imagine that on such an occasion the demand for tickets is so great that they finally run out, so that many local and foreign visitors, including persons of high degree, were turned away, since they had not come ... with tickets.

"His Majesty appeared at half past seven and was welcomed with loud cheers on the part of all present. The gentlemen members of the Estates themselves collected the tickets, ensuring the requisite degree of order, so that no one might be turned away if he had a ticket and no one might push his way in without one." In the *Diary of the Bohemian Coronation*, published in Prague in 1791, it is said that the Imperial family did not enter their boxes until after 8 o'clock, "whither they were accompanied by general and joyful shouts of 'vivat' as they passed through the streets, the selfsame shouts being heard when Their Excellencies entered the theater itself."

In Franz Alexander von Kleist's *Fantasies on a Journey to Prague*, published in Dresden in 1792, the author notes that the music of *La Clemenza di Tito* is "entirely worthy of its master" and "especially pleasing here is the andante, where his melodies are sufficiently beautiful to entice the celestial beings themselves to earth."

Later performances before a local, middle-class audience proved a success for the

illness during which he had to complete the final part of it.

"The Estates had spared no expense in performing the same, they had sent their entrepreneur to Italy, from where the latter had brought back with him a prima donna and a leading male singer. The title of the opera itself was 'La Clemenza di Tito.' Admission was free, and many tickets had been distributed. The house was filled with a large

Deutsche Oper am Rhein,
Düsseldorf, September 15,
1967
Titus (William Holley) and chorus. Producer: Georg Reinhardt. Designer: Heinrich Wendel. Costumes: Günter Kappel. Conductor: Günther Wich
Mazzolà: "A magnificent chamber leading into a vast amphitheater, the interior of which can be seen through several arches. In the arena, prisoners prepare to be thrown to the wild animals. During the chorus, Titus enters, preceded by lictors, and followed by a retinue of senators, patricians, and members of the Praetorian Guard. Annius and Servilia enter later from different directions" (II, 16).

opera. "All the pieces were applauded," Mozart wrote to his wife in Baden on October 7, 1791.

A commemorative opera

In the eighteenth century, an *opera seria* was a regular part of coronation celebrations, an element in the arsenal of events that added luster to celebrations in princely houses. It gave the coronation the same outward glamor as official celebratory poems. Stage works such as *The Marriage of Figaro* or *Don Giovanni*, or even *The Magic Flute*, would have been felt to be inappropriate on such an occasion, and would even have been a disruptive element in the ceremony. Mozart showed that he could conform in being able to carry out a commission (as was usual at the time) in the shortest possible space of time. In doing so he showed his commitment to an artistic genre whose greatest successes lay in the past, although it was still a living art form in Romance countries. It achieved its impact first and foremost through brilliant coloratura singing. The coloratura passages help to make clear the affections and are suited to the character of the figures on stage. In this way the arias have a twofold function, being both ornamental and an expression of feeling. The coloratura writing is not applied indiscriminately to any word, as was often the case in Mozart's youthful operas, but is deployed in a way that reveals the composer as a tone-painter and psychologist of human emotions. Virtuoso instrumental solos are to be found in Sextus's aria "Parto, ma tu ben mio" (No. 9) and in Vitellia's rondo "Non più di fiori vaghe catene" (No. 23). The first of these is written for obbligato clarinet, the second for obbligato basset-horn. In both of them the composer displays a melodic gift and tonal sense. Vocal line and solo instrument overlap with each other seamlessly. The ensembles aim at psychological contrast. A decorative element of immense power and colorfulness is one of the essential aspects of *opera seria* and suitable as such for a coronation. The Overture is, so to speak, attuned to this mood of high festivity. Mozart has brought nuance and shade to *opera seria*. Gluck and his reform opera may have been his model, but the Salzburg composer writes "more" music, refusing to sacrifice it to the drama.

On December 28, 1791 Constanze Mozart wrote to Luigi Simonetti, first tenor at the Bonn court of the Elector Maximilian, informing him that he would soon be receiving the full score of *La Clemenza di Tito*. She was only awaiting his news before instructing the copyist to proceed. As the price she suggested 100 Kremnitz ducats, a considerable sum for the time—it corresponds to around 3,500 dollars at today's prices.

The first vocal score was prepared by Siegfried Schmiedt and published in 1795 by Breitkopf & Härtel of Leipzig. It was typeset, and included an engraving, *The Burning Capitol*, by Johann Adolf Rossmässler. Other vocal scores were published by T. Mollo & Co of Vienna in 1798 (German and Italian text), Nicolaus Simrock of Bonn in 1800 (prepared by C.G. Neefe and including both Italian and German text), Breitkopf & Härtel in 1803 (August Eberhard Müller), and Stamperia chymique of Vienna in 1804. The first full score with German and Italian words did not

Teatro Colón, Buenos Aires, July 11, 1969
Sextus: Teresa Berganza.
Vitellia: Heather Harper.
Annius: Norma Lerer.
Producer: Joachim Herz.
Designer: Alfred Siercke.
Conductor: Peter Maag
Scene in Act I: Siercke's sets create a three-dimensional impression. The cyclorama is used to establish a picture of ancient Rome with the Capitol.

La Clemenza di Tito

Cologne Opera, 1971
(Premiere: September 10,
1969)
Titus: Werner Hollweg.
Producer and designer: Jean-
Pierre Ponnelle. Conductor:
István Kertész

appear until 1809 and was published in Leipzig by Breitkopf & Härtel. J. Frey published a later score, around 1820, with Italian and French text. The old Mozart Edition brought out the work in December 1882, the Neue Mozart-Ausgabe in 1970.

Renowned productions

The first Viennese production of *La Clemenza di Tito* took place on December 29, 1794 in the Kärntnertortheater. In the *Wiener Zeitung* of December 13, 1794 we read that, "The highest authorities of the Imperial and Royal Court Theater have graciously allowed the undersigned [Constanze Mozart] to organize a musical academy for her own benefit during the present advent season. For this purpose she has chosen one of the best and final works of her late husband, the Imperial and Royal Court music composer, Wolfgang Amade Mozart, whose premature death is as sad for her as it is for art, the music in question being that which he wrote for the Metastasian opera 'La Clemenza di Tito,' and which has not yet been performed here. The general acclaim which has always greeted Mozart's musical works encourages her to hope that the venerable public will honor with its presence a performance of one of her husband's final masterpieces. The day of the performance, and the names of the singers, will be made known at the appropriate time by means of the usual playbills.   Mozart, née Weber."

A concert performance of *La Clemenza di Tito* was given in the Graz Schauspielhaus on September 4, 1795 "for the benefit of Mozart's widow and son." The *Grätzer Zeitung* described the event in its edition of August 28, 1795: "Since it has become clear during the last few years that our venerable local public has developed a taste for Mozart's music, attempts have been made to obtain his final work, the serious opera, 'La Clemenza di Tito,' which he wrote in Prague for the coronation celebrations of the late emperor, His Serene Highness Leopold II, in order to surprise our venerable music lovers in this academy with a masterpiece which, except in Vienna and Prague, is still entirely unknown."

Hamburg heard *La Clemenza di Tito* on February 7, 1796, Berlin on February 28, 1796 (in a concert performance which included highlights of the opera and which was given for Constanze Mozart's benefit). It was presented in Dresden on May 26, 1796 in Friedrich Rochlitz's German translation and in Kassel in March 1797; Budapest saw the piece on June 11, 1798, and on September 8, 1798 it was given in a concert performance in Vienna's Freihaustheater. (The performance was repeated on March 25, 1799). Emanuel Schikaneder wrote on the program: "Mozart's work is beyond all praise. On

Deutsche Oper, Berlin, October 25, 1974
Producer: Winfried Bauern-feind. Conductor: Eugen Jochum
Günter Walbeck's set design for the "Great Audience Chamber," including elements from the world of arts and crafts

hearing this music, as with every other piece that he wrote, one feels only too keenly what art has lost with his death." Constanze's sister Josepha, whose first husband Franz de Paula Hofer had died in 1796 and who had married Friedrich Sebastian Mayer in 1797, sang Servilia, and her husband took the part of Publius.

Further performances of the opera were given in 1798 in Altona, Brünn (modern Brno) (October 4) and Bautzen (December 3). Johann Jakob Ihlee translated *La Clemenza di Tito* into German, probably for a performance in Frankfurt on August 22, 1799. The Frankfurt sets were designed in a classicistic style by Giorgio Fuentes, a successful set-painter particularly highly admired by Goethe, who visited him many times and tried to engage him for Weimar. Anton Radl made two colored mezzotints, based on Fuentes's designs and entitled "Titus in the Senate, Forgiving the Conspirators" and "An Open Space near the Capitol." Christian August Vulpius translated Mazzolà's text into German for a performance in Weimar on December 21, 1799.

In 1801 performances are recorded in Leipzig (January), Munich (February 10), Dessau (August 10), Berlin (October 16), and Bremen (December). Also in 1801, the "law

student" Ignaz von Seyfried provided a free translation of the opera for the Royal and Imperial Theater an der Wien, whose director, Herr Emanuel Schikaneder, held the royal charter. Mannheim heard *La Clemenza di Tito* on August 8, 1802, when it was performed with additional music by Domenico Cimarosa, Joseph Weigl and Peter von Winter; a performance at the Vienna Kärntnertortheater on April 12, 1804 incorporated music by Weigl; and Munich's production on July 21, 1805 had added numbers by von Winter, Johann Christian Cannabich, Joseph Weigl, and Johann Simon Mayr. London heard its first performance of *La Clemenza di Tito* on March 27, 1806 in Italian, in a benefit performance for Elizabeth Billington. "Adapted to the modern stage ... by S[erafino] Buonaiuti," it was performed at the King's Theatre in the Haymarket. During the fall of 1806 a benefit performance for Marianna Sessi was given in Italian in Lisbon's Teatro S. Carlo. Amsterdam and Naples heard the work in 1809 (the latter at the Teatro San Carlo on May 13), and on May 20, 1816 *La Clemenza di Tito* was given in Italian in the Théâtre Royal Italien in Paris. Milanese audiences heard the piece on December 26, 1816 at the Teatro Rè, and on December 26, 1818 at La Scala. A Russian translation was

La Clemenza di Tito

Salzburg Festival, July 29,
1976 (Felsenreitschule)
Vitellia: Carol Neblett.
Sextus: Tatiana Troyanos.
Producer and designer: Jean-
Pierre Ponnelle. Conductor:
James Levine
Emotive passion and enor-
mous extavagance charac-
terized this production in
the Felsenreitschule. It
tended unmistakably toward
Romanticism and grand
opera.

Salzburg Festival,
August 3, 1977
Sextus: Tatiana Troyanos.
Publius: Kurt Rydl. Titus:
Werner Hollweg. Annius:
Anne Howells. Servilia:
Catherine Malfitano. Pro-
ducer and designer: Jean-
Pierre Ponnelle. Conductor:
James Levine (Revival of
the 1976 production)

heard in St. Petersburg on April 24, 1817 and in Moscow on July 23, 1818.

Goethe's set-designer, Friedrich Christian Beuther, created classicistic sets for the Grand Ducal Court Theater in Weimar in 1816, and his designs for the Electoral Court Theater in Kassel in 1820 adopted a similar approach.

A Danish translation (by Niels Thoroup Bruun) was given in Copenhagen on January 29, and a Swedish translation (by Anders Lindberg) in Stockholm on June 23, 1823. On February 15, 1824 Munich saw a revised version of the opera by the Bavarian theater poet and actor Cäsar Max Heigel under the title *King Garibald*. This version was performed to celebrate the twenty-fifth anniversary of the accession of His Majesty King Maximilian Joseph of Bavaria. Additional numbers were composed by the Munich assistant kapellmeister Joseph Hartmann Stuntz.

Louis XII ou La Route de Reims was the title of a pasticcio made up of numbers from *La Clemenza di Tito, The Abduction from the Seraglio*, and *Idomeneo*. Adapted by Jules-Henri Vernoy de Saint-Georges and Joseph-François Stanislas Maizony de Lauréal it was performed on June 7, 1825 in the Théâtre Royal de l'Odéon as an *opéra-comique* in three acts.

La Clemenza di Tito was performed in Hungarian in Budapest in 1830 in a transla-tion by Elek Pály. Carl Bayer created monu-mental sets for a production in Darmstadt in 1859; a pen-and-ink and watercolor entitled *Entrance to the "Circus"* has survived of the sets. In 1871 Hermann Mendel revised the German text, and in 1891 Václav Juda No-votný translated the opera into Czech for the first time for a production in Prague on November 19, 1891. In the same year Jovan Grčić translated the work into Serbian. Wil-helm Kienzl revised the opera for the Royal Court Theater in Munich on April 12, 1893; prose dialogue was used. Anton Rudolph adapted the text for performances in Mann-heim in November 1919. *La Clemenza di Tito* was first performed in English, in a transla-tion by Evelyn and Maisie Radford, at the Falmouth Theater on November 12, 1930; the performance was repeated at London's West Central Hall on February 28, 1931. Joseph Braunstein arranged the opera for Vienna Radio in 1931; and about 1940 Wilhelm Meckbach translated and adapted the opera into German. A new stage version and new translation were prepared by Hans Curjel and Bernhard Paumgartner in 1949, and a further German translation was made by Kurt Honolka in 1971. Folke Abenius translated Mazzolà's text for a production in Göteborg (Gothenburg) on March 17, 1974. In 1976 Walther Dürr produced a literal translation of the Italian text, and Lucette Dausqué translated the opera into French for

Opéra de Lyon, April 22, 1983
Titus: Anthony Rolfe Johnson. Vitellia: Rosalind Plowright. Sextus: Margarita Zimmermann. Annius: Rachel Ann Morgan. Servilia: Rosemary Musoleno. Publius: Dimitri Kavrakos. Producer: Pierre Strosser. Designer: Patrice Cauchetier. Conductor: Theodor Guschlbauer
The Lyons production achieved its impact chiefly through special lighting effects.

La Clemenza di Tito

Wuppertal Opera,
June 8, 1986
Producer and designer: Pet Halmen. Conductor: Peter Gülke
"Having worked closely with Jean-Pierre Ponnelle both in Zurich and on the film of *Tito* in Rome, the designer Pet Halmen had spectacular ideas to offer. Vast symbols superseded each other in suggestively light-filled spaces, from the plunging winged genius of the Overture to enormous statues of warriors, battle chargers, and mothers, and finally to visions of the Colosseo and Trojan's Column. Wafting gauzes and colored walls enclosed the acting area which, in the final scene, was meaningfully transformed into the setting for an oratorio. And, although a newcomer to opera production, Halmen presented a concept of the work that was a plausible attempt to go beyond all stylization and to reveal it as a product of the *Sturm und Drang*. In achieving this aim he made highly conscious use of costume as a means of impeding the action and of reinforcing it," Klaus Kirchberg wrote in *Opernwelt* in May 1986.

a production seen at the Opéra de Lyon during the 1982-83 season. In 1984 David Stivender translated the piece for the Metropolitan Opera Guild New York.

One of the most influential pre-war productions was designed by Leo Pasetti for the Munich National Theater in 1936. The producer was Kurt Barré and the conductor Wilhelm Sieben. Following the end of the Second World War *La Clemenza di Tito* has been taken up into the repertories of more and more of the world's leading opera houses. A selection of important productions may be listed here:

1949: Salzburg Festival. Producer: Hans Curjel. Sets and costumes: Hans Erni. Conductor: Josef Krips.

1962: Prinzregententheater, Munich. Producer: Hans Hartleb. Designer: Helmut Jürgens. Costumes: Sophia Schroeck. Conductor: Meinhard von Zallinger.

Jean-Pierre Ponnelle has enjoyed considerable success with his stagings of the opera, which he has both produced and designed. His productions are set in a Baroque framework that allows rapid changes of scene and which is underlined by a highly musical lighting plot. Ponnelle's productions have

been seen in Cologne in 1969-70 (conducted by István Kertész, this production was later seen at the Sadler's Wells Theatre in 1969 and at the 1981 Edinburgh Festival), in Munich's Cuvilliés Theater in 1971 (conducted by Reynald Giovaninetti), at the 1976 Salzburg Festival (conducted by James Levine), at the New York Met in 1985 (again conducted by Levine), and at the Zurich Opera House in 1986 (conducted by Nikolaus Harnoncourt).

1969: Teatro Colón, Buenos Aires. Producer: Joachim Herz. Designer: Alfred Siercke. Conductor: Peter Maag (Leopold Hager in 1980).

1974: Royal Opera House, Covent Garden, London. Producer: Anthony Besch. Designer: John Stoddart. Conductor: Colin Davis. This production was seen at La Scala, Milan, in 1976.

1974: Aix-en-Provence Festival. Producer: Antoine Bourseiller. Designer: Oskar Gustin. Costumes: Gian-Maurizio Fercioni. Conductor: Alberto Erede.

1974: Deutsche Oper, Berlin. Producer: Winfried Bauernfeind. Designer: Günter Walbeck. Conductor: Eugen Jochum.

274

Wuppertal Opera, June 8, 1986
Titus: Edmund Barham/Alexander Stevenson. Vitellia: Kathleen McCalla. Servilia: Claudia Visca. Sextus: Cornelia Kallisch. Annius: Katharina Dau. Publius: Hartmut Bauer. Producer and designer: Pet Halmen. Conductor: Peter Gülke

Writing in *Musica* magazine in 1986, Dieter Rexroth described Pet Halmen's debut as a producer: "Halmen did all he could to restore to the title role a sense of human seriousness and sombre emotion by giving special emphasis to Tito's agonized indecision. Dramatic credibility gained from the fact that Titus (Edmund Barham) was made to seem passionately concerned about the views of posterity." Halmen's visual imagination was said to involve little more than "designing showcases in whose aseptic ambiance porcelain figures come to life. Of course, danger lurks in such a uniform perspective. The scene in which the Capitol is gutted by fire becomes questionable in the Wuppertal *Tito* because of the apparent aesthetization of brute force: circlets of flame issue from monumental plaster statues of the imperial horse and the grief-stricken populace, but these flames do not so much symbolize danger as trivialize it like a party trick—the scenery usurps the symbol here. The actors, decked out in an economical Prussian variant of the Zurich Mozart costumes, move to and fro in this high-ceilinged, sparsely furnished, and atmospherically cold space as though in a shop window. In the twist that he gives to the production Halmen perpetuates the allusive artificiality of *opera seria*."

1976: Theater an der Wien, Vienna. Producer: Federik Mirdita. Designer: Matthias Kralj. Conductor: Julius Rudel.

1978: Deutsche Oper, Berlin. Producer: Ruth Berghaus. Designer: Marie-Luise Strandt. Conductor: Wolfgang Rennert. Marie-Luise Strandt used a revolving stage within an artificial and severely austere framework, a whitewashed, rectangular shell with several storeys and tiny rooms.

1982: Théâtre de la Monnaie, Brussels. Producer and designer: Karl-Ernst Herrmann. Conductor: Sylvain Cambreling.

1982: Ludwigsburg Festival (German translation by Kurt Honolka). Producer and designer: Ernst Poettgen. Conductor: Wolfgang Gönnenwein. The Ludwigsburg stage was sparsely furnished with Ionic columns and set pieces. The production was notable for being played in modern dress.

1983: Auditorium Maurice Ravel, Lyons. Producer: Pierre Strosser. Designer: Patrice Cauchetier. Conductor: Theodor Guschlbauer.

1983: Holland Festival, Amsterdam. Producer and designer: Filippo Sanjust. Conductor: Hans Vonk.

1983: Nantes Opera. Producer: Jean-José Rieu. Designer: Claire Belloc. Conductor: Vittorio Negri.

1985: Opera House, Bonn. Producer: Maria Francesca Siciliani. Designer: Uberto Bertacca. Conductor: Yehudi Menuhin.

1986: Wuppertal Opera. Producer and designer: Pet Halmen. Conductor: Peter Gülke.

1987: Grand Théâtre, Geneva. Producer: François Rochaix. Designer: Ezio Toffolutti. Conductor: Roderick Brydon.

1987: Opéra-Comique, Paris. Producer: Federik Mirdita. Designer: Rudolf Riescher. Costumes: Gera Graf. Conductor: Christopher Hogwood.

Select Bibliography

Standard Reference Works

Rudolph Angermüller and Otto Schneider, *Mozart-Bibliographie (bis 1970)*, Bärenreiter-Verlag, Kassel, Basel, Tours, London, 1976; *Mozart-Bibliographie 1971-1975 mit Nachträgen zur Mozart-Bibliographie bis 1970*, Kassel etc., 1978; *Mozart-Bibliographie 1976-1980 mit Nachträgen zur Mozart-Bibliographie bis 1975*, Kassel etc., 1982; *Mozart-Bibliographie 1981-1985 mit Nachträgen zur Mozart-Bibliographie bis 1980*, Kassel etc., 1987
For individual operas see the prefaces to the relevant volumes of the new Mozart edition (*Neue Ausgabe sämtlicher Werke*), Bärenreiter-Verlag, Kassel, etc., 1955

General literature on Mozart's musical dramas

Anna Amalie Abert, *Die Opern Mozarts*, Möseler, Wolfenbüttel and Zurich, 1970
Hermann Abert, *W.A. Mozart*, revised and enlarged edition of Otto Jahn's *Mozart*, 7th edition, ed. Anna Amalie Abert, Breitkopf und Härtel, Leipzig, 1966, Index compiled by Erich Kapst
Henry Barraud, *Les cinq grands Opéras*, Editions du Seuil, Paris, 1972
Christopher Benn, *Mozart on the Stage*, Ernest Benn, London, 1946, 2nd ed., 1947; Coward-McCann, New York, 1947
Marcel Brion, *Mozart*, Amiot-Dumont, Paris, 1955
Heinrich Bulthaupt, *Dramaturgie der Oper*, Breitkopf und Härtel, Leipzig, 1887
Hermann Cohen, *Die dramatische Idee in Mozarts Operntexten*, Bruno Cassirer, Berlin, 1915
Leopold Conrad, *Mozarts Dramaturgie der Oper*, Triltsch, Würzburg, 1943
Andrea Della Corte, *Tutto il teatro di Mozart*, ed. Radio italiana, Turin, 1957
Edward Joseph Dent, *Mozart's Operas. A Critical Study*, Chatto and Windus, London, 1913. 2nd ed. Oxford University Press, London, 1947
Alfred Einstein, *Mozart. Sein Charakter. Sein Werk*, S. Fischer Verlag, Frankfurt, 1968. English translation: *Mozart. His Character, his Work...*, by Arthur Mendel and Nathan Broder, Oxford University Press, New York, 1945
Aloys Greither, *Die sieben grossen Opern Mozarts. Versuche über das Verhältnis der Texte zur Musik*, L. Schneider, Heidelberg, 1956

Spike Hughes, *Famous Mozart Operas. An Analytical Guide for the Opera-goer and Arm-chair Listener*, Robert Hale, London, 1957, 1959; Citadel Press, New York, 1959
Stefan Kunze, *Mozarts Opern*, Reclam, Stuttgart, 1984
Ernst Lert, *Mozart auf dem Theater*, Schuster & Loeffler, Berlin, 1918; new edition Deutsche Verlagsanstalt, Stuttgart, 1921
Alfred Loewenberg, *Annals of Opera, 1597-1940*, compiled from the original sources ... with an introduction by Edward J. Dent, W. Heffer & Sons, Cambridge, 1943; 2nd ed. revised and corrected by Franck Walker, 2 vols., Societas Bibliographica, Geneva, 1955; reprinted Roman & Littlefield, New York, 1970.
←William Somervell Mann, *The Operas of Mozart*, Cassell, London, 1977
Hans Merian, *Mozarts Meisteropern*, Leipzig, 1900 [1905].
Ivan Nagen, *Autonomie und Gnade: über Mozarts Opern*, 2nd ed., Hanser, Munich and Vienna, 1985
Carl Niessen (ed.), *Mozart auf dem Theater*, catalogue of special exhibition at the Wallraf-Richartz-Museum, Cologne, 1957
Frits Noske, *The Signifier and the Signified: Studies in the Operas of Mozart and Verdi*, Nijhoff, The Hague, 1977
Charles Osborne, *The Complete Operas of Mozart: a Critical Guide*, Gollancz, London, 1978
Alexander D. Oulibischeff (Ulybyshev), *Mozarts Opern. Kritische Erläuterungen*, Breitkopf und Härtel, Leipzig, 1848
Roland Tenschert, Mozart. *Ein Leben für die Oper*, Frick, Vienna, 1941, 1942, 1945; English translation by Emily Anderson, *Wolfgang Amadeus Mozart*, Karl Gordon, Salzburg, 1952
Horst Weber, "Studien zu Mozarts Musiktheater. Mozarts Verhältnis zum Theater und seine Wirkung auf die Beziehung von Musik und Bühne in dessen dramatischen Werken," Ph.D. diss., Vienna, 1968
Théodore de Wyzewa and Georges de Saint-Foix, *Wolfgang Amédée Mozart. Sa vie musicale et son œuvre... Essai de biographie critique*, 5 vols. (vols 3-5 by G. de Saint-Foix), Paris, 1912-1946

Die Schuldigkeit des Ersten Gebots KV 35

Herbert Klein, "Unbekannte Mozartiana von 1766/67," in: *Mozart-Jahrbuch 1957*, Salzburg, 1958, pp. 168-185
Stefan Kunze, "Tradition und Originalität in Mozarts Frühwerk," in: *W.A. Mozart. Die Schuldigkeit des Ersten Gebots* [Program of the Municipal Theater, Bern], 1978/79, pp. 4-5, 7
Carl Ferdinand Pohl, "Mozarts erstes dramatisches Werk," in: *Allgemeine Musikalische Zeitung* 3 (1865), New Series, no. 14, 5.4.1865, cols. 225-233

David Allen Ruch, "Mozart's 'The Obligation of the First Commandment' K. 35. An Historical Analysis and Performance Edition," M.A. thesis, California State University, Fullerton, California, 1973

Appolo et Hyacinth KV 38

Dietrich Berke, "Apollo und Hyacinth," in: *Programm der Mozart-woche 1975*, Salzburg, 1.24.-2.2.1975, pp. 12-16

Sibylle Dahms, "Apollo und Hyacinth," in: *Programm der Mozart-woche 1981*, Salzburg, 1.23.-2.1.1981, pp. 19-24

Willy Krienitz, "Mozarts 'Apollo und Hyazinth,'" in: *Allgemeine Musikzeitung* 60 (1933), pp. 233-234

Roland Tenschert, "Mozarts 'Apollo und Hyazinthus,'" in: *Schwei-zerische Musikzeitung* 75 (1935), pp. 546-549

— "Die Oper des Elfjährigen," in: *Wiener Figaro* 10 (1939), October/November 1939, pp. 8-9

— "Das Duett Nr. 8 aus Mozarts 'Apollo et Hyacinthus' und das Andante aus der Sinfonia KV. 43 Vergleichende Studie," in: *Mozart-Jahrbuch 1958*, Salzburg, 1959, pp. 59-65

Bastien and Bastienne KV 50 (46 b)

Hermann Aicher, "Bastien und Bastienne und das Salzburger Marionettentheater," in: *Mozart und die Landstrasse*, special issue of the Landstrasser Heimatmuseum, Vienna, 1969, pp. 19-20

Rudolph Angermüller, "Johann Andreas Schachtners 'Bastienne'-Libretto," in: *Mitteilungen der Internationalen Stiftung Mozar-teum* 22 (1974), fasc. 1/2, pp. 4-28

— "Mozart und Rousseau. Zur Textgrundlage von Bastien und Bastienne," in: *Mitteilungen der Internationalen Stiftung Mozarteum* 23 (1975), fasc. 1/2, pp. 22-37

Karl Arnold, "Mozart und die Landstrasse. 200 Jahre 'Bastien und Bastienne' und 'Waisenhausmesse,'" special publication of the Landstrasser Heimatmuseum, Vienna, 1968

Alfred Loewenberg, "Some Stray Notes on Mozart. II. An Unknown Edition of the 'Bastien und Bastienne' Text," in: *Music & Letters* 23 (1942), pp. 319-321

— "'Bastien and Bastienne' once More," in: *Music & Letters* 25 (1944), pp. 176-181

Alfred Orel, "Zu Mozarts 'Bastien und Bastienne,'" in: *Wiener Figaro* 2 (1944), no. 5/6, May/June 1944, pp. 1-8

— "Die Legende um Mozarts 'Bastien et Bastienne,'" in: *Schwei-zerische Musikzeitung* 91 (1951), pp. 137-143

La Finta Semplice KV 51 (46 a)

Rudolph Angermüller, "Ein neuentdecktes Salzburger Libretto (1769) zu Mozarts 'La Finta semplice,'" in: *Die Musikforschung* 31 (1978), pp. 318-322

— "La Finta semplice. Goldoni/Coltellinis Libretto zu Mozarts erster Opera buffa (italienisch-deutsch)," in: *Mitteilungen der Internationalen Stiftung Mozarteum* 30 (1982), fasc. 3/4, pp. 15-72

— "Die vorgesehenen Sänger für die Wiener (1768) und Salzburger (1769) Erstaufführung von Mozarts 'La Finta semplice,'" in: *Wiener Figaro* 50 (November 1983), pp. 3-17

Peter Epstein, "Mozarts erste Oper: La finta semplice," in: *Die Musik* 20 (1927/28), 2nd semiannual vol., fasc. 7, April 1928, pp. 508-512

Bernhard Paumgartner, "La finta semplice—Das schlaue Mäd-chen—La fausse ingénue. Opera buffa in 3 Akten von W.A. Mozart (KV 51)," in: *Internationale Stiftung Mozarteum, Mozart- Festwoche 1956* (Program), pp. 3-7

Géza Rech, "Mozarts 'La Finta semplice,'" in: *Österreichische Musikzeitschrift* 11 (1956), pp. 12-14

Mitridate, Rè di Ponto KV 87 (74 a)

Jean-Michel Brèque, "Mithridate, de Racine à Mozart," in: *L'Avant-Scène Opéra*, no. 54, Paris, July 1983, pp. 8-13

Friedrich Chrysander, "Mitridate, italienische Oper von Mozart," in: *Allgemeine Musikalische Zeitung*, Leipzig 16 (1881), no. 50, 12.14.1881, cols. 785-788, no. 51, 12.21.1881, cols. 801-802, no. 52, 12.28.1881, cols. 817-821, 17 (1882), no. 1, 1.4.1882, cols. 8-12, no. 2, 1.11.1882, cols. 25-27, no. 3, 1.18.1882, cols. 36-42, no. 4, 1.25.1882, cols. 54-59, no. 5, 2.1.1882, cols. 70-74, no. 6, 2.8.1882, cols. 85-89, no. 7, 2.15.1882, cols. 103-107, no. 8, 22.2.1882, cols. 122-124, no. 52, 27.12.1882, col. 893

Jean-Claude Fall, "Une Tragédie rectifiée," in: *L'Avant-Scène Opéra*, no. 54, Paris, July 1983, pp. 78-81

Pierre Flinois, "Mithridate, une haute figure historique," in: *L'Avant-Scène Opéra*, no. 54, Paris, July 1983, pp. 4-7

Alain Gueulette, "L'Expérience italienne du jeune Mozart à l'élabo-ration de Mithridate," in: *L'Avant-Scène Opéra*, no. 54, Paris, July 1983, pp. 18-23

Carl Maria Haslbruner, "'Mithridates,' die vergessene Mozart-Oper," in: *Wiener Musikzeitung* 1 (1935), no. 10, August 1935, pp. 13-14. A.C. Keys, "Two Eighteenth-Century Racinian Oper-as," in: *Music & Letters* 59 (1978), pp. 1-9

Betulia liberata KV 118 (74 c)

Rudolph Angermüller, "Mozart und Metastasio," in: *Mitteilungen der Internationalen Stiftung Mozarteum* 26 (1978), fasc. 1/2, pp. 12-36

Gerhard Croll, "I fratelli Haydn," in: *Chigiana* 36 (1979), new series, no. 16, Florence, 1984, pp. 53-64

Luigi Ferdinando Tagliavini, "La Betulia liberata," in: Program of the 16th German Mozart Festival, Hanover, 1967, pp. 36-42

Ascanio in Alba KV 111

Sibylle Dahms, "Mozarts Festa teatrale 'Ascanio in Alba,'" in: *Österreichische Musikzeitschrift* 31 (1976), pp. 15-24

Hans Engel, "Hasses Ruggiero und Mozarts Festspiel Ascanio," in: *Mozart-Jahrbuch 1960/61*, Salzburg, 1961, pp. 29-42

Kathleen Kuzmick Hansell, "Opera und Ballet at the Regio Ducal Teatro of Milan, 1771-1776: A Musical and Social History," Ph.D. diss., University of California, Berkeley, 1980

Klaus Hortschansky, "Mozarts Ascanio in Alba und der Typus der Serenata," in: *Analecta Musicologica* 18 (1978), pp. 148-159

Giuseppe Parini, *Descrizione delle feste celebrate in Milano per le nozze delle LL. Altezze Reali l'Arciduca Ferdinando d'Austria e l'Arciduchessa Maria Beatrice d'Este fatta per ordine della R. Corte l'anno delle medesime nozze MDCCLXXI da Giuseppe Parini*, Società tipografica de' Classici italiani, Milan, 1825

Peter Otto Schneider, "Mozarts 'Ascanio in Alba'—szenisch: Bern," in: *Musica* 15 (1961), pp. 448-450

Il Sogno di Scipione KV 126

Josef-Horst Lederer, "Uraufführung einer Mozart-Oper," in: *Öster-reichische Musikzeitschrift* 34 (1979), pp. 26-27

— "Il Sogno di Scipione," in: *Programm der Mozartwoche 1979*, Salzburg, 20.1.-28.1.1979, pp. 24-28

Lucio Silla KV 135

Rudolph Angermüller, *W.A. Mozart. Lucio Silla. Faksimiledruck des Librettos von G. de Gamerra. Mailand, 1772*, With an introduction to the work by Rudolph Angermüller, Munich, 1975

Select Bibliography

Ernst Krause, "Mozart und die Opera seria. Zu Aufführungen des 'Lucius Silla,' 'Idomeneo,' und 'Titus,'" in: *Musik und Gesellschaft* 6 (1956), fasc. 3, March 1956, pp. 12-16

Bernhard Paumgartner, "Zu Mozarts Drama per musica 'Lucia Silla,'" in: Programm of "Lucio Silla" at the Salzburg Festival, 1964

Ernest Warburton, "'Lucio Silla' by Mozart and J.C. Bach," in: *The Musical Times* 126 (1985), 726-730

La Finta Giardiniera KV 196

Anna Amalie Abert, "'La Finta Giardiniera' und 'Zaide' als Quellen für spätere Opern Mozarts," in: *Musik und Verlag. Karl Vötterle zum 65. Geburtstag*, Kassel, 1968, pp. 113-122

Rudolph Angermüller, "Wer war der Librettist von 'La Finta Giardiniera?'" in: *Mozart-Jahrbuch 1976/77*, Kassel, 1978, pp. 1-8

Dietrich Berke, "Zur Entstehung und Überlieferung von Mozarts 'La Finta giardiniera'" in: *Jahrbuch der Bayerischen Staatsoper* [Munich], 1979, pp. 30-34

Frédéric Ligier, "Etude analytique et comparative des airs de: L'infedeltà delusa de Haydn et de La finta giardiniera de Mozart," M.A. thesis in musicology, Université de Paris IV Sorbonne, 1984. Volker Mattern, "Das dramma giocoso 'La Finta giardiniera.' Ein Vergleich der Vertonungen von Pasquale Anfossi und Wolfgang Amadeus Mozart," Ph.D. diss., Heidelberg, 1984

Robert Münster, "Die verstellte Gärtnerin. Neue Quellen zur authentischen Singspielfassung von W.A. Mozarts La Finta giardiniera," in: *Die Musikforschung* 18 (1965), pp. 138-153

— "Die Singspielfassung von W.A. Mozarts 'La finta giardiniera' in den Augsburger Aufführungen von 1780," in: *Acta Mozartiana* 13 (1966), fasc. 2, pp. 43-48

— « W.A. Mozarts 'Gärtnerin aus Liebe.' Italienische opera buffa und deutsches Singspiel," in: Program of the 19th German Mozart Festival, organized by the German Mozart Society, Augsburg, 1970, pp. 22-35

— "Mozarts Münchener Aufenthalt 1774/75 und die Opera buffa 'La finta giadiniera,'" in: *Acta Mozartiana* 22 (1975), fasc. 2, pp. 21-33, 35-37

Il Rè Pastore

Klaus Hortschansky, "'Il Re Pastore.' Zur Rezeption eines Librettos in der Mozart-Zeit," in: *Mozart-Jahrbuch 1978/79*, Kassel, 1979, pp. 61-70

Pierluigi Petrobelli, "'Il Rè pastore': una serenata," in: *Mozart-Jahrbuch 1984/85*, Kassel, 1986, pp. 109-114

Zaide (The Seraglio) KV 344 (336 b)

Alfred Einstein, "Die Text-Vorlage zu Mozarts 'Zaide,'" in: *Acta Musicologica* 8 (1936), fasc. I/II, pp. 30-37

Robert Hirschfeld, "Mozart's 'Zaide' in der Wiener Hofoper," in: *Zeitschrift der Internationalen Musikgesellschaft* 4 (1902/3), pp. 66-71

Werner Hollweg, "Mozarts 'Zaide' im Theater an der Wien," in: *Österreichische Musikzeitschrift* 38 (1983), pp. 215-217

Friedrich-Heinrich Neumann, "Zur Vorgeschichte der Zaide," in: *Mozart-Jahrbuch 1962/63*, Salzburg, 1964, pp. 216-247

Walter Senn, "Mozarts 'Zaide' und der Verfasser der vermutlichen Textvorlage," in: *Festschrift Alfred Orel zum 70. Geburtstag 1959*, Vienna, 1960, pp. 173-186

Idomeneo KV 366

Of fundamental importance is the miscellary: *Wolfgang Amadeus Mozart. Idomeneo 1781-1981. Essays, Forschungsberichte, Katalog mit der Rede zur Eröffnung der Ausstellung von Wolfgang Hildesheimer.* Essays edited by Rudolph Angermüller and Robert Münster; Exhibition and Catalogue: Robert Münster; with the assistance of Margot Attenkofer, Munich, 1981. The volume contains the following contributions: "Das Libretto zu Mozarts 'Idomeneo.' Quellen und Umgestaltung der Fabel" (Kurt Kramer); "'Idomeneo' auf der Opern- und Schauspielbühne des 18. und frühen 19. Jahrhunderts" (Rudolph Angermüller); "Hat Mozart das Libretto zu 'Idomeneo' ausgewählt?" (Daniel Heartz); "Mozarts Münchener Aufenthalt 1780/81 und die Uraufführung des 'Idomeneo'" (Robert Münster); "Das Münchener 'Idomeneo'-Orchester von 1781" (Robert Münster); "Die Musik im 'Idomeneo'" (Walter Gerstenberg); Editionen, Aufführungen und Bearbeitungen des 'Idomeneo'" (Rudolph Angermüller); "Die 'Idomeneo'-Bearbeitung von Lothar Wallerstein und Richard Strauss" (Stephan Kohler); "Die 'Idomeneo'-Bearbeitung von Ermanno Wolf-Ferrari (1931)" (Helmut Hell); "'Idomeneo' in Glyndebourne unter Fritz Busch (1951)" (Sena Jurinac); "Einführung in Mozarts 'Idomeneos': Zu meiner Bearbeitung (1954)" (Winfried Zillig); "Mozarts 'Idomeneo': Ein Gespräch bei den Salzburger Festspielen 1973" (Karl Böhm-Walter Gerstenberg); "Bekenntnis zu 'Idomeneo'" (Wolfgang Sawallisch); "Gedanken zu meiner 'Idomeneo'-Inszenierung in Salzburg" (Oscar Fritz Schuh); "'Mozart ist das Wichtigste in meinem Leben:' aus einem Gespräch mit Jean-Pierre Ponnelle zur Zürcher Inszenierung 1980" (Jean-Pierre Ponnelle); "Inhalt und Musiknummern des Mozartschen 'Idomeneo'" (Rudolph Angermüller); Bibliography (Rudolph Angermüller); 'Idomeneo' Discography (Ulrich Hein).

Anna Amalie Abert, "Idomeneo zwischen opera buffa und Singspiel," in: *Mozart-Jahrbuch 1973/74*, Salzburg, 1975, pp. 158-166

— "Mozarts italianità in Idomeneo und Titus," in: *Analecta Musicologica* 18 (1978), pp. 205-216

Rudolph Angermüller, "Bemerkungen zum Idomeneus-Stoff," in: *Mozart-Jahrbuch 1973/74*, Salzburg, 1975, pp. 279-297

Margret Dietrich, "'Wiener Fassungen' des 'Idomeneo,'" in: *Mozart-Jahrbuch 1973/74*, Salznurg, 1975, pp. 56-76

Walther Dürr, "'Idomeneo': Sprache und Musik," in: *Mozart-Jahrbuch 1973/74*, Salzburg, 1975, pp. 180-190

Cuthbert Girdlestone, "Idoménée... Idomeneo. Transformations d'un thème 1699-1781," in: *Recherches sur la musique française classique* 13 (Paris, 1973), pp. 102-132

Daniel Heartz, "The Genesis of Mozart's Idomeneo," in: *Mozart-Jahrbuch 1967*, Salzburg, 1968, pp. 150-164

— "Idomeneus Rex", in: *Mozart-Jahrbuch 1973/74*, Salzburg, 1975, pp. 7-15

Kurt Kramer, "Antike und christliches Mittelalter in Varescos 'Idomeneo,' dem Librettisten zu Mozarts gleichnamiger Oper," in: *Mitteilungen der Internationalen Stiftung Mozarteum* 28 (1980), fasc. 1/2, pp. 6-20

Jean-Victor Hocquard, *Idoménée, Re di Creta, K.V. 366* Paris, 1982. (Les grands Opéras de Mozart)

C. Mazouer, "'Idomeneo, re di Creta': Mozart et la tragédie," in: *Revue Belge de Musicologie* 36-38 (1982-1984), pp. 133-144

Robert Münster, "Neues zum Münchner 'Idomeneo' 1781," in: *Acta Mozartiana* 29 (1982), fasc. 1, pp. 10-20

Don J. Neville, "'Idomeneo' and 'La Clemenza di Tito': Opera seria and 'Vera Opera'," in: *Studies in Music from the University of Western Ontario* 2 (1977), pp. 138-166; 3 (1978), pp. 97-126; 5 (1980), pp. 99-121; 6 (1981), pp. 112-146; 8 (1983), pp. 107-136

Eduard Reeser, "'Idomeneo' auf dem Theater," in: *Mozart-Jahrbuch 1973/74*, Salzburg, 1975, pp. 46-55

The Abuction from the Seraglio KV 384

Rudolph Angermüller, "'Les Époux Esclaves ou Bastien et Bastienne à Alger.' Zur Stoffgeschichte der 'Entführung aus dem Serail,'" in: *Mozart-Jahrbuch 1978/79*, Kassel, 1979, pp. 70-88

Howard Wesley Balk, "The Mozart Operas and the Director: The Dramatic Meaning of Mozart's Operatic Music, Including a Directiorial Analysis of the Abduction from the Seraglio," Ph.D. diss., Yale University, New Haven, Conn., 1965

Liselotte Blumenthal, *Mozarts englisches Mädchen*, Berlin, 1979. (Transactions of the Saxon Academy of Sciences, Leipzig. Philological-historical Series, vol. 120, fasc. 1.)

Gerhard Croll, "Mozarts 'Entführung aus dem Serail.' Vorbemerkungen zu einem Jubiläum im Jahre 1982," in: *Österreichische Musikzeitschrift* 35 (1980), pp. 351-356

Margaret Ross Griffel, "'Turkish' Opera from Mozart to Cornelius," Ph.D. diss., Columbia University, New York, 1975

Jean-Victor Hocquard, *L'Enlèvement au Sérail (Die Entführung aus dem Serail) précédé de Zaide*, Aubier Montaigne, Paris, 1980. (Les grands Opéras de Mozart.)

Christoph-Hellmut Mahling, "Die Gestalt des Osmin in Mozarts 'Entführung.' Vom Typus zur Individualität," in: *Archiv für Musikwissenschaft* 30 (1973), fasc. 3, 2nd quarter, pp. 96-108

Hanneliese Oelbermann, "Mozarts 'Entführung aus dem Serail' auf der Wiener und Hamburger Bühne," Ph.D. diss., Hamburg, 1945

Walter Preibisch, "Quellenstudien zu Mozarts 'Entführung aus dem Serail.' Ein Beitrag zur Geschichte der Türkenoper," in: *Sammelbände der Internationale Musik-Gesellschaft* 10 (1908/09), ed. Max Seiffert, Breitkopf & Härtel, Leipzig, pp. 430-476

Albert Protz, *Die Entführung aus dem Serail*, Lienau, Berlin 1959, 1961. (Die Oper. Schriftenreihe zum Musikunterricht in den mittleren und höheren Schulen.)

Cesare Questa, *Il Ratto dal Serraglio. Euripide. Plauto. Mozart. Rossini*, Pàtron Bologna, 1979

Christopher Raeburn, "Die Entführungsszene aus 'Die Entführung aus dem Serail,'" in: *Mozart-Jahrbuch 1964*, Salzburg, 1965, pp. 130-137

Géza Rech, "Bretzner contra Mozart," in: *Mozart-Jahrbuch 1969/70*, Salzburg, 1971, pp. 186-205

Wolfgang Sulzer, "Bretzner oder Stephanie d.J. Wer schrieb den Text zu Mozarts 'Entführung'?," in: *Wiener Figaro* 49 (June 1982), pp. 6-34

— "Bretzner gegen Mozart? Ein Protest und seine Folgen," in: *Acta Mozartiana* 29 (1982), fasc. 3, pp. 53-59

L'Oca del Cairo KV 422

Rudolph Genée, "Mozarts Partitur-Entwurf seiner Oper 'L'Oca del Cairo,'" in: *Mitteilungen für die Mozart-Gemeinde in Berlin*, vol. 1, fasc. 9, March 1900, pp. 271-277

Virgilio Mortari, "L'Oca del Cairo di W.A. Mozart," in: *Rivista Musicale Italiana* 40 (1936), pp. 477-481

Hans Ferdinand Redlich, "L'Oca del Cairo," in: *The Music Review* 2 (1941), pp. 122-131

Wolfgang Rehm, "Mozarts Opern-Fragment 'L'Oca del Cairo' und Gazzanigas Opern-Einakter 'Don Giovanni.' Zur Konzertanten Opernaufführung am Mittwoch, dem 20. Jänner," in: *Programm der Mozartwoche 1985*, Salzburg, 1.25.-2.3.1985, pp. 94-138, 152-156

Paul Graf Waldersee, "Varesco's L'Oca del Cairo, nach der Originalhandschrift herausgegeben," in: *Allgemeine Musikalische Zeitung*, Leipzig 17 (1882), no. 44, 11.1.1882, cols. 693-698, no. 45, 11.8.1882, cols. 710-715, no. 46, 11.15.1883, cols. 728-734, no. 47, 11.22.1882, cols. 745-750

Lo Sposo Deluso ossia La Rivalità di Tre Donne per un Solo Amante KV 430 (424 a)

Anonymous, "Eine neuaufgefundene Oper von Mozart," in: *Neue Wiener Musikzeitung* 1 (1852), p. 212

Ernst Reichert, "Don Pedros Heimkehr," in: *Schweizer Musikzeitung* 91 (1951), pp. 249-250

Willi Wöhler, "Mozarts Opernfragmente. Zum 175. Todestage Wolfgang Amadeus Mozarts," in: *Salve Hospes. Braunschweiger Blätter für Musik* 16 (1966), fasc. 12, December 1966, pp. 195-200

Der Schauspieldirektor KV 486

Otto Erich Deutsch, "Mozart und die Schönbrunner Orangerie," in: *Österreichische Musikzeitschrift* 9 (1954), pp. 37-42. Addenda *Österreichische Musikzeitschrift* 12 (1957), pp. 384-386, 13 (1958), p. 3

Rudolph Genée, "Zur Geschichte des Mozartschen Schauspieldirektor und der verschiedenen Bearbeitungen," in: *Mitteilungen für die Mozartgemeinde in Berlin 1896*, fasc. 2, April 1896, pp. 60-62

Stefan Kunze, "Mozarts Schauspieldirektor," in: *Mozart-Jahrbuch 1962/63*, Salzburg, 1964, pp. 156-167

Albert Philipp M(a)clane, "Mozart's 'Der Schauspieldirektor.' An Introduction and Translation of the Original Libretto," Ph.D. diss., University of Washington, Seattle, Washington, 1976

Christopher Raeburn, "Die textlichen Quellen des 'Schauspieldirektor,'" in: *Österreichische Musikzeitschrift* 13 (1958), pp. 4-10

Heinz Schuler, "Mozarts 'Schauspieldirektor.' Gestalten der Uraufführung in der Silhouette," in: *Wiener Figaro* 50 (November 1983), pp. 20-27

The Marriage of Figaro KV 492

Wye Jamison Allanbrook, *Rhythmic Gesture in Mozart. Le Nozze di Figaro and Don Giovanni*, University of Chicago Press, Chicago, 1983

Rudolph Angermüller, *Figaro*. With a contribution by Wolfgang Pütz, "'Le Nozze di Figaro' auf dem Theater," Munich, 1986. [With extensive bibliography.]

Harry R. Beard, "Figaro in England. Productions of Mozart's Opera and the Early Adaptations of it in England before 1850," in: *Maske und Kothurn* 10 (1964), pp. 498-513

Frédéric Mathais Breydert, *Le Génie créateur de W.A. Mozart. Essais sur l'instauration musicale des personnages dans "Les Noces de Figaro," "Don Juan," et "La Flûte enchantée,"* preface by Guy Ferchault, Alsatia, Paris, 1956

Brigid Brophy, "Figaro and the Limitations of Music," in: *Music & Letters* 51 (1970), pp. 26-36

Paolo Emilio Carapezza, *Figaro e Don Giovanni: due folle giornate*, S.F. Flaccovio, Palermo, 1974

Peggie Cochrane and Quita Chavez, *The Marriage of Figaro*, A. & C. Black, London, 1962. (Opera Pocket Books, 2)

Margit Finda, "Mozarts 'Le Nozze di Figaro' auf den Wiener Bühnen," Ph.D. diss., Vienna, 1966

Bernd Gallob, "Mozarts 'Figaro' und Grundformen menschlichen Verhaltens," Ph.D. diss., Vienna, 1970

Jean-Victor Hocquard, *Le Nozze di Figaro de Mozart*, Paris, 1979. (Les grands opéras de Mozart.)

Eduard von Jan, "Figaro," in: *Romanische Forschungen* 56 (1942), pp. 325-344

Karl-Heinz Köhler, "Figaro-Miscellen: einige dramaturgische Mitteilungen zur Quellensituation," in: *Mozart-Jahrbuch 1968/70*, Salzburg, 1970, pp. 119-131

Siegmund Levarie, *Mozart's "Le nozze di Figaro": A Critical Analysis*, Chicago University Press, Chicago, 1952

Ann Livermore, "Rousseau, Beaumarchais, and Figaro," in: *The Musical Quartely* 57 (1971), pp. 466-490

Select Bibliography

Frank Merkling, *The Opera News Book of Figaro*, New York, [1967]. Massimo Mila, *Le Nozze di Figaro*, Turin, 1970

Frits R. Noske, "Social Tensions in Le Nozze di Figaro," in: *Music & Letters* 55 (1969), pp. 45-62

Le Nozze de Figaro. Articles by Lorenzo Arruga, Fedele d'Amico, Giorgio Gualerzi, Guido Piemont, Carlo Marinelli, Sergio Martinotti, Milan, 1974

Martine Ollivier Smith, "Beaumarchais et Mozart: essai d'étude comparée entre le Mariage de Figaro et Les Noces de Figaro," Ph.D. diss., Université de Paris III, 1974

Sonja Puntscher-Riekmann, *Mozart, ein bürgerlicher Künstler. Studien zu den Libretti "Le Nozze di Figaro," "Don Giovanni," und "Così fan tutte,"* Böhlau-Verlag, Vienna, Cologne, and Graz, 1982. (Junge Wiener Romanistik, 4)

Gunter Reiss, "Die Thematik der Komödie in 'Le Nozze di Figaro,'" in: *Mozart-Jahrbuch 1965/66*, Salzburg, 1967, pp. 164-178

Wolfgang Ruf, *Die Rezeption von Mozarts "Le Nozze di Figaro" bei den Zeitgenossen*, Steiner, Wiesbaden, 1977 (Beihefte zum Archiv für Musikwissenschaft, 16)

Hans Ludwig Scheel, "'Le Mariage de Figaro' von Beaumarchais und das Libretto der 'Nozze di Figaro' von Lorenzo Da Ponte," in: *Die Musikforschung* 28 (1975), pp. 156-173

Erich Schenk, "Zur Tonsymbolik in Mozarts 'Figaro,'" in: *Neues Mozart-Jahrbuch"* 1 (1941), pp. 114-134

Alan Tyson, "Le nozze di Figaro: Lessons from the Autograph Score," in: *The Musical Times* 122 (1981), pp. 456-461

Thomas Walton, *Beaumarchais, da Ponte and Figaro. Mozart's The Marriage of Figaro*, in: *Sadler's Wells Opera Books*, John Lane, The Bodley Head, London, 1948, no. 5, pp. 40-48

Il Dissoluto Punito o sia Don Giovanni KV 527

Otello Andolfi, *Don Giovanni di Wolfgang Mozart*, A.F. Formiggini, Rome, 1930

Rudolph Angermüller, "'Les Mystères d'Isis' (1801) und 'Don Juan' (1805, 1834) auf der Bühne der Pariser Oper," in: *Mozart-Jahrbuch 1980-83*, Kassel, 1983, pp. 32-97

— *Don Juan-Register*, Munich, 1987

Christof Bitter, *Wandlungen in den Inszenierungsformen des "Don Giovanni" von 1787 bis 1928. Zur Problematik des musikalischen Theaters in Deutschland*, Bosse, Regensburg 1961. (Forschungsbeiträge zur Musikwissenschaft, 10.)

Fedele d'Amico, *Attorno al "Don Giovanni" di Mozart*, Rome, 1971

Max Chop, *Don Juan. Opera buffa in zwei Aufzügen. Geschichtlich, szenisch und musikalisch analysiert mit zahlreichen Notenbeispielen*, Leipzig, 1912

Friedrich Chrysander, "Die Oper Don Giovanni von Gazzaniga und von Mozart," in: *Vierteljahrsschrift für Musikwissenschaft* 4 (1888), pp. 351-435

Rolf Dammann, "Die 'Register-Arie' in Mozarts Don Giovanni," in: *Archiv für Musikwissenschaft* 33 (1976), fasc. 4, pp. 278-308, and 34 (1977), fasc. 1, pp. 56-78

Don Juan. Analyse d'un mythe. 2 vols., Paris, 1974

Walther Dürr, "Überlegungen zu einer Übersetzung des Don Giovanni," in: *Mozart-Jahrbuch 1971/72*, Salzburg, 1973, pp. 81-88

Hans Heinrich Eggebrecht, *Versuch über die Wiener Klassik. Die Tanzszene in Mozarts Don Giovanni*, Steiner, Wiesbaden, 1971. (Beihefte zum Archiv für Musikwissenschaft, ed. H.H. Eggebrecht, 12)

Karl Engel, *Die Don Juan-Sage auf der Bühne*, Pierson, Dresden and Leipzig, 1887

Theodor Epstein, *Don Giovanni von Mozart. Eine Studie zur Oper auf Grundlage des da Ponte'schen Textes, nebst einer verbesserten Übersetzung des letzteren*, André Offenbach, Frankfurt/Main, 1870

Arturo Farinelli, *Don Giovanni*, Fratelli Bocca, Milan, 1946

Rudolf von Freisauff, *Mozarts Don Juan 1787-1887. Ein Beitrag zur Geschichte dieser Oper*, Salzburg, 1887

Hiltrud Gnüg, *Don Juans theatralische Existenz. Typ und Gattung*, Fink, Munich, 1974

Charles Gounod, *Le Don Juan de Mozart*, Paris, 1890. German translation by Adolf Klages, Leipzig, 1890. English translation by Windeyer Clark and J.T. Hutchinson, R. Cocks & Co., London, 1895

Sabine Henze-Döhring, *Opera seria, opera buffa und Mozarts Don Giovanni. Zur Gattungskonvergenz in der italienischen Oper des 18. Jahrhunderts*, Laaber, Rome, 1986. (Analecta Musicologica, 24)

Nicholas John (ed.), *Don Giovanni*, London and New York, [1983]. (Opera Guide, 18)

Pierre Jean Jouve, *Le Don Juan de Mozart*, Fribourg, 1942; Paris, 1948. English translation by Eric E. Smith, Vincent Stuart, London, 1957.

Friedrich Kugler, *Bemerkungen über Don Juan und Figaro*, Cologne, 1854

Stefan Kunze, *Don Giovanni vor Mozart. Die Tradition der Don Giovanni-Opern im italienischen Buffo-Theater des 18. Jahrhunderts*, Fink, Munich, 1972. (Münchener Universitäts-Schriften. Reihe der Philosophischen Fakultät, 10)

François Lesure, "Le manuscrit de Don Giovanni," in: *Autour de Mozart. La Revue Musicale*, no. 313, Paris, 1978, pp. 55-62

Giovanni Macchia, *Vita, avventure e morte di Don Giovanni*, Bari, 1966. (Universale Laterza, 48.) 2nd edition: Turin, 1978 (Piccola Biblioteca Einaudi, 334)

Oscar Mandel, *The Theater of Don Juan. A Collection of Plays and Views, 1630-1963*, University of Nebraska Press, Lincoln, NE, 1963

Gregorio Marañón, *Don Juan — Legende und Wirklichkeit*, Holle, Darmstadt & Geneva, 1954

Massimo Mila, *Il Don Giovanni di Mozart. Corso monografico di storia della musica*, G. Giappichelli, Turin, 1971

Mozart's Don Giovanni in Prague, Prague, 1987, with contributions by Jiří Hilmera ("The Theatre of Mozart's Don Giovanni"), Tomislav Volek ("Prague Operatic Traditions and the Origin of don Giovanni"), Věra Ptáčková ("Scenography of Don Giovanni in Prague"), Vlasta Koubaská ("Table of Selected Don Giovanni Productions at Prague Theatres")

Franz Walter Müller, "Zur Genealogie von Leporellos Liste," in: *Beiträge zur romanischen Philologie* 9 (1970), fasc. 2, pp. 199-228. Paul Nettl, *Mozart in Böhmen*. Published as the 2nd complete, revised, and augmented edition of Procházak's *Mozart in Prag*, Prague, 1938

Pierluigi Petrobelli, "Don Giovanni in Italia. La fortuna dell'opera ed il influsso," in: *Analecta Musicologica* 18 (1978), pp. 30-51

Gualterio Petrucci, *Il "Don Giovanni" di Mozart*, W. Modes, Rome, 1913

Carroll Milton Proctor, "The Singspiel and the Singspiel Adaptation of Mozart's Don Giovanni: an Eighteenth-Century Manuscript," Ph.D. diss., University of Iowa, Ames, Iowa, 1979

Otto Rank, *Die Don-Juan-Gestalt*, Internationaler Psychoanalytischer Verlag, Leipzig, Vienna, and Zurich, 1924

— *The Don Juan Legend*, translated and edited with an introduction by David G. Winter, Princeton University Press, Princeton and London, 1975

Wolfgang Rehm, "Zur Dramaturgie von Mozarts 'Don Giovanni.' Die beiden Fassungen Prag 1787 und Wien 1788—ein philologisches Problem?," in: *Hamburger Jahrbuch für Musikwissenschaft* 5 (1981), pp. 247-254

Pierre-Jean Remy, *Don Giovanni. Mozart*. Losey [Paris, 1979]

Jacques Rouché, *La Mise en scène de "Don Juan'*, Paris, 1934

Jean Rousset, *Le Mythe de Don Juan*, Paris, [1978] (U Prisme)

Alfons Rosenberg, *Don Giovanni. Mozarts Oper und Don Juans Gestalt*, Prestel, Munich, 1968

Julian Rushton, *W.A. Mozart: Don Giovanni*, Cambridge University Press, Cambridge, 1981. (Cambridge Opera Handbooks)

Armand E. Singer, *The Don Juan Theme, Versions and Criticism: a Bibliography*, West Virginia University, 1965

Paul Stefan, *Don Giovanni. Die Opernlegende von Don Juan, den Versucher und Sucher*, Reichner, Vienna, Leipzig, and Zürich, 1938

Louis Viardeot, "Das autographe Manuskript des 'Don Giovanni' von Mozart," in: *Neue Wiener Musikzeitung* 5 (1856), no. 9, 2.7.1856, p. 33, no. 10, 2.14.1856, pp. 37-38, no. 12, 2.28.1856, p. 46, no. 13, 3.6.1856, pp. 49-50, no. 14, 3.13.1856, pp. 52-53, and in: *Revue et Gazette musicale de Paris* 23 (1856), no. 2, 1.13.1856, pp. 12-13, no. 4, 1.27.1856, pp. 27-29

Karin Werner-Jensen, *Studien zur "Don Giovanni"-Rezeption im 19. Jahrhundert (1800-1850)*, Schneider, Tutzing, 1980. (Frankfurt Beiträge zur Musikwissenschaft, 8)

Brigitte Wittmann (ed.), *Don Juan. Darstellung und Deutung*, Darmstadt, 1976 (Wege der Forschung, 282)

Alfred Freiherr von Wolzogen, *Über die szenische Darstellung von Mozarts Don Juan mit Berücksichtigung des ursprünglichen Textbuches von Lorenzo da Ponte*, Breslau, 1860

— *Don Juan. Auf Grundlage der neuen Text-Übersetzung von B. von Gugler [nach dem Italienischen des Lorenzo da Ponte] neu szeniert und mit Erläuterungen versehen*, Leuckart, Breslau, 1869

Così fan tutte o sia La Scuola degli Amanti KV 588

Of fundamental importance is the miscellany *Così fan tutte: Beiträge zur Wirkungsgeschichte von Mozarts Oper*, edited for the Forschungsinstitut für Musiktheater, Universität Bayreuth, by Susanne Vill, Bayreuth, 1978 (Schriften zum Musiktheater, 2) with the following contributions: "Mozarts 'musikalische Regie'—eine musikdramatische Analyse" (Ludwig Finscher; "Dokumentation zur Uraufführung" (Margret Dietrich); "Gegen Unwahrscheinlichkeit und Frivolität: Die Bearbeitungen im 19. Jahrhundert" (Klaus Hortschansky); "Bemerkungen zu französischen Bearbeitungen des 19. Jahrhunderts" (Rudolph Angermüller); "Das Aufführungsmaterial des Frankfurter Opernarchivs" (Nikolaus Westphal); "Così fan tutte im Angebot der Musikverleger" (Karin Werner-Jensen); "Die Popularisierung der Unmoral: Così fan tutte in der Belletristik" (Hans-Peter Glöckner); "Ein seltenes Beispiel der Rezeption in der philosophischen Ästhetik" (Gisela Glagla); "Die Berichterstattung in den Musikzeitschriften und Tageszeitungen des 19. Jahrhunderts" (Heinz Zietsch); "Mozarts 'Reigen': Zur Wirkungsgeschichte im Fin de siècle" (Horst Weber); "Tendenzen der Fabel: Così fan tutte im Opernführer" (Klaus Hortschansky); "Zwischen Kritik und Provokation: Così fan tutte in den Programmheften" (Peter Ackermann); "Sichtbarer Gesang? Die Konzeption von Lothar Wallerstein und Ludwig Sievert 1928" (Christa Jost); "Meinungen zum Thema: Die Inszenierungen von Carl Ebert 1955; Günther Rennert 1972; Jean-Pierre Ponnelle 1972; András Fricsay 1974" (Susanne Vill); "Das Spiel mit der Wahrheit. Götz Friedrichs Hamburger Inszenierung 1975 und das Berliner Konzept 1962" (Gisela Glagla); "Così fan tutte auf der Schallplatte—Bemerkungen zu einer medienspezifischen Rezeption" (Wolf Kunold); "Publikumsdramaturgie im Musiktheater. Zu Fragen von Rezeption und Kommunikation musikalischer Bühnenwerke" (Volker Klotz); "Aufführungsstatistik 1790-1975" (Susanne Vill); Bibliography (Susanne Vill, Thomas Siedhoff)

Peter Ackermann, "'Così fan tutte.' Zur Rezeption von Mozarts Oper in der Musikwissenschaft," in: *Mitteilungen der Internationalen Stiftung Mozarteum* 33 (1985), fasc. 1-4, pp. 17-24

Gabriele Brandstetter, "So machen's alle. Die frühen Übersetzungen von Da Pontes und Mozarts 'Così fan tutte' für deutsche Bühnen," in: *Die Musikforschung* 35 (1982), pp. 27-44

Edward Joseph Dent, "Mozart's Così fan tutte," in: *Sadler's Wells Opera Books*, London, 1945/46, no. 2, pp. 14-22

Götz Friedrich, "Zur Inszenierungskonzeption 'Così fan tutte.' Komische Oper Berlin 1962," in: *Jahrbuch der Komischen Oper Berlin* 3 (1962/63), pp. 34-56

Nicholas John (ed.), *Così fan tutte*, London and New York, 1983. (Opera Guide, 22)

Kurt Kramer, "Da Ponte's 'Così fan tutte,'" in: *Nachrichten der Akademie der Wissenschaften in Göttingen. I. Philologisch-Historische Klasse 1973*, no. 1

René Leibowitz, "'Così fan tutte' ou La Tragédie sous forme de jeu—Les opéras de Mozart en 1956," in: R. Leibowitz: *Histoire de l'opéra*, Paris, 1959, pp. 49-84

Richard Strauss, *Mozarts "Così fan tutte,"* Vienna, 1911. (Novellen, 24)

Alfred Freiherr von Wolzogen, "Mozart's 'Così fan tutte' auf der deutschen Bühne," in: *Deutsche Musikzeitung* 2 (Vienna, 1961), pp. 137-140, 145-148

The Magic Flute KV 620

Anonymous, Mozart und Schikaneder. *Ein theatralisches Gespräch über die Aufführung der Zauberflöte*, Vienna, 1801

Gloria J. Ascher, *Die Zauberflöte und Die Frau ohne Schatten. Ein Vergleich zwischen zwei Operndichtungen der Humanität*, Francke, Bern, and Munich, 1972

Jacques Chailley, "*La Flûte enchantée. Opéra maçonnique. Essai d'explication du livret et de la musique*, Robert Laffont, Paris, 1968. English translation by Herbert Weinstock, *The Magic Flute, Masonic Opera...*, Gollancz, London, 1972. French editions Paris, 1975 (Les Introuvables, 12) and Paris, 1983 (Nouvelle édition revue et augmentée)

Max Chop, *Die Zauberflöte. Geschichtlich, szenisch und musikalisch analysiert mit zahlreichen Notenbeispielen*, Reclam, Leipzig, 1913, new ed. 1922

Thilo Cornelissen, *Mozarts Zauberflöte*, Lienau, Berlin, 1940 (Die Werkstatt der höheren Schule); 2nd edition, Berlin, 1963. (Die Oper. Schriftenreihe über musikalische Werke)

Decker, Herbert, "Dramaturgie und Szene in Mozarts Zauberflöte," Ph.D. diss., Munich, 1947, published by Bosse, Regensburg, 1949

Edward Joseph Dent, *Mozart's Opera The Magic Flute: Its History and Interpretation*, Cambridge, 1911

Friedrich Götz, *Die humanistische Idee der "Zauberflöte": Ein Beitrag zur Dramaturgie der Oper*, Dresden, 1954. (Studienmaterial für die künstlerischen Lehranstalten der Deutschen Demokratischen Republik. Reihe Theater und Tanz, 10)

Gernot Gruber, "Das Autograph der 'Zauberflöte,'" in: *Mozart-Jahrbuch 1967*, Salzburg, 1968, pp. 127-149

Kurt Honolka, *Papageno. Emanuel Schikaneder. Der große Theatermann der Mozart-Zeit*, Residenz-Verlag, Salzburg and Vienna, 1984

Karl-Heinz Köhler, "Die Aussagefähigkeit des Berliner Mozartnachlasses (Überlieferung—Wirkungsgeschichte—Schaffensprinzipien)—Studien zum Mozartbild der Gegenwart," Habil. thesis, Martin-Luther-Universität, Halle-Wittenberg, [1981]

— "Zu den Methoden und einigen Ergebnissen der philologischen Analyse der 'Zauberflöte,'" in: *Mozart-Jahrbuch 1980-83*, Kassel, 1983, pp. 283-287

Egon Komozynski, *Emanuel Schikaneder. Ein Beitrag zur Geschichte des deutschen Theaters*, Doblinger, Vienna, 1951, 2nd ed. Vienna, 1955

Rupert Lee, *Mozart: The Magic Flute*, Boosey & Hawkes, London, 1947. (Covent Garden Opera Series)

Massimo Mila, *Il Flauto magico di Mozart. Corso monografico di storia della musica*, G. Giappichelli, Turin, 1974

Siegfried Morenz, *Die Zauberflöte. Eine Studie zum Lebenszusammenhang Ägypten-Antike-Abendland*, Böhlau-Verlag, Münster and Cologne, 1952. (Münstersche Forschungen, 5)

Mozart.—Ist die Zauberflöte ein Machwerk?, Munich, 1978. (Musik-Konzepte, 3)

Paul Nettl, *Mozart und die königliche Kunst. Die freimaurerische Grundlage der Zauberflöte*, Wunder, Berlin, 1932. Revised and

Select Bibliography

expanded edition: Musik und Freimaurerei, Bechtle, Esslingen 1956

Christoph Peter, *Die Sprache der Musik in Mozarts Zauberflöte*, Verlag Freies Geistesleben, Stuttgart, 1983

Friedrich Oberkogler, *Wolfgang Amadeus Mozart. Die Zauberflöte. Märchenoper und Mysterienspiel. Eine musikalisch-geisteswissenschaftliche Werkbesprechung*, Vienna: the author, 1975

Alfons Rosenberg, *Die Zauberflöte. Geschichte und Deutung von Mozarts Oper*, Prestel, München 1964. 2nd enlarged edition: Munich, 1972

Wolfram Skalicki, "Das Bühnenbild der 'Zauberflöte,'" Ph.D. diss., Vienna, 1950; also in: *Maske und Kothurn* 2 (1956), fasc. 1, pp. 2-34, fasc. 2, pp. 142-165

Paul Stefan, *Die Zauberflöte. Herkunft, Bedeutung, Geheimnis*, Reichner, Vienna, Leipzig, and Zürich, 1937

Hermann Wolfgang von Waltershausen, *Die Zauberflöte. Eine operndramatische Studie*, Drei Masken Verlag, Munich, 1920. (Musikalische Stillehre in Einzeldarstellungen, 1)

La Clemenza di Tito KV 621

Walther Dürr, "Zur Dramaturgie des 'Titus.' Mozarts Libretto und Metastasio," in: *Mozart-Jahrbuch 1978/79*, Kassel, 1979, pp. 55-61

Joseph Heinz Eibl, "'...una porcheria tedesca'? Zur Uraufführung von Mozarts 'La clemenza di Tito,'" in: *Österreichische Musikzeitschrift* 31 (1976) pp. 329-334

Franz Giegling, "Zu den Rezitativen von Mozarts Oper 'Titus,'" in: *Mozart-Jahrbuch 1967*, Salzburg, 1968, pp. 121-126

— "Metastasios Oper 'La Clemenza di Tito' in der Bearbeitung durch Mazzolà," in: *Mozart-Jahrbuch 1968/70*, Salzburg, 1970, pp. 88-94

— "'La Clemenza di Tito.' Metastasio-Mazzolà-Mozart," in: *Österreichische Musikzeitschrift* 31 (1976), pp. 321-329

Daniel Heartz, "Mozart and his Italian Contemporaries: 'La Clemenza di Tito,'" in: *Mozart-Jahrbuch 1978/79*, Kassel, 1979, pp. 275-293

— "Mozarts 'Titus' und die italienische Oper um 1800," in: *Hamburger Jahrbuch für Musikwissenschaft* 5 (1981), pp. 255-266

Helga Lühning, "Zur Entstehungsgeschichte von Mozarts 'Titus,'" in: *Die Musikforschung* 27 (1974), pp. 300-318

— *Titus-Vertonungen im 18. Jahrhundert. Untersuchungen zur Tradition der Opera seria von Hasse bis Mozart*, Laaber, Rome, 1983. (Analecta Musicologica, 20)

Marita MacClymonds, "Mozarts 'La Clemenza di Tito' and Opera seria in Florence as a Reflection of Leopold II's Musical Taste," in: *Mozart-Jahrbuch 1984/85*, Salzburg, 1986, pp. 61-70

Robert Moberly and Christopher Raeburn, "The Mozart Version of La Clemenza di Tiro," in: *The Music Review* 31 (1970), pp. 285-294

Don J. Neville, "La Clemenza di Tito: Metastasio, Mazzolà and Mozart," in: *Studies in Music from the University of Western Ontario*, London (Ontario) 1 (1976), pp. 124-148

James Paul Parakilas, "Mozarts 'Tito' and the Music of Rhetorical strategy," Ph.D. diss., Cornell University Ithaca, N.Y., 1979

Alan Tyson, "'La Clemenza di Tito' and its Chronology," in: *The Musical Times* 116 (1975), pp. 221-227

Tomislav Volek, "Über den Ursprung von Mozarts Oper 'La Clemenza di Tito,'" in: *Mozart-Jahrbuch 1959*, Salzburg, 1960, pp. 274-286

Adam Wandruszka, "'Die Clementia Austriaca' und der aufgeklärte Absolutismus. Zum politischen und ideellen Hintergrund von 'La Clemenza di Tito,'" in: *Österreichische Musikzeitschrift* 31 (1976), pp. 186-193

William J. Weichlein, "A Comparative Study of Five Musical Settings of 'La Clemenza di Tito,'" Ph.D. diss., University of Michigan, Ann Arbor, Michigan

Index

Index of Names

The numbers in italics refer to the captions

Abenius, Folke 273
Abert, Hermann (1871-1927) 140
Adam, Adolphe Charles
(1803-1856) 141; *141*
Adam, Klaus *190*
Adamberger, Johann Valentin
(1743-1804) 100, 102, 104f., 106, 130
Adamberger, Maria Anna (Nanni),
née Jaquet (1752-1804) 130
Adlgasser, Anton Cajetan
(1729-1777) 11, 13
Adorno, Theodor Wiesengrund
(1903-1969) *201*
Affligio (Afflisio), Giuseppe
(1722-1788) 25, 26, 28f.
Agricola, Johann Friedrich
(1720-1774) 71
Ahlersmeyer, Mathieu (1896-1979) *150*
Ahnsjö, Claes H. (b. 1942) *65, 78*
Aicher, Anton (1859-1930) *21*
Aicher, Friedl (b. 1904) *17, 21, 109*
Aicher, Gretl *21*
Albert, Alfred *170*
Albertarelli, Francesco
(late 18th century) 165
Alberti, Ignaz (fl. c. 1780-1801) 222;
223
Albrecht, Johann Friedrich Ernst
(1752-1814) 266
Albrecht, Sophie, née Baumer
(1757-1840) 266
Aldrovandini, Giuseppe
(c. 1673-1707) 31
Aler, John *67*
Alexander the Great
(356-323 B.C.) 72
Alexander, Roberta (b. 1957) *67, 194*
Algarotti, Francesco (1712-1764) 42
Allegrante, Maddalena (1750-1802) 71,
198
Allen, Thomas (b. 1944) *195*
Altén, Martin (1764-1830) 117
Amara (Armaganian), Lucine
(b. 1927) *185*

Amicis Buonsol(l)azzi, Anna de
ʼ(c. 1733-1816) 50, 51, 52, 54
Anders, Peter (1908-1954) *108*
Andrade, Rosario *191*
André, Johann (1741-1799) 98
André, Johann Anton (1775-1842) 75,
76
Andrésen, Ivar (1896-1940) *103*
Anfossi, Pasquale (1727-1797) 55, 59,
68
Anheisser, Siegfried 64, 73
Anton, Johann Daniel (b. 1801) 204
Antonini, Signora 263
Apell, David August von (1754-1832) 87
Appia, Adolphe (1862-1928) 142
Aquistapace, Jean *241*
Araiza, Francisco (b. 1950) *252*
Aravantinos, Panos (1886-1930) 232
Arnold, Heinz (b. 1906) *89*
Artaxerxes III. Ochus (358-337? B.C.) 37
Artois, Count Charles d' (1757-1836)
see Charles X
Aruhn, Britt-Marie (b. 1943) *69*
Asaf'yev, Boris 22
Assmann, Arno (1908-1979) 152
Asti von Astenburg, Marianne d', née
Troger 51, 54
Auersperg, Prince Karl (1720-1800) 82
Augér, Arleen (b. 1939) *33*
Ayars, Ann *180*

Babbini, Cherubino 266
Baccaloni, Salvatore (1900-1969) *107,
176, 180*
Bach, Johann Christian (1735-1782) 55
Baciu, Ilie *115*
Baglioni, Antonio (fl. 1786-1794) 164,
263
Bahner, Willi 121; *119*
Bailey, J. *168*
Baillot, Denis 168
Bailly, Alexandre *102*
Baker, Janet (b. 1933) *208*
Baltsa, Agnes (b. 1944) *214*
Barbaux, Christiane (b. 1953?) *260*
Barbier, Jules (1822-1901) 211

Barham, Edmund *275*
Barilli, Luigi (c. 1767-1824) 209
Barré, Kurt 274; *85, 87, 148, 267*
Barth, Ruodi (b. 1921) *35, 212*
Bassano, Gaspare (fl. 18th century) 32
Bassi, Luigi (1766-1825) 164, 165; *164*
Bastin, Jules (b. 1934) *260*
Batelli, Vincenzo (1786-1856) *230*
Battle, Kathleen (b. 1950) *194*
Battu, Léon (1799-1870) 131
Baudo, Serge (b. 1927) *216*
Bauer, Fritz 152
Bauer, Hartmut *275*
Bauer, Karl (1900-1982) 152
Bauer-Ecsy, Leni (b. 1909) *64, 207*
Bäuerle, Adolf (1786-1859) 140; *141*
Bauernfeind, Winfried (b. 1935) 274;
271
Bauernfeld, Joseph von 222
Beaumarchais, Pierre-Augustin Caron de
(1732-1799) 133, 134, 136, 146; *132,
134, 136*
Beaumont, Adolphe 226
Beaumont, William 117
Bechtold, Rudolf 64
Becke, Johann Baptist (1743-1817) 71,
72, 80f.
Bedini, Domenico (fl. 18th century) 263
Beethoven, Ludwig van (1770-1827) 7,
205
Behrens, Anke *212*
Beilke, Irma (b. 1904) *107, 153*
Béjart, Maurice (b. 1927) *192*
Belloc, Claire 275
Belloc, Teresa (1784-1855) *230*
Benda, Georg (1722-1795) 109
Benedetti, Pietro (Piero)
(c. 1585-1649) 32
Benedict, Sir Julius (1804-1885) 117
Benelli, Ugo (b. 1935) *69*
Benucci, Francesco (c. 1745-1825) 123,
137, 165, 197, 199
Berbié, Jeanne (Jane) (b. 1931/34) *62,
63*
Berchtold von Sonnenburg, Nannerl 28
Berganza, Teresa (b. 1935) *269*

Index

Berger, Erna (b. 1900) *103*

Berger (= Bamberger), Ludwig (1892-1969) 64

Berger (= Bamberger), Rudolf (1874-1915) 64

Berghaus, Ruth (b. 1927) 275; *94*

Bergman, Ingmar (b. 1918) 235

Berke, Dietrich (b. 1938) 64

Berman, Eugene (1899-1972) *185*

Bernadič, Drago *246*

Bernasconi, Antonia (1741-1803) 26, 32, 34

Berner, Felix (1738-1787) 19, 20

Berry, Walter (b. 1929) *191, 209*

Bertacca, Uberto 275

Bertati, Giovanni (1736-1815) 163

Besch, Anthony (b. 1924) 274; *208*

Besson, Benno (b. 1922) *258*

Beuther, Friedrich Christian (1777-1856) 140, 231, 273; *138, 234*

Bianchi, Francesco (c. 1752-1810) 59

Bianchini, Charles (1860-1905) 102

Bibiena *see* Galli-Bibiena

Bibikov, Vasilij Il'ic (1740-1787) 133

Bie, Oscar (1864-1938) 64

Bieber, Leo (b. 1908) *110*

Bignens, Max *112*

Billington, Elizabeth (?1765/68-1818) 271

Bilt, Peter van der (b. 1936) *23*

Birke, Susanne (b. 1956) *36*

Bisson, Alexandre Charles Auguste (1848-1912) 226

Bittner, Norbert (1786-1851) 168

Blache, Maria 42

Bloch, John W. 117

Blom, Eric Walter (1888-1959) 131

Blomstedt, Herbert (b. 1927) *111*

Blume, Heinrich (1788-1856) 168

Böhlke, Edgard M. (b. 1940) *115*

Böhm, Gotthard (b. 1936) *257*

Böhm, Johann 226

Böhm, Johann Heinrich (1740-1792) 63, 75, 97

Böhm, Karl (1894-1981) 95, 146, 147, 175, 211; *90, 94, 96, 106, 107, 109, 132, 150, 185, 191, 197, 203, 206, 207, 210, 211*

Böhme, Günther E. *262*

Boesch, Christian (b. 1941) *221*

Boguslawski, Wojciech (1757-1829) 226

Boky, Colette (b. 1935) *64*

Boldogh, Lajos 131

Bondini, Pasquale (1737?-1789) 116, 164

Bondini, Teresa 164

Bondy, Luc (b. 1948) *219*

Bonini, Emilia *265*

Bonnet, Horst *115*

Bonno, Giuseppe (1710-1788) 71

Borowski, Dávid *193*

Boschot, Adolphe (1871-1955) 140

Bosquet, Thierry (b. 1937) *192*

Bourdet, Gildas 66; *67, 68*

Bourseiller, Antoine (b. 1930) 274

Braithwaite, Nicholas (b. 1939) *191*

Brand, Erich *147*

Brass, Kurt (b. 1923) 160

Braun, Helena (b. 1903) *153*

Braunhofer, Maria Anna (1748-1819) 13, 72

Braunstein, Joseph 273

Brecht, Bertolt (1898-1956) 188; *256*

Breicha, Anton Daniel 138

Breitkopf & Härtel 40, 45, 47, 55, 63, 87, 90, 168, 201, 269f.

Brender à Brandis, Gerrit 117

Brenner, Peter (b. 1930) *78*

Bretzner, Christoph Friedrich (1748-1807) 98f., 100, 107f., 116, 200-204; *97*

Breuer, Hans *146*

Brieff, J. 63

Brioschi, (designer) 140; *141*

Brioschi, Anton (1855-1920) 208, 231; *199*

Brioschi, Carlo (1826-1895) 169; *172, 198*

Brock, Hannes *66*

Brockmann, Johann Franz Hieronymus (1745-1812) 130

Broissin, Nicole *63*

Bronsgeest, Cornelis (1878-1957) 131

Broschi, Carlo known as Farinelli, (1705-1782) 71

Brown, Zack *161*

Browne, M.F. 73

Brownlee, John (1901-1969) *204*

Brückner, Max *145*

Brühl, Count Karl Friedrich Moritz Paul von (1772-1837) *231, 232*

Bründl, Joseph Anton (b. 1749) 16

Brumaire, Jacqueline (b. 1921) *62, 205*

Brunelli, Bruno 39

Bruscantini, Sesto (b. 1919) *206*

Bruun, Niels Thoroup (1778-1828) 117, 226, 273

Brydon, Roderick (b. 1939) 275

Bučar, Franjo 117

Buchholz, Ernst 152

Büchner, Eberhard (b. 1939) *94*

Budden, Julian (b. 1924) 76

Buenzod, Emmanuel *206*

Bünte, Gerhard *105*

Buonaiuti, Serafino 271

Burghard, Herrmann *198*

Burney, Charles (1726-1814) 60

Burrows, Stuart (b. 1933) *260*

Bury, John (b. 1925) 179; *191*

Busch, Fritz (1890-1951) 95; *88, 103, 150, 174, 180, 181, 183*

Buschbeck, Gandolf (b. 1926) *74*

Büscher, Carl *139*

Businger, Toni (b. 1934) *162, 211*

Bussani, Dorothea, née Sardi (1763-after 1810) 137, 197, 198

Bussani, Francesco (1743-after 1807) 123, 137, 165, 197, 199; *137*

Bychkov, Semyon 66; *67, 68*

Cachemaille, Gilles *67, 194*

Caigniez, Louis-Charles (1762-1842) 89

Caldara, Antonio (1670-1736) 31, 261

Calderón de la Barca, Pedro (1600-1681) 208

Calegari, Giuseppe (c. 1750-1812) 38

Calvesi, Vincenzo (late 18th century) 197, 199

Calzabigi, Raniero de (1714-1795) 42, 59, 64

Cambon, Charles (1802-1875) *170, 171*

Cambreling, Sylvain (b. 1948) 275; *56, 69, 195, 260*

Campi, Gaetano (fl. 18th century) 263f.

Cannabich, Johann Christian (1731-1798) 55, 79, 80, 81, 271

Carat(t)oli, Francesco (c. 1705-1772) 26

Caribaldi (Garibaldi), Gioacchino (1743-after 1792) 26

Carnuth, Walther *108*

Caroline, Princess of Nassau-Weilburg (1743-1787) 55

Carré, Michel (1819-1872) 211

Carrère-Xanrof, Marguerite *173*

Carroll, Christina *180*

Casa d'Arte Caramba *176*

Casazza, Giulio *see* Gatti

Caselli, Francesco 34

Casoni, Bianca-Maria *28*

Cassandre *see* Mouron, Adolphe

Cassello, Kathleen (b. 1958) *13*

Castelbarco, Count Carlo Ercole 54

Casti, Giambattista (1724-1803) 130

Castiglione, Federico 49

Castil-Blaze, François-Henry-Joseph (1784-1857) 140, 168, 169, 210; *169*

Catherine II, empress (1729/1762-1796) 133

Cauchetier, Patrice (b. 1944) 275; *273*

Cavalieri, Catarina (1755-1801) 100, 102, 104, 123, 130, 165, 224; *125*

Cebotari, Maria (1910-1949) *150*

Ceccato, Aldo *211*

Chagall, Marc (1887-1985) 233, *250*

Chaperon, Philippe (1823-1907) *170*

Charles VI, emperor (1685/1711-1740) 39, 46, 261

Charles X, king, formerly Count d'Artois (1757/1824-1830/1836) 89, 133f.

Chéreau, Patrice (b. 1944) 55, *56*

Chéreau, Pierre *241*

Chéret, Joseph L. *170, 171*

Cherubini, Luigi (1760-1842) 133

Chevalier, Françoise 66; *67, 68*

Chmelenský, Josef Krasoslaw 226

Chodowiecki, Daniel Nikolaus (1726-1801) *134, 139*

Chris, Xenia *28*

Christiansen, Rolf (b. 1914) 146; *155*

Christin, Judith *252*

Chung, Myung-Whun *162*

Cicognani, Giuseppe 32

Cigna-Santi, Vittorio Amedeo (1725-1785) 31f.; *31*

Cimarosa, Domenico (1749-1801) 131, 198, 211, 271; *131*

Clerico, Giovanni 95

Colloredo, Count Hieronymus von, prince-archbishop (1753/1772-1803/1812) 46, 47, 60, 79, 98, 102, 134, 221; *98*

Coltellini, Marco (1707-1777) 28f.; *25*

Condò, Nucci (b. 1946) *252*

Conrad, Leopold 56

Consoli, Tommaso (1753-after 1811) 71, 72

Conwell, Julia *65*

Conz, Bernhard (b. 1906)   147; *28, 48, 64, 74*
Cook, Jean   *64*
Copley, John   *161, 162, 190*
Corazza, Rémy   *62*
Corena, Fernando (1916-1984)   *110*
Corneille, Pierre (1606-1684)   31, 262
Corrodi, Anneliese   *251*
Cortolezis, Fritz (1878-1934)   90
Cotrubas, Ileana (b. 1939)   *23, 249*
Cousins, Michaël (b. 1940)   *115*
Coutance, Guy   *216*
Cowdrick, Kathryn   *252*
Cox, John   *252, 254*
Crage, Basil   144; *144*
Craig, Edward Gordon (1872-1966)   142
Cramer, Carl Friedrich (1752-1807)   109
Crasnaru, Georg-Emil (b. 1941)   *256*
Crémont, Pierre   89
Croll, Gerhard (b. 1927)   40
Csampai, Attila (b. 1949)   *194*
Cuberli, Lella (b. 1945)   *56*
Curjel, Hans (1896-1974)   273, 274; *268*
Curzi, Cesare (b. 1926)   *64*
Czettel, Ladislav   *154*

Daffinger, Moritz Michael
   (1790-1849)   *236*
Dalayrac, Nicolas (1753-1809)   103
Dalla Rosa, Saverio   *see* Rosa
Dal Prato, Vincenzo (1756-1815?)   80
Dam, Mogens   117
Damiani, Luciano (b. 1923)   238, 248;
   110, 252
Dammers, Michael   144
Damonte, Magali (b. 1960)   *216*
d'Andrade, Francisco (1859-1921)   169f.;
   173
Danovsky, B.   226
Danzi, Innozenz (c. 1730-1798)   81
Da Ponte, Lorenzo (1749-1838)   7, 8,
   118, 123, 130, 134, 136, 137, 139, 160,
   163, 164, 165, 168f., 198, 200, 201,
   202, 207, 208, 210, 215, 219; *122,
   123, 133, 136, 151, 163, 184, 185,
   187, 193, 197, 204, 206, 208, 212,
   214*
Dargomyzhsky, Alexander1869)   *22*
Dau, Katharina   *275*
Daubner, Georg (1865-1926)   144, *145*
Dauer, Johann Ernst (1746-1812)   100,
   104, 105, 106
Dausqué, Lucette   273
David, Antoine (b. 1951)   *115*
David, Yoram   *114*
Davies, Dennis Russell (b. 1944)   160;
   158
Davis, Andrew (b. 1944)   *252, 254*
Davis, Colin (b. 1927)   274; *186, 190,
   192*
Daydé, Bernhard (b. 1921)   *62, 63, 96,
   109*
Dean, Stafford (b. 1937)   *191, 192*
Debrois, Johann   266
Decker, Willy (b. 1950)   *160*
Dehmel, Wolfram (b. 1938)   *212*
Delamboye, Hubert (b. 1945)   *256*
della Francesca, Piero   *see* Piero
Delmas, Francisque   *172*

Delsenbach, Johann Adam
   (1687-1765)   *222*
Dent, Edward Joseph (1876-1957)   7,
   117, 226
de Pian   *see* Pian
Dermota, Anton (b. 1910)   *206*
Deschamps, Emile (1791-1871)   168;
   169
Despléchin, Edouard-Désiré-Joseph
   (1802-1870)   *170, 171*
Destouches, Philippe Néricault
   (1680-1754)   29
Destrais, Charles   117
d'Ettore, Guglielmo (1740-1771)   32
Devrient, Eduard (1801-1877)   207
Diderot, Denis (1713-1784)   66
Diemann, Kurt   76
Diettrich, Inge   *91, 212*
Dimond, William   117
Dincklage, Irmgard von   17
Dingelstedt, Franz von (1814-1881)   *237*
Dittersdorf, Karl Ditters von
   (1739-1799)   131
Dobbs, Mattiwilda (b. 1925)   *110*
Doderer, Claudia (b. 1957)   *160*
Doebbelin, Karl Theophilus
   (1727-1793)   98
Dohnányi, Christoph von (b. 1929)   *256*
Donath, Helen (b. 1940)   *249*
Dönch, Karl (b. 1915)   207
Donizetti, Gaetano (1797-1848)   141
Donohue-Schmeiser, Dwyla   *249*
Dooley, William (b. 1932)   *48*
Dowd, F. Harrison   *64*
Drath, Johannes (1902-1983)   *151*
Drésa, Jacques (1869-1929)   *241*
Dressel, Heinz (b. 1902)   *155*
Dudley, William   192
Dülberg, Ewald (1888-1933)   175, 232;
   177, 243
Durazzo, Giacomo (1717-1794)   19
Dürr, Karl-Friedrich   *158*
Dürr, Walther (b. 1932)   273
Duschek, Franz Xaver (1731-1799)   136,
   164
Duschek, Josepha (1754-1834)   137
Dusserrat, Michel (b. 1947)   *257*

Eberhardi, Teresa (fl. 18th century)   26
Eberlin, Johann Ernst (1702-1762)   11, 15
Ebert, Carl (1887-1980)   *88, 110, 155,
   180, 181, 183, 206, 246*
Eda-Pierre, Christiane (b. 1932)   *260*
Egk, Werner (1901-1983)   152
Ehlers, Wilhelm (1774-1845)   131, 168
Eibl, Joseph Heinz (1905-1982)   59
Einstein, Alfred (1880-1952)   34, 57, 67,
   76
Eissler, Franz   *178*
Elias, Rosalind (b. 1929)   *209*
Ellis, Brent (b. 1946)   *191*
Elson, Charles (Louis Charles,
   1848-1920)   *184*
Elzin, Serge   *22*
Engel, Hans   44f.
Engel, Johann Jakob (1741-1802)   225
Enriquez, Franco   *186, 188, 189*
Enzinger, Christian (1755-?)   16
Erede, Alberto (b. 1909)   274
Erismann, Hans (b. 1911)   121

Erni, Hans (b. 1909)   274; *268*
Ernst, Johann (1755-?)   16
Erté, Romain   *205*
Esser, Hermin (b. 1928)   *91*
Esterházy, Anton von, prince
   (1738-1794)   266
Ettore, Guglielmo d'   *see* d'Ettore
Eugen(e), Prince (1663-1736)   98
Euller, Erwin   *16*
Evangelatos, Daphne   *65, 260*
Evans, Sir Geraint (b. 1922)   *132, 155,
   185, 186, 190, 206, 246*
Everding, August (b. 1928)   *112, 253*

Falchini, Gertrude (fl. 18th century)   42,
   43
Fanfani, Raniero   *230*
Fanto, Leonhart (b. 1874)   146; *150*
Fantozzi, Maria   *see* Marchetti
Fassbaender, Brigitte (b. 1939)   *197*
Faulkner, Julia (b. 1957)   *68*
Favart, Charles-Simon (1710-1792)   19;
   19
Favart, Marie-Justine-Benoîte
   (1727-1772)   19; *19*
Favier (Fabier), Jean   41f.
Fellini, Federico (b. 1920)   *69*
Felsenstein, Walter (1901-1975)   146;
   153, 190, 248
Fenneker, Josef (1895-1956)   146
Fercioni, Gian-Maurizio   274
Ferdinand, archduke of Austria
   (1754-1806)   41, 42, 43, 50, 54
Ferrandini, Giovanni (1710-1791)   38
Ferrarese del Bene, Adriana
   see Gabriel(l)i
Ferrier, Paul (1843-1920)   226
Fesemayr, Maria Anna (1743-1782?)   13,
   28, 72
Fielding, David (b. 1948)   *95*
Fierz, Gerold   *30, 92*
Finscher, Ludwig (b. 1930)   140
Firmian, Count Carlo di (1716-1782)   31,
   51
Firmian, Count Leopold Anton von
   (1679-1744)   31
Firmian, Count Leopold III. Ernst von
   (1708-1783)   51
Fischer, Iván   *193*
Fischer, Johann Ignaz Ludwig
   (1745-1825)   100, 102, 104, 105, 106
Fischer von Erlach, Josef Emanuel
   (1693-1742)   *222*
Fischietti, Domenico
   (c. 1720-after 1800)   71
Flemming, Charlotte   *91*
Flipse, Maarten   *258*
Flothow, Friedrich von (1812-1883)   174
Forzano, Giovacchino (1884-1970)   *176*
Franceschini, Girolamo
   (1820-1859?)   131; *128*
Francis I, emperor (1708-1765)   41
Franz, Cornel   *213*
Franzen, Hans (b. 1935)   *144*
Frasel, Wilhelm   222
Freni, Mirella (b. 1936)   *185*
Frey, Gaby   160
Frey, Jacques-Joseph (1781-1838)   140,
   201, 270
Frey, Willi (1901-1986)   *105*

Index

Freyer, Achim (b. 1934) *160, 256*
Fricsay, András 215
Frieberth, Franz Karl (1736-1816) 76
Friedländer-Abel, Hedwig von
  (1863-?) *208*
Friedman, Martin *254*
Friedrich, Götz (b. 1930) 160, 215; *211*
Friedrich Wilhelm II, king
  (1744-1797) 225
Friedrich Wilhelm III, king
  (1770/1797-1840) 88
Frigerio, Ezio (b. 1930) *65, 157, 195*
Fröhlich, Christian (b. 1949) *116*
Fronsac, Duc de 134
Fuchs, Ernst (b. 1930) 233
Fuchs, Felix 16
Fuchs, Johann Nepomuk
  (1842-1899) 63, 90
Fuentes, Giorgio (1756-1821) (1765?-
  1829?) 140, 271; *138, 234, 263, 264*
Fürstenberg, Joseph Maria, prince 139
Furlanetto, Ferruccio (b. 1949) *194*
Furtwängler, Wilhelm (1886-1954) 232;
  103, 184, 244

Gabriel(l)i, Francesca, known as Adriana
  Ferraresi del Bene (c. 1750-after
  1799) 139, 197, 198
Gabry, Edith (b. 1927) *43*
Gál, Hans (1890-1987) 95; *88*
Galliari, brothers 51
Galliari, Bernardino (1707-1794) 43
Galliari, Fabrizio (1709-1790) 43, *52*
Galliari, Giovanni Antonio
  (1714-1783) 43
Galli-Bibiena, family: Giuseppe
  (1696-1757), Antonio (1700-1774),
  Francesco (1659-1739) 229; *223*
Gallusser, Werner (b. 1932) 121
Galuppi, Baldassare (1706-1785) 71
Gamerra, Giovanni de (1743-1803) 49,
  55, 56, 198, 225, 226; *49*
Gandolf, Walter 146
Garnerey, Auguste (-Simon
  1785-1824) *167*
Gasparini, Quirino (1721-1778) 31
Gassmann, Leopold Florian
  (1729-1774) *230*
Gatti, Luigi (1740-1817) 118
Gatti-Casazza, Giulio *176, 240*
Gaul, Franz (1837-1906) *81, 238*
Gauthier-Villars, Henry (1859-1931) 22
Gazzaniga, Giuseppe (1743-1818) 163
Geiger, Andreas (1765-1856) 168
Geiger-Torel, Hermann *152*
Geis, Josef *200*
Geister, Jutta (b. 1957) *36*
Gellhorn, Peter *110, 185*
Genée, Rudolph (1824-1914) 131
Generali, Pietro (1773-1832) 211
Genzmer, W. 93
Gérard, Rolf *204, 206*
Gerhäuser, Emil 174; *147*
Gerl, Barbara, née Reisinger
  (1770-1806) 222
Gerl, Franz Xaver (1764-1827) 221, 222
Germani, Don Ferdinando 51
Gessner, Friedrich 131
Ghiaurov, Nicolai (b. 1929) *190*

Giai, Giovanni Antonio
  (c. 1690-1764) 31
Gibson, Alexander Drummond
  (b. 1926) *208*
Gielen, Josef (1890-1968) *88*
Gieseke, Karl Ludwig (1761-1833) 202,
  221, 222; *223*
Gilsault, Claire *115*
Giotto di Bondone (1266?-1337) *254*
Giovaninetti, Reynald (b. 1932) 274
Girard, André (b. 1913) *62, 63*
Giraudeau, Jean (b. 1916) *62, 63*
Girelli-Aquilar, Antonia Maria
  (fl. 1752-1772) 42, 43
Giustiniani, prince 59
Gliese, Rochus (1891-1978) *200*
Gliewe, Helene 175
Gluck, Christoph Willibald (1714-
  1787) 25, 26, 40, 57, 71, 77, 87, 98,
  103, 104, 107, 109, 269; *169*
Glückselig, Karl-Egon, (Gorvin, Carl)
  (b. 1912) 17; *14*
Gmeiner, Klaus (b. 1932) 17
Göbbel, Wolfgang (b. 1953) *95*
Gobbi, Tito (1913-1984) *186*
Godin, Guy *63*
Goeke, Leo *252*
Goethe, Johann Wolfgang von (1749-
  1832) 38, 131, 140, 202, 229, 231,
  271, 273; *138, 225, 234, 241, 263*
Goethe, Katharina Elisabeth, née Textor
  (1731-1808) 203
Goldoni, Carlo (1707-1793) 28f; *25*
Gollmick, Friedrich Carl (1796-1866) 75,
  76
Gomez, Jill (b. 1942) *55*
Gondolf, Walter (b. 1912) *156*
Gönnenwein, Wolfgang (b. 1933) 275
Goosens, Korneel 22
Gottlieb, Anna (Marianna, Nannina,
  1774-1856) 137, 222; *223*
Graf, Gera 275
Graf, Herbert (1903-1973) 147; *104,
  154, 184, 185, 244, 245, 246*
Graf, Max (1873-1958) 174
Granzer, Robert 74
Grčić, Jovan 273
Gresse, André (1868-1937) *102, 172*
Grist, Reri (b. 1932) *110, 132, 211*
Grist, William 131
Grobe, Donald (1929-1986) *64*
Gropius, Wilhelm 169
Groszer, Christoph *48*
Gruber, Franz 142; *142*
Gruberova, Edita (b. 1946) *55, 112*
Grübler, Ekkehard (b. 1928) *43, 48, 78,
  113*
Gründgens Gustaf (1899-1963) 146;
  149
Grützke, Johannes (b. 1937) 160; *158*
Guardasoni, Domenico
  (1731?-1806) 165, 262f., 266
Guarini, Giovan(ni) Battista
  (1538-1612) 42
Guarrera, Frank (b. 1923) *204*
Gubisch, Gérard 117
Güden, Hilde (b. 1917) *180*
Guglielmi, Pietro Alessandro
  (1728-1804) 71
Gülke, Peter (b. 1935) 275; *274, 275*

Günther, Friedrich 116
Günther, Sophie, née Huber
  (b. 1754 deb. 1767) 116
Günzel, Paul (b. 1944) *16*
Günzel-Dworski, Maria 17; *16*
Gui, Vittorio (1885-1975) 95; *206, 246*
Gulyás, Dénes (b. 1954) *193*
Guschlbauer, Theodor (b. 1939) 275;
  257, 273
Gustin, Oskar 274

Haberkorn, Friedrich 168
Hacker, Georg (1865-?) 144, *145*
Hadrabová, Eva (1902-1973) *87*
Haefliger, Ernst (b. 1919) *91, 110, 246*
Haferung, Paul *202*
Hägelin, Franz Carl (1735-1809) 134
Hagemann, Carl (1871-1945) 232
Hagenauer, Ignaz Joachim
  (1749-1824) 118
Hagenauer, Johann Lorenz
  (1712-1792) 20, 25, 26
Hagen-Groll, Walter (b. 1927) *36*
Hager, Leopold (b. 1935) 17, 22, 45, 47,
  55, 64, 73, 274; *23, 32, 33, 43, 77*
Hager, Paul *91*
Hahn, Reynaldo (1875-1947) *241*
Hain, Karl 226
Hainl, Georges *170*
Halévy, Ludovic (1833-1908) 131
Hall, Peter (b. 1930) *191*
Hallstein, Ingeborg (b. 1937) *74*
Halmen, Pet (b. 1943) 35, 275; *30, 55,
  218, 274, 275*
Hamari, Julia (b. 1942) *218*
Hamilton, David *191*
Hampe, Michael (b. 1935) 219; *194,
  214, 215*
Hampson, Thomas *218*
Hansell, Kathleen Kuzmick 55
Hansen, Wilhelm 29
Hanslick, Eduard (1825-1904) 205f.
Harambašič, August 226
Hardt-Warden, Bruno (1883-1954) 131
Harley, Mister *168*
Harnoncourt, Nikolaus (b. 1929) 35,
  274; *30, 55, 92, 95, 218, 258*
Harny de Guerville 19; *19*
Harper, Heather (b. 1930) *269*
Harper, James *74*
Hartleb, Hans (b. 1910) 274
Hartmann, Georges (d. 1900) 22
Hartmann, Rudolf (b. 1900) 214; *108,
  151, 200*
Hartwig, Erich (1887-?) 144
Harwood, Elizabeth (b. 1938) *208*
Haseleu, Werner (b. 1935) *111, 218*
Hasse, Johann Adolf (1699-1783) 40, 41,
  42, 44, 71
Hasselt-Barth, Wilhelmine Marie von
  (1813-1881) 140; *141*
Hassloch, Christiane Elisabeth
  (1764-1829) 87f.
Hassloch, Theodor 88
Hasslwander, Josef (1812-1878) 140;
  141
Haudek, Trude *16*
Hauptner, Thuiskon (1821-1889) 121
Hawkes, Ruth 117
Hawkes, Thomas 117

Haydn, Johann Michael (1737-1806) 11, 40, 72
Haydn, Joseph (1732-1809) 76, 98, 197
Hebert, Bliss 95
Heckel, Carl Ferdinand (1800-1870) 63, 89; *58*
Heckroth, Hein (1901-1970) *180, 181*
Heger, Robert (b. 1886) 95; *89*
Hegi, Franz (1774-1850) *98*
Heichele, Hildegard *160*
Heidenreich, Joseph 224
Heigel, Cäsar Max (1783-after 1829) 273
Heil, Georg *240*
Hein, Richard *85, 149*
Heinrich, Reinhard *114*
Heinrich, Rudolf (b. 1926) 147, 152; *132, 248*
Heinrichs, Helmut 152
Heinse, Friedrich 198
Held, Michael 139
Henderson, William James (1855-1937) *240*
Henneberg, Johann Baptist (1768-1822) 222
Herklots, Carl Alexander (1759-1830) 204
Hermann, Roland (b. 1936) *92*
Herrmann, Karl-Ernst (b. 1936) 160, 275; *69, 195, 219, 260*
Herrmann, Ursel (b. 1943) *69*
Herz, Joachim (b. 1924) 274; *216, 269*
Hevesi, Sándor 117
Heyduck, Peter (b. 1924) *32, 33*
Higgins, John *33*
Hinton, Stephen *114*
Hirsch, Georges *62, 63, 205*
Hirschel-Protsch, Günter *175*
Hirschfeld, Robert (1858-1914) 76; *239*
Hirsti, Marianne *256*
Hlawa, Stefan (1896-1977) 146; *27, 91, 153*
Hnewkowský, Sebastián 226
Hockney, David (b. 1937) 233; *252, 254*
Hofer, Franz de Paula (1755-1796) 224
Hofer, later Mayer, Josepha (1758-1819) 222, 271; *223*
Höfermeyer, Walter *151*
Hoffmann, Ernst Theodor (1766-1822) 205
Hoffmann, Frank *112*
Hoffmann, Josef (1831-1904) 231; *237*
Hoffmeister, Franz Anton (1754-1812) & Kühnel 63
Hofmann, Vlastislav (1884-?) *178*
Hofmüller, Max 175
Hofstätter, Felix (1744-1814) 72
Hogwood, Christopher (b. 1941) 275
Hoheisel, Tobias (b. 1956) *95*
Holley, William *268*
Hollweg, Werner (b. 1936) *13, 77, 92, 95, 270, 272*
Holm, Richard (b. 1912) *248*
Holmen, Tor 117
Holschneider, Andreas (b. 1931) 121
Holtei, Karl von (1797-1880) 204
Holtzmann, Thomas (b. 1927) *112*
Holzmeister, Clemens (1886-1983) 175f.; *184*
Holzbauer, Ignaz (1711-1781) 198

Homer 79
Honolka, Kurt (b. 1913) 273, 275
Horn, Charles Edward (1786-1849) 226
Horner, Harry *246, 247*
Hornung, Joseph 28
Hörth, Franz Ludwig *177, 240, 272*
Howells, Anne *272*
Huberty, Albert *241*
Hüni-Mihacsek, Felicie (1896-1976) *108, 151*
Hurka, Friedrich Franz 116

Iffland, August Wilhelm (1759-1814) *229*
Ihlee, Johann Jakob (1762-1827) 271
Imbault, Jean-Jérôme (1753-1832) 139
Ingerslev-Jensen, Povl 29
Israel, Zwi 117

Jacob, Walter *183*
Jacquin, Emilian Gottfried von (1767-1792) 138, 164, 165
Jaenicke, Gabriele *114*
Jahn, Gertrude *43*
Jahn, Otto (1813-1869) 207
Jahnn, Hans Henny (1894-1959) 64
Jakameit, Rosemarie *89*
Jambon, Marcel *102*
Jan, Eduard von 133
Janisch, Flora *16*
Janowitz, Gundula (b. 1937) *197*
Jara, Jorge *219*
Jaresch, August (1902-1984) *27*
Jautz, Dominik Joseph (1737-1806) 104, 105
Jax, Gerhard (b. 1944) *36*
Jennings, Diane (b. 1955) *13*
Jerger, Alfred (1889-1976) *186*
Joachim, Heinz (b. 1902) *110*
Jochum, Eugen (1902-1987) 274; *149, 271*
Johnson, Anthony Rolfe *56, 67, 273*
Jommelli, Niccolò (1714-1774) 50, 71, 98
Jorgulesco, Jonel *154*
Joseph II, emperor (1741/1765-1790) 25f., 54, 75, 97, 100, 129, 130, 134, 165, 198, 221, 248, 262
Joséphine de Beauharnais, empress (1763-1814) 168
Jürgens, Helmut (1902-1963) 274; *89*
Jungheinrich, Hans-Klaus 69
Jungmann, Josef (1773-1847) 117
Jurinac, Sena (b. 1921) *88*

Kalbeck, Max (1850-1921) 21f., 63, 144
Kalenberg, Josef (1886-1962) *87*
Kalkbrenner, Christian (1755-1806) 168
Kallisch, Cornelia *275*
Kalliwoda, Wilhelm (1827-1893) 207
Kamahora, Yoko (b. 1957) *116*
Kaplan, Emanuel *22*
Kaposy, Andor (b. 1922) *81*
Kappel, Günter *268*
Karajan, Herbert von (b. 1908) 152; *158, 187, 190, 194, 252*
Karl Theodor, elector 79, 80, 81, 82, 167
Kaslík, Václav *249*
Kaufmann, Julie (b. 1957) *114*

Kautsky, Hans (Johann) (1827-1896) 142; *106, 107, 198, 240*
Kautsky, Robert *106, 107*
Kavrakos, Dimitri *273*
Kehr, Klaus Peter 160
Keilberth, Joseph (1908-1968) 152
Keller, Carl (1784-1855) *242*
Kempe, Rudolf (1910-1976) *186*
Kenny, Yvonne (b. 1950) *30, 93*
Kern, Adele (b. 1901) *108, 151*
Kertész, István (1929-1973) 274; *156, 270*
Kesting, Jürgen (b. 1940) *191*
Kienlin, Jules 226; *241*
Kienzl, Wilhelm (1857-1931) 273
Kiessling, Richard 89f.
Kindermann, Heinz (1894-1985) 211
Kipnis, Alexander (1891-1978) *244*
Kirchberg, Klaus *274*
Kistler, Johann Michael 222
Klee, Bernhard (b. 1936) *65, 112, 158*
Kleiber, Eleonore *218, 258*
Klein, Cäsar (1876-1954) 146
Klein, Johann Baptist *229*
Klein, Peter *105*
Klein, Rudolf (b. 1920) *95*
Kleinmichel, Richard (1846-1901) 63
Kleist, Franz Alexander von (1769-1797) 268
Klemperer, Otto (1885-1973) 146; *149, 177, 243*
Klink, Max *212*
Kmentt, Waldemar (b. 1929) *207*
Knappertsbusch, Hans (1888-1965) *87, 148, 200*
Kniepert, Erni (b. 1911) *74*
Knigge, Adolf Freiherr von (1752-1796) 116, 139
Knigge, Philippine Eregine (1775-1841) 139
Knoll, Waldemar (1829-1909) 169
Koegler, Horst (b. 1927) 66; *35*
Köhler, Franz Heinrich 205
Köhler, Siegfried (b. 1923) *256*
Köhler-Helffrich, Heinrich (1904-1960) 17; *14*
Kokkos, Yannis (b. 1944) *216, 258*
Kokoschka, Oskar (1886-1980) 233; *245*
Kölle, Gustav *141*
Kollo, René (b. 1937) *252*
Kondrak, Erich *251*
Körner, Thomas 160
Köstlinger, Josef (b. 1946) *13*
Kozlowska, Joanna (b. 1959) *69*
Kozma, Lajos (b. 1938) *209*
Kralj, Matthias 275
Kramer, Christopher 117
Kramer, Kurt 198
Kraus, Georg Melchior (1737-1806) 229
Kraus, Gottfried (b. 1936) *17, 23*
Kraus, Walther (b. 1902) 17; *17*
Krause, Tom (b. 1934) *209, 217*
Krauss, Clemens (1893-1954) 144, 211f.; *148, 151, 153, 179, 200, 201*
Krauss, Fritz (1883-1976) *87*
Krebs, Johann Baptist (1774-1851) 204
Krehbiel, Edward 131
Krenn, Werner (b. 1943) *43*
Krips, Josef (1902-1974) 274; *250, 268*

Index

Krombholč, Jaroslav (b. 1918) *249*
Krücke Adolf 121
Krüger, Wilhelm 142
Kubelik, Rafael (b. 1914) *180, 251*
Kucharz, Johann Baptist
  (1751-1829) 139, 225
Kufferath, Maurice (1852-1919) 117;
  102
Küfferle, Rinaldo 117
Kukely, Julia *193*
Kullberg, Hermann Anders 226
Kumpf, Hubert (1756-1811) 221
Künast, Adolph W. 63
Kuntzsch, Matthias (b. 1935) 251
Kunz, Erich (b. 1909) *206*
Kupfer, Harry *111, 114, 218, 254, 258*
Kuppelwieser, Robert (b. 1903) 45
Kurz, Siegfried (b. 1930) 45; *254*
Küster, Karin *27*
Kutzschbach, Hermann 93
Kuvichinsky, Semen 117

La Bruce, Evelyn *64*
La Bruyère, Jean de (1645-1696) 31
Lachnith, Ludwig Wenzel
  (1746-1820) 226
Lagrange, Michèle (b. 1947) *216*
Laloy, Louis (1874-1944) 90
Lampugnani, Giovanni Battista
  (1706-1781) 71
Langan, Kevin (b. 1955) *115*
Langdon, Michael (b. 1920) *186*
Lange, Joseph (1751-1827) 130
Lankow, Edward (1838-1940) *240*
Lapissida, Raoul *102*
Laschi, Filippo 26
Laschi-Mombelli, Luisa
  (c. 1760-c. 1790) 137, 165; *137*
Laubenthal, Horst (b. 1939) *74*
Laudon, Gideon von (1716-1790) 98
Lautenschläger, Karl August
  (1843-1906) 144, 169
Lavastre, Jean-Baptiste *170, 171*
Lavaudant, Georges *115*
Lawrence, Robert 117
Layer, Friedmann (b. 1941) *160, 212,
  252*
Lazaridis, Stefanos *190*
Lazzari, Virgilio (1887-1953) *178*
Leavitt, Max 22
Le Bailly de Saint-Paulin,
  Antoine-François 210
Lebois, Michel (b. 1939) *257*
Lechner, Julius K. (?-1895) *100*
Lefler, Heinrich (1863-1918) 76, 142,
  144, 208, 231; *143, 145*
Legal, Ernst (1881-1955) 64
Legrand, Jean-Pierre (1734-1809) 80
Lehmann, Hans-Peter (b. 1934) *113*
Lehmann, Lilli (1848-1929) *173*
Lehmann, Reinhard (b. 1937) *155*
Lehnhoff, Nikolaus (b. 1939) *256*
Lehrberger, Thomas (b. 1934) *22*
Lelash, Marjorie 117
Le Maigat, Pierre-Yves (b. 1941) *216*
Le Noir, Jean-Claude-Pierre 133
Lenz, Leopold (c. 1803-1862) 89f.
Leopold II, emperor (1747/1790-
  1792) 41, 55, 167, 262, 263, 266,
  268, 270

Le Picq, Carlo (1744?-1806?) 41f., 51
Lerer, Norma (b. 1942?) *269*
Le Roux, Francois (b. 1955) *216*
Lert, Ernst (1883-1955) *241*
Leug, Peter *18*
Levi, Hermann (1839-1900) 7, 90
Levine, James (b. 1943) 274; *93, 221,
  272*
Levysohn, Salomon 117
Lewicki, Ernst (1863-1937) 90, 93
Lewis, Richard (b. 1914) *88, 180, 185,
  206*
Lichtenthal, Peter (1780-1853) 89
Liebeneiner, Wolfgang *155*
Liebermann, Rolf (b. 1910) 152
Liebstoeckl, Hans 170
Liesenheimer, Reinhard *66*
Ligabue, Ilva *185*
Lindberg, Anders 273
Lipp, Maria Magdalena, wife of M. Haydn
  (1745?-1827) 13, 28, 72
Lippert, Carl 139, 167
Littig, Rebecca (b. 1951) *115*
Ljubimov, Juri (b. 1917) *193*
Lobasà, Monique *74, 249*
Lobensommer, Karl (b. 1949) *13*
Loes, Joseph Benedikt Edler von
  (1739-1798) 71
Löffler, Eduard (b. 1896) 144; *85, 149,
  152*
Lolli, Giuseppe Francesco
  (1701-1778) 164
Lorengar, Pilar (b. 1921) *91, 246*
Lorenstrong, Pilar *33*
Löschenkohl, Hieronymus
  (1753-1807) *125, 130, 137*
Losey, Joseph (1909-1984) *191*
Louis XVI, king (1754/1774-1793) 133f.
Löwlein, Hans (b. 1909) 146
Ludwig I, king (1786/1825-1848/68) 90
Ludwig, Christa (b. 1928) *207*
Ludwig, Heinz *155*
Ludwig, Wolf-Dieter (b. 1928) *187*
Lugiati, Pietro (1724-1788) 118
Lumpe, Vera *116*
Lunt, Alfred (1893-1977) *204*
Lütkemeyer, professor *150*
Lutzer, Jenny (1816-1827) 140; *141*
Luxon, Benjamin (b. 1937) *252*
Luz, Angelika (b. 1956) *13*
Luzzati, Emanuele (b. 1921) 179; *186,
  188, 189*
Lyser, Johann Peter (1803-1870) 207
Lyubimov, Yuri *193*

Maag, Peter (b. 1919) 274; *91, 269*
Maazel, Lorin (b. 1930) *111, 112, 191*
Mackerras, Charles Alan (b. 1925)
Madra, Barbara (b. 1957) *69, 219*
Magnus, Josef (b. 1909) *17, 187*
Magnusson, Lars *117*
Mahler, Gustav (1860-1911) 144, 170,
  207f., 211, 231; *239*
Mahlknecht, Karl (1810-1893) 140; *141*
Mahnke, Adolph (1891-1945) *150*
Mahnke, Gustav 146
Mair, Joseph 15f.
Maizony de Lauréal, Joseph-François
  Stanislas 89, 273
Major, Malvina (b. 1943) *69*

Makart, Hans (1840-1884) 142; *199*
Malfitano, Catherine (b. 1948) *272*
Malis, David *252*
Mallabrera, André (b. 1934) *62, 63*
Malone, Carol (b. 1940) *111*
Malta, Alexander (b. 1939) *194*
Mandaus, Luděk (b. 1898) *181*
Mandini, Maria, née Piccinelli
  (fl. 1780s) 137; *137*
Mandini, Paolo Stefano
  (1757-1842) 123, 137
Mandini, Stefano (1750-c. 1810) 137
Mangelsdorff, Simone (1931-1973) *43*
Mann, Erika (1905-1969) 17
Manservisi, Rosa 60
Manzuoli, Giovanni (c. 1725-c. 1780)
  42, 43
Marcello, Benedetto (1686-1739) 130
Marchetti-Fantozzi, Maria
  (1767-1801) 263
Marcuse, Ludwig 152
Marelli, Marco Arturo (b. 1949) *114,
  194*
Maria Beatrice Riccarda, princess
  of Modena (1750-1829) 41
Maria Christina, archduchess
  (1742-1798) 129
Maria Fedorovna, empress 133
Maria Louise, empress (1745-1792) 266
Maria Theresa, empress (1717/1740-
  1780) 41, 42, 43, 54, 71, 75
Marie-Antoinette, queen
  (1755-1793) 134
Marischka, Hubert (1882-1959) 131
Marius, General Gaius (156-86 B.C.) 49
Markt, F.S. 88
Marshall, Margaret (b. 1953) *214*
Martin, Karl Heinz (1888-1948) *178*
Martini, Giambattista (1706-1784) 38
Martín y Soler, Vicente
  (1754-1806) 163, 198, 221
Mas, Margaret (b. 1926?) *62*
Maschek, Vincenz (1755-1831) 139
Masson, Ernst (b. 1936) *212*
Matiasek, Hellmuth (b. 1931) *43*
Matuschek, S. *256*
Maurenbrecher, Wilhelm *145*
Maximilian III Joseph, elector
  (1727-1777) 50, 59, 63
Maximilian I Joseph, king
  (1756/1799-1825) 273
Maximilian Franz, archduke 71, 72f.,
  269
Maximowna, Ita (b. 1914) 147, 179;
  195, 197, 210, 211
Mayer, Friedrich Sebastian
  (1773-1835) 271
Mayer, Gerhard *43*
Mayer, Josepha see Hofer
Meyer, Tony *67*
Mayr, Albert Michael von 11, 51
Mayr, Anton 63
Mayr, Johann Simon (1763-1845) 121,
  271
Mazza, Giovanni 51
Mazzolà, Caterino (c.1740/50-1806) 262,
  263, 266, 271; *261, 268*
Mazzoni, Antonio Maria (1717-1785) 71
McCalla, Kathleen *275*
McCauley, Barry (b. 1950) *69*

McDaniel, Barry (b. 1930) *74*
Meckbach, Wilhelm 94, 273
Mehlich, Ernst (1888-?) *175*
Mehta, Zubin (b. 1936) *110*
Meisel, Karl (1775-1853) 231
Meissner, Joseph (1725?-1795) 13, 28
Mekler, Mani *252*
Melbye, Mikael (b. 1956) *256*
Melchinger, Siegfried (b. 1906) 152; *213*
Melis, György (b. 1923) *193*
Mellen, Constance 95
Meltzer, Andrew *217*
Mendel, Hermann (1834-1876) 90, 273
Mendelssohn Bartholdy, Felix (1809-1847) 21
Mentzer, Susanne *195*
Menuhin, Yehudi (b. 1916) 275
Mercker, Karl-Ernst (b. 1933) *65*
Mesmer, Anton (1734-1815) 21
Messel, Oliver (b. 1905) 233; *88, 110, 155, 246*
Metastasio, Pietro (1698-1782) 32, 38f., 42, 46, 49, 71, 72, 87, 261f., 266; *37, 46, 71, 261*
Meyer, G.M. jr. 89
Meyer, Jan Coenraad 226
Meyer, Jean *182*
Micelli, Catarina 164
Michaelis, Rolf (b. 1933) *187*
Mienci, Daniella (fl. 18th century) 52
Mihule, Wenzel 202
Milianti, Alain 66; *67, 68*
Miller, Kevin *110, 246*
Miller, Mildred (b. 1924) *154*
Milnes, Rodney *117*
Milnes, Sherrill (b. 1935) *191*
Mirdita, Federik (b. 1932) 275
Mithradates VI of Pontos (132/111-63 B.C.) 31, 49
Molcho, Samy (b. 1936) 66
Molière, Jean-Baptiste, born Poquelin (1622-1673) 163
Molina *see* Tirso de Molina
Moline, Pierre-Louis (c. 1740-1821) 117
Mölk, Franz von 60
Moll, Christian Hieronymus (1750-?) 222
Moll, Kurt (b. 1938) *96, 117*
Mollo, Tranquillo (1767-1837) 269
Mombelli, Luisa *see* Laschi-Mombelli
Mommaer, Carmen *18*
Monreale, Leonardo (b. 1924) *185*
Monsy, Marguerite *241*
Montarsolo, Paolo (b. 1925) *186*
Montgomery, Kenneth (b. 1943) *191*
Moore, Henry (1896-1986) *178*
Mora, Alois (1872-1947) *174*
Moralt, Rudolf (1902-1958) 147
Morel de Chédeville, Etienne 226
Morella, Francesco 165
Morgan, Rachel Ann (b. 1950) *273*
Morgnoni, Bassano 51, 52, 54
Mortari, Virgilio (b. 1902) 121
Moser, Edda (b. 1941) 33
Moser, Jakob (1751-?) 16
Moshinsky, Elijah *117*
Mostar, Herrmann (b. 1901) 152
Motta, Francesco 51
Motta, Gustave 117
Mouron, Adolphe Jean-Marie known as

Cassandre (1901-1968) *182*
Mozart, Anna Maria, Wolfgang's mother (1720-1778) 25, 34, 38, 41f., 50f., 54f., 59, 62f., 266
Mozart, Carl, Wolfgang's son (1784-1858) 224, 270
Mozart, Constanze, Wolfgang's wife (1762-1842) 107, 127, 139, 164, 198, 222, 269, 270, 271
Mozart, Leopold, Wolfgang's father (1719-1787) 11, 13, 15, 20, 25, 28, 34, 35, 38, 41f., 50f., 57, 59, 62f., 71, 75, 79, 80, 82, 99, 100, 103, 107, 118, 119, 136f., 266; *37, 122*
Mozart, Maria Anna (Nannerl), Wolfgang's sister, (1751-1829) 25, 50, 55, 60, 82, 136f., 165, 266
Mühldorfer, Joseph (1800-1863) *237*
Müller, August Eberhard (1767-1817) 87, 168, 269; *262*
Müller, Johann Heinrich Friedrich (1738-1815) 19f., 97; *19*
Müller, Wenzel (1759-1835) 231
Munch, Edvard (1863-1944) *183*
Münster, Robert (b. 1928) 59
Murphy, Richard 117
Murray, Ann (b. 1949) *30, 55, 218*
Muschietti, Pietro 32
Musoleno, Rosemary (b. 1959) *273*
Mussbach, Peter *116*
Muszely, Melitta (b. 1928) *48*
Muti, Riccardo (b. 1941) *195, 214, 215*
Mutze, Oswald 131
Muzika, Frantisek (1900-1974) *181*
Mysliweczek, Joseph (1737-1781) 72

Nafé, Alicia (b. 1947) *260*
Napoleon Bonaparte, emperor (1769-1821) 230
Nattier, Jean-Marc (1685-1766) *136*
Naujok, Barbara *158*
Neblett, Carol (b. 1946) *272*
Nebucadnezzar (605-562 B.C.) 37
Neefe, Christian Gottlob (1748-1798) 167, 201, 269
Negri, Vittorio (b. 1923) 275
Neher, Caspar (1897-1962) 147, 132; *88, 90, 108, 206, 244*
Nejedlý, Adalbert 226
Nemeth, Maria (1899-1967) *87*
Nemetz-Fiedler, Kurt *91*
Nero, emperor (37/54-58) 261
Nestroy, Johann (1801-1861) *236, 258*
Neugebauer, Hans (b. 1916) *156*
Neukirchen, Alfons *132*
Neumann, Günter (b. 1938) *114*
Nicolai, Claudio *218, 219*
Niefind, Dagmar *194*
Niehoff, Beatrice *258*
Niemetschek, Franz Xaver (1766-1849) 197f., 262 f.
Niese, Carl Friedrich 90, 93, 207
Nilsson, Birgit (b. 1918) *88*
Nissen, Georg Nikolaus (1761-1826) 21, 198
Noguera, Louis *62*
Nolan, Sir Sidney *117*
Northern, Michael *88*
Norwich, John Julius *183*
Nourrit, Adolphe (1802-1839) *169*

Nouseul, Johann Joseph 222
Novotná Jarmila (b. 1907) *244*
Novotný, Václav Juda (1849-1922) 273
Nuitter, Charles (1828-1899) 226

Ober, William B. 76
O'Brien, Timothy *117*
Oehlmann, Werner (b. 1901) *64, 108*
Offermann, Sabine *87*
Ohms-Quennet, Elly (b. 1909) *155*
O'Kelly, Michael (1762-1826) 137
Onofrio, Giuseppe 50, 52
Orel, Arkady *22*
Orff, Carl (1895-1982) 152
Orsini-Rosenberg, Count Franz Xaver Wolf von (1723-1796) 99, 100, 118, 165
Ortes, Giovanni Maria, abbot 42
Orth, Norbert (b. 1939) *96*
Orthmann, Erich (b. 1894) *149*
Ortlepp, Ernst (1800-1864) 205
Ostrčil, Otakar (1879-1935) *178*
Otto, Teo (1904-1968) 144, 177f., 238; *149, 187, 249*
Ozawa, Seiji (b. 1935) *209*

Pabst, Peter (b. 1944) *117*
Pachl, Peter P. (b. 1953) *193*
Pack, Robert 117
Paër, Ferdinando (1771-1839) 211
Pagano, Mauro (b. 1951) *65, 194, 214, 215*
Paisiello, Giovanni (1740-1816) 55, 59, 199
Pallavicini-Centurioni, Count Giovanni Luca (1697-1773) 38, 41, 42
Palmer, Felicity (b. 1944) *92*
Pály, Elek 273
Panerai, Rolando (b. 1924) *197, 211*
Pankok, Bernhard (1872-1943) 144, 174, 231; *147, 240*
Panzacchi, Domenico de (1733-after 1805) 80
Parbs, Florian (b. 1952) *13*
Parini, Giuseppe, abbot (1729-1799) 31, 34, 42f.; *41*
Parker, Patricia *252*
Pascal, Prosper 117
Pasetti, Carlo (1613-1679) *267*
Pasetti, Leo (1882-1937) 64, 144. 175, 274; *85, 87, 148, 200, 267*
Pasqualio, Benedetto 31
Patzak, Julius (1898-1974) *268*
Paul, Olga 22
Paul Petrovich, Grand Duke, later Emperor Paul I (1754/1796-1801) 100, 133
Paumgarten, Countess Josefa von (1762-1817) 79
Paumgartner, Bernhard (1887-1971) 29, 45, 64, 95, 131, 273; *22, 27, 28, 43, 64*
Pavarotti, Luciano (b. 1935) *93*
Pavesi, Stefano (1779-1850) 211
Pedroni, Giovanni (1762-1842) *265*
Peduzzi, Richard (b. 1943) *56*
Pekenino, Michele *136*
Pena, Costa Joaquim (1873-1944) 117
Pergolesi, Giovanni Battista (1710-1736) 22
Perigo, Giovanni *166*

Index

Perillo, Salvatore (c. 1731-?)   29
Perini, Carolina   263
Pernerstorfer, Alois (1912-1978)   *27*
Peters, Reinhard (b. 1926)   *192*
Petersen, Arvid   117
Petrobelli, Pierluigi (b. 1932)   73
Petrosellini, Giuseppe (1727-c. 1799)   59; *59*
Petrova, Ekaterina   *22*
Petzold, Richard (1907-1974)   64
Pezzino, Leonard (b. 1948)   *216*
Pezzl, Johann (1756-1823)   79
Pfitzner, Hans (1869-1949)   *145*
Pian, Antonio de (1784-1851)   168, 231; *235*
Piero della Francesca (c. 1416-1492)   *195*
Pignotti, L.   208f.
Pinza, Ezio (1872-1957)   *154, 178*
Piper, John (b. 1903)   179; *183*
Piranesi, Giambattista (1720-1778)   231; *55*
Pirchan, Emil (1884-1957)   175
Pistrucci, Filippo   *230*
Pitt, Suzan   *256*
Pittman, Josiah   117
Planché, James Robinson (1796-1880)   226
Pleyer, Friedrich (b. 1937)   *213*
Plowright, Rosalind (b. 1949)   *273*
Poelzig, Hans (1869-1939)   175; *177*
Poettgen, Ernst Ludwig (b. 1922)   35, 275; *35, 36, 64*
Poggi, later Baglioni, Clementina   26
Poggi, Domenico (?-c. 1790)   26
Poisson, Alain   *257*
Pokorný, Marcel   *23*
Polignac, Duchesse Yolande de (1749-1793)   134
Pollak, Egon (1879-1933)   *148, 177*
Poniatowski, Prince Stanisław (1732-1798)   129
Ponnelle, Jean-Pierre (b. 1932)   35, 55, 152, 238, 248, 251, 274; *30, 55, 92, 93, 115, 158, 191, 209, 217, 218, 221, 270, 272, 274*
Ponziani, Felice (?-c. 1826)   164
Popp, Lucia (b. 1939)   *218*
Porpora, Nicola (1686-1768)   31
Porter, Andrew   *93*
Possart, Ernst von   7
Poulson, Lani (b. 1953)   *69*
Prey, Hermann (b. 1929)   *197, 207, 252*
Pritchard, John (b. 1921)   *88, 183, 185, 186, 188, 189*
Prod'homme, Jacques-Gabriel (1871-1956)   226; *241*
Pruett, Jerome (b. 1941)   *219*
Puchberg, Michael (1741-1822)   197
Puchmayer, Antonin Jaroslaw   226
Pudlich, Robert (1905-1962)   146
Purgmaaten, R.   *27*
Pusar, Ana   *216*

Quaglio, Angelo (1828-1890)   167; *166*
Quaglio, Giuseppe (1747-1828)   229; *223*
Quaglio, Lorenzo (1730-1804)   80, 82, 229

Quaglio, Simon (1795-1878)   231; *100*
Quittmeyer, Susan   *161*

Raaff, Anton (c. 1711-1797)   79, 80, 82, 105
Racine, Jean (1639-1699)   31, 262; *30*
Rader, Hannes (b. 1940)   *77*
Radford, Evelyn   273
Radford, Maisie   273
Radl, Anton (1774-1852)   271
Raffael(l)i(j), Michel (b. 1929)   147
Raffelsberger, Ernst (b. 1961)   *36*
Raftery, J. Patrick (b. 1961)   *69*
Raimondi, Ruggero (b. 1941)   *190, 191, 192*
Raimund, Ferdinand (1790-1836)   231; *258*
Raine, Patricia   *18, 66*
Rambaud, Edmond   *241*
Ramberg, Johann Heinrich (1763-1840)   140; *139*
Ramey, Samuel (b. 1940)   *194*
Raninger, Walter (b. 1926)   *27*
Rauzzini, Venanzio (1746-1810)   50, 52, 54
Ravel, Maurice (1875-1937)   90, 275
Rech, Géza (b. 1910)   *27*
Rehkemper, Heinrich (1894-1949)   *151*
Rehm, Wolfgang (b. 1929)   73
Reichmann, Theodor (1850-1903)   169
Reichssiegel, Florian (1735-1793)   40
Reiner, Fritz (1850-1903)   *154*
Reinhard, Andreas (b. 1939)   *117*
Reinhardt, Georg (b. 1919)   *28, 91, 212, 268*
Reinking, Wilhelm (b. 1896)   146, 232; *105, 151*
Reiter, Ronny (Veronica) (1939-1980)   *187*
Rellstab, Ludwig (1799-1860)   205
Rennert, Günther (1911-1978)   147, 152, 214, 233, 275; *96, 109, 132, 185, 190, 197, 207, 210, 211, 250, 251*
Rennert, Wolfgang (b. 1922)   274
Rethberg, Elisabeth (1894-1976)   *154*
Reucker, Alfred (1869-1958)   *150*
Reuter, Rolf (b. 1926)   *114, 258*
Reutter, Georg the Younger (1708-1772)   39
Rexroth, Dieter   *218, 275*
Rhode, Johann Gottlieb (1762-1827)   204
Riccarda, Maria   *see* Maria
Ricci, Filippo   *230*
Richault, Charles Simon (1780-1866)   140
Richter-Forgách, Thomas (b. 1940)   *213*
Riescher, Rudolf   275
Rietz, Julius (1812-1877)   201
Rieu, Jean-José   275
Rigaud de Vaudreuil, Marquis Louis Philippe (1724-1802)   134
Rimsky-Korsakov, Nikolai (1844-1908)   *22*
Rischbieter, Henning (b. 1927)   *249*
Ritter-Ciampi, Gabrielle (1886-1974)   *241*
Rochaix, François (b. 1942)   275
Rochlitz, Johann Friedrich (1769-1842)   167, 203f., 270; *98*
Rogers, Nathaniel (1788-1844)   *136*
Rohs, Marta (1909-1963)   *268*

Rolandi, Gianna (b. 1952)   *115, 161*
Roller, Alfred (1864-1935)   94, 144, 170f., 214, 231; *83, 84, 87, 146, 239*
Roller, Ulrich   *106, 107*
Ronconi, Domenico (1772-1839)   *265*
Rosa, Saverio dalla (1745-1821)   118
Rosbaud, Hans (1895-1962)   *182*
Rose, Jürgen   *210, 253*
Rosenbaum, Therese (1774-1837)   *230*
Rosenshein, Neil (b. 1947)   *68*
Rosenstock, Joseph (1895-1985)   *85*
Rossi, Carlo   22
Rossini, Gioacchino (1792-1868)   7, 211
Rossmässler, Johann Adolf (1770-1821)   269
Rothenberger, Anneliese (b. 1924)   *209*
Rother, Arthur Martin (1885-1972)   93
Rottonara, Francesco Angelo (1848-1938)   142, 231
Rousseau, Jean-Jacques (1712-1778)   19, 77
Rovescalli, Antonio (1864-?)   *176*
Rubé, Auguste (Alfred?) (1815-1899)   *170*
Rudel, Julius (b. 1921)   275
Rudolph, Anton (1890-1971)   29, 64, 76, 131, 273
Ruepp, Odo   *108, 151*
Ruiz, Emilio Serrano y (1850-1939)   32
Ruppel, Karl Heinz (b. 1900)   *153*
Rychtarik, Richard   *244*
Rydl, Kurt (b. 1947)   *117, 272*

Sabatier, Pierre   *63*
Sacchetti, Lorenzo (1759-1836)   230
Sacchetti, Vincenzo   230
Sacco, Johanna, née Richard (1754-1802)   130
Sacher, Paul (b. 1906)   130; *110*
Sachse, Leopold   *242*
Saint-Foix, Georges de (1874-1954)   56
Salamoni, Giuseppe   51
Sales, Pietro Pompeo (c. 1729-1797)   60
Salieri, Antonio (1750-1825)   97, 103, 104, 118, 129, 130, 137, 163, 199, 224; *230*
Salter, Lionel (b. 1914)   95, 117
Sander, Alexander (b. 1940)   *193*
Sanjust, Filippo   275; *111, 112*
Sanquirico, Alessandro (1777-1849)   *166, 265*
Santori, Signore   *176*
Saporiti-Codecasa, Teresa (1763-1869)   164
Sarti, Giuseppe (1729-1802)   71
Sau(e)rau, Joseph Gottfried (1720-1775)   60
Savary, Jérôme (b. 1942)   *257*
Savio, Johann Baptist   20
Sawallisch, Wolfgang (b. 1923)   *78, 249, 253*
Scarlatti, Alessandro (1660-1724)   31
Schaaf, Johannes (b. 1933)   95; *95, 117*
Schachtner, Johann Andreas (1731-1795)   20ff., 75, 76, 79, 82; *19, 75*
Scha(c)k, Benedikt (1758-1826)   221, 222
Scha(c)k, Elisabeth, née Weinhold   222
Schäfer, Edgar (b. 1947)   *116*
Schaffer, Josef   229; *226*
Schaffer, Peter   229; *226*

Schaffkotsch, Count Franz
    (c. 1900-1943) 17; *16*
Schalk, Franz (1863-1931) *146, 243*
Schaller, Stephan 17
Schatzdorfer, Günther *77*
Schavernoch, Hans (b. 1945) *258*
Scheder, Gerolf (b. 1940) *114*
Scheepers, Sepp (b. 1932) *74*
Scheffler, Karl *177*
Scheibner, Andreas *216*
Scheidemantel, Karl (1859-1923) 208
Schenk, Otto (b. 1930) *210, 258*
Schiedenhofen auf Stumm und
    Triebenbach, Johann Baptist Joachim
    Ferdinand von (1747-1823) 71
Schikaneder, Emanuel (1751-1812) 75,
    131, 170, 221f., 225, 226, 230f., 238,
    248, 251, 270f.; *77, 128, 221, 222,
    223, 225, 233, 240, 242, 246, 248,
    251, 252, 253, 257*
Schikaneder, Urban (1746-1818) 222,
    223
Schillings, Max von (1868-1933) 174
Schink, Johann Friedrich
    (1755-1835) 109, 167
Schinkel, Karl Friedrich
    (1782-1841) 230, 232, 248; *232, 233,
    234, 250, 254*
Schleifer, Karl 17, 64
Schlesinger, Maurice (1798-1871) 89
Schmidt, Eberhard *254, 258*
Schmidt, Jacques (b. 1933) *56*
Schmidt, Ludwig 116
Schmidt, Manfred (b. 1928) *28*
Schmidt, Trudeliese (b. 1941) *92, 93*
Schmidt-Isserstedt, Hans
    (1900-1973) 64; *105, 155*
Schmidt-Lindner, August 121
Schmieder, Heinrich Gottlieb
    (1763?-after 1811) 165, 201
Schmiedt, Siegfried (c. 1756-1799) 269
Schmückle, Hans-Ulrich (b. 1916) 152
Schnabel, Manfred (b. 1927) *114*
Schneider, Carl Friedrich 98
Schneider, Louis (1861-1934) 131
Schneider, Peter (b. 1939) *115*
Schneider-Siemssen, Günther
    (b. 1926) *17, 187, 190*
Schneider, Hanns-Martin (b. 1930) *13*
Schock, Rudolf (1915-1986) *88*
Schoff, Dean *256*
Schöffler, Paul (b. 1897) *150, 206*
Schønwandt, Michael *219*
Schoppe, Julius (1795-1868) 168
Schoras, Dietrich (b. 1939) *193*
Schrattenbach, Count Sigismund
    Christoph von, prince-archbishop
    (1698/1753-1771) 13, 28, 46, 79
Schreiber, Wolfgang *55*
Schreier, Peter (b. 1935) *33, 94, 95,
    191, 194, 197*
Schröder, Friedrich Ludwig
    (1744-1816) 99, 167, 201
Schroeck, Sophia (b. 1931) 152, 274;
    156
Schröter, Bernhard (b. 1928) *216*
Schubert, Franz (1797-1828) *169*
Schuh, Oscar Fritz (1904-1984) 146,
    147, 238f.; *90, 105, 108, 151, 187,
    190, 203, 206, 244, 249*

Schuk, Lydia *22*
Schulz, Werner (b. 1929) *115*
Schuman, Patricia (b. 1952) *195, 219*
Schumann, Karl (b. 1925) *78*
Schünemann, Georg (1884-1945) 140,
    201; *200*
Schütz, Johannes (b. 1950) *116*
Schwarz, Carl Benjamin
    (1757-1813) *224*
Schwarzenberg, Elisabeth (b. 1933) *91*
Schwarzkopf, Elisabeth (b. 1915) *207*
Schwind, Moritz von (1804-1871) 141,
    169; *141, 239*
Sciutti, Graziella (b. 1927) *64, 207*
Sébastian, Georges (b. 1903) *205*
Sebastiani, Franz Josef (1722-1772) 76
Seconda, Friedrich *224*
Seeau, Count Joseph Anton von
    (1713-1799) 59f., 79ff.
Seeauer, P. Beda (1716-1785) 28
Seibel, Klauspeter *213*
Seidelmann, Eugen 89f.
Seidl, Teresa *115*
Seinsheim, Count Joseph Maria von
    (1707-1787) 80f.
Seligmann, Adalbert Franz
    (1862-1954) 174
Sellner, Gustav Rudolf (b. 1905) 95,
    147; *94*
Seneca, Lucius Annaeus
    (c. 4 B.C.-65) 261
Senff, (Bartholomäus) Bartholf Wilhelm
    (1815-1900) 63
Senn, Walter (1904-1981) 75
Serbelloni, Vittoria Duchessa 25
Serrano y Ruiz *see* Ruiz
Sessi, Marianna (1776-1847) 271
Seyfried, Ignaz von (1776-1841) 224,
    271
Sgourda, Antigone (b. 1938) *91*
Shakespeare, William (1564-1616) 99,
    167; *247*
Sharp, Martha (b. 1947) *116*
Siciliani, Maria Francesca *275*
Sieben, Wilhelm (1881-1971) 274; *267*
Siebert, Dorothea *27*
Siepi, Cesare (b. 1923) *154, 185*
Siercke, Alfred 274; *269*
Sievert, Ludwig (1887-1968) 144, 175,
    211, 214, 232; *108, 148, 151, 179,
    201, 241*
Silveri, Paolo (b. 1913) *180*
Simoneau, Léopold (b. 1918) *88, 185*
Simonetti, Luigi 269
Simons, Rainer 22, 142; *143*
Simrock, Nicolaus (1752-1833) 87, 88,
    117, 140, 167, 201, 202, 226, 269
Singer, Gustav 144
Skalicki, Wolfram *233, 234, 237*
Skalicky, Jan *35*
Škor, František *178*
Slevogt, Max (1868-1932) 170; *173,
    174*
Smith-Mayer, Carolyn *111*
Soldan, Kurt 140
Soleri, Ferruccio *65*
Soliman II, sultan (1520-1566) 97
Solti, Georg (b. 1912) *88, 117, 157,
    183, 186, 245*
Solvay, Lucien 117; *102*

Solzi, Adamo 42, 43
Sönnerstedt, Bernhard 22
Spiess, Christian Heinrich
    (1755-1799) 167
Spitzeder, Franz Anton (1735-1796) 13,
    28, 72
Spork, Johann Wenzel
    (1724-1804) 26
Squarciapino, Franca *195*
Stabile, Mariano (1888-1968) *176*
Stadler, Matthias 16
Stahl, Robert 152
Stangenburg, Harry *146*
Stantz, Ferdinand von 21
Starhemberg, Count Ernst Rüdiger von
    (1638-1683) 98
Starzer, Joseph (1726/27-1787) 51
Stegmann, Carl David (1751-1826) 201f.
Stegmayer, Matthäus (1771-1820) 131
Stehlé, Jean-Marc 258
Steibelt, Daniel (1765-1823) 211
Stein, Horst (b. 1928) *117, 192*
Stein, Peter (b. 1937) *69*
Steinkauler, Walter 90f.
Stephanie, Anna Maria, née Mika
    (1751-1802) 130
Stephanie, Johann Gottlieb the Younger
    (1741-1800) 75f., 98, 99, 100, 102,
    103, 106, 130, 131; *97, 129*
Stern, Ernst (1876-1954) 174
Sterneck, Berthold (1893?-1943) *104*
Stevens, Risë (b. 1913) *154*
Stevenson, Alexander (b. 1944) *116,
    275*
Stich-Randall, Teresa (b. 1927) *63, 185*
Stieber, Hans (1886-1969) 131
Stiedry, Fritz (1883-1968) *204*
Stief, Sebastian (1811-1889) *10*
Stierle, Johann Franz Joseph the Elder
    (1741-after 1800) 63; *59*
Stivender, David 274
Stoddart, John 274; *208*
Storace, Ann Selina (1766-1817) 123,
    137
Strandt, Marie-Louise 275; *94*
Strauss, Richard (1864-1949) 94, 103,
    211, 219; *83, 84, 85, 186*
Strehler, Giorgio (b. 1921) 238, 239f.,
    248; *110, 157, 195, 252*
Stressel, Albert 117
Strnad, Oskar (1879-1935) 175, 232;
    104, 178, 243
Strohbach, Hans (?-1949) 144, 146; *150*
Štros, Ladislav (b. 1926) *23*
Strosser, Pierre (b. 1943) 275; *273*
Stubenrauch, Philipp von
    (1784-1848) *230*
Studer, Cheryl *256*
Stuntz, Joseph Hartmann
    (1793-1859) 273
Stürmer, Johann Heinrich
    (1774-1855) *231*
Suard, Jean-Baptiste (1733-1817) 133
Suardi, Felicità 50, 52
Sudlik, Mária *193*
Suetonius (c. 70-after 128) 261, 262
Sukis, Lilian *78*
Sulla, Lucius Cornelius (138-78 B.C.) 49f.
Sullivan, Brian *246, 247*
Süssmayr, Franz Xaver (1766-1803) 222

Index

Sutherland, Graham (b. 1903) *187*
Sutherland, Joan (b. 1926) *185*
Svoboda, Josef (b. 1920) 233; *249, 251*
Swift, Basil 22
Sykora, Peter *111, 254*
Szenkar, Eugen (1891-1977) 144; *152, 241*
Szewczuk, Edith *155*
Szmytka, Elzbieta *69, 219*

Tagliavini, Luigi Ferdinando
  (b. 1929) 35, 45
Talankin, Vladimir *22*
Talich, Václav (1883-1961) *181*
Talvela, Martti (b. 1935) *111*
Tamburini, Antonio (1800-1876) *168*
Tamschick, Rüdiger *213*
Tappy, Eric (b. 1931) *55, 63*
Tarchi, Angelo (1759-1814) 32
Tasso, Torquato (1544-1595) 42
Tate, Jeffrey *161, 258*
Te Kanawa, Kiri (b. 1944) *161*
Tenschert, Roland (1894-1970) 17; *16, 17*
Tesi, Vittoria (1700-1775) 50
Teyber, Therese (1760-1830) 55, 100, 104f., 123
Thau, Pierre (b. 1933) *195*
Thierry, Joseph (1812-1866) 170
Thoenert, Medardus (1754-1814) 165
Thonus, J.P. von 63
Thoroup, Adam Gottlob 208
Thun, Maria Wilhelmine
  (1747-1800) 104
Thuring, Henri Joseph 168
Tibaldi, Giuseppe Luigi
  (1729-after 1790) 42, 43
Tichy, Vassily *22*
Tiepolo, Giovanni Battista (1696-1770)
Tietjen, Heinz (1881-1967) *175*
Tipton, Thomas (b. 1926) *64*
Tirso de Molina (Fray Gabriel Téllez)
  (1583?-1648) 163
Titus Flavius Vespasianus Augustus,
  emperor (39-81) 261
Toffolutti, Ezio 275
Tomaszewski, Rolf *111*
Tomowa-Sintow, Anna (b. 1941) *191, 194*
Topitz-Feiler, Jetti *16*
Törneroos, Anders 226
Torzewski, Marek (b. 1960) *69*
Tozzi, Antonio (c. 1736-after 1812) 60
Tracey, Edmund 117
Tramezzani, Signore *265*
Travaglia, Pietro 263
Treitschke, Georg Friedrich
  (1776-1842) *88, 204*
Trinkle, Johann David *229*
Troger, Leopold 51
Troller, Georg 93
Troyanos, Tatiana (b. 1938) *217, 272*
Tucker, Richard (1913-1975) *204*
Turnau, Josef *178*
Tutein, Karl *85*

Uccello, Paolo (1397-1475) *254*
Ude, Armin *216*
Ulïbïshev, Alexander Dmitryevich 205
Umlauf, Ignaz (1746-1796) 97, 100, 104

Uppman, Theodor (b. 1920) *247*
Urban, Josef (1872-1933) 231; *176*
Ursuleac, Viorica (b. 1899) *200*
Uttini, Francesco Antonio
  (1723-1795) 71

Valeri, Diego 121
Valesi, Giovanni *see* Wallishauser
Vallotti, Francesco Antonio
  (1697-1780) 38
Van Allan, Richard 192
Vanaud, Marcel *160, 195, 219*
Vande(n?)burg, Howard *89*
van Dam, José (b. 1940) *195*
van der Walt *see* Walt
Varady, Julia (b. 1941) *78, 194*
Varesco, Gianbattista, abbott
  (1735-1805) 79, 80, 87, 89, 118ff.; *79, 118*
Varese, Anna Francesca 32
Vargas, Milagro *158*
Vargo, Gustav 45, 131
Varona, José (b. 1930) *96, 109*
Vaughan, Denis Edward (b. 1926) 73
Velázquez, Diego (1599-1660) *195*
Vercoe, Rosemary *206*
Verdi, Giuseppe (1813-1901) 7
Vergier, Jean-Pierre (b. 1944)
Vergne, Alphonse 89
Vernet, Horace *167*
Vernoy de Saint Georges,
  Jules-Henri 89, 273
Vidal, Paul-Antoine
  (1863-1931) 117; *102, 172*
Viljakainen, Railli (b. 1954) *158*
Villeneuve, Louise 197, 198
Virgil (c. 70-19 B.C.) 79
Visca, Claudia *275*
Vogel, Manfred *28*
Vogler, Georg Joseph, abbé
  (1749-1814) 139
Voigt, Deborah *252*
Völker, Wolf (1896-1981) 160; *106, 107*
Volkmer, Hans (1870-?) *173*
Voltaire, François Marie Arouet
  (1694-1778) 261
Vonderthon, Joseph 16
Vonk, Hans (b. 1924) 275; *216*
Vulpius, Christian August (1762-1827)
  131, 139, 203, 229, 271

Wälterlin, Oskar (1895-1961) 121
Wagner, Richard (1813-1883) 7, 169, 205; *103, 173, 177*
Wakhevitch, Georges (1907-1985) *156, 190*
Walbeck, Günter (b. 1939) 274; *271*
Waldburg-Zeil, Count Ferdinand
  Christoph (1719-1786) 59
Waldersee, Count Paul von
  (1831-1906) 90
Walker, David *192*
Walker, Raymond 117
Wallace, Ian (b. 1919) *180*
Wallberg, Heinz (b. 1923) 147
Wallerstein, Lothar (1882-1949) 94, 144, 211f.; *83, 84, 85, 87, 148, 179, 201, 243*
Wallishauser, Johann Baptist known as
  Valesi, Giovanni (1735-1811) *230*

Walt, Deon van der (b. 1958) *117*
Walter, Bruno (1876-1962) *104, 178, 244, 247*
Walter, Franz 139
Walter, Johann Ignaz (1755-1822) 100
Warrack, John *188, 189*
Wäser, Hermann 203
Watts, Helen (b. 1927) *33*
Weber, later Lange, Aloisia 55, 57, 113, 130, 165; *128*
Weber, Fridolin (1733-1799) 55
Weber, Ludwig (1899-1974) *108*
Weber, Maria Cäcilia (1727-1793) 224
Weber, Wolfgang (b. 1935) *32, 33*
Wechsler, Gil *93*
Weidmann, Joseph (1742-1810) 130
Weigl, Joseph (1766-1846) 137, 271
Weikert, Ralf (b. 1940) *113*
Weiser, Ignaz Anton von
  (1701-1785) 11; *10, 11*
Weiskern, Friedrich Wilhelm
  (1710-1768) 19ff.; *19*
Weiss, Karl Joseph 76
Welitsch, Ljuba (b. 1913) *180*
Wendel, Heinz (Heinrich) Ernst
  (b. 1923) 17; *14, 28, 91, 268*
Wendling, Dorothea (1735-1811) 80
Wendling, Elisabeth (1746-1794) 80
Wendling, Johann Baptist
  (1723-1797) 82
Wenzel, Johann 87
Wernigk, William *104*
Wetzelberger, Bertil (1892-1967) *108*
Wich, Günther (b. 1928) *35, 91, 268*
Widl, P. Rufinus (1731-1798) 15; *15*
Wieland, Christoph Martin
  (1733-1813) 57
Wild, Franz (1791-1860) 168
Wilder, Victor (1835-1892) 121
Wildermann, Hans (1884-1954) 175, 232; *86*
Wilke, Elisabeth *216*
Willer, Luise *151*
Willert, Joachim *218*
Wilson, Hamish *180, 181*
Wimmer, Jakob Anton (1725-1793) 15
Winbergh, Gösta (b. 1943) *194, 218*
Winckelmann, Johann Joachim
  (1717-1768) *91*
Windgassen, Peter (b. 1947) 215
Winkler, Georg C. (b. 1902) *224*
Winkler, Hermann 78
Winter, Felix (1722-1772) 28
Winter, Peter von (1754-1825) 226, 271; *253*
Wise, Patricia (b. 1943) *65*
Wöhler, Willi (b. 1917) 121
Wolf-Ferrari, Ermanno (1876-1948) 94f.
Wolzogen, Alfred von (1823-1883) 131
Wood, Anne (b. 1907) 117
Wood, Peter *192*
Wranitzky, Paul (1756-1808) 221
Wüllner, Franz (1832-1902) 22
Wyzewa, Théodore de (1862-1917) 56

Ximenes de Principi d'Aragona,
  Don Giuseppe (1718-1784) 38

Yakar, Rachel (b. 1938) *35, 55, 92*
Young, Alexander (b. 1920) *88*

Zadek, Hilde (b. 1917)   *268*
Zadek, Peter (b. 1926)   160; *158*
Zallinger, Meinhard von (1897-?)   274; *248*
Zara, Meredith   *35*
Zaun, Fritz (1893-1966)   *155*
Zeffirelli, Franco (b. 1923)   188; *186, 189*
Zemlinsky, Alexander von (1871-1942)   142; *143*

Zierfuss, Ferdinand   64
Zillig, Winfried (1905-1963)   95
Zimmermann, Jörg (b. 1933)   *94*
Zimmermann, Margarita (b. 1947)   *273*
Zimmermann, Reinhard   *218*
Zinzendorf, Count Johann Karl (1739-1813)   137, 165, 200
Znamenacek, Wolfgang (1913-1953)   *183*
Zonca, Giovanni Battista (1728-1808)   82
Zonca, Giuseppe (1715-1772)   71

Zorn, Timm   *66*
Zuccalmaglio, Anton Wilhelm Florentin von (1808-1869)   89
Zucchelli, Carlo   *167*
Zulehner, Karl (c. 1770-1830)   167, 200
Zylis-Gara, Teresa (b. 1936)   *190, 191*

Index of illustrated production, in chronological order

The Abduction from the Seraglio
Berlin (1789)   98
Munich (1825)   100
Vienna (1840/54)   100
Berlin (1884)   100
Paris (1903)   102
Königsberg (1932)   104
Salzburg (1935)   104
Hamburg (1937)   105
Munich (1939)   108
Salzburg (1939)   106, 107
Salzburg (1955)   108
Glyndebourne (1956)   110
Salzburg (1958)   109
Salzburg (1965)   110
Dresden (1976)   111
Paris (1976)   96, 109
Bregenz (1980)   113
Munich (1980)   112
Salzburg (1980)   111
Hagen (1981)   114
Salzburg (1981)   112
East Berlin (1982)   114
Bremen (1982)   115
Lyons (1982/83)   115
Kassel (1986)   116
London (1987)   117
Salzburg (1987)   117

Apollo et Hyacinthus
Salzburg (1935)   16
Linz (1937)   16
Wuppertal (1942)   14
Salzburg (1975)   17

Ascanio in Alba
Salzburg (1958)   41
Salzburg (1967)   43

Bastien and Bastienne
Salzburg (1913)   21
Salzburg (1928)   22
Salzburg (1969)   22
Hagen (1980-81)   18

Betulia liberata
Salzburg (1988)   36

La Clemenza di Tito
Frankfurt am Main (1799)   265
Milan (1818)   265
Mainz (1933)   265
Munich (1936)   267

Salzburg (1949)   268
Düsseldorf (1967)   268
Buenos Aires (1969)   269
Cologne (1971)   270
Berlin (1974)   271
Salzburg (1976)   272
Salzburg (1977)   272
Brussels (1982)   260
Lyons (1982-83)   273
Wuppertal (1986)   274, 275

Così fan tutte
Vienna (end of the 19th century)   198, 199
Munich (1927)   201
Frankfurt am Main (1928)   201
Munich (1941)   200
Posen (1942)   202
Vienna (1943)   203
New York (1951)   204
Paris (1952)   205
Glyndebourne (1954)   206
Salzburg (1953)   206
Salzburg (1960)   207
Edinburgh (1967)   208
Salzburg (1969)   209
Salzburg (1972)   210
Hamburg (1975)   211
Vienna (1975)   210
Düsseldorf (1976)   212
Salzburg (1976)   197, 211
Freiburg im Breisgau (1978)   213
Würzburg (1978)   212
Ulm (1979)   213
Salzburg (1982)   214, 215
Dresden (1983)   216
Lyons (1983)   216
San Francisco (1983)   217
East Berlin (1984)   218
Brussels (1984)   219
Zurich (1986)   218

Don Giovanni
Vienna (c. 1810)   166
Milan (1816)   166
Paris (1834)   169
Paris (first quarter of the 19th century)   167
Paris (1866)   170
Vienna (1869)   172
Paris (1902)   172, 173
Salzburg (1923)   177
Dresden (1924)   174

Breslau (1925)   175
Frankfurt am Main (1926)   179
Berlin (1928)   177
Milan (1929)   176
New York (1929)   176
Prague (1934)   175, 178
Salzburg (1934)   178
Glyndebourne (1936)   180, 181
Prague (1937)   181
Glyndebourne (1948)   180
Paris/Aix-en-Provence (1949)   182
Salzburg (1950)   175
Glyndebourne (1951)   183
Frankfurt am Main (1952)   183
New York (1953)   184
Salzburg (1953)   184
New York (1957)   185
Glyndebourne (1960)   185
Salzburg (1960)   187
London (1965)   186
Salzburg (1966)   187
London (1967)   186
Glyndebourne (1967)   186, 188

La Finta Giardiniera
Versailles (1963)   62
Salzburg (1965)   64
Munich (1979)   65
Salzburg (1979)   64
Schwetzingen (1979)   64
Salzburg (1980)   64
Hagen (1983)   66
Aix-en-Provence (1984)   67
Lyons (1985)   68
Brussel (1986)   69

La Finta Semplice
Salzburg (1956)   27
Salzburg (1960)   28

Idomeneo
Vienna (1879)   81
Breslau (1931)   83
Mannheim (1931)   85
Munich (1931)   87
Vienna (1931)   84, 86, 87
Munich (1936)   85
Glyndebourne (1951)   88
Salzburg (1951)   88
Munich (1955)   89
Salzburg (1956)   90
Salzburg (1961-62)   91
Düsseldorf (1964)   91

Index

Cologne (1971) 92
Munich (1975) 78
Salzburg (1976) 94
Zurich (1980) 92
East Berlin (1981) 94
New York (1982) 93
Salzburg (1984) 93
Vienna (1987) 95

Lucio Silla
Milan (1772) 52
Salzburg (1964) 48
Zurich (1981) 55

The Magic Flute
Vienna (1791) 223
Munich (1794) 229
Weimar (1794) 225
Vienna (1812) 230
Berlin (1816) 232-34
Milan (1816) 230
Weimar (1818) 234
Vienna (1818) 235
Vienna (1822) 236
Mannheim (1834) 237
Vienna (1874) 238
Vienna (1906) 239
New York (1912) 240
Stuttgart (1919) 240
Frankfurt am Main (1921) 241
Paris (1922) 241
Salzburg (1928) 243
Berlin (1929) 243
New York (1941) 244
Salzburg (1949-52) 244
New York (1950) 247
East Berlin (1954) 248

Salzburg (1955) 245
Glyndebourne (1956) 246
New York (1956) 246
Prague (1961) 249
New York (1967) 250
Salzburg (1967) 249
Munich (1970) 251
Salzburg (1974) 252
Glyndebourne (1978) 252, 254
Munich (1978) 253
Salzburg (1978-86) 221
Dresden (1979) 254
Hamburg (1982) 256
Wiesbaden (1983) 256
Bregenz (1985) 257
East Berlin (1986) 258
Geneva (1987) 258
Vienna (1988) 258

The Marriage of Figaro
Vienna (1838) 141
Vienna (second half of
   the 19th century) 141
Hamburg (1894) 142
Vienna (1905) 143
Berlin (c. 1910) 144
Düsseldorf (c. 1910) 145
Strasbourg (1911) 145
Stuttgart (1912) 147
Salzburg (1922) 146
Frankfurt am Main (1924) 148
Munich (1927) 148
Mannheim (1930) 149
Berlin (1931) 149
Dresden (1934) 150
Hamburg (1940) 151
Munich (1940) 151

Rio de Janeiro (1942) 152
Salzburg (1942) 153
Nashville (Tennessee) (1946) 154
Freiburg im Breisgau (1951) 155
New York (1951) 154
Glyndebourne (1958) 155
Düsseldorf (1963) 155
Paris (1964) 156
Cologne (1965) 156
Paris/Versailles (1972) 157
Salzburg (1979) 158
Stuttgart (1983) 159
Brussels (1984) 160
San Francisco (1986) 161

Mitridate, Rè di Ponto
Düsseldorf (1971-72) 35
Salzburg (1971) 32, 33
Schwetzingen (1983) 30
Zurich (1983) 30

L'Oca del Cairo
Salzburg (1936) 119

Der Schauspieldirektor
Vienna (1786) 130
Vienna (1858) 128
Tokyo (1987) 131

Die Schuldigkeit des Ersten Gebots
Salzburg (1987) 13

Zaide
Salzburg (1968) 74
Vienna (1983) 77

Photo credits

The publishers wish to thank all the photographers who collaborated on this book, as well as the museums, archives, and other institutions which supplied additional photographic material. The illustrations not listed below were kindly put at our disposal by the International Mozart Foundation, Salzburg. The numbers refer to the pages.

Gérard Amsellem, Lyons   67, 68, 115 below, 216 above, 273
Bavarian State Opera, Munich   200 right, 251
Beth Bergman, New York   93 above
Bibliothèque et Archives de l'Opéra, Paris   102, 109 left, 156 above, 156 below right, 157, 167 right, 169, 172 below, 173 below left, 182, 205
— Erich Lessing, Magnum   96
Bibliothèque Nationale, Paris   24, 167 left, 168 right, 170, 171
Bregenz Festival, Bregenz   257
— Landesfremdenverkehrsverband Vorarlberg, Bregenz   113
Covent Garden Archives, The Royal Opera House, London   168 left, 173 above left, 186 above left, 192 below
— Reg Wilson   186 below
— Donald Southern   190 below
Deutsche Oper am Rhein, Düsseldorf   35, 91 below, 268 below
Deutsches Theatermuseum, Munich   166 below, 200 left, 223 below, 234 below, 265 above
Erwin Döring, Dresden   111 above, 216 below
Glyndebourne Festival Opera, archive, Glyndebourne   88 right, 180 above right, 180 below, 181 above, 183 above, 188, 189, 206 below
— Antony Armstrong Jones   110 above, 246 above
— Guy Gravett   155 below left, 185 below, 186 above right, 191 above, 252 below
Grand Théâtre, Geneva   192 above
— Marc van Appelghem   259
Pet Halmen, Munich   274, 275
Klaus Hennch, Kilchberg   132
Oliver Herrmann, Berlin   69, 195 above, 260
Historisches Museum Vienna   125, 130, 137, 165, 227, 230 left
Herbert Huber, Salzburg   13
Hungarian State Opera, Budapest   193 below
Thomas Huther, Kassel   116 left
Institut für Theater-, Film- und Fernsehwissenschaft at the University of Cologne   85 below, 101 below, 138, 140 above, 141 above, 142, 143, 144, 145 above and below, 147, 148 above and below, 149 above and below, 150 above, 152, 155 above, 155 below right, 156 below left, 159, 164, 174, 175, 177 above and below, 179, 180 above left, 183 below, 187 above, 224, 225, 236, 241 above, 249 above, 263, 267, 271
Anne Kirchbach, Starberg   65 above and below, 112 above
Arwid Lagenpusch, Berlin   114 below, 218 above, 258 left
Siegfried Lauterwasser, Überlingen   194 above
Paul Leclaire, Cologne   270
Klaus Lefebvre, Bremen   115 above
Metropolitan Opera Guild, New York   154 above
— Frank Dunand   250
— Sedge Lebland   154 below, 204
Metropolitan Opera Association, New York   176 above, 240 above left and right, 244 above, 247 above and below

— Sedge Lebland   184 below, 246 below
— Louis Mélançon   185 above
Mathias Michell, MM-Vision, Munich   36
Victor Mory, Vienna   258 right
Museo Teatrale alla Scala, Milan   230 right
Stefan Odry, Cologne   92 above
Opéra National de Belgique, Brussels
— J.P. Bouduin   160
Opernhaus, Zurich   55, 92 below
Österreichische Nationalbibliothek, Bildarchiv, Vienna   98, 136 right, 222
Österreichische Nationalbibliothek, Theatersammlung, Vienna   81, 128, 198, 203, 238, 239
Pinacoteca Brera, Milan   53 above and below
Stuart Robinson, Aquarius, Hastings   117
H. Roger-Viollet, Paris   62, 63
Salzburg Festival, archive, Salzburg   23, 28, 32, 33, 43, 48, 64, 74, 88 left, 90 above and below, 91 above, 93 below, 94 above, 110 below, 111 below, 112 below, 116 right, 153, 158, 184 above, 190 above, 191 below, 196, 206 above, 209, 210 above, 211 right, 214, 215, 220, 244 below, 249 below, 252 above, 268 above, 272 above and below
Salzburg Marionette Theater, Salzburg   16 above, 17, 109 right, 187 below
San Francisco Opera, San Francisco
— Marty Sohl   161
— David Powers   162, 217
Susan Schimmert-Ramme, Zurich   218 below
Marion Schöne, State Opera, Berlin   94 below
Scottish Opera, Edinburgh   208
Marianne Sobczak, Wetter/Ruhr   18, 66, 114 above
Staatsbibliothek Preussischer Kulturbesitz, Berlin   139 left and right
Staatsgalerie, Stuttgart   173 above right
Staatstheater, Dresden   254
Staatstheater, Kassel
— Peter P. Pachl   193 above
Städtisches Reiss-Museum, Mannheim   229, 237 above
Eduard Straub, Meerbusch   30, 256 below
Teatro alla Scala, Milan   195 below
Teatro Colón, Buenos Aires   269
Joachim Thode, Mönkeberg/Kiel   194 below, 256 above
Sabine Toepffer, Munich   78, 89
Tradhart Ltd., Shipley, West Yorkshire   255
Abisag Tüllmann, Frankfurt am Main   56, 219
Vienna Festival, Vienna   77
Axel Zeininger, Vienna   95

Author's archive   131, 141 below

Copyright:
© 1988 by COSMOPRESS, Geneva   245
© 1988 by PRO LITTERIS, Zurich and ADAGP, Paris   182, 250
© 1988 by Dietrich Alfred Roller   83, 84, 146, 239
© 1988 by Frank Tornquist   90, 203, 244 below

QM LIBRARY
(MILE END)

Setting: TransfoTexte SA, Lausanne
Photolithographs, printing, and binding: Dai Nippon Printing Co., Tokyo
Design and Production: Emma Staffelbach
Editorial: Martha Swiderski-Ritchie

Printed in Japan

Y TEI

ML 410. M7 ANG

QM Library

||||||||||||||||||||||||||||||||||||||
23 1372040 2

WITHDRAWN
FROM STOCK
QMUL LIBRARY

ML 410. M7 ANG